The CERT® C
Coding Standard

Second Edition

The SEI Series in Software Engineering

Software Engineering Institute of Carnegie Mellon University and Addison-Wesley

Software Engineering Institute | **Carnegie Mellon**

Visit **informit.com/sei** for a complete list of available publications.

The SEI Series in Software Engineering is a collaborative undertaking of the Carnegie Mellon Software Engineering Institute (SEI) and Addison-Wesley to develop and publish books on software engineering and related topics. The common goal of the SEI and Addison-Wesley is to provide the most current information on these topics in a form that is easily usable by practitioners and students.

Titles in the series describe frameworks, tools, methods, and technologies designed to help organizations, teams, and individuals improve their technical or management capabilities. Some books describe processes and practices for developing higher-quality software, acquiring programs for complex systems, or delivering services more effectively. Other books focus on software and system architecture and product-line development. Still others, from the SEI's CERT Program, describe technologies and practices needed to manage software and network security risk. These and all titles in the series address critical problems in software engineering for which practical solutions are available.

Make sure to connect with us!
informit.com/socialconnect

 Addison Wesley | |

The CERT® C Coding Standard

98 Rules for Developing Safe, Reliable, and Secure Systems

Second Edition

Robert C. Seacord

✦✦ Addison-Wesley

Upper Saddle River, NJ • Boston • Indianapolis • San Francisco
New York • Toronto • Montreal • London • Munich • Paris • Madrid
Capetown • Sydney • Tokyo • Singapore • Mexico City

The SEI Series in Software Engineering

Many of the designations used by manufacturers and sellers to distinguish their products are claimed as trademarks. Where those designations appear in this book, and the publisher was aware of a trademark claim, the designations have been printed with initial capital letters or in all capitals.

CMM, CMMI, Capability Maturity Model, Capability Maturity Modeling, Carnegie Mellon, CERT, and CERT Coordination Center are registered in the U.S. Patent and Trademark Office by Carnegie Mellon University.

ATAM; Architecture Tradeoff Analysis Method; CMM Integration; COTS Usage-Risk Evaluation; CURE; EPIC; Evolutionary Process for Integrating COTS Based Systems; Framework for Software Product Line Practice; IDEAL; Interim Profile; OAR; OCTAVE; Operationally Critical Threat, Asset, and Vulnerability Evaluation; Options Analysis for Reengineering; Personal Software Process; PLTP; Product Line Technical Probe; PSP; SCAMPI; SCAMPI Lead Appraiser; SCAMPI Lead Assessor; SCE; SEI; SEPG; Team Software Process; and TSP are service marks of Carnegie Mellon University.

Special permission to reproduce portions of material from the CERT Secure Coding Standards website, © 2007 by Carnegie Mellon University, in this book is granted by the Software Engineering Institute.

For information about buying this title in bulk quantities, or for special sales opportunities (which may include electronic versions; custom cover designs; and content particular to your business, training goals, marketing focus, or branding interests), please contact our corporate sales department at corpsales@pearsoned.com or (800) 382-3419.

For government sales inquiries, please contact governmentsales@pearsoned.com.

For questions about sales outside the U.S., please contact international@pearsoned.com.

Visit us on the Web: informit.com/aw

Cataloging-in-Publication Data is on file with the Library of Congress.

ISBN-13: 978-0-321-98404-3
ISBN-10: 0-321-98404-8
Text printed in the United States on recycled paper at Courier in Westford, Massachusetts.
First printing, April 2014

To my wife, Rhonda, and our children, Chelsea and Jordan, and their children.

Contents

Preface

The CERT® C Coding Standard, Second Edition, provides rules for coding in the C programming language. The goal of these rules is to develop safe, reliable, and secure systems, for example, by eliminating undefined behaviors that can lead to unexpected program behaviors and exploitable vulnerabilities. Conformance to the coding rules defined in this standard are necessary (but not sufficient) to ensure the safety, reliability, and security of software systems developed in the C programming language. It is also necessary, for example, to have a safe and secure design. Safety-critical systems typically have stricter requirements than are imposed by this coding standard, for example, requiring that all memory be statically allocated. However, the application of this coding standard will result in high-quality systems that are reliable, robust, and resistant to attack.

Each rule consists of a *title*, a *description*, and *noncompliant code examples* and *compliant solutions*. The title is a concise, but sometimes imprecise, description of the rule. The description specifies the normative requirements of the rule. The noncompliant code examples are examples of code that would constitute a violation of the rule. The accompanying compliant solutions demonstrate equivalent code that does not violate the rule or any other rules in this coding standard.

A well-documented and enforceable coding standard is an essential element of coding in the C programming language. Coding standards encourage programmers to follow a uniform set of rules determined by the requirements of the project and organization rather than by the programmer's familiarity.

Once established, these standards can be used as a metric to evaluate source code (using manual or automated processes).

CERT's coding standards are being widely adopted by industry. Cisco Systems, Inc., announced its adoption of the CERT C Secure Coding Standard as a baseline programming standard in its product development in October 2011 at Cisco's annual SecCon conference. Recently, Oracle has integrated all of CERT's secure coding standards into its existing Secure Coding Standards. Note that this adoption is the most recent step of a long collaboration: CERT and Oracle previously worked together in authoring *The CERT® Oracle Secure Coding Standard for Java* (Addison-Wesley, 2011).

■ Scope

The CERT® C Coding Standard, Second Edition, was developed specifically for versions of the C programming language defined by

- ISO/IEC 9899:2011, *Programming Languages—C, Third Edition* [ISO/IEC 9899:2011]
- ISO/IEC 9899:2011/Cor.1:2012, Technical Corrigendum 1

The CERT® C Coding Standard, Second Edition, updates and replaces *The CERT® C Secure Coding Standard* (Addison-Wesley, 2008). The scope of the first edition of this book is C99 (the second edition of the C Standard) [ISO/IEC 9899:1999]. Although the rules in this book were developed for C11, they can also be applied to earlier versions of the C programming language, including C99. Variations between versions of the C Standard that would affect the proper application of these rules are noted where applicable.

Most rules have a noncompliant code example that is a C11-conforming program to ensure that the problem identified by the rule is within the scope of the standard. However, the best solutions to coding problems are often platform specific. In many cases, this standard provides appropriate compliant solutions for both POSIX and Windows operating systems. Language and library extensions that have been published as ISO/IEC technical reports or technical specifications are frequently given precedence, such as those described by ISO/IEC TR 24731-2, *Extensions to the C Library—Part II: Dynamic Allocation Functions* [ISO/IEC TR 24731-2:2010]. In many cases, compliant solutions are also provided for specific platforms such as Linux or OpenBSD. Occasionally, interesting or illustrative implementation-specific behaviors are described.

Rationale

A coding standard for the C programming language can create the highest value for the longest period of time by focusing on the C Standard (C11) and the relevant post-C11 technical reports.

The C Standard documents existing practice where possible. That is, most features must be tested in an implementation before being included in the standard. *The CERT® C Coding Standard, Second Edition,* has a different purpose: to establish a set of best practices, which sometimes requires introducing new practices that may not be widely known or used when existing practices are inadequate. To put it a different way, *The CERT® C Coding Standard, Second Edition,* attempts to drive change rather than just document it.

For example, the optional but normative Annex K, "Bounds-Checking Interfaces," introduced in C11, is gaining support but at present is implemented by only a few vendors. It introduces functions such as memcpy_s(), which serve the purpose of security by adding the destination buffer size to the API. A forward-looking document could not reasonably ignore these functions simply because they are not yet widely implemented. The base C Standard is more widely implemented than Annex K, but even if it were not, it is the direction in which the industry is moving. Developers of new C code, especially, need guidance that is usable on and makes the best use of the compilers and tools that are now being developed.

Some vendors have extensions to C, and some also have implemented only part of the C Standard before stopping development. Consequently, it is not possible to back up and discuss only C99, C95, or C90. The vendor support equation is too complicated to draw a line and say that a certain compiler supports exactly a certain standard. Whatever demarcation point is selected, different vendors are on opposite sides of it for different parts of the language. Supporting all possibilities would require testing the cross-product of each compiler with each language feature. Consequently, we have selected a demarcation point that is the most recent in time so that the rules defined by the standard will be applicable for as long as possible. As a result of the variations in support, source-code portability is enhanced when the programmer uses only the features specified by C99. This is one of many trade-offs between security and portability inherent to C language programming.

The value of forward-looking information increases with time before it starts to decrease. The value of backward-looking information starts to decrease immediately.

For all of these reasons, the priority of this standard is to support new code development using C11 and the post-C11 technical reports that have not been incorporated into the C Standard. A close-second priority is supporting remediation of old code using C99 and the technical reports.

This coding standard does make contributions to support older compilers when these contributions can be significant and doing so does not compromise other priorities. The intent is not to capture all deviations from the C Standard but to capture only a few important ones.

Issues Not Addressed

A number of issues are not addressed by this coding standard.

Coding Style. Coding style issues are subjective, and it has proven impossible to develop a consensus on appropriate style guidelines. Consequently, *The CERT® C Coding Standard, Second Edition,* does not require the enforcement of any particular coding style but only suggests that development organizations define or adopt style guidelines and apply these guidelines consistently. The easiest way to apply a coding style consistently is to use a code-formatting tool. Many interactive development environments (IDEs) provide such capabilities.

Controversial Rules. In general, the CERT coding standards try to avoid the inclusion of controversial rules that lack a broad consensus.

■ Who Should Read This Book

The CERT® C Coding Standard, Second Edition, is primarily intended for developers of C language programs but may also be used by software acquirers to define the requirements for bespoke software. This book is of particular interest to developers who are interested in building high-quality systems that are reliable, robust, and resistant to attack.

While not intended for C++ programmers, this book may also be of some value because the vast majority of issues identified for C language programs are also issues in C++ programs, although in many cases the solutions are different.

■ History

The idea of a CERT secure coding standard arose at the Spring 2006 meeting of the C Standards Committee (more formally, ISO/IEC JTC1/SC22/WG14) in Berlin, Germany [Seacord 2013a]. The C Standard is an authoritative document, but its audience is primarily compiler implementers, and, as noted by many, its language is obscure and often impenetrable. A secure coding standard would be targeted primarily toward C language programmers and would provide actionable guidance on how to code securely in the language.

The CERT C Secure Coding Standard was developed on the CERT Secure Coding wiki (http://www.securecoding.cert.org) following a community-based development process. Experts from the community, including members of the WG14 C Standards Committee, were invited to contribute and were provided with edit privileges on the wiki. Members of the community can register for a free account on the wiki and comment on the coding standards and the individual rules. Reviewers who provide high-quality comments are frequently extended edit privileges so that they can directly contribute to the development and evolution of the coding standard. Today, the CERT Secure Coding wiki has 1,576 registered contributors.

This wiki-based community development process has many advantages. Most important, it engages a broad group of experts to form a consensus opinion on the content of the rules. The main disadvantage of developing a secure coding standard on a wiki is that the content is constantly evolving. This instability may be acceptable if you want the latest information and are willing to entertain the possibility that a recent change has not yet been fully vetted. However, many software development organizations require a static set of rules and recommendations that they can adopt as requirements for their software development process. Toward this end, a stable snapshot of the CERT C Secure Coding Standard was produced after two and a half years of community development and published as *The CERT® C Secure Coding Standard*. With the production of the manuscript for the book in June 2008, version 1.0 (the book) and the wiki versions of the secure coding standard began to diverge.

The CERT C secure coding guidelines were first reviewed by WG14 at the London meeting in April 2007 and again at the Kona, Hawaii, meeting in August 2007.

The topic of whether INCITS PL22.11 should submit the CERT C Secure Coding Standard to WG14 as a candidate for publication as a type 2 or type 3 technical report was discussed at the J11/U.S. TAG Meeting, April 15, 2008, as reported in the minutes. J11 is now Task Group PL22.11, Programming Language C, and this technical committee is the U.S. Technical Advisory Group to ISO/IEC JTC 1 SC22/WG14. A straw poll was taken on the question, "Who has time to work on this project?" for which the vote was 4 (has time) to 12 (has no time). Some of the feedback we received afterwards was that although the CERT C Secure Coding Standard was a strong set of guidelines that had been developed with input from many of the technical experts at WG14 and had been reviewed by WG14 on several occasions, WG14 was not normally in the business of "blessing" guidance to developers. However, WG14 was certainly in the business of defining normative requirements for tools such as compilers.

Armed with this knowledge, we proposed that WG14 establish a study group to consider the problem of producing analyzable secure coding guidelines for the C language. The study group first met on October 27, 2009. CERT contributed an automatically enforceable subset of the C secure coding rules to ISO/IEC for use in the standardization process.

Participants in the study group included analyzer vendors such as Coverity, Fortify, GammaTech, Gimpel, Klocwork, and LDRA; security experts; language experts; and consumers. A new work item to develop and publish ISO/IEC TS 17961, C Secure Coding Rules, was approved for WG14 in March 2012, and the study group concluded. Roberto Bagnara, the Italian National Body representative to WG 14, later joined the WG14 editorial committee. *ISO/IEC TS 17961:2013(E), Information Technology—Programming Languages, Their Environments and System Software Interfaces—C Secure Coding Rules* [ISO/IEC TS 17961:2013] was officially published in November 2013 and is available for purchase at the ISO store (http://www.iso.org/iso/catalogue_detail.htm?csnumber=61134).

◼ ISO/IEC TS 17961 C Secure Coding Rules

The purpose of ISO/IEC TS 17961 is to establish a baseline set of requirements for analyzers, including static analysis tools and C language compilers, to be applied by vendors that wish to diagnose insecure code beyond the requirements of the language standard. All rules are meant to be enforceable by static analysis. The criterion for selecting these rules is that analyzers that implement these rules must be able to effectively discover secure coding errors without generating excessive false positives.

To date, the application of static analysis to security has been performed in an ad hoc manner by different vendors, resulting in nonuniform coverage of significant security issues. ISO/IEC TS 17961 enumerates secure coding rules and requires analysis engines to diagnose violations of these rules as a matter of conformance to the specification. These rules may be extended in an implementation-dependent manner, which provides a minimum coverage guarantee to customers of any and all conforming static analysis implementations.

ISO/IEC TS 17961 specifies rules for secure coding in the C programming language and includes code examples for each rule. Noncompliant code examples demonstrate language constructs that have weaknesses with potentially exploitable security implications; such examples are expected to elicit a diagnostic from a conforming analyzer for the affected language construct. Compliant examples are expected not to elicit a diagnostic. ISO/IEC TS 17961 does not specify the mechanism by which these rules are enforced or any particular coding style to be enforced.

Table P–1. ISO/IEC TS 17961 Compared with Other Standards

Coding Standard	C Standard	Security Standard	Safety Standard	International Standard	Whole Language
CWE	None/all	Yes	No	No	N/A
MISRA C2	C89	No	Yes	No	No
MISRA C3	C99	No	Yes	No	No
CERT C99	C99	Yes	No	No	Yes
CERT C11	C11	Yes	Yes	No	Yes
ISO/IEC TS 17961	C11	Yes	No	Yes	Yes

Table P–1 shows how ISO/IEC TS 17961 relates to other standards and guidelines. Of the publications listed, ISO/IEC TS 17961 is the only one for which the immediate audience is analyzers and not developers.

A conforming analyzer must be capable of producing a diagnostic for each distinct rule in the technical specification upon detecting a violation of that rule in isolation. If the same program text violates multiple rules simultaneously, a conforming analyzer may aggregate diagnostics but must produce at least one diagnostic. The diagnostic message might be of the form

```
Accessing freed memory in function abc, file xyz.c, line nnn.
```

ISO/IEC TS 17961 does not require an analyzer to produce a diagnostic message for any violation of any syntax rule or constraint specified by the C Standard. Conformance is defined only with respect to source code that is visible to the analyzer. Binary-only libraries, and calls to them, are outside the scope of these rules.

An interesting aspect of the technical specification is the portability assumptions, known within the group as the "San Francisco rule" because the assumptions evolved at a meeting hosted by Coverity at its headquarters. The San Francisco rule states that a conforming analyzer must be able to diagnose violations of guidelines for at least one C implementation but does not need to diagnose a rule violation if the result is documented for the target implementation and does not cause a security flaw. Variations in quality of implementation permit an analyzer to produce diagnostics concerning portability issues. For example, the following program fragment can produce a diagnostic, such as the mismatch between %d and long int:

```
long i; printf ("i = %d", i);
```

This mismatch might not be a problem for all target implementations, but it is a portability problem because not all implementations have the same representation for int and long.

In addition to other goals already stated, *The CERT® C Coding Standard, Second Edition,* has been updated for consistency with ISO/IEC TS 17961. Although the documents serve different audiences, consistency between the documents should improve the ability of developers to use ISO/IEC TS 17961– conforming analyzers to find violations of rules from this coding standard.

The Secure Coding Validation Suite (https://github.com/SEI-CERT/scvs) is a set of tests developed by CERT to validate the rules defined in ISO/IEC TS 17961. These tests are based on the examples in this technical specification and are distributed with a BSD-style license.

■ Tool Selection and Validation

Although rule checking can be performed manually, with increasing program size and complexity, it rapidly becomes infeasible. For this reason, the use of static analysis tools is recommended.

When choosing a compiler (which should be understood to include the linker), a C-compliant compiler should be used whenever possible. A conforming implementation will produce at least one diagnostic message if a preprocessing translation unit or translation unit contains a violation of any syntax rule or constraint, even if the behavior is also explicitly specified as *undefined* or *implementation-defined*. It is also likely that any analyzers you may use assume a C-compliant compiler.

When choosing a source code analysis tool, it is clearly desirable that the tool be able to enforce as many of the recommendations on the wiki as possible. Not all recommendations are enforceable; some are strictly meant to be informative.

Although CERT recommends the use of an ISO/IEC TS 17961–conforming analyzer, the Software Engineering Institute, as a federally funded research and development center (FFRDC), is not in a position to endorse any particular vendor or tool. Vendors are encouraged to develop conforming analyzers, and users of this coding standard are free to evaluate and select whichever analyzers best suit their purposes.

Completeness and Soundness

It should be recognized that, in general, determining conformance to coding rules is computationally undecidable. The precision of static analysis has practical limitations. For example, the halting theorem of computer science states that programs exist in which exact control flow cannot be determined statically. Consequently, any property dependent on control flow—such as halting—may be indeterminate for some programs. A consequence of undecidability is that it may be impossible for any tool to determine statically whether a given rule is satisfied in specific circumstances. The widespread presence of such code may also lead to unexpected results from an analysis tool.

However checking is performed, the analysis may generate

- *False negatives:* Failure to report a real flaw in the code is usually regarded as the most serious analysis error, as it may leave the user with a false sense of security. Most tools err on the side of caution and consequently generate false positives. However, in some cases, it may be deemed better to report some high-risk flaws and miss others than to overwhelm the user with false positives.

- *False positives:* The tool reports a flaw when one does not exist. False positives may occur because the code is too complex for the tool to perform a complete analysis. The use of features such as function pointers and libraries may make false positives more likely.

To the greatest extent feasible, an analyzer should be both complete and sound with respect to enforceable rules. An analyzer is considered sound with respect to a specific rule if it cannot give a false-negative result, meaning it finds all violations of a rule within the entire program. An analyzer is considered complete if it cannot issue false-positive results, or false alarms. The possibilities for a given rule are outlined in Figure P–1.

False Positives

		Y	N
False Negatives	**N**	Complete with false positives	Complete and sound
	Y	Incomplete with false positives	Incomplete

Figure P–1. False-negative and false-positive possibilities

Compilers and source code analysis tools are *trusted* processes, meaning that a degree of reliance is placed on the output of the tools. Accordingly, developers must ensure that this trust is not misplaced. Ideally, trust should be achieved by the tool supplier running appropriate validation tests such as the Secure Coding Validation Suite.

False Positives

Although many rules list common exceptions, it is difficult if not impossible to develop a complete list of exceptions for each guideline. Consequently, it is important that source code comply with the *intent* of each rule and that tools, to the greatest extent possible, minimize false positives that do not violate the intent of the rule. The degree to which tools minimize false-positive diagnostics is a quality-of-implementation issue.

Taint Analysis

Taint and Tainted Sources

Certain operations and functions have a domain that is a subset of the type domain of their operands or parameters. When the actual values are outside of the defined domain, the result might be undefined or at least unexpected. If the value of an operand or argument may be outside the domain of an operation or function that consumes that value, and the value is derived from any external input to the program (such as a command-line argument, data returned from a system call, or data in shared memory), that value is tainted, and its origin is known as a *tainted source*. A tainted value is not necessarily known to be out of the domain; rather, it is not known to be in the domain. Only values, and not the operands or arguments, can be tainted; in some cases, the same operand or argument can hold tainted or untainted values along different paths. In this regard, taint is an attribute of a value that is assigned to any value originating from a tainted source.

Restricted Sinks

Operands and arguments whose domain is a subset of the domain described by their types are called restricted sinks. Any integer operand used in a pointer arithmetic operation is a restricted sink for that operand. Certain parameters of certain library functions are restricted sinks because these functions perform address arithmetic with these parameters, or control the allocation of a resource, or pass these parameters on to another restricted sink. All string input parameters to library functions are restricted sinks because it is possible to pass in a character sequence that is not null terminated. The exceptions are input parameters to strncpy() and strncpy_s(), which explicitly allow the source character sequence not to be null terminated.

Propagation

Taint is propagated through operations from operands to results unless the operation itself imposes constraints on the value of its result that subsume the constraints imposed by restricted sinks. In addition to operations that propagate the same sort of taint, there are operations that propagate taint of one sort of an operand to taint of a different sort for their results, the most notable example of which is strlen() propagating the taint of its argument with respect to string length to the taint of its return value with respect to range.

Although the exit condition of a loop is not normally considered to be a restricted sink, a loop whose exit condition depends on a tainted value propagates taint to any numeric or pointer variables that are increased or decreased by amounts proportional to the number of iterations of the loop.

Sanitization

To remove the taint from a value, the value must be sanitized to ensure that it is in the defined domain of any restricted sink into which it flows. Sanitization is performed by replacement or termination. In replacement, out-of-domain values are replaced by in-domain values, and processing continues using an in-domain value in place of the original. In termination, the program logic terminates the path of execution when an out-of-domain value is detected, often simply by branching around whatever code would have used the value.

In general, sanitization cannot be recognized exactly using static analysis. Analyzers that perform taint analysis usually provide some extralinguistic mechanism to identify sanitizing functions that sanitize an argument (passed by address) in place, return a sanitized version of an argument, or return a status code indicating whether the argument is in the required domain. Because such extralinguistic mechanisms are outside the scope of this coding standard, we use a set of rudimentary definitions of sanitization that is likely to recognize real sanitization but might cause nonsanitizing or ineffectively sanitizing code to be misconstrued as sanitizing. The following definition of sanitization presupposes that the analysis is in some way maintaining a set of constraints on each value encountered as the simulated execution progresses: a given path through the code sanitizes a value with respect to a given restricted sink if it restricts the range of that value to a subset of the defined domain of the restricted sink type. For example, sanitization of signed integers with respect to an array index operation must restrict the range of that integer value to numbers between zero and the size of the array minus one.

This description is suitable for numeric values, but sanitization of strings with respect to content is more difficult to recognize in a general way.

■ Rules versus Recommendations

This book contains 98 coding *rules*. The CERT Coding Standards wiki also has 178 recommendations at the time of writing. Rules are meant to provide normative requirements for code, whereas recommendations are meant to provide guidance that, when followed, should improve the safety, reliability, and security of software systems. However, a violation of a recommendation does not necessarily indicate the presence of a defect in the code.

Rules and recommendations are collectively referred to as *guidelines*. Rules must meet the following criteria:

1. Violation of the guideline is likely to result in a defect that may adversely affect the safety, reliability, or security of a system, for example, by introducing a security flaw that may result in an exploitable vulnerability.

2. The guideline does not rely on source code annotations or assumptions of programmer intent.

3. Conformance to the guideline can be determined through automated analysis (either static or dynamic), formal methods, or manual inspection techniques.

Recommendations are suggestions for improving code quality. Guidelines are defined to be recommendations when all of the following conditions are met:

1. Application of a guideline is likely to improve the safety, reliability, or security of software systems.

2. One or more of the requirements necessary for a guideline to be considered a rule cannot be met.

Figure P–2 shows how the 98 rules and 178 recommendations are organized.

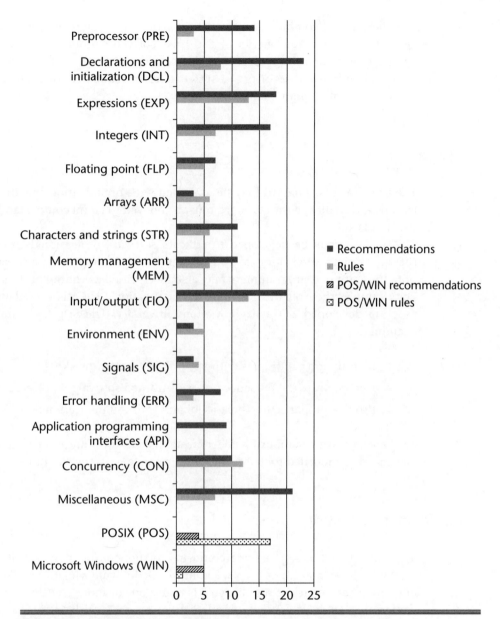

Figure P–2. CERT C coding guidelines

The wiki also contains two platform-specific annexes at the time of writing, one for POSIX and one for Windows, which have been omitted from this book because they are not part of the core standard.

The set of recommendations that a particular development effort adopts depends on the requirements of the final software product. Projects with stricter requirements may decide to dedicate more resources to ensuring the safety, reliability, and security of a system and consequently are likely to adopt a broader set of recommendations.

■ Usage

The rules in this standard may be extended with organization-specific rules. However, the rules in the standard must be obeyed to claim conformance with the standard.

Training may be developed to educate software professionals regarding the appropriate application of coding standards. After passing an examination, these trained programmers may also be certified as coding professionals. For example, the Software Developer Certification (SDC) is a credentialing program developed at Carnegie Mellon University. The SDC uses authentic examination to

1. Identify job candidates with specific programming skills
2. Demonstrate the presence of a well-trained software workforce
3. Provide guidance to educational and training institutions

Once a coding standard has been established, tools and processes can be developed or modified to determine conformance with the standard.

■ Conformance Testing

To ensure that the source code conforms to this coding standard, it is necessary to have measures in place that check for rule violations. The most effective means of achieving this goal is to use one or more ISO/IEC TS 17961–conforming analyzers. Where a rule cannot be checked by a tool, a manual review is required.

The Source Code Analysis Laboratory (SCALe) provides a means for evaluating the conformance of software systems against this and other coding standards. CERT coding standards provide a normative set of rules against which software systems can be evaluated. Conforming software systems should demonstrate improvements in the safety, reliability, and security over nonconforming systems.

The SCALe team at the CERT Division of Carnegie Mellon University's Software Engineering Institute analyzes a developer's source code and provides a detailed report of findings to guide the code's repair. After the developer has addressed these findings and the SCALe team determines that the product version conforms to the standard, the CERT Program issues the developer a certificate and lists the system in a registry of conforming systems. This report details the SCALe process and provides an analysis of selected software systems.

Conformance

Conformance to *The CERT® C Coding Standard* requires that the code not contain any violations of the rules specified in this book. If an exceptional condition is claimed, the exception must correspond to a predefined exceptional condition, and the application of this exception must be documented in the source code.

Conformance with the recommendations on the wiki is not necessary to claim conformance with *The CERT® C Coding Standard*. Conformance to the recommendations will, in many cases, make it easier to conform to the rules; eliminating many potential sources of defects.

Deviation Procedure

Strict adherence to all rules is unlikely and, consequently, deviations associated with specific rule violations are necessary. Deviations can be used in cases where a true-positive finding is uncontested as a rule violation but the code is nonetheless determined to be correct. An uncontested true-positive finding may be the result of a design or architecture feature of the software or may occur for a valid reason that was unanticipated by the coding standard. In this respect, the deviation procedure allows for the possibility that coding rules are overly strict [Seacord 2012].

Deviations are not granted for reasons of performance or usability. A software system that successfully passes conformance testing must not contain defects or exploitable vulnerabilities. Deviation requests are evaluated by the lead assessor, and if the developer can provide sufficient evidence that deviation will not result in a vulnerability, the deviation request is accepted. Deviations are used infrequently because it is almost always easier to fix a coding error than it is to provide an argument that the coding error does not result in a vulnerability.

■ System Qualities

The goal of this coding standard is to produce safe, reliable, and secure systems. Additional requirements might exist for safety-critical systems, such as the absence of dynamic memory allocation. Other software quality attributes of interest include portability, usability, availability, maintainability, readability, and performance.

Many of these attributes are interrelated in interesting ways. For example, readability is an attribute of maintainability; both are important for limiting the introduction of defects during maintenance that can result in security flaws or reliability issues. In addition, readability aids code inspection by safety officers. Reliability and availability require proper resources management, which also contributes to the safety and security of the system. System attributes such as performance and security are often in conflict, requiring trade-offs to be considered.

■ How This Book Is Organized

This book is organized into 14 chapters containing rules in specific topic areas, three appendices, a bibliography, and an index. The first appendix is a glossary of terms used through this book. Terms that are listed in the glossary are printed in **bold font** the first time they appear and then in normal font in subsequent appearances. The second appendix lists the undefined behaviors from the C Standard, Annex J, J.2 [ISO/IEC 9899:2011], numbered and classified for easy reference. These numbered undefined behaviors are referenced frequently from the rules. The third appendix contains unspecified behaviors from the C Standard, Annex J, J.1 [ISO/IEC 9899:2011]. These unspecified behaviors are occasionally referenced from the rules as well. The bibliography is a compendium of the small bibliography sections from each rule as well as other references cited throughout the book.

Most rules have a consistent structure. Each rule in this standard has a unique *identifier,* which is included in the title. The title and the introductory paragraphs define the rule and are typically followed by one or more pairs of *noncompliant code examples* and *compliant solutions.* Each rule also includes a *risk assessment, related guidelines,* and a *bibliography* (where applicable). Rules may also include a table of *related vulnerabilities.* Recommendations on the CERT Coding Standards wiki are organized in a similar fashion.

Identifiers

Each rule and recommendation is given a unique identifier, which consists of three parts:

- A three-letter mnemonic representing the section of the standard
- A two-digit numeric value in the range of 00 to 99
- The letter *C* indicating that this is a C language guideline

The three-letter mnemonic is used to group similar coding practices and to indicate to which category a coding practice belongs.

The numeric value is used to give each coding practice a unique identifier. Numeric values in the range of 00 to 29 are reserved for recommendations, and values in the range of 30 to 99 are reserved for rules. Rules and recommendations are frequently referenced from the rules in this book by their identifier and title. Rules can be found in the book's table of contents, whereas recommendations can be found only on the wiki.

Noncompliant Code Examples and Compliant Solutions

Noncompliant code examples illustrate code that violates the guideline under discussion. It is important to note that these are only examples, and eliminating all occurrences of the example does not necessarily mean that the code being analyzed is now compliant with the guideline.

Noncompliant code examples are typically followed by compliant solutions, which show how the noncompliant code example can be recoded in a secure, compliant manner. Except where noted, noncompliant code examples should contain violations only of the rule under discussion. Compliant solutions should comply with all secure coding rules but may on occasion fail to comply with a recommendation.

Exceptions

Any rule or recommendation may specify a small set of exceptions detailing the circumstances under which the guideline is not necessary to ensure the safety, reliability, or security of software. Exceptions are informative only and are not required to be followed.

Risk Assessment

Each guideline in *The CERT® C Coding Standard, Second Edition,* contains a risk assessment section that attempts to provide software developers with an indication of the potential consequences of not addressing violations of a particular rule in their code (along with some indication of expected remediation costs). This information may be used to prioritize the repair of rule violations by a development team. The metric is designed primarily for remediation projects. It is generally assumed that new code will be developed to be compliant with the entire coding standard and applicable recommendations.

Each rule and recommendation has an assigned *priority.* Priorities are assigned using a metric based on Failure Mode, Effects, and Criticality Analysis (FMECA) [IEC 60812]. Three values are assigned for each rule on a scale of 1 to 3 for severity, likelihood, and remediation cost.

- **Severity**—How serious are the consequences of the rule being ignored?

Value	Meaning	Examples of Vulnerability
1	Low	Denial-of-service attack, abnormal termination
2	Medium	Data integrity violation, unintentional information disclosure
3	High	Run arbitrary code

- **Likelihood**—How likely is it that a flaw introduced by ignoring the rule can lead to an exploitable vulnerability?

Value	Meaning
1	Unlikely
2	Probable
3	Likely

- **Remediation Cost**—How expensive is it to comply with the rule?

Value	Meaning	Detection	Correction
1	High	Manual	Manual
2	Medium	Automatic	Manual
3	Low	Automatic	Automatic

The three values are then multiplied together for each rule. This product provides a measure that can be used in prioritizing the application of the rules. The products range from 1 to 27, although only the following 10 distinct values are possible: 1, 2, 3, 4, 6, 8, 9, 12, 18, and 27. Rules and recommendations with a priority in the range of 1 to 4 are Level 3 rules, 6 to 9 are Level 2, and 12 to 27 are Level 1. The following are possible interpretations of the priorities and levels:

Level	Priorities	Possible Interpretation
L1	12, 18, 27	High severity, likely, inexpensive to repair
L2	6, 8, 9	Medium severity, probable, medium cost to repair
L3	1, 2, 3, 4	Low severity, unlikely, expensive to repair

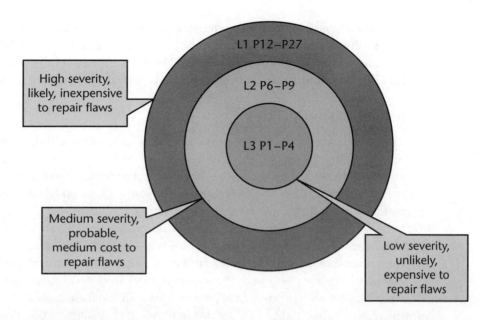

Figure P–3. Levels of compliance

Specific projects may begin remediation by implementing all rules at a particular level before proceeding to lower priority rules, as shown in Figure P–3.

Automated Detection

On the wiki, both rules and recommendations frequently have sections that describe automated detection. These sections provide additional information on analyzers that can automatically diagnose violations of coding guidelines. Most automated analyses for the C programming language are neither sound nor complete, so the inclusion of a tool in this section typically means that the tool can diagnose some violations of this particular rule. Although the Secure Coding Validation Suite can be used to test the ability of analyzers to diagnose violations of rules from ISO/IEC TS 17961, no currently available conformance test suite can assess the ability of analyzers to diagnose violations of the rules in this book. Consequently, the information in automated detection sections on the wiki may be

- Provided by the vendors
- Determined by CERT by informally evaluating the analyzer
- Determined by CERT by reviewing the vendor documentation

Where possible, we try to reference the exact version of the tool for which the results were obtained. Because these tools evolve continuously, this information can rapidly become dated and obsolete. Consequently, this information has been omitted from this book and is maintained only on the wiki.

Related Vulnerabilities

The related vulnerabilities sections on the wiki contain a link to search for related vulnerabilities on the CERT Web site. Whenever possible, CERT Vulnerability Notes are tagged with a keyword corresponding to the unique ID of the coding guideline. This search provides you with an up-to-date list of real-world vulnerabilities that have been determined to be at least partially caused by a violation of this specific guideline. These vulnerabilities are labeled as such only when the vulnerability analysis team at the CERT/CC is able to evaluate the source code and precisely determine the cause of the vulnerability. Because many vulnerability notes refer to vulnerabilities in closed-source software systems, it is not always possible to provide this additional analysis. Consequently, the related vulnerabilities field tends to be somewhat sparsely populated.

To find the latest list of related vulnerabilities, enter the following URL:

https://www.kb.cert.org/vulnotes/bymetric?searchview&query=FIELD+ KEYWORDS+contains+XXXNN-X

where XXXNN-X is the ID of the rule or recommendation for which you are searching.

Specific vulnerability (VU) identifiers and common vulnerabilities and exposures (CVE) identifiers are referenced throughout this book. You can create a unique URL to get more information on specific vulnerabilities by appending the relevant ID to the end of a fixed string. For example, to find more information about

- *VU#551436*, "Mozilla Firefox SVG viewer vulnerable to integer overflow," you can append 551436 to https://www.kb.cert.org/vulnotes/id/ and enter the resulting URL in your browser: https://www.kb.cert.org/ vulnotes/id/551436
- *CVE-2006-1174*, you can append CVE-2006-1174 to http://cve.mitre .org/cgi-bin/cvename.cgi?name= and enter the resulting URL in your browser: http://cve.mitre.org/cgi-bin/cvename.cgi?name= CVE-2006-1174

Related vulnerability sections are included only for specific rules in this book, when the information is both relevant and interesting.

Related Guidelines

This section contains links to guidelines in related standards, technical specifications, and guideline collections such as *Information Technology— Programming Languages, Their Environments and System Software Interfaces—C Secure Coding Rules* [ISO/IEC TS 17961:2013]; *Information Technology— Programming Languages—Guidance to Avoiding Vulnerabilities in Programming Languages through Language Selection and Use* [ISO/IEC TR 24772:2013]; *MISRA C 2012: Guidelines for the Use of the C Language in Critical Systems* [MISRA C:2012]; and CWE IDs in MITRE's Common Weakness Enumeration (CWE) [MITRE 2013].

You can create a unique URL to get more information on CWEs by appending the relevant ID to the end of a fixed string. For example, to find more information about CWE-192, "Integer Coercion Error," you can append 192.html to http://cwe.mitre.org/data/definitions/ and enter the resulting URL in your browser: http://cwe.mitre.org/data/definitions/192.html.

The other referenced technical specifications, technical reports, and guidelines are commercially available.

Bibliography

Most rules have a small bibliography section that lists documents and sections in these documents that provide information relevant to the rule.

■ Automatically Generated Code

If a code-generating tool is to be used, it is necessary to select an appropriate tool and undertake validation. Adherence to the requirements of this document may provide one criterion for assessing a tool.

Coding guidance varies depending on how code is generated and maintained. Categories of code include the following:

- Tool-generated, tool-maintained code that is specified and maintained in a higher-level format from which language-specific source code is generated. The source code is generated from this higher-level description and then provided as input to the language compiler. The generated source code is never viewed or modified by the programmer.

- Tool-generated, hand-maintained code that is specified and maintained in a higher-level format from which language-specific source code is generated. It is expected or anticipated, however, that at some point in the development cycle, the tool will cease to be used and the generated source code will be visually inspected and/or manually modified and maintained.

■ Hand-coded code is manually written by a programmer using a text editor or interactive development environment; the programmer maintains source code directly in the source-code format provided to the compiler.

Source code that is written and maintained by hand must have the following properties:

■ Readability
■ Program comprehension

These requirements are not applicable for source code that is never directly handled by a programmer, although requirements for correct behavior still apply. Reading and comprehension requirements apply to code that is tool generated and hand maintained but do not apply to code that is tool generated and tool maintained. Tool-generated, tool-maintained code can impose consistent constraints that ensure the safety of some constructs that are risky in hand-generated code.

■ Government Regulations

Developing software to secure coding rules is a good idea and is increasingly a requirement. The National Defense Authorization Act for Fiscal Year 2013, Section 933, "Improvements in Assurance of Computer Software Procured by the Department of Defense," requires evidence that government software development and maintenance organizations and contractors are conforming, in computer software coding, to approved secure coding standards of the Department of Defense (DoD) during software development, upgrade, and maintenance activities, including through the use of inspection and appraisals.

DoD acquisition programs are specifying *The Application Security and Development Security Technical Implementation Guide (STIG)*, Version 2, Release 1 [DISA 2008] in requests for proposal (RFPs). Section 2.1.5, "Coding Standards," requires that "the Program Manager will ensure the development team follows a set of coding standards."

The proper application of this standard would enable a system to comply with the following requirements from the *Application Security and Development STIG* [DISA 2008]:

- **(APP2060.1: CAT II)** The Program Manager will ensure the development team follows a set of coding standards.

- **(APP2060.2: CAT II)** The Program Manager will ensure the development team creates a list of unsafe functions to avoid and document this list in the coding standards.

- **(APP3550: CAT I)** The Designer will ensure the application is not vulnerable to integer arithmetic issues.

- **(APP3560: CAT I)** The Designer will ensure the application does not contain format string vulnerabilities.

- **(APP3570: CAT I)** The Designer will ensure the application does not allow Command Injection.

- **(APP3590.1: CAT I)** The Designer will ensure the application does not have buffer overflows.

- **(APP3590.2: CAT I)** The Designer will ensure the application does not use functions known to be vulnerable to buffer overflows.

- **(APP3590.3: CAT II)** The Designer will ensure the application does not use signed values for memory allocation where permitted by the programming language.

- **(APP3600: CAT II)** The Designer will ensure the application has no canonical representation vulnerabilities.

- **(APP3630.1: CAT II)** The Designer will ensure the application is not vulnerable to race conditions.

- **(APP3630.2: CAT III)** The Designer will ensure the application does not use global variables when local variables could be used.

Training programmers and software testers will satisfy the following requirements:

- **(APP2120.3: CAT II)** The Program Manager will ensure developers are provided with training on secure design and coding practices on at least an annual basis.

- **(APP2120.4: CAT II)** The Program Manager will ensure testers are provided annual training.

- (**APP2060.3: CAT II**) The Designer will follow the established coding standards established for the project.
- (**APP2060.4: CAT II**) The Designer will not use unsafe functions documented in the project coding standards.
- (**APP5010: CAT III**) The Test Manager will ensure at least one tester is designated to test for security flaws in addition to functional testing.

Acknowledgments

This book was made possible through a broad community effort. First I would like to thank those who contributed guidelines to this book, including Arbob Ahmad, Juan Alvarado, Dave Aronson, Abhishek Arya, Berin Babcock-McConnell, Roberto Bagnara, Bruce Bayha, Joe Black, Jodi Blake, Jill Britton, Levi Broderick, Hal Burch, J. L. Charton, Steve Christey, Ciera Christopher, Geoff Clare, Frank Costello, Joe Damato, Stephen C. Dewhurst, Susan Ditmore, Chad Dougherty, Mark Dowd, Apoorv Dutta, Emily Evans, Xiaoyi Fei, William Fithen, Hallvard Furuseth, Jeff Gennari, Andrew Gidwani, Ankur Goyal, Douglas A. Gwyn, Shaun Hedrick, Michael Howard, Sujay Jain, Christina Johns, Pranjal Jumde, Andrew Keeton, David Kohlbrenner, Takuya Kondo, Masaki Kubo, Pranav Kukreja, Richard Lane, Stephanie Wan-Ruey Lee, Jonathan Leffler, Pengfei Li, Fred Long, Justin Loo, Gregory K. Look, Larry Maccherone, Aditya Mahendrakar, Lee Mancuso, John McDonald, James McNellis, Randy Meyers, Dhruv Mohindra, Nat Lyle, Bhaswanth Nalabothula, Todd Nowacki, Adrian Trejo Nuñez, Bhadrinath Pani, Vishal Patel, David M. Pickett, Justin Pincar, Thomas Plum, Abhijit Rao, Raunak Rungta, Dan Saks, Alexandre Santos, Brendan Saulsbury, Jason Michael Sharp, Astha Singhal, Will Snavely, Nick Stoughton, Alexander E. Strommen, Glenn Stroz, Dean Sutherland, Kazunori Takeuchi, Chris Tapp, Chris Taschner, Mira Sri Divya Thambireddy, Melanie Thompson, Elpiniki Tsakalaki, Ben Tucker, Fred J. Tydeman, Abhishek Veldurthy, Wietse Venema, Alex Volkovitsky, Michael Shaye-Wen Wang, Grant Watters, Tim Wilson, Eric Wong, Lutz Wrage, Shishir Kumar Yadav, Gary Yuan, Ricky Zhou, and Alen Zukich.

I would also like to thank the following reviewers: Stefan Achatz, Arbob Ahmad, Laurent Alebarde, Kevin Bagust, Greg Beeley, Arjun Bijanki, John Bode,

Konrad Borowski, Stewart Brodie, Jordan Brown, Andrew Browne, G. Bulmer, Kyle Comer, Sean Connelly, Ale Contenti, Tom Danielsen, Eric Decker, Mark Dowd, T. Edwin, Brian Ewins, Justin Ferguson, William L. Fithen, Stephen Friedl, Hallvard Furuseth, Shay Green, Samium Gromoff, Kowsik Guruswamy, Jens Gustedt, Peter Gutmann, Douglas A. Gwyn, Richard Heathfield, Darryl Hill, Paul Hsieh, Ivan Jager, Steven G. Johnson, Anders Kaseorg, Matt Kraai, Piotr Krukowiecki, Jerry Leichter, Nicholas Marriott, Frank Martinez, Scott Meyers, Eric Miller, Charles-Francois Natali, Ron Natalie, Adam O'Brien, Heikki Orsila, Balog Pal, Jonathan Paulson, P. J. Plauger, Leslie Satenstein, Kirk Sayre, Neil Schellenberger, Michel Schinz, Eric Sosman, Chris Tapp, Andrey Tarasevich, Josh Triplett, Yozo Toda, Pavel Vasilyev, Ivan Vecerina, Zeljko Vrba, David Wagner, Henry S. Warren, Colin Watson, Zhenyu Wu, Drew Yao, Christopher Yeleighton, and Robin Zhu.

Thanks also to the team at Addison-Wesley, including Kim Boedigheimer, assistant editor; Caroline Senay, production editor; Julie B. Nahil, full-service production manager; Deborah Thompson, copy editor; Christopher Guzikowski, executive editor; John Fuller, managing editor; and Stephane Nakib, product marketing manager.

I also want to thank Peter Gordon, who approved this project but retired before it was completed, presumably to avoid dealing with me again. I first met Peter Gordon in 1999 at the restaurant in the Los Angeles Hilton (the one near the airport) for breakfast to discuss our first collaboration, *Building Systems from Commercial Components*, along with one of my coauthors on the project, Kurt Wallnau. I don't remember the details of the discussion, but I do recall that Peter's skills went well beyond breakfast, as we also dined at a seafood restaurant in Santa Monica on that very same trip.

Since that time, Peter and I have collaborated on eight book projects over 14 years. From dinner in Boston's Back Bay to lunch in Tokyo, Peter had a profound impact on me and provided a steadier hand at guiding my career over that period than anyone else. While most of my memories of Peter remain food related, I benefited greatly from his excellent guidance and knowledge of marketing technical books, such as his advice to "make the cover red and put some numbers in the title." More important, even though Peter had the opportunity to work with such notable authors as Donald Knuth and myself, he remained humble. Peter, I hope you enjoy your retirement and that I'll have a chance to break bread with you again soon.

I also want to thank the remainder of the CERT team, including Tamara Butler, Pamela Curtis, Gina DeCola, Ed Desautels, Shannon Haas, Paul Ruggiero, Osona Steave, Tracey Tamules, and Pennie Walters, for their support and assistance, without which this book could not have been completed. And last but not least, we would like to thank our in-house editor, Carol J. Lallier, who helped make this work possible.

Special thanks are also extended to Archie Andrews, Mark Sherman, Bill Wilson, and Rich Pethia.

Contributors

Aaron Ballman is a security software engineer at CERT. He is an active developer on the Clang open source C, C++, and Objective-C compiler, focusing primarily on frontend development. Aaron has more than a decade of experience writing commercial compilers for various programming languages, as well as developing cross-platform C and C++ frameworks. He is the author of *Ramblings on REALbasic* (2009).

John Benito is an independent consultant providing software development, project management, and software testing. He is the current convener of ISO/IEC JTC 1/SC 22/WG14, the ISO group responsible for Standard C, the initial convener of ISO/IEC JTC 1/SC 22 WG 23 (was OWG Vulnerabilities), the project editor for the Technical Report 24772, and a member of the INCITS PL22.11 (ANSI C) technical committee. John previously was a member of INCITS PL22.16 (ANSI C++) and the ISO Java Study group. He has been in software development, project management, and testing for more than 38 years. John has been participating in International Standards development for the past 24 years and is the recipient of the INCITS Exceptional International Leadership Award.

David Keaton is the chairman of the ANSI C Committee, the U.S. segment of the international committee that standardizes the C programming language. He has been a voting member of the committee since 1990. David has written compilers for everything from embedded systems to supercomputers. He has two patents related to compiler-assisted security mechanisms.

Dan Plakosh was the lead software engineer for the Systems Engineering Department at the Naval Surface Warfare Center (NSWCDD) before joining the SEI. Dan has more than 15 years of software development experience in defense, research, and industry. Dan's principal areas of expertise include real-time distributed systems, network communications and protocols, systems engineering, real-time 2D and 3D graphics, and UNIX OS internals. Much of Dan's recent experience has been redesigning legacy-distributed systems to use the latest distributed communication technologies.

Martin Sebor is a technical leader in the C and C++ compiler tool chain group in the Network Operating Systems Group at Cisco Systems, Inc., where he works on compilers and related development tools as well as the Cisco networking operating system IOS. Among Martin's responsibilities is leading the development and deployment of Cisco Secure Coding Standards. Martin's expertise includes the C and C++ languages and development tools and the POSIX standard. Martin is Cisco's representative to the C and C++ international standards committees (PL22.11 and PL22.16 subgroups of the INCITS technical committee for Programming Languages, PL22).

David Svoboda is a software security engineer at CERT. He has been the primary developer on a diverse set of software development projects at Carnegie Mellon University since 1991. His projects have ranged from hierarchical chip modeling and social organization simulation to automated machine translation (AMT). His KANTOO AMT software, developed in 1996, is still in production and use at Caterpillar. He has taught secure coding in C and C++ all over the world to various groups in the military, government, and banking industries. David also participates in the ISO/IEC JTC1/SC22/WG14 working group for the C programming language and the ISO/IEC JTC1/SC22/WG21 working group for C++.

About the Author

Robert C. Seacord is the secure coding technical manager in the CERT Division of Carnegie Mellon University's Software Engineering Institute (SEI). The CERT Program is a trusted provider of operationally relevant cybersecurity research and innovative and timely responses to our nation's cybersecurity challenges. The Secure Coding Initiative works with software developers and software development organizations to eliminate vulnerabilities resulting from coding errors before they are deployed. Robert is also an adjunct professor in the School of Computer Science and the Information Networking Institute at Carnegie Mellon University.

He is the author of eight books, including *Secure Coding in C and C++*, Second Edition (Addison-Wesley, 2013), and *Java Coding Guidelines: 75 Recommendations for Reliable and Secure Programs* (Addison-Wesley, 2014). He has also published more than 40 papers on software security, component-based software engineering, Web-based system design, legacy-system modernization, component repositories and search engines, and user interface design and development. Robert has been teaching secure coding in C and C++ to private industry, academia, and government since 2005. He started programming professionally for IBM in 1982, working in communications and operating system software, processor development, and software engineering. Robert also has worked at the X Consortium, where he developed and maintained code for the Common Desktop Environment and the X Window System. He represents Carnegie Mellon University (CMU) at the ISO/IEC JTC1/SC22/WG14 international standardization working group for the C programming language.

Chapter 1

Preprocessor (PRE)

Chapter Contents

Risk Assessment Summary

Rule	Severity	Likelihood	Remediation Cost	Priority	Level
PRE30-C	Low	Unlikely	Medium	P2	L3
PRE31-C	Low	Unlikely	Low	P3	L3
PRE32-C	Low	Unlikely	Medium	P2	L3

■ PRE30-C. Do not create a universal character name through concatenation

The C Standard supports universal character names that may be used in identifiers, character constants, and **string** literals to designate characters that are not in the basic character set. The universal character name \U*nnnnnnnn* designates the character whose 8-digit short identifier (as specified by ISO/IEC 10646) is *nnnnnnnn*. Similarly, the universal character name \u*nnnn* designates the character whose 4-digit short identifier is *nnnn* (and whose 8-digit short identifier is 0000*nnnn*).

The C Standard, 5.1.1.2, paragraph 4 [ISO/IEC 9899:2011], says,

> If a character sequence that matches the syntax of a universal character name is produced by token concatenation (6.10.3.3), the behavior is undefined.

See also **undefined behavior** 3 in Appendix B.

In general, avoid universal character names in identifiers unless absolutely necessary.

Noncompliant Code Example

This code example is noncompliant because it produces a universal character name by token concatenation:

```
#define assign(uc1, uc2, val) uc1##uc2 = val

void func(void) {
  int \u0401;
  /* ... */
  assign(\u04, 01, 4);
  /* ... */
}
```

Compliant Solution

This compliant solution uses a universal character name but does not create it by using token concatenation:

```
#define assign(ucn, val) ucn = val;

void func(void) {
  int \u0401;
  /* ... */
  assign(\u0401, 4);
  /* ... */
}
```

Risk Assessment

Creating a universal character name through token concatenation results in undefined behavior.

Rule	Severity	Likelihood	Remediation Cost	Priority	Level
PRE30-C	Low	Unlikely	Medium	P2	L3

Bibliography

[ISO/IEC 10646:2012]	
[ISO/IEC 9899:2011]	5.1.1.2, "Translation Phases"

■ PRE31-C. Avoid side effects in arguments to unsafe macros

An **unsafe function-like macro** is one whose expansion results in evaluating one of its parameters more than once or not at all. Never invoke an unsafe macro with arguments containing an assignment, increment, decrement, volatile access, input/output, or other expressions with **side effects** (including function calls, which may cause side effects).

The documentation for unsafe macros should warn against invoking them with arguments with side effects, but the responsibility is on the programmer using the macro. Because of the risks associated with their use, it is recommended that the creation of unsafe function-like macros be avoided (see "PRE00-C. Prefer inline or static functions to function-like macros").

This rule is similar to "EXP44-C. Do not rely on side effects in operands to sizeof, _Alignof, or _Generic."

Noncompliant Code Example

One problem with unsafe macros is side effects on macro arguments, as shown by this noncompliant code example:

```
#define ABS(x) (((x) < 0) ? -(x) : (x))

void func(int n) {
  /* Validate that n is within the desired range */
  int m = ABS(++n);

  /* ... */
}
```

The invocation of the ABS() macro in this example expands to

```
m = (((++n) < 0) ? -(++n) : (++n));
```

The resulting code is well defined but causes n to be incremented twice rather than once.

Compliant Solution

In this compliant solution, the increment operation ++n is performed before the call to the unsafe macro.

```
#define ABS(x) (((x) < 0) ? -(x) : (x)) /* UNSAFE */

void func(int n) {
  /* Validate that n is within the desired range */
  ++n;
  int m = ABS(n);

  /* ... */
}
```

Note the comment warning programmers that the macro is unsafe. The macro can also be renamed ABS_UNSAFE() to make it clear that the macro is unsafe. This compliant solution, like all the compliant solutions for this rule, has undefined behavior if the argument to ABS() is equal to the minimum (most negative) value for the signed integer type (see "INT32-C. Ensure that operations on signed integers do not result in overflow" for more information).

Compliant Solution

This compliant solution follows the guidance of "PRE00-C. Prefer inline or static functions to function-like macros" by defining an inline function iabs() to replace the ABS() macro. Unlike the ABS() macro, which operates on operands of any type, the iabs() function will truncate arguments of types wider than int whose value is not in range of the latter type.

```
#include <complex.h>
#include <math.h>

static inline int iabs(int x) {
  return (((x) < 0) ? -(x) : (x));
}

void func(int n) {
  /* Validate that n is within the desired range */
```

```
int m = iabs(++n);

  /* ... */
}
```

Compliant Solution

A more flexible compliant solution is to declare the ABS() macro using a _Generic selection. To support all arithmetic data types, this solution also makes use of inline functions to compute integer absolute values (see "PRE00-C. Prefer inline or static functions to function-like macros" and "PRE12-C. Do not define unsafe macros").

According to the C Standard, 6.5.1.1, paragraph 3 [ISO/IEC 9899:2011]:

> The controlling expression of a generic selection is not evaluated. If a generic selection has a generic association with a type name that is compatible with the type of the controlling expression, then the result expression of the generic selection is the expression in that generic association. Otherwise, the result expression of the generic selection is the expression in the default generic association. None of the expressions from any other generic association of the generic selection is evaluated.

Because the expression is not evaluated as part of the generic selection, the use of a macro in this solution is guaranteed to evaluate the macro parameter v only once.

```
#include <complex.h>
#include <math.h>

static inline long long llabs(long long v) {
  return v < 0 ? -v : v;
}
static inline long labs(long v) {
  return v < 0 ? -v : v;
}
static inline int iabs(int v) {
  return v < 0 ? -v : v;
}
static int sabs(short v) {
  return v < 0 ? -v : v;
}
static inline int scabs(signed char v) {
  return v < 0 ? -v : v;
}
```

```
#define ABS(v)  _Generic(v, signed char : scabs, \
                            short : sabs, \
                            int : iabs, \
                            long : labs, \
                            long long : llabs, \
                            float : fabsf, \
                            double : fabs, \
                            long double : fabsl, \
                            double complex : cabs, \
                            float complex : cabsf, \
                            long double complex : cabsl)(v)

void func(int n) {
  /* Validate n is within the desired range */
  int m = ABS(++n);
  /* ... */
}
```

Generic selections were introduced in C11 and are not available in C99 and earlier editions of the C standard.

Compliant Solution (GCC)

GCC's __typeof extension makes it possible to declare and assign the value of the macro operand to a temporary of the same type and perform the computation on the temporary, consequently guaranteeing that the operand will be evaluated exactly once. Another GCC extension, known as *statement expression*, makes it possible for the block statement to appear where an expression is expected:

```
#define ABS(x) __extension__ ({ __typeof (x) tmp = x; \
                                tmp < 0 ? -tmp : tmp; })
```

Note that relying on such extensions makes code nonportable and violates "MSC14-C. Do not introduce unnecessary platform dependencies."

Noncompliant Code Example (assert())

The assert() macro is a convenient mechanism for incorporating diagnostic tests in code (see "MSC11-C. Incorporate diagnostic tests using assertions"). Expressions used as arguments to the standard assert() macro should not have side effects. The behavior of the assert() macro depends on the definition of the **object-like macro** NDEBUG. If the macro NDEBUG is undefined, the assert() macro is defined to evaluate its expression argument and, if the result of the expression compares equal to 0, call the abort() function. If NDEBUG is defined, assert is defined to expand to ((void)0). Consequently, the expression in the assertion is not evaluated and no side effects it may have had otherwise take place in non-debugging executions of the code.

This noncompliant code example includes an `assert()` macro containing an expression (index++) that has a side effect:

```
#include <assert.h>
#include <stddef.h>

void process(size_t index) {
  assert(index++ > 0); /* Side effect */
  /* ... */
}
```

Compliant Solution (assert())

This compliant solution avoids the possibility of side effects in assertions by moving the expression containing the side effect outside of the `assert()` macro:

```
#include <assert.h>
#include <stddef.h>

void process(size_t index) {
  assert(index > 0); /* No side effect */
  ++index;
  /* ... */
}
```

Exceptions

PRE31-EX1: An exception can be made for invoking an unsafe macro with a function call argument provided that the function has no side effects. However, it is easy to forget about obscure side effects that a function might have, especially library functions for which source code is not available; even changing `errno` is a side effect. Unless the function is user written and does nothing but perform a computation and return its result without calling any other functions, it is likely that many developers will forget about some side effect. Consequently, this exception must be used with great care.

Risk Assessment

Invoking an unsafe macro with an argument that has side effects may cause those side effects to occur more than once. This practice can lead to unexpected program behavior.

Rule	Severity	Likelihood	Remediation Cost	Priority	Level
PRE31-C	Low	Unlikely	Low	P3	L3

Related Guidelines

ISO/IEC TR 24772:2013	Pre-processor Directives [NMP]
MISRA C:2012	Rule 20.5 (advisory)

Bibliography

[ISO/IEC 9899:2011]	6.5.1.1, "Generic selection"
[Plum 1985]	Rule 1-11
[Dewhurst 2002]	Gotcha 28: "Side Effects in Assertions"

■ PRE32-C. Do not use preprocessor directives in invocations of function-like macros

Invocations of **function-like macros** must not include preprocessor directives, such as #define, #ifdef, and #include. Doing so results in undefined behavior, according to the C Standard, 6.10.3, paragraph 11 [ISO/IEC 9899:2011]:

> The sequence of preprocessing tokens bounded by the outside-most matching parentheses forms the list of arguments for the function-like macro. The individual arguments within the list are separated by comma preprocessing tokens, but comma preprocessing tokens between matching inner parentheses do not separate arguments. If there are sequences of preprocessing tokens within the list of arguments that would otherwise act as preprocessing directives, the behavior is undefined.

See also undefined behavior 93 in Appendix B.

This rule also applies to the use of preprocessor directives in arguments to a function where it is unknown whether or not the function is implemented using a macro. For example, standard library functions, such as `memcpy()`, `printf()`, and `assert()`, may be implemented as macros.

Noncompliant Code Example

In this noncompliant code example [GCC Bugs], the programmer uses pre-processor directives to specify platform-specific arguments to `memcpy()`. However, if `memcpy()` is implemented using a macro, the code results in undefined behavior.

```
#include <string.h>

void func(const char *src) {
  /* Validate the source string; calculate size */
  char *dest;
  /* malloc() destination string */
  memcpy(dest, src,
    #ifdef PLATFORM1
      12
    #else
      24
    #endif
  );
  /* ... */
);
```

Compliant Solution

In this compliant solution [GCC Bugs], the appropriate call to `memcpy()` is determined outside the function call:

```
#include <string.h>

void func(const char *src) {
  /* Validate the source string; calculate size */
  char *dest;
  /* malloc() destination string */
  #ifdef PLATFORM1
    memcpy(dest, src, 12);
  #else
    memcpy(dest, src, 24);
  #endif
  /* ... */
}
```

Risk Assessment

Including preprocessor directives in macro arguments is undefined behavior.

Rule	Severity	Likelihood	Remediation Cost	Priority	Level
PRE32-C	Low	Unlikely	Medium	P2	L3

Bibliography

[GCC Bugs]	"Non-bug"
[ISO/IEC 9899:2011]	6.10.3, "Macro Replacement"

Chapter 2

Declarations and Initialization (DCL)

Chapter Contents

Risk Assessment Summary

Rule	Severity	Likelihood	Remediation Cost	Priority	Level
DCL30-C	High	Probable	High	P6	L2
DCL31-C	Low	Unlikely	Low	P3	L3
DCL36-C	Medium	Probable	Medium	P8	L2
DCL37-C	Low	Unlikely	Low	P3	L3
DCL38-C	Low	Unlikely	Low	P3	L3
DCL39-C	Low	Unlikely	High	P1	L3
DCL40-C	Low	Unlikely	Medium	P2	L3
DCL41-C	Medium	Unlikely	Medium	P4	L3

■ DCL30-C. Declare objects with appropriate storage durations

Every object has a storage duration that determines its lifetime: *static*, *thread*, *automatic*, or *allocated*.

According to the C Standard, 6.2.4, paragraph 2 [ISO/IEC 9899:2011]:

> The lifetime of an object is the portion of program execution during which storage is guaranteed to be reserved for it. An object exists, has a constant address, and retains its last-stored value throughout its lifetime. If an object is referred to outside of its lifetime, the behavior is undefined. The value of a pointer becomes indeterminate when the object it points to reaches the end of its lifetime.

Do not attempt to access an object outside of its lifetime. Attempting to do so is undefined behavior and can lead to an exploitable **vulnerability** (see also undefined behavior 9 in Appendix B).

Noncompliant Code Example (Differing Storage Durations)

In this noncompliant code example, the address of the variable c_str with automatic storage duration is assigned to the variable p, which has static storage duration. The assignment is valid, but it is invalid for c_str to go out of scope while p holds its address, as happens at the end of dont_do_this().

```
#include <stdio.h>

const char *p;
void dont_do_this(void) {
  const char c_str[] = "This will change";
  p = c_str; /* Dangerous */
}

void innocuous(void) {
  printf("%s\n", p);
}

int main(void) {
  dont_do_this();
  innocuous();
  return 0;
}
```

Compliant Solution (Same Storage Durations)

In this compliant solution, p is declared with the same storage duration as c_str, preventing p from taking on an **indeterminate value** outside of this_is_OK():

```
void this_is_OK(void) {
  const char c_str[] = "Everything OK";
  const char *p = c_str;
  /* ... */
}
/* p is inaccessible outside the scope of string c_str */
```

Alternatively, both p and c_str could be declared with static storage duration.

Compliant Solution (Differing Storage Durations)

If it is necessary for p to be defined with static storage duration but c_str with a more limited duration, then p can be set to NULL before c_str is destroyed. This practice prevents p from taking on an indeterminate value, although any references to p must check for NULL.

```
const char *p;
void is_this_OK(void) {
  const char c_str[] = "Everything OK?";
  p = c_str;
  /* ... */
  p = NULL;
}
```

Noncompliant Code Example (Return Values)

In this noncompliant code sample, the function init_array() returns a pointer to a character array with automatic storage duration, which is accessible to the caller:

```
char *init_array(void) {
  char array[10];
  /* Initialize array */
  return array;
}
```

Some compilers generate a **diagnostic message** when a pointer to an object with automatic storage duration is returned from a function, as in this example. Programmers should compile code at high warning levels and resolve any diagnostic messages (see "MSC00-C. Compile cleanly at high warning levels").

Compliant Solution (Return Values)

The solution, in this case, depends on the intent of the programmer. If the intent is to modify the value of array and have that modification persist outside the scope of init_array(), the desired behavior can be achieved by declaring array elsewhere and passing it as an argument to init_array():

```
#include <stddef.h>

void init_array(char *array, size_t len) {
  /* Initialize array */
  return;
}

int main(void) {
  char array[10];
  init_array(array, sizeof(array) / sizeof(array[0]));
  /* ... */
  return 0;
}
```

Noncompliant Code Example (Output Parameter)

In this noncompliant code example, the function squirrel_away() stores a pointer to local variable local into a location pointed to by function parameter ptr_param. Upon the return of squirrel_away(), the pointer ptr_param points to a variable that has an expired lifetime.

```
void squirrel_away(char **ptr_param) {
  char local[10];
  /* Initialize array */
  *ptr_param = local;
}

void rodent(void) {
  char *ptr;
  squirrel_away(&ptr);
  /* ptr is live but invalid here */
}
```

Compliant Solution (Output Parameter)

In this compliant solution, the variable local has static storage duration; consequently, ptr can be used to reference the local array within the rodent() function:

```
char local[10];

void squirrel_away(char **ptr_param) {
  /* Initialize array */
  *ptr_param = local;
}

void rodent(void) {
  char *ptr;
  squirrel_away(&ptr);
  /* ptr is valid in this scope */
}
```

Risk Assessment

Referencing an object outside of its lifetime can result in an attacker being able to execute arbitrary code.

Rule	Severity	Likelihood	Remediation Cost	Priority	Level
DCL30-C	High	Probable	High	P6	L2

Related Guidelines

ISO/IEC TR 24772:2013	Dangling References to Stack Frames [DCM]
ISO/IEC TS 17961:2013	Escaping of the address of an automatic object [addrescape]

Bibliography

[Coverity 2007]	
[ISO/IEC 9899:2011]	6.2.4, "Storage Durations of Objects"

■ DCL31-C. Declare identifiers before using them

The C11 Standard requires type specifiers and forbids implicit function declarations. The C90 Standard allows implicit typing of variables and functions. Consequently, some existing legacy code uses implicit typing. Some C compilers still support legacy code by allowing implicit typing, but it should not be used for new code. Such an **implementation** may choose to assume an implicit declaration and continue translation to support existing programs that use this feature.

Noncompliant Code Example (Implicit `int`)

C no longer allows the absence of type specifiers in a declaration. The C Standard, 6.7.2 [ISO/IEC 9899:2011], states:

> At least one type specifier shall be given in the declaration specifiers in each declaration, and in the specifier-qualifier list in each `struct` declaration and type name.

This noncompliant code example omits the type specifier:

```
extern foo;
```

Some C implementations do not issue a diagnostic for the violation of this constraint. These nonconforming C translators continue to treat such declarations as implying the type `int`.

Compliant Solution (Implicit `int`)

This compliant solution explicitly includes a type specifier:

```
extern int foo;
```

Noncompliant Code Example (Implicit Function Declaration)

Implicit declaration of functions is not allowed: every function must be explicitly declared before it can be called. In C90, if a function is called without an explicit prototype, the compiler provides an implicit declaration.

The C90 Standard [ISO/IEC 9899:1990] includes this requirement:

> If the expression that precedes the parenthesized argument list in a function call consists solely of an identifier, and if no declaration is visible for this identifier, the identifier is implicitly declared exactly as if, in the innermost block containing the function call, the declaration `extern int identifier();` appeared.

If a function declaration is not visible at the point at which a call to the function is made, C90-compliant platforms assume an implicit declaration of

```
extern int identifier();
```

This declaration implies that the function may take any number and type of arguments and return an `int`. However, to conform to the current C Standard, programmers must explicitly prototype every function before invoking it. An implementation that conforms to the C Standard may or may not perform implicit function declarations, but C does require a **conforming** implementation to issue a diagnostic if it encounters an undeclared function being used.

In this noncompliant code example, if `malloc()` is not declared, either explicitly or by including `stdlib.h`, a compiler that conforms only to C90 may implicitly declare `malloc()` as `int malloc()`. If the platform's size of `int` is 32 bits, but the size of pointers is 64 bits, the resulting pointer would likely be truncated as a result of the implicit declaration of `malloc()` returning a 32-bit integer.

```
#include <stddef.h>
/* #include <stdlib.h> is missing */

int main(void) {
  for (size_t i = 0; i < 100; ++i) {
    /* int malloc() assumed */
```

```
      char *ptr = (char *)malloc(0x10000000);
      *ptr = 'a';
    }
    return 0;
}
```

Compliant Solution (Implicit Function Declaration)

This compliant solution declares malloc() by including the appropriate header file:

```
#include <stdlib.h>

int main(void) {
    for (size_t i = 0; i < 100; ++i) {
        char *ptr = (char *)malloc(0x10000000);
        *ptr = 'a';
    }
    return 0;
}
```

For more information on function declarations, see "DCL07-C. Include the appropriate type information in function declarators."

Noncompliant Code Example (Implicit Return Type)

Do not declare a function with an implicit return type. For example, if a function returns a meaningful integer value, declare it as returning int. If it returns no meaningful value, declare it as returning void.

```
#include <limits.h>
#include <stdio.h>

foo(void) {
    return UINT_MAX;
}

int main(void) {
    long long int c = foo();
    printf("%lld\n", c);
    return 0;
}
```

Because the compiler assumes that foo() returns a value of type int for this noncompliant code example, UINT_MAX is incorrectly converted to -1.

Compliant Solution (Implicit Return Type)

This compliant solution explicitly defines the return type of `foo()` as `unsigned int`. As a result, the function correctly returns `UINT_MAX`.

```
#include <limits.h>
#include <stdio.h>

unsigned int foo(void) {
  return UINT_MAX;
}

int main(void) {
  long long int c = foo();
  printf("%lld\n", c);
  return 0;
}
```

Risk Assessment

Because implicit declarations lead to less stringent type checking, they can introduce unexpected and erroneous behavior. Occurrences of an omitted type specifier in existing code are rare and the consequences are generally minor, perhaps resulting in **abnormal program termination**.

Rule	Severity	Likelihood	Remediation Cost	Priority	Level
DCL31-C	Low	Unlikely	Low	P3	L3

Related Guidelines

ISO/IEC TR 24772:2013	Subprogram Signature Mismatch [OTR]
MISRA C:2012	Rule 8.1 (required)

Bibliography

[ISO/IEC 9899:1990]	
[ISO/IEC 9899:2011]	6.7.2, "Type Specifiers"
[Jones 2008]	

■ DCL36-C. Do not declare an identifier with conflicting linkage classifications

Linkage can make an identifier declared in different scopes or declared multiple times within the same scope refer to the same object or function. Identifiers are classified as *externally linked*, *internally linked*, or *not linked*. These three kinds of linkage have the following characteristics [Kirch-Prinz 2002]:

- *External linkage:* An identifier with external linkage represents the same object or function throughout the entire program; that is, in all compilation units and libraries belonging to the program. The identifier is available to the linker. When a second declaration of the same identifier with external linkage occurs, the linker associates the identifier with the same object or function.

- *Internal linkage:* An identifier with internal linkage represents the same object or function within a given translation unit. The linker has no information about identifiers with internal linkage. Consequently, these identifiers are internal to the translation unit.

- *No linkage:* If an identifier has no linkage, then any further declaration using the identifier declares something new, such as a new variable or a new type.

According to the C Standard, 6.2.2 [ISO/IEC 9899:2011], linkage is determined as follows:

If the declaration of a file scope identifier for an object or a function contains the storage class specifier `static`, the identifier has internal linkage.

For an identifier declared with the storage-class specifier `extern` in a scope in which a prior declaration of that identifier is visible, if the prior declaration specifies internal or external linkage, the linkage of the identifier at the later declaration is the same as the linkage specified at the prior declaration. If no prior declaration is visible, or if the prior declaration specifies no linkage, then the identifier has external linkage.

If the declaration of an identifier for a function has no storage-class specifier, its linkage is determined exactly as if it were declared with the storage-class specifier `extern`. If the declaration of an identifier for an object has file scope and no storage-class specifier, its linkage is external.

The following identifiers have no linkage: an identifier declared to be anything other than an object or a function; an identifier declared to be a function parameter; a block scope identifier for an object declared without the storage-class specifier `extern`.

Table 2–1. Assigned Linkage

		Second		
		static	No linkage	extern
First	static	Internal	Undefined	Internal
	No linkage	Undefined	No linkage	External
	extern	Undefined	Undefined	External

Use of an identifier (within one translation unit) classified as both internally and externally linked is undefined behavior (see also undefined behavior 8 in Appendix B). A translation unit includes the source file together with its headers and all source files included via the preprocessing directive #include.

Table 2–1 identifies the linkage assigned to an object that is declared twice in a single translation unit. The column designates the first declaration and the row designates the redeclaration.

Noncompliant Code Example

In this noncompliant code example, i2 and i5 are defined as having both internal and external linkage. Future use of either identifier results in undefined behavior.

```
int i1 = 10;        /* Definition, external linkage */
static int i2 = 20; /* Definition, internal linkage */
extern int i3 = 30; /* Definition, external linkage */
int i4;             /* Tentative definition, external linkage */
static int i5;      /* Tentative definition, internal linkage */

int i1; /* Valid tentative definition */
int i2; /* Undefined, linkage disagreement with previous */
int i3; /* Valid tentative definition */
int i4; /* Valid tentative definition */
int i5; /* Undefined, linkage disagreement with previous */

int main(void) {
  /* ... */
  return 0;
}
```

Compliant Solution

This compliant solution does not include conflicting definitions:

```
int i1 = 10;         /* Definition, external linkage */
static int i2 = 20;/* Definition, internal linkage */
extern int i3 = 30; /* Definition, external linkage */
int i4;              /* Tentative definition, external linkage */
static int i5;       /* Tentative definition, internal linkage */

int main(void) {
  /* ... */
  return 0;
}
```

Risk Assessment

Use of an identifier classified as both internally and externally linked is undefined behavior.

Rule	Severity	Likelihood	Remediation Cost	Priority	Level
DCL36-C	Medium	Probable	Medium	P8	L2

Related Guidelines

MISRA-C	Rule 8.2 (required)
	Rule 8.4 (required)
	Rule 17.3 (mandatory)

Bibliography

[Banahan 2003]	Section 8.2, "Declarations, Definitions and Accessibility"
[ISO/IEC 9899:2011]	6.2.2, "Linkages of Identifiers"
[Kirch-Prinz 2002]	

■ DCL37-C. Do not declare or define a reserved identifier

According to the C Standard, 7.1.3 [ISO/IEC 9899:2011],

- All identifiers that begin with an underscore and either an uppercase letter or another underscore are always reserved for any use.
- All identifiers that begin with an underscore are always reserved for use as identifiers with file scope in both the ordinary and tag name spaces.
- Each macro name in any of the following subclauses (including the future library directions) is reserved for use as specified if any of its associated headers is included, unless explicitly stated otherwise.
- All identifiers with external linkage (including future library directions) and errno are always reserved for use as identifiers with external linkage.
- Each identifier with file scope listed in any of the following subclauses (including the future library directions) is reserved for use as a macro name and as an identifier with file scope in the same name space if any of its associated headers is included.

Additionally, subclause 7.31 defines many other reserved identifiers for future library directions.

No other identifiers are reserved. (Note that the POSIX standard extends the set of identifiers reserved by the C Standard to include an open-ended set of its own. See *Portable Operating System Interface [POSIX®], Base Specifications, Issue 7*, section 2.2, "The Compilation Environment" [IEEE Std 1003.1-2013].) The behavior of a program that declares or defines an identifier in a context in which it is reserved or that defines a reserved identifier as a macro name is undefined (see also undefined behavior 106 in Appendix B).

Noncompliant Code Example (Header Guard)

A common, but noncompliant, practice is to choose a reserved name for a macro used in a preprocessor conditional guarding against multiple inclusions of a header file (see also "PRE06-C. Enclose header files in an inclusion guard"). The name may clash with reserved names defined by the implementation of the C standard library in its headers or with reserved names implicitly predefined by the compiler even when no C standard library header is included.

```
#ifndef _MY_HEADER_H_
#define _MY_HEADER_H_

/* Contents of <my_header.h> */

#endif /* _MY_HEADER_H_ */
```

Compliant Solution (Header Guard)

This compliant solution avoids using leading underscores in the name of the header guard:

```
#ifndef MY_HEADER_H
#define MY_HEADER_H

/* Contents of <my_header.h> */

#endif /* MY_HEADER_H */
```

Noncompliant Code Example (File Scope Objects)

In this noncompliant code example, the names of the file scope objects _max_limit and _limit both begin with an underscore. Because _max_limit is static, this declaration might seem to be impervious to clashes with names defined by the implementation. However, because the header <stddef.h> is included to define size_t, a potential for a name clash exists. (Note, however, that a conforming compiler may implicitly declare reserved names regardless of whether any C standard library header is explicitly included.) In addition, because _limit has external linkage, it may clash with a symbol with the same name defined in the language runtime library even if such a symbol is not declared in any header. Consequently, it is unsafe to start the name of any file scope identifier with an underscore even if its linkage limits its visibility to a single translation unit.

```
#include <stddef.h>

static const size_t _max_limit = 1024;
size_t _limit = 100;

unsigned int getValue(unsigned int count) {
  return count < _limit ? count : _limit;
}
```

Compliant Solution (File Scope Objects)

In this compliant solution, names of file scope objects do not begin with an underscore:

```
#include <stddef.h>

static const size_t max_limit = 1024;
size_t limit = 100;

unsigned int getValue(unsigned int count) {
  return count < limit ? count : limit;
}
```

Noncompliant Code Example (Reserved Macros)

In this noncompliant code example, because the C standard library header <inttypes.h> is specified to include <stdint.h>, the name MAX_SIZE conflicts with a standard macro of the same name, used to denote the upper limit of size_t. In addition, although the name INTFAST16_LIMIT_MAX is not defined by the C standard library, it is a reserved identifier because it begins with the INT prefix and ends with the _MAX suffix (see the C Standard, 7.31.10).

```
#include <inttypes.h>
#include <stdio.h>

static const int_fast16_t INTFAST16_LIMIT_MAX = 12000;

void print_fast16(int_fast16_t val) {
  enum { MAX_SIZE = 80 };
  char buf[MAX_SIZE];
  if (INTFAST16_LIMIT_MAX < val) {
    sprintf(buf, "The value is too large");
  } else {
    snprintf(buf, MAX_SIZE, "The value is %" PRIdFAST16, val);
  }
}
```

Compliant Solution (Reserved Macros)

This compliant solution avoids redefining reserved names or using reserved prefixes and suffixes:

```
#include <inttypes.h>
#include <stdio.h>
```

```
static const int_fast16_t MY_INTFAST16_UPPER_LIMIT = 12000;

void print_fast16(int_fast16_t val) {
  enum { BUFSIZE = 80 };
  char buf[BUFSIZE];
  if (MY_INTFAST16_UPPER_LIMIT < val) {
    sprintf(buf, "The value is too large");
  } else {
    snprintf(buf, BUFSIZE, "The value is %" PRIdFAST16, val);
  }
}
```

Noncompliant Code Example (Identifiers with External Linkage)

In addition to symbols defined as functions in each C standard library header, identifiers with external linkage include errno and math_errhandling, among others, regardless of whether any of them are masked by a macro of the same name.

This noncompliant example provides definitions for the C standard library functions malloc() and free(). Although this practice is permitted by many traditional implementations of UNIX (for example, the Dmalloc library), it is undefined behavior according to the C Standard. Even on systems that allow replacing malloc(), doing so without also replacing aligned_alloc(), calloc(), and realloc() is likely to cause problems.

```
#include <stddef.h>

void *malloc(size_t nbytes) {
  void *ptr;
  /* Allocate storage from own pool and set ptr */
  return ptr;
}

void free(void *ptr) {
  /* Return storage to own pool */
}
```

Compliant Solution (Identifiers with External Linkage)

The compliant, portable solution avoids redefining any C standard library identifiers with external linkage. In addition, it provides definitions for all memory allocation functions:

```
#include <stddef.h>

void *my_malloc(size_t nbytes) {
```

```
    void *ptr;
    /* Allocate storage from own pool and set ptr */
    return ptr;
}
void *my_aligned_alloc(size_t alignment, size_t size) {
    void *ptr;
    /* Allocate storage from own pool, align properly, set ptr */
    return ptr;
}

void *my_calloc(size_t nelems, size_t elsize) {
    void *ptr;
    /* Allocate storage from own pool, zero memory, and set ptr */
    return ptr;
}

void *my_realloc(void *ptr, size_t nbytes) {
    /* Reallocate storage from own pool and set ptr */
    return ptr;
}

void my_free(void *ptr) {
    /* Return storage to own pool */
}
```

Noncompliant Code Example (errno)

According to the C Standard, 7.5, paragraph 2 [ISO/IEC 9899:2011], the behavior of a program is undefined when

> a macro definition of errno is suppressed in order to access an actual object, or the program defines an identifier with the name errno.

See Appendix B, undefined behavior 114.

The errno identifier expands to a modifiable **lvalue** that has type int but is not necessarily the identifier of an object. It might expand to a modifiable lvalue resulting from a function call, such as *errno(). It is unspecified whether errno is a macro or an identifier declared with external linkage. If a macro definition is suppressed to access an actual object, or if a program defines an identifier with the name errno, the behavior is undefined.

Legacy code is apt to include an incorrect declaration, such as the following:

```
extern int errno;
```

Compliant Solution (errno)

The correct way to declare errno is to include the header <errno.h>:

```
#include <errno.h>
```

Implementations conforming to C are required to declare errno in <errno.h>, although some historic implementations failed to do so.

Exceptions

DCL37-EX1: Provided that a library function can be declared without reference to any type defined in a header, it is permissible to declare that function without including its header provided that declaration is compatible with the standard declaration.

```
/* Not including stdlib.h */
void free(void *);

void func(void *ptr) {
  free(ptr);
}
```

Such code is compliant because the declaration matches what stdlib.h would provide and does not redefine the reserved identifier. However, it would not be acceptable to provide a definition for the free() function in the preceding example.

Risk Assessment

Using reserved identifiers can lead to incorrect program operation.

Rule	Severity	Likelihood	Remediation Cost	Priority	Level
DCL37-C	Low	Unlikely	Low	P3	L3

Related Guidelines

ISO/IEC TS 17961:2013	Using identifiers that are reserved for the implementation [resident]

Bibliography

[IEEE Std 1003.1-2013]	Section 2.2, "The Compilation Environment"
[ISO/IEC 9899:2011]	7.1.3, "Reserved Identifiers" 7.31.10, "Integer Types <stdint.h>"

■ DCL38-C. Use the correct syntax when declaring a flexible array member

Flexible array members are a special type of array in which the last element of a structure with more than one named member has an incomplete array type; that is, the size of the array is not specified explicitly within the structure. This "struct hack" was widely used in practice and supported by a variety of compilers. Consequently, a variety of different syntaxes have been used for declaring flexible array members. For conforming C implementations, use the syntax guaranteed valid by the C Standard.

Flexible array members are defined in the C Standard, 6.7.2.1, paragraph 18 [ISO/IEC 9899:2011], as follows:

> As a special case, the last element of a structure with more than one named member may have an incomplete array type; this is called a *flexible array member*. In most situations, the flexible array member is ignored. In particular, the size of the structure is as if the flexible array member were omitted except that it may have more trailing padding than the omission would imply. However, when a . (or ->) operator has a left operand that is (a pointer to) a structure with a flexible array member and the right operand names that member, it behaves as if that member were replaced with the longest array (with the same element type) that would not make the structure larger than the object being accessed; the offset of the array shall remain that of the flexible array member, even if this would differ from that of the replacement array. If this array would have no elements, it behaves as if it had one element but the behavior is undefined if any attempt is made to access that element or to generate a pointer one past it.

Structures with a flexible array member can be used to produce code with defined behavior. However, some restrictions apply, as follows:

1. The incomplete array type *must* be the last element within the structure.

2. There cannot be an array of structures that contain a flexible array member.

3. Structures that contain a flexible array member cannot be used as a member of another structure except as the last element of that structure.

4. The structure must contain at least one named member in addition to the flexible array member.

"MEM33-C. Allocate and copy structures containing a flexible array member dynamically" describes how to allocate and copy structures containing flexible array members.

Noncompliant Code Example

Before the introduction of flexible array members in the C Standard, structures with a one-element array as the final member were used to achieve similar functionality. This noncompliant code example illustrates how `struct flexArrayStruct` is declared in this case.

This noncompliant code example attempts to allocate a flexible array-like member with a one-element array as the final member. When the structure is instantiated, the size computed for `malloc()` is modified to account for the actual size of the dynamic array.

```
#include <stdlib.h>

struct flexArrayStruct {
  int num;
  int data[1];
};

void func(size_t array_size) {
  /* Space is allocated for the struct */
  struct flexArrayStruct *structP
    = (struct flexArrayStruct *)
      malloc(sizeof(struct flexArrayStruct)
          + sizeof(int) * (array_size - 1));
  if (structP == NULL) {
    /* Handle malloc failure */
  }

  structP->num = array_size;

  /*
   * Access data[] as if it had been allocated
   * as data[array_size].
   */
  for (size_t i = 0; i < array_size; ++i) {
    structP->data[i] = 1;
```

```
    }
}
```

This example has undefined behavior when accessing any element other than the first element of the data array (see the C Standard, 6.5.6). Consequently, the compiler can generate code that does not return the expected value when accessing the second element of data.

This approach may be the only alternative for compilers that do not yet implement the standard C syntax.

Compliant Solution

This compliant solution uses a flexible array member to achieve a dynamically sized structure:

```c
#include <stdlib.h>

struct flexArrayStruct{
  int num;
  int data[];
};

void func(size_t array_size) {
  /* Space is allocated for the struct */
  struct flexArrayStruct *structP
    = (struct flexArrayStruct *)
     malloc(sizeof(struct flexArrayStruct)
         + sizeof(int) * array_size);
  if (structP == NULL) {
    /* Handle malloc failure */
  }

  structP->num = array_size;

  /*
   * Access data[] as if it had been allocated
   * as data[array_size].
   */
  for (size_t i = 0; i < array_size; ++i) {
    structP->data[i] = 1;
  }
}
```

This compliant solution allows the structure to be treated as if its member data[] were declared to be data[array_size] in a manner that conforms to the C Standard.

Risk Assessment

Failing to use the correct syntax when declaring a flexible array member can result in undefined behavior, although the incorrect syntax will work on most implementations.

Rule	Severity	Likelihood	Remediation Cost	Priority	Level
DCL38-C	Low	Unlikely	Low	P3	L3

Bibliography

[ISO/IEC 9899:2011]	6.5.6, "Additive Operators" 6.7.2.1, "Structure and Union Specifiers"
[McCluskey 2001]	"Flexible Array Members and Designators in C9X"

■ DCL39-C. Avoid information leakage in structure padding

The C Standard, 6.7.2.1, discusses the layout of structure fields. It specifies that non-bit-field members are aligned in an implementation-defined manner and that there may be padding within or at the end of a structure. Furthermore, initializing the members of the structure does not guarantee initialization of the padding bytes. The C Standard, 6.2.6.1, paragraph 6 [ISO/IEC 9899:2011], states:

> When a value is stored in an object of structure or union type, including in a member object, the bytes of the object representation that correspond to any padding bytes take unspecified values.

> When passing a pointer to a structure across a trust boundary to a different trusted domain, programmers must ensure that the padding bytes of these structures do not contain sensitive information.

Noncompliant Code Example

This noncompliant code example runs in kernel space and copies data from struct test to user space. However, padding bytes may be used within the structure, for example, to ensure the proper alignment of the structure members.

These padding bytes may contain sensitive information, which may then be leaked when the data is copied to user space.

```c
#include <stddef.h>

struct test {
  int a;
  char b;
  int c;
};

/* Safely copy bytes to user space */
extern int copy_to_user(void *dest, void *src, size_t size);

void do_stuff(void *usr_buf) {
  struct test arg = {.a = 1, .b = 2, .c = 3};
  copy_to_user(usr_buf, &arg, sizeof(arg));
}
```

Noncompliant Code Example (memset())

The padding bytes can be explicitly initialized by calling memset():

```c
#include <string.h>

struct test {
  int a;
  char b;
  int c;
};

/* Safely copy bytes to user space */
extern int copy_to_user(void *dest, void *src, size_t size);

void do_stuff(void *usr_buf) {
  struct test arg;

  /* Set all bytes (including padding bytes) to zero */
  memset(&arg, 0, sizeof(arg));

  arg.a = 1;
  arg.b = 2;
  arg.c = 3;

  copy_to_user(usr_buf, &arg, sizeof(arg));
}
```

However, compilers are free to implement arg.b = 2 by setting the low byte of a 32-bit register to 2, leaving the high bytes unchanged, and storing all 32 bits of the register into memory. This could leak the high-order bytes resident in the register to a user.

Compliant Solution

This compliant solution serializes the structure data before copying it to an untrusted context:

```
#include <stddef.h>

struct test {
  int a;
  char b;
  int c;
};

/* Safely copy bytes to user space */
extern int copy_to_user(void *dest, void *src, size_t size);

void do_stuff(void *usr_buf) {
  struct test arg = {.a = 1, .b = 2, .c = 3};
  /* May be larger than strictly needed */
  unsigned char buf[sizeof(arg)];
  size_t offset = 0;

  memcpy(buf + offset, &arg.a, sizeof(arg.a));
  offset += sizeof(arg.a);
  memcpy(buf + offset, &arg.b, sizeof(arg.b));
  offset += sizeof(arg.b);
  memcpy(buf + offset, &arg.c, sizeof(arg.c));
  offset += sizeof(arg.c);

  copy_to_user(usr_buf, buf, offset /* size of info copied */);
}
```

This code ensures that no uninitialized padding bytes are copied to unprivileged users. Note that the structure copied to user space is now a packed structure and that the copy_to_user() function would need to unpack it to re-create the original padded structure.

Compliant Solution (Padding Bytes)

Padding bytes can be explicitly declared as fields within the structure. This solution is not portable, however, because it depends on the implementation and target memory architecture. The following solution is specific to the x86-32 architecture:

```
#include <assert.h>
#include <stddef.h>

struct test {
  int a;
  char b;
  char padding_1, padding_2, padding_3;
  int c;
};

/* Safely copy bytes to user space */
extern int copy_to_user(void *dest, void *src, size_t size);

void do_stuff(void *usr_buf) {
  /* Ensure c is the next byte after the last padding byte */
  static_assert(offsetof(struct test, c) ==
                offsetof(struct test, padding_3) + 1,
                "Structure contains intermediate padding");
  /* Ensure there is no trailing padding */
  static_assert(sizeof(struct test) ==
                offsetof(struct test, c) + sizeof(int),
                "Structure contains trailing padding");
  struct test arg = {.a = 1, .b = 2, .c = 3};
  arg.padding_1 = 0;
  arg.padding_2 = 0;
  arg.padding_3 = 0;
  copy_to_user(usr_buf, &arg, sizeof(arg));
}
```

The C Standard static_assert() macro accepts a constant expression and an **error message**. The expression is evaluated at compile time and, if false, the compilation is terminated and the error message is output (see "DCL03-C. Use a static assertion to test the value of a constant expression" for more details). The explicit insertion of the padding bytes into the struct should ensure that no additional padding bytes are added by the compiler and, consequently, both static assertions should be true. However, it is necessary to validate these assumptions to ensure that the solution is correct for a particular implementation.

Compliant Solution (Structure Packing—GCC)

GCC allows specifying declaration attributes using the keyword _attribute_((_packed_)). When this attribute is present, the compiler will not add padding bytes for memory alignment unless otherwise required to by the _Alignas alignment specifier, and it will attempt to place fields at adjacent memory offsets when possible.

```
#include <stddef.h>

struct test {
  int a;
  char b;
  int c;
} _attribute_((_packed_));

/* Safely copy bytes to user space */
extern int copy_to_user(void *dest, void *src, size_t size);

void do_stuff(void *usr_buf) {
  struct test arg = {.a = 1, .b = 2, .c = 3};
  copy_to_user(usr_buf, &arg, sizeof(arg));
}
```

Compliant Solution (Structure Packing—Microsoft Visual Studio)

Microsoft Visual Studio supports #pragma pack() to suppress padding bytes [MSDN]. The compiler adds padding bytes for memory alignment depending on the current packing mode but still honors alignment specified by _declspec(align()). In this compliant solution, the packing mode is set to 1 in an attempt to ensure all fields are given adjacent offsets:

```
#include <stddef.h>

#pragma pack(push, 1) /* 1 byte */
struct test {
  int a;
  char b;
  int c;
};
#pragma pack(pop)

/* Safely copy bytes to user space */
extern int copy_to_user(void *dest, void *src, size_t size);

void do_stuff(void *usr_buf) {
  struct test arg = {1, 2, 3};
  copy_to_user(usr_buf, &arg, sizeof(arg));
}
```

The pack pragma takes effect at the first struct declaration after the pragma is seen.

Risk Assessment

Padding bytes might contain sensitive data because the C Standard allows any padding bytes to take **unspecified values**. A pointer to such a structure could be passed to other functions, causing information leakage.

Rule	Severity	Likelihood	Remediation Cost	Priority	Level
DCL39-C	Low	Unlikely	High	P1	L3

Related Vulnerabilities

Numerous vulnerabilities in the Linux Kernel have resulted from violations of this rule. CVE-2010-4083 describes a vulnerability in which the semctl() system call allows unprivileged users to read uninitialized kernel stack memory, because various fields of a semid_ds struct declared on the stack are not altered or zeroed before being copied back to the user. CVE-2010-3881 describes a vulnerability in which structure padding and reserved fields in certain data structures in QEMU-KVM were not initialized properly before being copied to user space. A privileged host user with access to /dev/kvm could use this flaw to leak kernel stack memory to user space. CVE-2010-3477 describes a kernel information leak in act_police where incorrectly initialized structures in the traffic-control dump code may allow the disclosure of kernel memory to user space applications.

Bibliography

[Graff 2003]	
[ISO/IEC 9899:2011]	6.2.6.1, "General" 6.7.2.1, "Structure and Union Specifiers"
[Sun 1993]	

■ DCL40-C. Do not create incompatible declarations of the same function or object

Two or more incompatible declarations of the same function or object must not appear in the same program because they result in undefined behavior.

The C Standard, 6.2.7, mentions that two types may be distinct yet compatible and addresses precisely when two distinct types are compatible.

The C Standard identifies four situations in which undefined behavior (UB) may arise as a result of incompatible declarations of the same function or object:

- Two declarations of the same object or function specify types that are not compatible (see undefined behavior 15 in Appendix B).
- Two identifiers differ only in nonsignificant characters (see undefined behavior 31 in Appendix B).
- An object has its stored value accessed other than by an lvalue of an allowable type (see undefined behavior 37 in Appendix B).
- A function is defined with a type that is not compatible with the type (of the expression) pointed to by the expression that denotes the called function (see undefined behavior 41 in Appendix B).

Although the effect of two incompatible declarations simply appearing in the same program may be benign on most implementations, the effects of invoking a function through an expression whose type is incompatible with the function definition are typically catastrophic. Similarly, the effects of accessing an object using an lvalue of a type that is incompatible with the object definition may range from unintended information exposure to memory overwrite to a hardware trap.

Noncompliant Code Example (Incompatible Object Declarations)

In this noncompliant code example, the variable i is declared to have type int in file a.c but defined to be of type short in file b.c. The declarations are incompatible, resulting in undefined behavior 15. Furthermore, accessing the object using an lvalue of an incompatible type, as shown in function f(), is undefined behavior 37 with possible observable results ranging from unintended information exposure to memory overwrite to a hardware trap.

```
/* In a.c */
extern int i; /* UB 15 */

int f(void) {
  return ++i; /* UB 37 */
}

/* In b.c */
short i; /* UB 15 */
```

Compliant Solution (Incompatible Object Declarations)

This compliant solution has compatible declarations of the variable i:

```
/* In a.c */
extern int i;

int f(void) {
  return ++i;
}
```

```
/* In b.c */
int i;
```

Noncompliant Code Example (Incompatible Array Declarations)

In this noncompliant code example, the variable a is declared to have pointer type in file a.c but defined to have array type in file b.c. The two declarations are incompatible, resulting in undefined behavior 15. As before, accessing the object in function f() is undefined behavior 37 with the typical effect of triggering a hardware trap.

```
/* In a.c */
extern int *a;  /* UB 15 */

int f(unsigned int i, int x) {
  int tmp = a[i];    /* UB 37: read access */
  a[i] = x;          /* UB 37: write access */
  return tmp;
}
```

```
/* In b.c */
int a[] = { 1, 2, 3, 4 };  /* UB 15 */
```

Compliant Solution (Incompatible Array Declarations)

This compliant solution declares a as an array in a.c and b.c:

```
/* In a.c */
extern int a[];

int f(unsigned int i, int x) {
  int tmp = a[i];
  a[i] = x;
  return tmp;
}
```

```
/* In b.c */
int a[] = { 1, 2, 3, 4 };
```

Noncompliant Code Example (Incompatible Function Declarations)

In this noncompliant code example, the function f() is declared in file a.c with one prototype but defined in file b.c with another. The two prototypes are incompatible, resulting in undefined behavior 15. Furthermore, invoking the function is undefined behavior 41 and typically has catastrophic consequences.

```
/* In a.c */
extern int f(int a);  /* UB 15 */

int g(int a) {
  return f(a);  /* UB 41 */
}

/* In b.c */
long f(long a) {  /* UB 15 */
  return a * 2;
}
```

Compliant Solution (Incompatible Function Declarations)

This compliant solution has compatible prototypes for the function f():

```
/* In a.c */
extern int f(int a);

int g(int a) {
  return f(a);
}

/* In b.c */
int f(int a) {
  return a * 2;
}
```

Noncompliant Code Example (Incompatible Variadic Function Declarations)

In this noncompliant code example, the function buginf() is defined to take a variable number of arguments and expects them all to be signed integers, with a sentinel value of -1:

```
/* In a.c */
void buginf(const char *fmt, ...) {
    /* ... */
}

/* In b.c */
void buginf();
```

Although this code appears to be well defined because of the prototype-less declaration of buginf(), it exhibits undefined behavior in accordance with the C Standard, 6.7.6.3, paragraph 15 [ISO/IEC 9899:2011]:

> For two function types to be compatible, both shall specify compatible return types. Moreover, the parameter type lists, if both are present, shall agree in the number of parameters and in use of the ellipsis terminator; corresponding parameters shall have compatible types. If one type has a parameter type list and the other type is specified by a function declarator that is not part of a function definition and that contains an empty identifier list, the parameter list shall not have an ellipsis terminator and the type of each parameter shall be compatible with the type that results from the application of the default argument promotions.

Compliant Solution (Incompatible Variadic Function Declarations)

In this compliant solution, the prototype for the function buginf() is included in the scope in the source file where it will be used:

```
/* In a.c */
void buginf(const char *fmt, ...) {
    /* ... */
}

/* In b.c */
void buginf(const char *fmt, ...);
```

Noncompliant Code Example (Excessively Long Identifiers)

In this noncompliant code example, the length of the identifier declaring the function pointer bash_groupname_completion_function() in file bashline.h exceeds by 3 the minimum implementation limit of 31 significant initial characters in an external identifier, introducing the possibility of colliding with the `bash_groupname_completion_funct` integer variable defined in file b.c, which is exactly 31 characters long. On an implementation that exactly meets this limit, this is undefined behavior 31. It results in two incompatible declarations of the same function (see undefined behavior 15). In addition, invoking the function leads to undefined behavior 41 with typically catastrophic effects.

```
/* In bashline.h */
/* UB 15, UB 31 */
extern char *bash_groupname_completion_function(const char *, int);

/* In a.c */
#include "bashline.h"

void f(const char *s, int i) {
  bash_groupname_completion_function(s, i); /* UB 41 */
}

/* In b.c */
int bash_groupname_completion_funct; /* UB 15, UB 31 */
```

> NOTE The identifier bash_groupname_completion_function referenced here was taken from GNU Bash version 3.2.

Compliant Solution (Excessively Long Identifiers)

In this compliant solution, the length of the identifier declaring the function pointer `bash_groupname_completion()` in `bashline.h` is less than 32 characters. Consequently, it cannot clash with `bash_groupname_completion_funct` on any compliant platform.

```
/* In bashline.h */
extern char *bash_groupname_completion(const char *, int);

/* In a.c */
#include "bashline.h"

void f(const char *s, int i) {
  bash_groupname_completion(s, i);
}

/* In b.c */
int bash_groupname_completion_funct;
```

Risk Assessment

Rule	Severity	Likelihood	Remediation Cost	Priority	Level
DCL40-C	Low	Unlikely	Medium	P2	L3

Related Guidelines

ISO/IEC TS 17961:2013	Declaring the same function or object in incompatible ways [funcdecl]

Bibliography

[Hatton 1995]	Section 2.8.3
[ISO/IEC 9899:2011]	6.7.6.3, "Function Declarators (including Prototypes)" J.2, "Undefined Behavior"

■ DCL41-C. Do not declare variables inside a switch statement before the first case label

According to the C Standard, 6.8.4.2, paragraph 4 [ISO/IEC 9899:2011],

> A switch statement causes control to jump to, into, or past the statement that is the switch body, depending on the value of a controlling expression, and on the presence of a default label and the values of any case labels on or in the switch body.

If a programmer declares variables, initializes them before the first case statement, and then tries to use them inside any of the case statements, those variables will have scope inside the switch block but will not be initialized and will consequently contain indeterminate values.

Noncompliant Code Example

This noncompliant code example declares variables and contains executable statements before the first case label within the switch statement:

```
#include <stdio.h>

extern void f(int i);
```

```
void func(int expr) {
  switch (expr) {
    int i = 4;
    f(i);
  case 0:
    i = 17;
    /* Falls through into default code */
  default:
    printf("%d\n", i);
  }
}
```

Compliant Solution

In this compliant solution, the statements before the first case label occur before the switch statement:

```
#include <stdio.h>

extern void f(int i);

int func(int expr) {
  /*
   * Move the code outside the switch block; now the statements
   * will get executed.
   */
  int i = 4;
  f(i);

  switch (expr) {
    case 0:
      i = 17;
      /* Falls through into default code */
    default:
      printf("%d\n", i);
  }
  return 0;
}
```

Risk Assessment

Using test conditions or initializing variables before the first case statement in a switch block can result in **unexpected behavior** and undefined behavior.

Rule	Severity	Likelihood	Remediation Cost	Priority	Level
DCL41-C	Medium	Unlikely	Medium	P4	L3

Related Guidelines

MISRA C:2012	Rule 16.1 (required)

Bibliography

[ISO/IEC 9899:2011]	6.8.4.2, "The `switch` Statement"

Chapter 3

Expressions (EXP)

Chapter Contents

Risk Assessment Summary

Rule	Severity	Likelihood	Remediation Cost	Priority	Level
EXP30-C	Medium	Probable	Medium	P8	L2
EXP32-C	Low	Likely	Medium	P6	L2
EXP33-C	High	Probable	Medium	P12	L1
EXP34-C	High	Likely	Medium	P18	L1
EXP35-C	Low	Probable	Medium	P4	L3
EXP36-C	Low	Probable	Medium	P4	L3
EXP37-C	Medium	Probable	High	P4	L3
EXP39-C	Medium	Unlikely	High	P2	L3
EXP40-C	Low	Unlikely	Medium	P2	L3
EXP42-C	Medium	Probable	Medium	P8	L2
EXP43-C	Medium	Probable	High	P4	L3
EXP44-C	Low	Unlikely	Low	P3	L3
EXP45-C	Low	Likely	Medium	P6	L2

■ EXP30-C. Do not depend on the order of evaluation for side effects

Evaluation of an expression may produce side effects. At specific points during execution, known as **sequence points**, all side effects of previous evaluations are complete, and no side effects of subsequent evaluations have yet taken place. Do not depend on the order of evaluation for side effects unless there is an intervening sequence point.

The C Standard, 6.5, paragraph 2 [ISO/IEC 9899:2011], states:

If a side effect on a scalar object is unsequenced relative to either a different side effect on the same scalar object or a value computation using the value of the same scalar object, the behavior is undefined. If there are multiple allowable orderings of the subexpressions of an expression, the behavior is undefined if such an unsequenced side effect occurs in any of the orderings.

This requirement must be met for each allowable ordering of the subexpressions of a full expression; otherwise, the behavior is undefined (see undefined behavior 35 in Appendix B.)

The following sequence points are defined in the C Standard, Annex C [ISO/IEC 9899:2011]:

- Between the evaluations of the function designator and actual arguments in a function call and the actual call
- Between the evaluations of the first and second operands of the following operators:
  - Logical AND: **&&**
  - Logical OR: **||**
  - Comma: **,**
- Between the evaluations of the first operand of the conditional **?:** operator and whichever of the second and third operands is evaluated
- The end of a full declarator
- Between the evaluation of a full expression and the next full expression to be evaluated; the following are full expressions:
  - An initializer that is not part of a compound literal
  - The expression in an expression statement
  - The controlling expression of a selection statement (**if** or **switch**)
  - The controlling expression of a **while** or **do** statement
  - Each of the (optional) expressions of a **for** statement
  - The (optional) expression in a **return** statement
- Immediately before a library function returns
- After the actions associated with each formatted input/output function conversion specifier
- Immediately before and immediately after each call to a comparison function, and also between any call to a comparison function and any movement of the objects passed as arguments to that call

This rule means that statements such as

```
i = i + 1;
a[i] = i;
```

have defined behavior, and statements such as the following do not:

```
/* i is modified twice between sequence points */
i = ++i + 1;

/* i is read other than to determine the value to be stored */
a[i++] = i;
```

Note that not all instances of a comma in C code denote a usage of the comma operator. For example, the comma between arguments in a function call is not a sequence point. However, according to the C Standard, 6.5.2.2, paragraph 10 [ISO/IEC 9899:2011]:

> Every evaluation in the calling function (including other function calls) that is not otherwise specifically sequenced before or after the execution of the body of the called function is indeterminately sequenced with respect to the execution of the called function.

This rule means that the order of evaluation for function call arguments is unspecified and can happen in any order.

Noncompliant Code Example

Programs cannot safely rely on the order of evaluation of operands between sequence points. In this noncompliant code example, i is evaluated twice without an intervening sequence point, and so the behavior of the expression is undefined:

```
#include <stdio.h>

void func(int i, int *b) {
  int a = i + b[++i];
  printf("%d, %d", a, i);
}
```

Compliant Solution

These examples are independent of the order of evaluation of the operands and can be interpreted in only one way:

```
#include <stdio.h>

void func(int i, int *b) {
```

```
    int a;
    ++i;
    a = i + b[i];
    printf("%d, %d", a, i);
}
```

Alternatively:

```
#include <stdio.h>

void func(int i, int *b) {
  int a = i + b[i + 1];
  ++i;
  printf("%d, %d", a, i);
}
```

Noncompliant Code Example

The call to func() in this noncompliant code example has undefined behavior because there is no sequence point between the argument expressions:

```
extern void func(int i, int j);

void f(int i) {
  func(i++, i);
}
```

The first (left) argument expression reads the value of i (to determine the value to be stored) and then modifies i. The second (right) argument expression reads the value of i between the same pair of sequence points as the first argument, but not to determine the value to be stored in i. This additional attempt to read the value of i has undefined behavior.

Compliant Solution

This compliant solution is appropriate when the programmer intends for both arguments to func() to be equivalent:

```
extern void func(int i, int j);

void f(int i) {
  i++;
  func(i, i);
}
```

This compliant solution is appropriate when the programmer intends for the second argument to be 1 greater than the first:

```
extern void func(int i, int j);

void f(int i) {
  int j = i++;
  func(j, i);
}
```

Noncompliant Code Example

The order of evaluation for function arguments is unspecified. This noncompliant code example exhibits **unspecified behavior** but not undefined behavior:

```
extern void c(int i, int j);
int glob;

int a(void) {
  return glob + 10;
}

int b(void) {
  glob = 42;
  return glob;
}

void func(void) {
  c(a(), b());
}
```

It is unspecified what order a() and b() are called in; the only guarantee is that both a() and b() will be called before c() is called. If a() or b() rely on shared state when calculating their return value, as they do in this example, the resulting arguments passed to c() may differ between compilers or architectures.

Compliant Solution

In this compliant solution, the order of evaluation for a() and b() is fixed, and so no unspecified behavior occurs:

```
extern void c(int i, int j);
int glob;

int a(void) {
  return glob + 10;
}
```

```
int b(void) {
  glob = 42;
  return glob;
}

void func(void) {
  int a_val, b_val;

  a_val = a();
  b_val = b();

  c(a_val, b_val);
}
```

Risk Assessment

Attempting to modify an object multiple times between sequence points may cause that object to take on an unexpected value, which can lead to unexpected program behavior.

Rule	Severity	Likelihood	Remediation Cost	Priority	Level
EXP30-C	Medium	Probable	Medium	P8	L2

Related Guidelines

ISO/IEC TR 24772:2013	Operator Precedence/Order of Evaluation [JCW] Side-effects and Order of Evaluation [SAM]
MISRA C:2012	Rule 12.1 (advisory)

Bibliography

[ISO/IEC 9899:2011]	6.5, "Expressions" 6.5.2.2, "Function Calls" Annex C, "Sequence Points"
[Saks 2007]	
[Summit 2005]	Questions 3.1, 3.2, 3.3, 3.3b, 3.7, 3.8, 3.9, 3.10a, 3.10b, and 3.11

■ EXP32-C. Do not access a volatile object through a nonvolatile reference

An object that has volatile-qualified type may be modified in ways unknown to the implementation or have other unknown side effects. Referencing a volatile object by using a non-volatile lvalue is undefined behavior. The C Standard, 6.7.3 [ISO/IEC 9899:2011], states:

> If an attempt is made to refer to an object defined with a volatile-qualified type through use of an lvalue with non-volatile-qualified type, the behavior is undefined.

See undefined behavior 65 in Appendix B.

Noncompliant Code Example

In this noncompliant code example, a volatile object is accessed through a non-volatile-qualified reference, resulting in undefined behavior:

```
#include <stdio.h>

void func(void) {
  static volatile int **ipp;
  static int *ip;
  static volatile int i = 0;

  printf("i = %d.\n", i);

  ipp = &ip; /* May produce a warning diagnostic */
  ipp = (int**)&ip;
  /* Constraint violation; may produce a warning diagnostic */
  *ipp = &i; /* Valid */
  if (*ip != 0) { /* Valid */
    /* ... */
  }
}
```

The assignment ipp = &ip is not safe because it allows the valid code that follows to reference the value of the volatile object i through the non-volatile-qualified reference ip. In this example, the compiler may optimize out the entire if block because *ip != 0 must be false if the object to which ip points is not volatile.

Compliant Solution

In this compliant solution, `ip` is declared `volatile`:

```
#include <stdio.h>

void func(void) {
  static volatile int **ipp;
  static volatile int *ip;
  static volatile int i = 0;

  printf("i = %d.\n", i);

  ipp = &ip;
  *ipp = &i;
  if (*ip != 0) {
    /* ... */
  }
}
```

Risk Assessment

Accessing an object with a volatile-qualified type through a reference with a non-volatile-qualified type is undefined behavior.

Rule	Severity	Likelihood	Remediation Cost	Priority	Level
EXP32-C	Low	Likely	Medium	P6	L2

Related Guidelines

ISO/IEC TR 24772:2013	Pointer Casting and Pointer Type Changes [HFC] Type System [IHN]
MISRA C:2012	Rule 11.8 (required)

Bibliography

[ISO/IEC 9899:2011]	6.7.3, "Type Qualifiers"

■ EXP33-C. Do not read uninitialized memory

Local, automatic variables assume unexpected values if they are read before they are initialized. The C Standard, 6.7.9, paragraph 10 [ISO/IEC 9899:2011], specifies:

> If an object that has automatic storage duration is not initialized explicitly, its value is indeterminate.

See undefined behavior 11 in Appendix B.

When local, automatic variables are stored on the program stack, for example, their values default to whichever values are currently stored in stack memory.

Additionally, some dynamic memory allocation functions do not initialize the contents of the memory they allocate; see Table 3–1.

Uninitialized automatic variables or dynamically allocated memory have indeterminate values, which for objects of some types can be a **trap representation**. Reading such trap representations is undefined behavior (see undefined behavior 10 and undefined behavior 12 in Appendix B); it can cause a program to behave in an unexpected manner and provide an avenue for attack. In many cases, compilers issue a warning diagnostic message when reading uninitialized variables (see "MSC00-C. Compile cleanly at high warning levels" for more information).

Table 3–1. Dynamic Memory Allocation Functions

Function	Initialization
aligned_alloc()	Does not perform initialization
calloc()	Zero-initializes allocated memory
malloc()	Does not perform initialization
realloc()	Copies contents from original pointer; may not initialize all memory

Noncompliant Code Example (Return-by-Reference)

In this noncompliant code example, the set_flag() function is intended to set the parameter, sign_flag, to the sign of number. However, the programmer neglected to account for the case where number is equal to 0. Because the local variable sign is uninitialized when calling set_flag() and is never written to by set_flag(), the comparison operation exhibits undefined behavior when reading sign.

```c
void set_flag(int number, int *sign_flag) {
  if (NULL == sign_flag) {
    return;
  }

  if (number > 0) {
    *sign_flag = 1;
  } else if (number < 0) {
    *sign_flag = -1;
  }
}

int is_negative(int number) {
  int sign;
  set_flag(number, &sign);
  return sign < 0;
}
```

Some compilers assume that when the address of an uninitialized variable is passed to a function, the variable is initialized within that function. Because compilers frequently fail to diagnose any resulting failure to initialize the variable, the programmer must apply additional scrutiny to ensure the correctness of the code.

This defect results from a failure to consider all possible data states (see "MSC01-C. Strive for logical completeness" for more information).

Compliant Solution (Return-by-Reference)

This compliant solution trivially repairs the problem by accounting for the possibility that number can be equal to zero.

Although compilers and **static analysis** tools often detect uses of uninitialized variables when they have access to the source code, diagnosing the problem is difficult or impossible when either the initialization or the use takes place in object code for which the source code is inaccessible. Unless doing so is prohibitive for performance reasons, an additional defense-in-depth practice worth considering is to initialize local variables immediately after declaration.

```
void set_flag(int number, int *sign_flag) {
  if (NULL == sign_flag) {
    return;
  }
  /* Account for number being 0 */
  if (number >= 0) {
    *sign_flag = 1;
  } else {
    *sign_flag = -1;
  }
}

int is_negative(int number) {
  int sign = 0; /* Initialize for defense-in-depth */
  set_flag(number, &sign);
  return sign < 0;
}
```

Noncompliant Code Example (Uninitialized Local)

In this noncompliant code example, the programmer mistakenly fails to set the local variable error_log to the msg argument in the report_error() function [Mercy 2006]. Because error_log has not been initialized, an indeterminate value is read. The sprintf() call copies data from the arbitrary location pointed to by the indeterminate error_log variable until a null byte is reached, which can result in a buffer overflow.

```
#include <stdio.h>

/* Get username and password from user, return -1 on error */
extern int do_auth(void);
enum { BUFFERSIZE = 24 };
void report_error(const char *msg) {
  const char *error_log;
  char buffer[BUFFERSIZE];

  sprintf(buffer, "Error: %s", error_log);
  printf("%s\n", buffer);
}

int main(void) {
  if (do_auth() == -1) {
    report_error("Unable to login");
  }
  return 0;
}
```

Noncompliant Code Example (Uninitialized Local)

In this noncompliant code example, the report_error() function has been modified so that error_log is properly initialized:

```
#include <stdio.h>
enum { BUFFERSIZE = 24 };
void report_error(const char *msg) {
  const char *error_log = msg;
  char buffer[BUFFERSIZE];

  sprintf(buffer, "Error: %s", error_log);
  printf("%s\n", buffer);
}
```

This example remains problematic because a buffer overflow will occur if the null-terminated byte string referenced by msg is greater than 16 characters, including the null terminator (see "STR31-C. Guarantee that storage for strings has sufficient space for character data and the null terminator" for more information).

Compliant Solution (Uninitialized Local)

In this compliant solution, the buffer overflow is eliminated by calling the snprintf() function:

```
#include <stdio.h>
enum { BUFFERSIZE = 24 };
void report_error(const char *msg) {
    char buffer[BUFFERSIZE];

  if (0 < snprintf(buffer, BUFFERSIZE, "Error: %s", msg))
    printf("%s\n", buffer);
  else
    puts("Unknown error");
}
```

Compliant Solution (Uninitialized Local)

A less error-prone compliant solution is to simply print the error message directly instead of using an intermediate buffer:

```
#include <stdio.h>

void report_error(const char *msg) {
  printf("Error: %s\n", msg);
}
```

Noncompliant Code Example (`mbstate_t`)

In this noncompliant code example, the function `mbrlen()` is passed the address of an automatic `mbstate_t` object that has not been initialized. This is undefined behavior 200 (see Appendix B) because `mbrlen()` dereferences and reads its third argument.

```
#include <string.h>
#include <wchar.h>

void func(const char *mbs) {
  size_t len;
  mbstate_t state;

  len = mbrlen(mbs, strlen(mbs), &state);
}
```

Compliant Solution (`mbstate_t`)

Before being passed to a multibyte conversion function, an `mbstate_t` object must be either initialized to the initial conversion state or set to a value that corresponds to the most recent shift state by a prior call to a multibyte conversion function. This compliant solution sets the `mbstate_t` object to the initial conversion state by setting it to all zeros.

```
#include <string.h>
#include <wchar.h>

void func(const char *mbs) {
  size_t len;
  mbstate_t state;

  memset(&state, 0, sizeof(state));
  len = mbrlen(mbs, strlen(mbs), &state);
}
```

Noncompliant Code Example (POSIX, Entropy)

In this noncompliant code example, described in "More Randomness or Less" [Wang 2012], the process ID, time of day, and uninitialized memory `junk` is used to seed a random number generator. This behavior is characteristic of some distributions derived from Debian Linux that use uninitialized memory as a source of entropy because the value stored in `junk` is indeterminate. However, because accessing an indeterminate value is undefined behavior, compilers may optimize out the uninitialized variable access completely, leaving only the time and process ID and resulting in a loss of desired entropy.

```
#include <time.h>
#include <unistd.h>
#include <stdlib.h>
#include <sys/time.h>

void func(void) {
  struct timeval tv;
  unsigned long junk;

  gettimeofday(&tv, NULL);
  srandom((getpid() << 16) ^ tv.tv_sec ^ tv.tv_usec ^ junk);
}
```

In security protocols that rely on unpredictability, such as RSA encryption, a loss in entropy results in a less secure system.

Compliant Solution (POSIX, Entropy)

This compliant solution seeds the random number generator by using the CPU clock and the real-time clock instead of reading uninitialized memory:

```
#include <time.h>
#include <unistd.h>
#include <stdlib.h>
#include <sys/time.h>

void func(void) {
  double cpu_time;
  struct timeval tv;

  cpu_time = ((double) clock()) / CLOCKS_PER_SEC;
  gettimeofday(&tv, NULL);
  srandom((getpid() << 16) ^ tv.tv_sec ^ tv.tv_usec ^ cpu_time);
}
```

Noncompliant Code Example (realloc())

The realloc() function changes the size of a dynamically allocated memory object. The initial size bytes of the returned memory object are unchanged, but any newly added space is uninitialized, and its value is indeterminate. As in the case of malloc(), accessing memory beyond the size of the original object is undefined behavior 181 (see Appendix B).

It is the programmer's responsibility to ensure that any memory allocated with `malloc()` and `realloc()` is properly initialized before it is used.

In this noncompliant code example, an array is allocated with `malloc()` and properly initialized. At a later point, the array is grown to a larger size but not initialized beyond what the original array contained. Subsequently accessing the uninitialized bytes in the new array is undefined behavior.

```c
#include <stdlib.h>
#include <stdio.h>
enum { OLD_SIZE = 10, NEW_SIZE = 20 };

int *resize_array(int *array, size_t count) {
  if (0 == count) {
    return 0;
  }

  int *ret = (int *)realloc(array, count * sizeof(int));
  if (!ret) {
    free(array);
    return 0;
  }

  return ret;
}

void func(void) {

  int *array = (int *)malloc(OLD_SIZE * sizeof(int));
  if (0 == array) {
    /* Handle error */
  }

  for (size_t i = 0; i < OLD_SIZE; ++i) {
    array[i] = i;
  }

  array = resize_array(array, NEW_SIZE);
  if (0 == array) {
    /* Handle error */
  }

  for (size_t i = 0; i < NEW_SIZE; ++i) {
    printf("%d ", array[i]);
  }
}
```

Compliant Solution (realloc())

In this compliant solution, the resize_array() helper function takes a second parameter for the old size of the array so that it can initialize any newly allocated elements:

```
#include <stdlib.h>
#include <stdio.h>
#include <string.h>

enum { OLD_SIZE = 10, NEW_SIZE = 20 };

int *resize_array(int *array, size_t old_count, size_t new_count) {
  if (0 == new_count) {
    return 0;
  }

  int *ret = (int *)realloc(array, new_count * sizeof(int));
  if (!ret) {
    free(array);
    return 0;
  }

  if (new_count > old_count) {
    memset(ret + old_count, 0, (new_count - old_count) * sizeof(int));
  }
  return ret;
}

void func(void) {

  int *array = (int *)malloc(OLD_SIZE * sizeof(int));
  if (0 == array) {
    /* Handle error */
  }

  for (size_t i = 0; i < OLD_SIZE; ++i) {
    array[i] = i;
  }

  array = resize_array(array, OLD_SIZE, NEW_SIZE);
  if (0 == array) {
    /* Handle error */
  }

  for (size_t i = 0; i < NEW_SIZE; ++i) {
    printf("%d ", array[i]);
  }
}
```

Exceptions

EXP33-EX1: Reading uninitialized memory by an lvalue of type `unsigned char` does not trigger undefined behavior. The `unsigned char` type is defined to not have a trap representation (see the C Standard, 6.2.6.1, paragraph 3), which allows for moving bytes without knowing if they are initialized. However, on some architectures, such as the Intel Itanium, registers have a bit to indicate whether or not they have been initialized. The C Standard, 6.3.2.1, paragraph 2, allows such implementations to cause a trap for an object that never had its address taken and is stored in a register if such an object is referred to in any way.

Risk Assessment

Reading uninitialized variables is undefined behavior and can result in unexpected program behavior. In some cases, these **security flaws** may allow the execution of arbitrary code.

Reading uninitialized variables for creating entropy is problematic because these memory accesses can be removed by compiler optimization. VU#925211 is an example of a vulnerability caused by this coding error.

Rule	Severity	Likelihood	Remediation Cost	Priority	Level
EXP33-C	High	Probable	Medium	P12	L1

Related Vulnerabilities

CVE-2009-1888 results from a violation of this rule. Some versions of SAMBA (up to 3.3.5) call a function that takes in two potentially uninitialized variables involving access rights. An attacker can **exploit** these coding errors to bypass the access control list and gain access to protected files [xorl 2009].

Related Guidelines

ISO/IEC TR 24772:2013	Initialization of Variables [LAV]
ISO/IEC TS 17961:2013	Referencing uninitialized memory [uninitref]
MITRE CWE	CWE-119, Improper Restriction of Operations within the Bounds of a Memory Buffer CWE-665, Improper Initialization

Bibliography

[Flake 2006]	
[ISO/IEC 9899:2011]	6.7.9, "Initialization" 6.2.6.1, "General" 6.3.2.1, "Lvalues, Arrays, and Function Designators"
[Mercy 2006]	
[VU#925211]	
[Wang 2012]	"More Randomness or Less"
[xorl 2009]	"CVE-2009-1888: SAMBA ACLs Uninitialized Memory Read"

■ EXP34-C. Do not dereference null pointers

Dereferencing a null pointer is undefined behavior.

On many platforms, dereferencing a null pointer results in abnormal program termination, but this is not required by the standard. See "Clever Attack Exploits Fully-Patched Linux Kernel" [Goodin 2009] for an example of a code execution exploit that resulted from a null pointer dereference.

Noncompliant Code Example

This noncompliant code example is derived from a real-world example taken from a vulnerable version of the libpng library as deployed on a popular ARM-based cell phone [Jack 2007]. The libpng library allows applications to read, create, and manipulate PNG (Portable Network Graphics) raster image files. The libpng library implements its own wrapper to malloc() that returns a null pointer on error or on being passed a 0-byte-length argument.

This code also violates "ERR33-C. Detect and handle standard library errors."

```c
#include <png.h> /* From libpng */
#include <string.h>

void func(png_structp png_ptr, int length, const void *user_data) {
  png_charp chunkdata;
  chunkdata = (png_charp)png_malloc(png_ptr, length + 1);
  /* ... */
  memcpy(chunkdata, user_data, length);
  /* ... */
}
```

If length has the value −1, the addition yields 0, and png_malloc() subsequently returns a null pointer, which is assigned to chunkdata. The chunkdata pointer is later used as a destination argument in a call to memcpy(), resulting in user-defined data overwriting memory starting at address 0. In the case of the ARM and XScale architectures, the 0x0 address is mapped in memory and serves as the exception vector table; consequently, dereferencing 0x0 did not cause an abnormal program termination.

Compliant Solution

This compliant solution ensures that the pointer returned by png_malloc() is not null. It also uses the unsigned type size_t to pass the length parameter, ensuring that negative values are not passed to func().

```
#include <png.h> /* From libpng */
#include <string.h>

void func(png_structp png_ptr, size_t length, const void *user_data) {
  png_charp chunkdata;
  if (length == SIZE_MAX) {
    /* Handle error */
  }
  chunkdata = (png_charp)png_malloc(png_ptr, length + 1);
  if (NULL == chunkdata) {
    /* Handle error */
  }
  /* ... */
  memcpy(chunkdata, user_data, length);
  /* ... */

}
```

Noncompliant Code Example

In this noncompliant code example, input_str is copied into dynamically allocated memory referenced by c_str. If malloc() fails, it returns a null pointer that is assigned to c_str. When c_str is dereferenced in memcpy(), the program exhibits undefined behavior. Additionally, if input_str is a null pointer, the call to strlen() dereferences a null pointer, also resulting in undefined behavior. This code also violates "ERR33-C. Detect and handle standard library errors."

```
#include <string.h>
#include <stdlib.h>
```

```
void f(const char *input_str) {
  size_t size = strlen(input_str) + 1;
  char *c_str = (char *)malloc(size);
  memcpy(c_str, input_str, size);
  /* ... */
  free(c_str);
  c_str = NULL;
  /* ... */
}
```

Compliant Solution

This compliant solution ensures that both `input_str` and the pointer returned by `malloc()` are not null.

```
#include <string.h>
#include <stdlib.h>

void f(const char *input_str) {
  size_t size;
  char *c_str;

  if (NULL == input_str) {
    /* Handle error */
  }

  size = strlen(input_str) + 1;
  c_str = (char *)malloc(size);
  if (NULL == c_str) {
    /* Handle error */
  }
  memcpy(c_str, input_str, size);
  /* ... */
  free(c_str);
  c_str = NULL;
  /* ... */
}
```

Noncompliant Code Example

This noncompliant code example is from a version of drivers/net/tun.c and affects Linux kernel 2.6.30 [Goodin 2009]:

```
static unsigned int tun_chr_poll(struct file *file,
                                 poll_table *wait) {
  struct tun_file *tfile = file->private_data;
  struct tun_struct *tun = __tun_get(tfile);
```

```
  struct sock *sk = tun->sk;
  unsigned int mask = 0;

  if (!tun)
    return POLLERR;

  DBG(KERN_INFO "%s: tun_chr_poll\n", tun->dev->name);

  poll_wait(file, &tun->socket.wait, wait);

  if (!skb_queue_empty(&tun->readq))
    mask |= POLLIN | POLLRDNORM;

  if (sock_writeable(sk) ||
      (!test_and_set_bit(SOCK_ASYNC_NOSPACE,
                         &sk->sk_socket->flags) &&
      sock_writeable(sk)))
    mask |= POLLOUT | POLLWRNORM;

  if (tun->dev->reg_state != NETREG_REGISTERED)
    mask = POLLERR;

  tun_put(tun);
  return mask;
}
```

The sk pointer is initialized to tun->sk before checking if tun is a null pointer. Because null pointer dereferencing is undefined behavior, the compiler (GCC in this case) can optimize away the if (!tun) check because it is performed after tun->sk is accessed, implying that tun is not null. As a result, this noncompliant code example is vulnerable to a null pointer dereference exploit because null pointer dereferencing can be permitted on several platforms, for example, by using mmap(2) with the MAP_FIXED flag on Linux and Mac OS X or by using the shmat() POSIX function with the SHM_RND flag [Liu 2009].

Compliant Solution

This compliant solution eliminates the null pointer deference by initializing sk to tun->sk following the null pointer check:

```
static unsigned int tun_chr_poll(struct file *file,
                                 poll_table *wait) {
  struct tun_file *tfile = file->private_data;
  struct tun_struct *tun = __tun_get(tfile);
```

```
    struct sock *sk;
    unsigned int mask = 0;

    if (!tun)
      return POLLERR;

    sk = tun->sk;

    /* The remaining code is omitted because it is unchanged... */
}
```

Risk Assessment

Dereferencing a null pointer is undefined behavior, typically abnormal program termination. In some situations, however, dereferencing a null pointer can lead to the execution of arbitrary code [Jack 2007], [van Sprundel 2006]. The indicated severity is for this more severe case; on platforms where it is not possible to exploit a null pointer dereference to execute arbitrary code, the actual severity is low.

Rule	Severity	Likelihood	Remediation Cost	Priority	Level
EXP34-C	High	Likely	Medium	P18	L1

Related Guidelines

ISO/IEC TR 24772:2013	Pointer Casting and Pointer Type Changes [HFC] Null Pointer Dereference [XYH]
ISO/IEC TS 17961:2013	Dereferencing an out-of-domain pointer [nullref]
MITRE CWE	CWE-476, NULL Pointer Dereference

Bibliography

[Goodin 2009]	
[Jack 2007]	
[Liu 2009]	
[van Sprundel 2006]	
[Viega 2005]	Section 5.2.18, "Null-Pointer Dereference"

■ EXP35-C. Do not modify objects with temporary lifetime

The C11 Standard [ISO/IEC 9899:2011] introduced a new term: *temporary lifetime*. Modifying an object with temporary lifetime is undefined behavior. According to subclause 6.2.4, paragraph 8:

> A non-lvalue expression with structure or union type, where the structure or union contains a member with array type (including, recursively, members of all contained structures and unions) refers to an object with automatic storage duration and *temporary* lifetime. Its lifetime begins when the expression is evaluated and its initial value is the value of the expression. Its lifetime ends when the evaluation of the containing full expression or full declarator ends. Any attempt to modify an object with temporary lifetime results in undefined behavior.

This definition differs from the C99 Standard (which defines modifying the result of a function call or accessing it after the next sequence point as undefined behavior) because a temporary object's lifetime ends when the evaluation containing the full expression or full declarator ends, so the result of a function call can be accessed. This extension to the lifetime of a temporary also removes a quiet change to C90 and improves compatibility with C++.

C functions may not return arrays; however, functions can return a pointer to an array or a `struct` or `union` that contains arrays. Consequently, if a function call returns by value a `struct` or `union` containing an array, do not modify those arrays within the expression containing the function call. Do not access an array returned by a function after the next sequence point or after the evaluation of the containing full expression or full declarator ends.

Noncompliant Code Example (C99)

This noncompliant code example conforms to the C11 Standard; however, it fails to conform to C99. If compiled with a C99-conforming implementation, this code has undefined behavior because the sequence point preceding the call to `printf()` comes between the evaluation of its arguments and the access by `printf()` of the string in the returned object.

```
#include <stdio.h>

struct X { char a[8]; };

struct X salutation(void) {
  struct X result = { "Hello" };
  return result;
}
```

```
struct X addressee(void) {
  struct X result = { "world" };
  return result;
}

int main(void) {
  printf("%s, %s!\n", salutation().a, addressee().a);
  return 0;
}
```

Compliant Solution

This compliant solution stores the structures returned by the call to addressee() before calling the printf() function. Consequently, this program conforms to C99 and C11.

```
#include <stdio.h>

struct X { char a[8]; };

struct X salutation(void) {
  struct X result = { "Hello" };
  return result;
}

struct X addressee(void) {
  struct X result = { "world" };
  return result;
}

int main(void) {
  struct X my_salutation = salutation();
  struct X my_addressee = addressee();

  printf("%s, %s!\n", my_salutation.a, my_addressee.a);
  return 0;
}
```

Noncompliant Code Example

This noncompliant code example attempts to retrieve an array and increment the array's first element. The array is part of a struct that is returned by a function call. Consequently, the array has temporary lifetime, and modifying the array is undefined behavior.

```
#include <stdio.h>

struct X { int a[6]; };

struct X addressee(void) {
  struct X result = { { 1, 2, 3, 4, 5, 6 } };
  return result;
}

int main(void) {
  printf("%x", ++(addressee().a[0]));
  return 0;
}
```

Compliant Solution

This compliant solution stores the structure returned by the call to
addressee() as my_x before calling the printf() function. When the array is
modified, its lifetime is no longer temporary but matches the lifetime of the
block in main().

```
#include <stdio.h>

struct X { int a[6]; };

struct X addressee(void) {
  struct X result = { { 1, 2, 3, 4, 5, 6 } };
  return result;
}

int main(void) {
  struct X my_x = addressee();
  printf("%x", ++(my_x.a[0]));
  return 0;
}
```

Risk Assessment

Attempting to modify an array or access it after its lifetime expires may result
in erroneous program behavior.

Rule	Severity	Likelihood	Remediation Cost	Priority	Level
EXP35-C	Low	Probable	Medium	P4	L3

Related Guidelines

ISO/IEC TR 24772:2013	Dangling References to Stack Frames [DCM]
	Side-effects and Order of Evaluation [SAM]

Bibliography

[ISO/IEC 9899:2011]	6.2.4, "Storage Durations of Objects"

■ EXP36-C. Do not cast pointers into more strictly aligned pointer types

Do not convert a pointer value to a pointer type that is more strictly aligned than the referenced type. Different alignments are possible for different types of objects. If the type-checking system is overridden by an explicit cast or the pointer is converted to a void pointer (void *) and then to a different type, the alignment of an object may be changed.

The C Standard, 6.3.2.3, paragraph 7 [ISO/IEC 9899:2011] states:

> A pointer to an object or incomplete type may be converted to a pointer to a different object or incomplete type. If the resulting pointer is not correctly aligned for the referenced type, the behavior is undefined.

See undefined behavior 25 in Appendix B.

If the misaligned pointer is dereferenced, the program may terminate abnormally. On some architectures, the cast alone may cause a loss of information even if the value is not dereferenced if the types involved have differing alignment requirements.

Noncompliant Code Example

In this noncompliant example, the char pointer &c is converted to the more strictly aligned int pointer ip. On some implementations, cp will not match &c. As a result, if a pointer to one object type is converted to a pointer to a different object type, the second object type must not require stricter alignment than the first.

```
#include <assert.h>

void func(void) {
  char c = 'x';
  int *ip = (int *)&c; /* This can lose information */
  char *cp = (char *)ip;

  /* Will fail on some conforming implementations */
  assert(cp == &c);
}
```

Compliant Solution (Intermediate Object)

In this compliant solution, the char value is stored into an object of type int so that the pointer's value will be properly aligned:

```
#include <assert.h>

void func(void) {
  char c = 'x';
  int i = c;
  int *ip = &i;

  assert(ip == &i);
}
```

Compliant Solution (C11, alignas())

This compliant solution uses the alignment specifier to declare the char object c with the same alignment as that of an object of type int. As a result, the two pointers reference equally aligned pointer types:

```
#include <stdalign.h>
#include <assert.h>

void func(void) {
  /* Align c to the alignment of an int */
  alignas(int) char c = 'x';
  int *ip = (int *)&c;
  char *cp = (char *)ip;
  /* Both cp and &c point to equally aligned objects */
  assert(cp == &c);
}
```

Noncompliant Code Example

The C Standard allows any object pointer to be cast to and from void *. As a result, it is possible to silently convert from one pointer type to another without the compiler diagnosing the problem by storing or casting a pointer to void * and then storing or casting it to the final type. In this noncompliant code example, loop_function() is passed the char pointer loop_ptr but returns an object of type int pointer:

```
int *loop_function(void *v_pointer) {
  /* ... */
  return v_pointer;
}

void func(char *loop_ptr) {
  int *int_ptr = loop_function(loop_ptr);
  /* ... */
}
```

This example compiles without warning. However, v_pointer can be more strictly aligned than an object of type int *.

Compliant Solution

Because the input parameter directly influences the return value, and loop_function() returns an object of type int *, the formal parameter v_pointer is redeclared to accept only an object of type int *:

```
int *loop_function(int *v_pointer) {
  /* ... */
  return v_pointer;
}

void func(int *loop_ptr) {
  int *int_ptr = loop_function(loop_ptr);
  /* ... */
}
```

Another solution is to ensure that loop_ptr points to an object returned by malloc() because this object is guaranteed to be suitably aligned for the *storage* of any type of object. However, this subtlety is easily missed when the program is modified in the future. It is easier and safer to let the type system document the alignment needs.

Noncompliant Code Example

Some architectures require that pointers are correctly aligned when accessing objects larger than a byte. However, it is common in system code that unaligned data (for example, the network stacks) must be copied to a properly aligned memory location, such as in this noncompliant code example:

```
#include <string.h>

struct foo_header {
  int len;
  /* ... */
};

void func(char *data, size_t offset) {
  struct foo_header *tmp;
  struct foo_header header;

  tmp = data + offset;
  memcpy(&header, tmp, sizeof(header));
  /* ... */
}
```

Assigning an unaligned value to a pointer that references a type that needs to be aligned is undefined behavior. An implementation may notice, for example, that `tmp` and `header` must be aligned and use an inline `memcpy()` that uses instructions that assume aligned data.

Compliant Solution

This compliant solution avoids the use of the `foo_header` pointer:

```
#include <string.h>

struct foo_header {
  int len;
  /* ... */
};

void func(char *data, size_t offset) {
  struct foo_header header;
  memcpy(&header, data + offset, sizeof(header));
  /* ... */
}
```

Exceptions

EXP36-EX1: Some hardware architectures have relaxed requirements with regard to pointer alignment. Using a pointer that is not properly aligned is correctly handled by the architecture, although there might be a performance penalty. On such an architecture, improper pointer alignment is permitted but remains an efficiency problem.

Risk Assessment

Accessing a pointer or an object that is not properly aligned can cause a program to crash or give erroneous information, or it can cause slow pointer accesses (if the architecture allows misaligned accesses).

Rule	Severity	Likelihood	Remediation Cost	Priority	Level
EXP36-C	Low	Probable	Medium	P4	L3

Related Guidelines

ISO/IEC TR 24772:2013	Pointer Casting and Pointer Type Changes [HFC]
ISO/IEC TS 17961:2013	Converting pointer values to more strictly aligned pointer types [alignconv]
MISRA C:2012	Rule 11.1 (required) Rule 11.2 (required) Rule 11.5 (advisory) Rule 11.7 (required)

Bibliography

[Bryant 2003]	
[ISO/IEC 9899:2011]	6.3.2.3, "Pointers"
[Walfridsson 2003]	Aliasing, Pointer Casts and GCC 3.3

■ EXP37-C. Call functions with the correct number and type of arguments

Do not call a function with the wrong number or type of arguments.

The C Standard identifies five distinct situations in which undefined behavior may arise as a result of invoking a function using a declaration that is incompatible with its definition or by supplying incorrect types or numbers of arguments.

- A pointer is used to call a function whose type is not compatible with the referenced type (see undefined behavior 26 in Appendix B).

- For a call to a function without a function prototype in scope, the number of arguments does not equal the number of parameters (see undefined behavior 38 in Appendix B).

- For a call to a function without a function prototype in scope where the function is defined with a function prototype, either the prototype ends with an ellipsis or the types of the arguments after promotion are not compatible with the types of the parameters (see undefined behavior 39 in Appendix B).

- For a call to a function without a function prototype in scope where the function is not defined with a function prototype, the types of the arguments after promotion are not compatible with those of the parameters after promotion, with certain exceptions (see undefined behavior 40 in Appendix B).

- A function is defined with a type that is not compatible with the type (of the expression) pointed to by the expression that denotes the called function (see undefined behavior 41 in Appendix B).

Functions that are appropriately declared (as in "DCL40-C. Do not create incompatible declarations of the same function or object") will typically generate a compiler diagnostic message if they are supplied with the wrong number or types of arguments. However, there are cases in which supplying the incorrect arguments to a function will, at best, generate compiler warnings. Although such warnings should be resolved, they do not prevent program compilation (see "MSC00-C. Compile cleanly at high warning levels").

Noncompliant Code Example

The header `<tgmath.h>` provides type-generic macros for math functions. Although most functions from the `<math.h>` header have a complex counterpart in `<complex.h>`, several functions do not. Calling any of the type-generic functions listed in Table 3–2 with complex values is undefined behavior.

Table 3-2. Functions That Should Not Be Called with Complex Values

atan2()	fdim()	ilogb()	logb()	rint()
cbrt()	floor()	ldexp()	lrint()	round()
ceil()	fma()	lgamma()	lround()	scalbn()
copysign()	fmax()	llrint()	nearbyint()	scalbln()
erf()	fmin()	llround()	nextafter()	tgamma()
erfc()	fmod()	log10()	nexttoward()	trunc()
exp2()	frexp()	log1p()	remainder()	
expm1()	hypot()	log2()	remquo()	

This noncompliant code example attempts to take the base-2 logarithm of a complex number, resulting in undefined behavior:

```
#include <tgmath.h>

void func(void) {
  double complex c = 2.0 + 4.0 * I;
  double complex result = log2(c);
}
```

Compliant Solution (Complex Number)

If the clog2() function is not available for an implementation as an extension, the programmer can take the base-2 logarithm of a complex number using log() instead of log2(), because log() can be used on complex arguments, as shown in this compliant solution:

```
#include <tgmath.h>

void func(void) {
  double complex c = 2.0 + 4.0 * I;
  double complex result = log(c)/log(2);
}
```

Compliant Solution (Real Number)

The programmer can use this compliant solution if the intent is to take the base-2 logarithm of the real part of the complex number:

```
#include <tgmath.h>

void func(void) {
  double complex c = 2.0 + 4.0 * I;
  double complex result = log2(creal(c));
}
```

Noncompliant Code Example

In this noncompliant example, the C standard library function strchr() is called through the function pointer fp declared without a prototype with incorrectly typed arguments. According to the C Standard, 6.3.2.3, paragraph 8 [ISO/IEC 9899:2011]:

> A pointer to a function of one type may be converted to a pointer to a function of another type and back again; the result shall compare equal to the original pointer. If a converted pointer is used to call a function whose type is not compatible with the referenced type, the behavior is undefined.

See undefined behavior 26 in Appendix B.

```
#include <stdio.h>
#include <string.h>

char *(*fp)();

int main(void) {
  const char *c;
  fp = strchr;
  c = fp('e', "Hello");
  printf("%s\n", c);
  return 0;
}
```

Compliant Solution

In this compliant solution, the function pointer fp, which points to the C standard library function strchr(), is declared with the correct parameters and is invoked with the correct number and type of arguments:

```
#include <stdio.h>
#include <string.h>
```

```
char *(*fp)(const char *, int);

int main(void) {
  const char *c;
  fp = strchr;
  c = fp("Hello",'e');
  printf("%s\n", c);
  return 0;
}
```

Noncompliant Code Example

In this noncompliant example, the function f() is defined to take an argument of type long but f() is called from another file with an argument of type int:

```
/* In another source file */
long f(long x) {
  return x < 0 ? -x : x;
}

/* In this source file, no f prototype in scope */
long f();

long g(int x) {
  return f(x);
}
```

Compliant Solution

In this compliant solution, the prototype for the function f() is included in the source file in the scope of where it is called, and the function f() is correctly called with an argument of type long:

```
/* In another source file */

long f(long x) {
  return x < 0 ? -x : x;
}

/* f prototype in scope in this source file */

long f(long x);

long g(int x) {
  return f((long)x);
}
```

Noncompliant Code Example (POSIX)

The POSIX function open() [IEEE Std 1003.1-2013] is a variadic function with the following prototype:

```
int open(const char *path, int oflag, ...);
```

The open() function accepts a third argument to determine a newly created file's access mode. If open() is used to create a new file, and the third argument is omitted, the file may be created with unintended access permissions (see "FIO06-C. Create files with appropriate access permissions").

In this noncompliant code example from a vulnerability in the useradd() function of the shadow-utils package CVE-2006-1174, the third argument to open() is accidentally omitted:

```
fd = open(ms, O_CREAT | O_EXCL | O_WRONLY | O_TRUNC);
```

Note that, technically, it is incorrect to pass a third argument to open() when not creating a new file (that is, with the O_CREAT flag not set).

Compliant Solution (POSIX)

In this compliant solution, a third argument is specified in the call to open():

```
#include <fcntl.h>

void func(const char *ms, mode_t perms) {
  /* ... */
  int fd;
  fd = open(ms, O_CREAT | O_EXCL | O_WRONLY | O_TRUNC, perms);
  if (fd == -1) {
    /* Handle error */
  }
}
```

Risk Assessment

Calling a function with incorrect arguments can result in unexpected or unintended program behavior.

Rule	Severity	Likelihood	Remediation Cost	Priority	Level
EXP37-C	Medium	Probable	High	P4	L3

Related Guidelines

ISO/IEC TR 24772:2013	Subprogram Signature Mismatch [OTR]
ISO/IEC TS 17961:2013	Calling functions with incorrect arguments [argcomp]
MISRA C:2012	Rule 8.2 (required) Rule 17.3 (mandatory)
MITRE CWE	CWE-628, Function Call with Incorrectly Specified Arguments CWE-686, Function Call with Incorrect Argument Type

Bibliography

[CVE]	CVE-2006-1174
[IEEE Std 1003.1-2013]	open()
[ISO/IEC 9899:2011]	6.3.2.3, "Pointers" 6.5.2.2, "Function Calls"
[Spinellis 2006]	Section 2.6.1, "Incorrect Routine or Arguments"

■ EXP39-C. Do not access a variable through a pointer of an incompatible type

Modifying a variable through a pointer of an incompatible type (other than unsigned char) can lead to unpredictable results. Subclause 6.2.7 of the C Standard states that two types may be distinct yet compatible and addresses precisely when two distinct types are compatible.

This problem is often caused by a violation of aliasing rules. The C Standard, 6.5, paragraph 7 [ISO/IEC 9899:2011], specifies those circumstances in which an object may or may not be aliased:

> An object shall have its stored value accessed only by an lvalue expression that has one of the following types:
>
> ■ a type compatible with the effective type of the object,
>
> ■ a qualified version of a type compatible with the effective type of the object,

- a type that is the signed or unsigned type corresponding to the effective type of the object,

- a type that is the signed or unsigned type corresponding to a qualified version of the effective type of the object,

- an aggregate or union type that includes one of the aforementioned types among its members (including, recursively, a member of a subaggregate or contained union), or

- a character type.

Accessing an object by means of any other lvalue expression (other than unsigned char) is undefined behavior 34 (see Appendix B).

Noncompliant Code Example

In this noncompliant example, an object of type float is incremented through an int *. The programmer can use the unit in the last place to get the next representable value for a floating-point type. However, accessing an object through a pointer of an incompatible type is undefined behavior.

```
#include <stdio.h>

void f(void) {
  if (sizeof(int) == sizeof(float)) {
    float f = 0.0f;
    int *ip = (int *)&f;
    (*ip)++;
    printf("float is %f\n", f);
  }
}
```

Compliant Solution

In this compliant solution, the standard C function nextafterf() is used to round toward the highest representable floating-point value:

```
#include <float.h>
#include <math.h>
#include <stdio.h>

void f(void) {
  float f = 0.0f;
  f = nextafterf(f, FLT_MAX);
  printf("float is %f\n", f);
}
```

Noncompliant Code Example

In this noncompliant code example, an array of two values of type short is treated as an integer and assigned an integer value. The resulting values are indeterminate.

```c
#include <stdio.h>

void func(void) {
  short a[2];
  a[0]=0x1111;
  a[1]=0x1111;

  *(int *)a = 0x22222222;

  printf("%x %x\n", a[0], a[1]);
}
```

When translating this code, an implementation can assume that no access through an integer pointer can change the array a, consisting of shorts. Consequently, printf() may be called with the original values of a[0] and a[1].

Compliant Solution

This compliant solution uses a union type that includes a type compatible with the effective type of the object:

```c
#include <stdio.h>

void func(void) {
  union {
    short a[2];
    int i;
  } u;

  u.a[0]=0x1111;
  u.a[1]=0x1111;
  u.i = 0x22222222;

  printf("%x %x\n", u.a[0], u.a[1]);
  /* ... */
}
```

The printf() behavior in this compliant solution is unspecified, but it is commonly accepted as an implementation extension (see unspecified behavior 11 in Appendix C).

This function typically outputs "2222 2222." However, there is no guarantee that this will be true, even on implementations that defined the unspecified behavior; values of type short need not have the same representation as values of type int.

Noncompliant Code Example

In this noncompliant code example, a gadget object is allocated, then realloc() is called to create a widget object using the memory from the gadget object. Although reusing memory to change types is acceptable, accessing the memory copied from the original object is undefined behavior.

```c
#include <stdlib.h>

struct gadget {
  int i;
  double d;
  char *p;
};

struct widget {
  char *q;
  int j;
  double e;
};

void func(void) {
  struct gadget *gp;
  struct widget *wp;

  gp = (struct gadget *)malloc(sizeof(struct gadget));
  if (!gp) {
    /* Handle error */
  }
  /* ... Initialize gadget ... */
  wp = (struct widget *)realloc(gp, sizeof(struct widget));
  if (!wp) {
    free(gp);
    /* Handle error */
  }
  if (wp->j == 12) {
    /* ... */
  }
}
```

Compliant Solution

This compliant solution reuses the memory from the gadget object but reinitializes the memory to a consistent state before reading from it:

```
#include <stdlib.h>
#include <string.h>

struct gadget {
  int i;
  double d;
  char *p;
};

struct widget {
  char *q;
  int j;
  double e;
};

void func(void) {
  struct gadget *gp;
  struct widget *wp;

  gp = (struct gadget *)malloc(sizeof (struct gadget));
  if (!gp) {
    /* Handle error */
  }
  /* ... */
  wp = (struct widget *)realloc(gp, sizeof(struct widget));
  if (!wp) {
    free(gp);
    /* Handle error */
  }
  memset(wp, 0, sizeof(struct widget));
  /* ... Initialize widget ... */

  if (wp->j == 12) {
    /* ... */
  }
}
```

Noncompliant Code Example

According to the C Standard, 6.7.6.2 [ISO/IEC 9899:2011], using two or more incompatible arrays in an expression is undefined behavior (see also undefined behavior 76 in Appendix B).

For two array types to be compatible, both should have compatible underlying element types, and both size specifiers should have the same constant value. If either of these properties is violated, the resulting behavior is undefined.

In this noncompliant code example, the two arrays a and b fail to satisfy the equal size specifier criterion for array compatibility. Because a and b are not equal, writing to what is believed to be a valid member of a might exceed its defined memory boundary, resulting in an arbitrary memory overwrite.

```
enum { ROWS = 10, COLS = 15 };

void func(void) {
  int a[ROWS][COLS];
  int (*b)[ROWS] = a;
}
```

Most compilers will produce a warning diagnostic if the two array types used in an expression are incompatible.

Compliant Solution

In this compliant solution, b is declared to point to an array with the same number of elements as a, satisfying the size specifier criterion for array compatibility:

```
enum { ROWS = 10, COLS = 15 };

void func(void) {
  int a[ROWS][COLS];
  int (*b)[COLS] = a;
}
```

Risk Assessment

Optimizing for performance can lead to aliasing errors that can be quite difficult to detect. Furthermore, as in the preceding example, unexpected results can lead to buffer overflow attacks, bypassing security checks, or unexpected execution.

Recommendation	Severity	Likelihood	Remediation Cost	Priority	Level
EXP39-C	Medium	Unlikely	High	P2	L3

Related Guidelines

ISO/IEC TS 17961:2013	Accessing an object through a pointer to an incompatible type [ptrcomp]
MITRE CWE	CWE-119, Improper Restriction of Operations within the Bounds of a Memory Buffer

Bibliography

[Acton 2006]	"Understanding Strict Aliasing"
[ISO/IEC 9899:2011]	6.5, "Expressions" 6.7.6.2, "Array Declarators"
[Walfridsson 2003]	Aliasing, Pointer Casts and GCC 3.3

■ EXP40-C. Do not modify constant objects

The C Standard, 6.7.3, paragraph 6 [ISO/IEC 9899:2011], states:

> If an attempt is made to modify an object defined with a const-qualified type through use of an lvalue with non-const-qualified type, the behavior is undefined.

See also undefined behavior 64 in Appendix B.

There are existing compiler implementations that allow const-qualified objects to be modified without generating a **warning message**.

Avoid casting away const qualification because doing so makes it possible to modify const-qualified objects without issuing diagnostics (see "EXP05-C. Do not cast away a const qualification" and "STR30-C. Do not attempt to modify string literals" for more details).

Noncompliant Code Example

This noncompliant code example allows a constant object to be modified:

```
const int **ipp;
int *ip;
const int i = 42;
```

```
void func(void) {
  ipp = &ip; /* Constraint violation */
  *ipp = &i; /* Valid */
  *ip = 0;   /* Modifies constant i (was 42) */
}
```

The first assignment is unsafe because it allows the code that follows it to attempt to change the value of the const object i.

Compliant Solution

The compliant solution depends on the intent of the programmer. If the intent is that the value of i is modifiable, then it should not be declared as a constant, as in this compliant solution:

```
int **ipp;
int *ip;
int i = 42;

void func(void) {
  ipp = &ip; /* Valid */
  *ipp = &i; /* Valid */
  *ip = 0; /* Valid */
}
```

If the intent is that the value of i is not meant to change, then do not write noncompliant code that attempts to modify it.

Risk Assessment

Modifying constant objects through nonconstant references is undefined behavior.

Rule	Severity	Likelihood	Remediation Cost	Priority	Level
EXP40-C	Low	Unlikely	Medium	P2	L3

Bibliography

[ISO/IEC 9899:2011]   6.7.3, "Type Qualifiers"

■ EXP42-C. Do not compare padding data

The C Standard, 6.7.2.1 [ISO/IEC 9899:2011], states:

> There may be unnamed padding within a structure object, but not at its beginning. … There may be unnamed padding at the end of a structure or union.

Subclause 6.7.9, paragraph 9, states that

> unnamed members of objects of structure and union type do not participate in initialization. Unnamed members of structure objects have indeterminate value even after initialization.

The only exception is that padding bits are set to zero when a static or thread-local object is implicitly initialized (paragraph 10):

> If an object that has automatic storage duration is not initialized explicitly, its value is indeterminate. If an object that has static or thread storage duration is not initialized explicitly, then …
>
> ■ if it is an aggregate, every member is initialized (recursively) according to these rules, and any padding is initialized to zero bits;
>
> ■ if it is a union, the first named member is initialized (recursively) according to these rules, and any padding is initialized to zero bits.

Because these padding values are unspecified, attempting a byte-by-byte comparison between structures can lead to incorrect results [Summit 1995].

Noncompliant Code Example

In this noncompliant code example, memcmp() is used to compare the contents of two structures, including any padding bytes:

```
#include <string.h>

struct s {
  char c;
  int i;
  char buffer[13];
};

void compare(const struct s *left, const struct s *right) {
```

```
  if (0 == memcmp(left, right, sizeof(struct s)))) {
    /* ... */
  }
}
```

Compliant Solution

In this compliant solution, all of the fields are compared manually to avoid comparing any padding bytes:

```
#include <string.h>

struct s {
  char c;
  int i;
  char buffer[13];
};

void compare(const struct s *left, const struct s *right) {
  if ((left && right) &&
      (left->c == right->c) &&
      (left->i == right->i) &&
      (0 == memcmp(left->buffer, right->buffer, 13))) {
    /* ... */
  }
}
```

Exceptions

EXP42-EX1: A structure can be defined such that the members are aligned properly or the structure is packed using implementation-specific packing instructions. This is true only when the members' data types have no padding bits of their own and when their object representations are the same as their value representations. This frequently is not true for the _Bool type or floating-point types and need not be true for pointers. In such cases, the compiler does not insert padding, and use of functions such as memcmp() is acceptable.

This compliant example uses the #pragma pack compiler extension from Microsoft Visual Studio to ensure the structure members are packed as tightly as possible:

```
#include <string.h>

#pragma pack(push, 1)
struct s {
  char c;
```

```
    int i;
    char buffer[13];
};
#pragma pack(pop)

void compare(const struct s *left, const struct s *right) {
  if (0 == memcmp(left, right, sizeof(struct s))) {
    /* ... */
  }
}
```

Risk Assessment

Comparing padding bytes, when present, can lead to unexpected program behavior.

Rule	Severity	Likelihood	Remediation Cost	Priority	Level
EXP42-C	Medium	Probable	Medium	P8	L2

Related Guidelines

ISO/IEC TS 17961:2013	Comparison of padding data [padcomp]

Bibliography

[ISO/IEC 9899:2011]	6.7.2.1, "Structure and Union Specifiers" 6.7.9, "Initialization"
[Summit 1995]	Question 2.8 Question 2.12

■ EXP43-C. Avoid undefined behavior when using `restrict`-qualified pointers

An object that is accessed through a `restrict`-qualified pointer has a special association with that pointer. This association requires that all accesses to that object use, directly or indirectly, the value of that particular pointer. The intended use of the `restrict` qualifier is to promote optimization, and deleting all instances of the qualifier from a program does not change its meaning (that is, observable behavior). In the absence of this qualifier, other pointers can alias this object. Caching the value in an object designated through a restrict-qualified pointer is safe at the beginning of the block in which the pointer is declared because no preexisting aliases may also be used to reference that object. The cached value must be restored to the object by the end of the block, where preexisting aliases again become available. New aliases may be formed within the block, but these must all depend on the value of the restrict-qualified pointer so that they can be identified and adjusted to refer to the cached value. For a restrict-qualified pointer at file scope, the block is the body of each function in the file [Walls 2006]. Developers should be aware that C++ does not support the restrict qualifier, but some C++ compiler implementations support an equivalent qualifier as an extension.

The C Standard [ISO/IEC 9899:2011] identifies the following undefined behavior:

> A restrict-qualified pointer is assigned a value based on another restricted pointer whose associated block neither began execution before the block associated with this pointer, nor ended before the assignment (6.7.3.1).

This is an oversimplification, however, and it is important to review the formal definition of *restrict* in subclause 6.7.3.1 of the C Standard to properly understand undefined behaviors associated with the use of restrict-qualified pointers.

Overlapping Objects

The restrict qualifier requires that the pointers do not reference overlapping objects. If the objects referenced by arguments to functions overlap (meaning the objects share some common memory addresses), the behavior is undefined.

Noncompliant Code Example

This code example is noncompliant because an assignment is made between two restrict-qualified pointers in the same scope:

```
int *restrict a;
int *restrict b;

extern int c[];
```

```
int main(void) {
  c[0] = 17;
  c[1] = 18;
  a = &c[0];
  b = &c[1];
  a = b; /* Undefined behavior */
  /* ... */
}
```

Note that undefined behavior occurs only when a is assigned to b. It is valid for a and b to point into the same array object, provided the range of elements accessed through one of the pointers does not overlap with the range of elements accessed through the other pointer.

Compliant Solution

One way to eliminate the undefined behavior is simply to remove the `restrict` qualification from the affected pointers:

```
int *a;
int *b;

extern int c[];

int main(void) {
  c[0] = 17;
  c[1] = 18;
  a = &c[0];
  b = &c[1];
  a = b; /* Defined behavior */
  /* ... */
}
```

restrict-Qualified Function Parameters

When calling functions that have `restrict`-qualified function parameters, it is important that the pointer arguments do not reference overlapping objects if one or more of the pointers are used to modify memory. Consequently, it is important to understand the semantics of the function being called.

Noncompliant Code Example

In this noncompliant code example, the function f() accepts three parameters. The function copies n integers from the int array referenced by the `restrict`-qualified pointer p to the int array referenced by the `restrict`-qualified pointer q. Because the destination array is modified during each execution of the function (for which n is nonzero), if the array is accessed through one of the pointer parameters, it cannot also be accessed through the other. Declaring these function parameters as restrict-qualified pointers allows aggressive optimization by the compiler but can also result in undefined behavior if these pointers refer to overlapping objects.

```c
#include <stddef.h>
void f(size_t n, int *restrict p, const int *restrict q) {
  while (n-- > 0) {
    *p++ = *q++;
  }
}

void g(void) {
  extern int d[100];
  /* ... */
  f(50, d + 1, d); /* Undefined behavior */
}
```

The function g() declares an array d consisting of 100 int values and then invokes f() to copy memory from one area of the array to another. This call has undefined behavior because each of d[1] through d[49] is accessed through both p and q.

Compliant Solution

In this compliant solution, the function f() is unchanged but the programmer has ensured that none of the calls to f() result in undefined behavior. The call to f() in g() is valid because the storage allocated to d is effectively divided into two disjoint objects.

```c
#include <stddef.h>

void f(size_t n, int *restrict p, const int *restrict q) {
  while (n-- > 0) {
    *p++ = *q++;
  }
}

void g(void) {
  extern int d[100];
  /* ... */
  f(50, d + 50, d); /* Defined behavior */
}
```

Noncompliant Code Example

In this noncompliant code example, the function add() adds the integer array referenced by the restrict-qualified pointers lhs to the integer array referenced by the restrict-qualified pointer rhs and stores the result in the restrict-qualified pointer referenced by res. The function f() declares an array a consisting of 100 int values and then invokes add() to copy memory from one area of the array to another. The call add(100, a, a, a) has undefined behavior because the object modified by res is accessed by lhs and rhs.

```
#include <stddef.h>

void add(size_t n, int *restrict res, const int *restrict lhs,
        const int * restrict rhs) {
  for (size_t i = 0; i < n; ++i) {
    res[i] = lhs[i] + rhs[i];
  }
}

void f(void) {
  int a[100];
  add(100, a, a, a); /* Undefined behavior */
}
```

Compliant Solution

In this compliant solution, an unmodified object is aliased through two restricted pointers. Because a and b are disjoint arrays, a call of the form add(100, a, b, b) has defined behavior, because array b is not modified within function add.

```
#include <stddef.h>
void add(size_t n, int *restrict res, const int *restrict lhs,
        const int *restrict rhs) {
  for (size_t i = 0; i < n; ++i) {
    res[i] = lhs[i] + rhs[i];
  }
}

void f(void) {
  int a[100];
  int b[100];
  add(100, a, b, b); /* Defined behavior */
}
```

Invoking Library Functions with `restrict`-Qualified Pointers

Ensure that `restrict`-qualified source and destination pointers do not reference overlapping objects when invoking library functions. For example, Table 3–3 lists C standard library functions that copy memory from a source object referenced by a `restrict`-qualified pointer to a destination object that is also referenced by a `restrict`-qualified pointer.

If the objects referenced by arguments to functions overlap (meaning the objects share some common memory addresses), the behavior is undefined (see also undefined behavior 68 in Appendix B). The result of the functions is unknown, and data may be corrupted. As a result, these functions must never be passed pointers to overlapping objects. If data must be copied between objects that share common memory addresses, a copy function guaranteed to work on overlapping memory, such as `memmove()`, should be used.

Noncompliant Code Example

In this noncompliant code example, the values of objects referenced by `ptr1` and `ptr2` become unpredictable after the call to `memcpy()` because their memory areas overlap:

```c
#include <string.h>

void func(void) {
  char c_str[]= "test string";
  char *ptr1 = c_str;
  char *ptr2;

  ptr2 = ptr1 + 3;
  /* Undefined behavior because of overlapping objects */
  memcpy(ptr2, ptr1, 6);
  /* ... */
}
```

Table 3–3. restrict Copy Functions

Standard C	Annex K
strcpy()	strcpy_s()
strncpy()	strncpy_s()
strcat()	strcat_s()
strncat()	strncat_s()
memcpy()	memcpy_s()
	strtok_s()

Compliant Solution

In this compliant solution, the call to memcpy() is replaced with a call to memmove(). The memmove() function performs the same operation as memcpy() when the memory regions do not overlap. When the memory regions do overlap, the *n* characters from the object pointed to by the source (ptr1) are first copied into a temporary array of *n* characters that does not overlap the objects pointed to by the destination (ptr2) or the source. The *n* characters from the temporary array are then copied into the object pointed to by the destination.

```
#include <string.h>

void func(void) {
  char c_str[]= "test string";
  char *ptr1 = c_str;
  char *ptr2;

  ptr2 = ptr1 + 3;
  memmove(ptr2, ptr1, 6);  /* Replace call to memcpy() */
  /* ... */
}
```

Similar solutions using memmove() can replace the string functions as long as care is taken regarding the byte size of the characters and proper null-termination of the copied string.

Calling Functions with restrict-Qualified Pointer to a const-Qualified Type

Ensure that functions that accept a restrict-qualified pointer to a const-qualified type do not modify the object referenced by that pointer. Formatted input and output standard library functions frequently fit this description. Table 3–4 lists of some of the common functions for which the format argument is a restrict-qualified pointer to a const-qualified type.

Table 3–4. restrict Format String Functions

Standard C	Annex K
printf()	printf_s()
scanf()	scanf_s()
sprintf()	sprintf_s()
snprintf()	snprintf_s()

For formatted output functions such as printf(), it is unlikely that a programmer would modify the format string. However, an attacker may attempt to do so if a program violates "FIO30-C. Exclude user input from format strings" and passes **tainted values** as part of the format string.

Noncompliant Code Example

In this noncompliant code example, the programmer is attempting to overwrite the format string with a string value read in from stdin such as "%d%f 1 3.3" and use the resulting modified string of "%s%d%f" to input the subsequent values of 1 and 3.3:

```c
#include <stdio.h>

void func(void) {
  int i;
  float x;
  char format[100] = "%s";
  /* Undefined behavior */
  int n = scanf(format, format + 2, &i, &x);
  /* ... */
}
```

Compliant Solution

The intended results are achieved by this compliant solution:

```c
#include <stdio.h>

void func(void) {
  int i;
  float x
  int n = scanf("%d%f", &i, &x); /* Defined behavior */
  /* ... */
}
```

Outer-to-Inner Assignments between Restricted Pointers

The assignment between restrict-qualified pointers declared in an inner nested block from an outer block has defined behavior.

Noncompliant Code Example

The assignment of restrict-qualified pointers to other restrict-qualified pointers within the same block has undefined behavior:

```
void func(void) {
  int * restrict p1;
  int * restrict q1;

  int * restrict p2 = p1; /* Undefined behavior */
  int * restrict q2 = q1; /* Undefined behavior */
}
```

Compliant Solution

The intended results can be achieved using an inner nested block, as shown in this compliant solution:

```
void func(void) {
  int * restrict p1;
  int * restrict q1;
  { /* Added inner block */
    int * restrict p2 = p1; /* Valid, well-defined behavior */
    int * restrict q2 = q1; /* Valid, well-defined behavior */
  }
}
```

Risk Assessment

The incorrect use of `restrict`-qualified pointers can result in undefined behavior that might be exploited to cause data integrity violations.

Rule	Severity	Likelihood	Remediation Cost	Priority	Level
EXP43-C	Medium	Probable	High	P4	L3

Related Guidelines

ISO/IEC TR 24772:2013	Passing Parameters and Return Values [CSJ]
ISO/IEC TS 17961:2013	Passing pointers into the same object as arguments to different restrict-qualified parameters [restrict]

Bibliography

[ISO/IEC 9899:2011]	6.7.3.1, "Formal Definition of `restrict`"
[Walls 2006]	

■ EXP44-C. Do not rely on side effects in operands to sizeof, _Alignof, or _Generic

Some operators do not evaluate their operands beyond the type information the operands provide. When using one of these operators, do not pass an operand which would otherwise yield a side effect, as the side effect will not be generated.

The sizeof operator yields the size (in bytes) of its operand, which may be an expression or the parenthesized name of a type. In most cases, the operand is not evaluated. A possible exception is when the type of the operand is a variable length array (VLA) type, in which case the expression is evaluated. When part of the operand of the sizeof operator is a VLA type, and when changing the value of the VLA's size expression would not affect the result of the operator, it is unspecified whether or not the size expression is evaluated (see unspecified behavior 22 in Appendix C).

The operand passed to _Alignof is never evaluated. The operand used in the controlling expression of a _Generic selection expression is never evaluated.

Providing an expression that appears to produce side effects may be misleading to programmers who are not aware that these expressions are not evaluated, and in the case of a VLA used in sizeof, have unspecified results. As a result, programmers may make invalid assumptions about program state, leading to errors and possible software vulnerabilities.

This rule is similar to "PRE31-C. Avoid side effects in arguments to unsafe macros."

Noncompliant Code Example (sizeof)

In this noncompliant code example, the expression a++ is not evaluated:

```
#include <stdio.h>
void func(void) {
  int a = 14;
  int b = sizeof(a++);
  printf("%d, %d\n", a, b);
}
```

Consequently, the value of a after b has been initialized is 14.

Compliant Solution (sizeof)

In this compliant solution, the variable a is incremented outside of the sizeof operation:

```
#include <stdio.h>

void func(void) {
  int a = 14;
  int b = sizeof(a);
  ++a;
  printf("%d, %d\n", a, b);
}
```

Noncompliant Code Example (sizeof, VLA)

In this noncompliant code example, the expression ++n in the initialization expression of a must be evaluated because its value affects the size of the VLA operand of the sizeof operator. However, in the initialization expression of b, the expression ++n % 1 evaluates to 0. This means that the value of n does not affect the result of the sizeof operator. Consequently, it is unspecified whether or not n will be incremented when initializing b.

```
#include <stddef.h>
#include <stdio.h>

void f(size_t n) {
  /* n must be incremented */
  size_t a = sizeof(int[++n]);

  /* n need not be incremented */
  size_t b = sizeof(int[++n % 1 + 1]);

  printf("%z, %z, %z\n", a, b, n);
  /* ... */
}
```

Compliant Solution (sizeof, VLA)

This compliant solution avoids changing the value of the variable n used in each sizeof expression and instead increments n safely afterwards:

```
#include <stddef.h>
#include <stdio.h>

void f(size_t n) {
  size_t a = sizeof(int[n + 1]);
  ++n;

  size_t b = sizeof(int[n % 1 + 1]);
  ++n;
  printf("%z, %z, %z\n", a, b, n);
  /* ... */
}
```

Noncompliant Code Example (_Generic)

This noncompliant code example attempts to modify a variable's value as part of the _Generic selection control expression. The programmer may expect that a is incremented, but because _Generic does not evaluate its control expression, the value of a is not modified.

```
#include <stdio.h>

#define S(val) _Generic(val, int : 2, \
                              short : 3, \
                              default : 1)
void func(void) {
  int a = 0;
  int b = S(a++);
  printf("%d, %d\n", a, b);
}
```

Compliant Solution (_Generic)

In this compliant solution, a is incremented outside of the _Generic selection expression:

```
#include <stdio.h>

#define S(val) _Generic(val, int : 2, \
                              short : 3, \
                              default : 1)
void func(void) {
  int a = 0;
  int b = S(a);
  ++a;
  printf("%d, %d\n", a, b);
}
```

Noncompliant Code Example (_Alignof)

This noncompliant code example attempts to modify a variable while getting its default alignment value. The user may have expected val to be incremented as part of the _Alignof expression, but because _Alignof does not evaluate its operand, val is unchanged.

```
#include <stdio.h>

void func(void) {
  int val = 0;
  /* ... */
  size_t align = _Alignof(++val);
  printf("%z, %d\n", align, val);
  /* ... */
}
```

Compliant Solution (_Alignof)

This compliant solution moves the expression out of the _Alignof operator:

```
#include <stdio.h>

void func(void) {
  int val = 0;
  /* ... */
  ++val;
  size_t align = _Alignof(val);
  printf("%z, %d\n", align, val);
  /* ... */
}
```

Risk Assessment

If expressions that appear to produce side effects are supplied to an operator that does not evaluate its operands, the results may be different than expected. Depending on how this result is used, it can lead to unintended program behavior.

Rule	Severity	Likelihood	Remediation Cost	Priority	Level
EXP44-C	Low	Unlikely	Low	P3	L3

■ EXP45-C. Do not perform assignments in selection statements

Do not use an assignment operator as the outermost expression in the contexts listed in Table 3–5 because doing so typically indicates programmer error and can result in unexpected behavior.

Table 3–5. Contexts in Which to Avoid Assignment Operator

Operator	Context
if	Controlling expression
while	Controlling expression
do ... while	Controlling expression
for	Second operand
?:	First operand
?:	Second or third operands, where the ternary expression is used in any of these contexts
&&	Either operand
||	Either operand
,	Second operand, when the comma expression is used in any of these contexts

Noncompliant Code Example

In this noncompliant code example, an assignment expression is the outermost expression in an if statement:

```
if (a = b) {
  /* ... */
}
```

Although the intent of the code may be to assign b to a and test the value of the result for equality to 0, it is frequently a case of the programmer mistakenly using the assignment operator = instead of the equals operator ==. Consequently, many compilers will warn about this condition, making this coding error detectable by adhering to "MSC00-C. Compile cleanly at high warning levels."

Compliant Solution (Unintentional Assignment)

When the assignment of b to a is not intended, this conditional block is now executed when a is equal to b:

```
if (a == b) {
  /* ... */
}
```

Compliant Solution (Intentional Assignment)

When the assignment is intended, this compliant solution explicitly uses inequality as the outermost expression while performing the assignment in the inner expression:

```
if ((a = b) != 0) {
  /* ... */
}
```

It is less desirable in general, depending on what was intended, because it mixes the assignment in the condition, but it is clear that the programmer intended the assignment to occur.

Noncompliant Code Example

In this noncompliant code example, the expression x = y is used as the controlling expression of the while statement:

```
do { /* ... */ } while (foo(), x = y);
```

The same result can be obtained using the for statement, which is specifically designed to evaluate an expression on each iteration of the loop, just before performing the test in its controlling expression:

```
for (; x; foo(), x = y) { /* ... */ }
```

Compliant Solution (Unintentional Assignment)

When the assignment of y to x is not intended, the conditional block should be executed only when x is equal to y, as in this compliant solution:

```
do { /* ... */ } while (foo(), x == y);
```

Compliant Solution (Intentional Assignment)

When the assignment is intended, this compliant solution can be used:

```
do { /* ... */ } while (foo(), (x = y) != 0);
```

Noncompliant Code Example

In this noncompliant code example, the expression p = q is used as the controlling expression of the while statement:

```
do { /* ... */ } while (x = y, p = q);
```

Compliant Solution

In this compliant solution, the expression x = y is not used as the controlling expression of the while statement:

```
do { /* ... */ } while (x = y, p == q);
```

Exceptions

EXP45-EX1: Assignment can be used where the result of the assignment is itself an operand to a comparison expression or relational expression. In this compliant example, the expression x = y is itself an operand to a comparison operation:

```
if ((x = y) != 0) { /* ... */ }
```

EXP45-EX2: Assignment can be used where the expression consists of a single primary expression. The following code is compliant because the expression x = y is a single primary expression:

```
if ((x = y)) { /* ... */ }
```

The following controlling expression is noncompliant because && is not a comparison or relational operator and the entire expression is not primary:

```
if ((v = w) && flag) { /* ... */ }
```

When the assignment of v to w is not intended, the following controlling expression can be used to execute the conditional block when v is equal to w:

```
if ((v == w) && flag) { /* ... */ };
```

When the assignment is intended, the following controlling expression can be used:

```
if (((v = w) != 0) && flag) { /* ... */ };
```

EXP45-EX3: Assignment can be used in a function argument or array index. In this compliant solution, the expression x = y is used in a function argument:

```
if (foo(x = y)) { /* ... */ }
```

Risk Assessment

Errors of omission can result in unintended program flow.

Recommendation	Severity	Likelihood	Remediation Cost	Priority	Level
EXP45-C	Low	Likely	Medium	P6	L2

Related Guidelines

ISO/IEC TR 24772:2013	Likely Incorrect Expression [KOA]
ISO/IEC TS 17961:2013	No assignment in conditional expressions [boolasgn]
MITRE CWE	CWE-480, Use of Incorrect Operator

Bibliography

[Hatton 1995]	Section 2.7.2, "Errors of Omission and Addition"

Chapter 4

Integers (INT)

Chapter Contents

Risk Assessment Summary

Rule	Severity	Likelihood	Remediation Cost	Priority	Level
INT30-C	High	Likely	High	P9	L2
INT31-C	High	Probable	High	P6	L2
INT32-C	High	Likely	High	P9	L2

continues

Rule	Severity	Likelihood	Remediation Cost	Priority	Level
INT33-C	Low	Likely	Medium	P6	L2
INT34-C	Low	Unlikely	Medium	P2	L3
INT35-C	Low	Unlikely	Medium	P2	L3
INT36-C	Low	Probable	High	P2	L3

■ INT30-C. Ensure that unsigned integer operations do not wrap

The C Standard, 6.2.5, paragraph 9 [ISO/IEC 9899:2011], states:

> A computation involving unsigned operands can never overflow, because a result that cannot be represented by the resulting unsigned integer type is reduced modulo the number that is one greater than the largest value that can be represented by the resulting type.

This behavior is more informally called **unsigned integer wrapping**. Unsigned integer operations can wrap if the resulting value cannot be represented by the underlying representation of the integer. Table 4–1 indicates which operators can result in wrapping.

The following sections examine specific operations that are susceptible to unsigned integer wrap. When operating on integer types with less precision than int, integer promotions are applied. The usual arithmetic conversions may also be applied to (implicitly) convert operands to equivalent types before

Table 4–1. Operators That May Cause Wrapping

Operator	Wrap	Operator	Wrap	Operator	Wrap	Operator	Wrap
+	Yes	-=	Yes	<<	Yes	<	No
-	Yes	*=	Yes	>>	No	>	No
*	Yes	/=	No	&	No	>=	No
/	No	%=	No			No	<=	No
%	No	<<=	Yes	^	No	==	No
++	Yes	>>=	No	~	No	!=	No
--	Yes	&=	No	!	No	&&	No
=	No	|=	No	un +	No	||	No
+=	Yes	^=	No	un -	Yes	?:	No

arithmetic operations are performed. Programmers should understand integer conversion rules before trying to implement secure arithmetic operations (see "INT02-C. Understand integer conversion rules").

Integer values must not be allowed to wrap, especially if they are used in any of the following ways:

- Integer operands of any pointer arithmetic, including array indexing
- The assignment expression for the declaration of a variable length array
- The postfix expression preceding square brackets [] or the expression in square brackets [] of a subscripted designation of an element of an array object
- Function arguments of type size_t or rsize_t (for example, an argument to a memory allocation function)
- In security-critical code

The C Standard defines arithmetic on atomic integer types as read-modify-write operations with the same representation as regular integer types. As a result, wrapping of atomic unsigned integers is identical to regular unsigned integers and should also be prevented or detected.

Addition

Addition is between two operands of arithmetic type or between a pointer to an object type and an integer type. This rule only applies to addition between two operands of arithmetic type (see "ARR37-C. Do not add or subtract an integer to a pointer to a non-array object" and "ARR30-C. Do not form or use out-of-bounds pointers or array subscripts").

Incrementing is equivalent to adding 1.

Noncompliant Code Example

This noncompliant code example can result in an unsigned integer wrap during the addition of the unsigned operands ui_a and ui_b. If this behavior is unexpected, the resulting value may be used to allocate insufficient memory for a subsequent operation or in some other manner that can lead to an exploitable vulnerability.

```
void func(unsigned int ui_a, unsigned int ui_b) {
  unsigned int usum = ui_a + ui_b;
  /* ... */
}
```

Compliant Solution (Precondition Test)

This compliant solution performs a precondition test of the operands of the addition to guarantee there is no possibility of unsigned wrap:

```
#include <limits.h>

void func(unsigned int ui_a, unsigned int ui_b) {
  unsigned int usum;
  if (UINT_MAX - ui_a < ui_b) {
    /* Handle error */
  } else {
    usum = ui_a + ui_b;
  }
  /* ... */
}
```

Compliant Solution (Postcondition Test)

This compliant solution performs a postcondition test to ensure that the result of the unsigned addition operation usum is not less than the first operand:

```
void func(unsigned int ui_a, unsigned int ui_b) {
  unsigned int usum = ui_a + ui_b;
  if (usum < ui_a) {
    /* Handle error */
  }
  /* ... */
}
```

Subtraction

Subtraction is between two operands of arithmetic type, two pointers to qualified or unqualified versions of compatible object types, or a pointer to an object type and an integer type. This rule only applies to subtraction between two operands of arithmetic type (see "ARR36-C. Do not subtract or compare two pointers that do not refer to the same array"; "ARR37-C. Do not add or subtract an integer to a pointer to a non-array object"; and "ARR30-C. Do not form or use out-of-bounds pointers or array subscripts" for information about pointer subtraction).

Decrementing is equivalent to subtracting 1.

Noncompliant Code Example

This noncompliant code example can result in an unsigned integer wrap during the subtraction of the unsigned operands ui_a and ui_b. If this behavior is unanticipated, it may lead to an exploitable vulnerability.

```
void func(unsigned int ui_a, unsigned int ui_b) {
  unsigned int udiff = ui_a - ui_b;
  /* ... */
}
```

Compliant Solution (Precondition Test)

This compliant solution performs a precondition test of the unsigned operands of the subtraction operation to guarantee there is no possibility of unsigned wrap:

```
void func(unsigned int ui_a, unsigned int ui_b) {
  unsigned int udiff;
  if (ui_a < ui_b){
    /* Handle error */
  } else {
    udiff = ui_a - ui_b;
  }
  /* ... */
}
```

Compliant Solution (Postcondition Test)

This compliant solution performs a postcondition test that the result of the unsigned subtraction operation udiff is not greater than the minuend:

```
void func(unsigned int ui_a, unsigned int ui_b) {
  unsigned int udiff = ui_a - ui_b;
  if (udiff > ui_a) {
    /* Handle error */
  }
  /* ... */
}
```

Multiplication

Multiplication is between two operands of arithmetic type.

Noncompliant Code Example

The Mozilla Foundation Security Advisory 2007-01 describes a heap buffer overflow vulnerability in the Mozilla Scalable Vector Graphics (SVG) viewer resulting from an unsigned integer wrap during the multiplication of the signed int value pen->num_vertices and the size_t value sizeof(cairo_pen_vertex_t) [VU#551436]. The signed int operand is converted to size_t prior to the multiplication operation so that the multiplication takes place between two size_t integers, which are unsigned (see "INT02-C. Understand integer conversion rules").

```
pen->num_vertices = _cairo_pen_vertices_needed(
  gstate->tolerance, radius, &gstate->ctm
);
pen->vertices = malloc(
  pen->num_vertices * sizeof(cairo_pen_vertex_t)
);
```

The unsigned integer wrap can result in allocating memory of insufficient size.

Compliant Solution

This compliant solution tests the operands of the multiplication to guarantee that there is no unsigned integer wrap:

```
pen->num_vertices = _cairo_pen_vertices_needed(
  gstate->tolerance, radius, &gstate->ctm
);

if (pen->num_vertices > SIZE_MAX / sizeof(cairo_pen_vertex_t)) {
  /* Handle error */
}
pen->vertices = malloc(
  pen->num_vertices * sizeof(cairo_pen_vertex_t)
);
```

Exceptions

INT30-EX1: Unsigned integers can exhibit modulo behavior (wrapping) when necessary for the proper execution of the program. It is recommended that the variable declaration be clearly commented as supporting modulo behavior and that each operation on that integer also be clearly commented as supporting modulo behavior.

INT30-EX2: Checks for wraparound can be omitted when it can be determined at compile time that wraparound will not occur. As such, the following operations on unsigned integers require no **validation**:

■ Operations on two compile-time constants
■ Operations on a variable and 0 (except division or remainder by 0)

- Subtracting any variable from its type's maximum; for example, any unsigned int may safely be subtracted from UINT_MAX
- Multiplying any variable by 1
- Division or remainder, as long as the divisor is nonzero
- Right-shifting any type maximum by any number no larger than the type precision; for example, UINT_MAX >> x is valid as long as 0 <= x < 32 (assuming that the precision of unsigned int is 32 bits)

INT30-EX3: The left-shift operator takes two operands of integer type. Unsigned left shift << can exhibit modulo behavior (wrapping). This exception is provided because of common usage, because this behavior is usually expected by the programmer, and because the behavior is well defined. For examples of usage of the left-shift operator, see "INT34-C. Do not shift an expression by a negative number of bits or by greater than or equal to the number of bits that exist in the operand."

Risk Assessment

Integer wrap can lead to buffer overflows and the execution of arbitrary code by an attacker.

Rule	Severity	Likelihood	Remediation Cost	Priority	Level
INT30-C	High	Likely	High	P9	L2

Related Vulnerabilities

CVE-2009-1385 results from a violation of this rule. The value performs an unchecked subtraction on the length of a buffer and then adds that many bytes of data to another buffer [xorl 2009]. This can cause a buffer overflow, which allows an attacker to execute arbitrary code.

A Linux kernel vmsplice exploit, described by Rafal Wojtczuk [Wojtczuk 2008], documents a vulnerability and exploit arising from a buffer overflow (caused by unsigned integer wrapping).

Related Guidelines

ISO/IEC TR 24772:2013	Arithmetic Wrap-around Error [FIF]
MITRE CWE	CWE-190, Integer Overflow or Wraparound

Bibliography

[Dowd 2006]	Chapter 6, "C Language Issues" ("Arithmetic Boundary Conditions," pp. 211–223)
[ISO/IEC 9899:2011]	6.2.5, "Types"
[Seacord 2013b]	Chapter 5, "Integer Security"
[Viega 2005]	Section 5.2.7, "Integer Overflow"
[VU#551436]	
[Warren 2002]	Chapter 2, "Basics"
[Wojtczuk 2008]	
[xorl 2009]	"CVE-2009-1385: Linux Kernel E1000 Integer Underflow"

■ INT31-C. Ensure that integer conversions do not result in lost or misinterpreted data

Integer conversions, both implicit and explicit (using a cast), must be guaranteed not to result in lost or misinterpreted data. This is particularly true for integer values that originate from untrusted sources and are used in any of the following ways:

- Integer operands of any pointer arithmetic, including array indexing;
- The assignment expression for the declaration of a variable length array;
- The postfix expression preceding square brackets [] or the expression in square brackets [] of a subscripted designation of an element of an array object; and
- Function arguments of type size_t or rsize_t (for example, an argument to a memory allocation function).

The only integer type conversions that are guaranteed to be safe for all data values and all possible conforming implementations are conversions of an integral value to a wider type of the same signedness. The C Standard, 6.3.1.3 [ISO/IEC 9899:2011], says,

When a value with integer type is converted to another integer type other than _Bool, if the value can be represented by the new type, it is unchanged.

Otherwise, if the new type is unsigned, the value is converted by repeatedly adding or subtracting one more than the maximum value that can be represented in the new type until the value is in the range of the new type.

Otherwise, the new type is signed and the value cannot be represented in it; either the result is implementation-defined or an implementation-defined signal is raised.

Typically, converting an integer to a smaller type results in truncation of the high-order bits.

Noncompliant Code Example (Unsigned to Signed)

Type range errors, including loss of data (truncation) and loss of sign (sign errors), can occur when converting from a value of an unsigned integer type to a value of a signed integer type. This noncompliant code example results in a truncation error on most implementations:

```
#include <limits.h>

void func(void) {
  unsigned long int u_a = ULONG_MAX;
  signed char sc;
  sc = (signed char)u_a; /* Cast eliminates warning */
  /* ... */
}
```

Compliant Solution (Unsigned to Signed)

Validate ranges when converting from an unsigned type to a signed type. This compliant solution can be used to convert a value of unsigned long int type to a value of signed char type:

```
#include <limits.h>

void func(void) {
  unsigned long int u_a = ULONG_MAX;
  signed char sc;
  if (u_a <= SCHAR_MAX) {
    sc = (signed char)u_a; /* Cast eliminates warning */
  } else {
    /* Handle error */
  }
}
```

Noncompliant Code Example (Signed to Unsigned)

Type range errors, including loss of data (truncation) and loss of sign (sign errors), can occur when converting from a value of a signed type to a value of an unsigned type. This noncompliant code example results in a loss of sign:

```
#include <limits.h>

void func(void) {
  signed int si = INT_MIN;
  /* Cast eliminates warning */
  unsigned int ui = (unsigned int)si;
  /* ... */
}
```

Compliant Solution (Signed to Unsigned)

Validate ranges when converting from a signed type to an unsigned type. This compliant solution converts a value of a signed int type to a value of an unsigned int type:

```
#include <limits.h>

void func(void) {
  signed int si = INT_MIN;
  unsigned int ui;
  if (si < 0) {
    /* Handle error */
  } else {
    ui = (unsigned int)si; /* Cast eliminates warning */
  }
  /* ... */
}
```

The C Standard, 6.2.5, paragraph 9 [ISO/IEC 9899:2011], provides the necessary guarantees to ensure this solution works on a conforming implementation:

> The range of nonnegative values of a signed integer type is a subrange of the corresponding unsigned integer type, and the representation of the same value in each type is the same.

Noncompliant Code Example (Signed, Loss of Precision)

A loss of data (truncation) can occur when converting from a value of a signed integer type to a value of a signed type with less precision. This noncompliant code example results in a truncation error on most implementations:

```
#include <limits.h>

void func(void) {
  signed long int s_a = LONG_MAX;
  signed char sc = (signed char)s_a; /* Cast eliminates warning */
  /* ... */
}
```

Compliant Solution (Signed, Loss of Precision)

Validate ranges when converting from a signed type to a signed type with less precision. This compliant solution converts a value of a signed long int type to a value of a signed char type:

```
#include <limits.h>

void func(void) {
  signed long int s_a = LONG_MAX;
  signed char sc;
  if ((s_a < SCHAR_MIN) || (s_a > SCHAR_MAX)) {
    /* Handle error */
  } else {
    sc = (signed char)s_a; /* Use cast to eliminate warning */
  }
  /* ... */
}
```

Conversion from a value of a signed integer type to a value of a signed integer type with less precision requires that both the upper and lower bounds are checked.

Noncompliant Code Example (Unsigned, Loss of Precision)

A loss of data (truncation) can occur when converting from a value of an unsigned integer type to a value of an unsigned type with less precision. This noncompliant code example results in a truncation error on most implementations:

```
#include <limits.h>

void func(void) {
  unsigned long int u_a = ULONG_MAX;
  unsigned char uc = (unsigned char)u_a; /* Cast eliminates warning */
  /* ... */
}
```

Compliant Solution (Unsigned, Loss of Precision)

Validate ranges when converting a value of an unsigned integer type to a value of an unsigned integer type with less precision. This compliant solution converts a value of an unsigned long int type to a value of an unsigned char type:

```
#include <limits.h>

void func(void) {
  unsigned long int u_a = ULONG_MAX;
  unsigned char uc;
  if (u_a > UCHAR_MAX) {
    /* Handle error */
  } else {
    uc = (unsigned char)u_a; /* Cast eliminates warning */
  }
  /* ... */
}
```

Conversions from unsigned types with greater precision to unsigned types with less precision require only the upper bounds to be checked.

Noncompliant Code Example (time_t Return Value)

The time() function returns the value (time_t)(-1) to indicate that the calendar time is not available. The C Standard requires only that the time_t type is a *real type* capable of representing time. (The integer and real floating types are collectively called real types.) It is left to the implementor to decide the best real type to use to represent time. If time_t is implemented as an unsigned integer type with less precision than a signed int, the return value of time() will never compare equal to the integer literal -1.

```
#include <time.h>

void func(void) {
  time_t now = time(NULL);
  if (now != -1) {
    /* Continue processing */
  }
}
```

Compliant Solution (`time_t` Return Value)

To ensure the comparison is properly performed, the return value of `time()` should be compared against –1 cast to type `time_t`:

```
#include <time.h>

void func(void) {
  time_t now = time(NULL);
  if (now != (time_t)-1) {
    /* Continue processing */
  }
}
```

This solution is in accordance with "INT18-C. Evaluate integer expressions in a larger size before comparing or assigning to that size."

Exceptions

INT31-EX1: The C Standard defines minimum ranges for standard integer types. For example, the minimum range for an object of type `unsigned short int` is 0 to 65,535, whereas the minimum range for `int` is –32,767 to +32,767. Consequently, it is not always possible to represent all possible values of an `unsigned short int` as an `int`. However, on the 32-bit x86 architecture, for example, the actual integer range is from –2,147,483,648 to +2,147,483,647, meaning that it is quite possible to represent all the values of an `unsigned short int` as an `int` for this architecture. As a result, it is not necessary to provide a test for this conversion on 32-bit x86. It is not possible to make assumptions about conversions without knowing the precision of the underlying types. If these tests are not provided, assumptions concerning precision must be clearly documented, as the resulting code cannot be safely ported to a system where these assumptions are invalid. A good way to document these assumptions is to use static assertions (see "DCL03-C. Use a static assertion to test the value of a constant expression").

INT31-EX2: Conversion from any integer type with a value between SCHAR_MIN and UCHAR_MAX to a character type is permitted provided the value represents a character and not an integer.

Conversions to unsigned character types are well defined by C to have modular behavior. A character's value is not misinterpreted by the loss of sign or conversion to a negative number. For example, the Euro symbol € is sometimes represented by bit pattern 0x80, which can have the numerical value 128 or –127 depending on the signedness of the type.

Conversions to signed character types are more problematic. The C Standard, 6.3.1.3, paragraph 3, says, regarding conversions:

> Otherwise, the new type is signed and the value cannot be represented in it; either the result is implementation-defined or an implementation-defined signal is raised.

Furthermore, subclause 6.2.6.2, paragraph 2, says, regarding integer modifications:

> If the sign bit is one, the value shall be modified in one of the following ways:
>
> ■ the corresponding value with sign bit 0 is negated (sign and magnitude);
>
> ■ the sign bit has the value $-(2M)$ (two's complement);
>
> ■ the sign bit has the value $-(2M - 1)$ (ones' complement).
>
> Which of these applies is implementation-defined, as is whether the value with sign bit 1 and all value bits zero (for the first two), or with sign bit and all value bits 1 (for ones' complement), is a trap representation or a normal value.[1]

Consequently the standard allows for this code to trap:

```
int i = 128; /* 1000 0000 in binary */
assert (SCHAR_MAX == 127);
signed char c = i; /* can trap */
```

However, platforms where this code traps or produces an unexpected value are rare. According to *The New C Standard: An Economic and Cultural Commentary* by Derek Jones [Jones 2008]:

> Implementations with such trap representations are thought to have existed in the past. Your author was unable to locate any documents describing such processors.

Risk Assessment

Integer truncation errors can lead to buffer overflows and the execution of arbitrary code by an attacker.

---

1. *Two's complement* is shorthand for "radix complement in radix 2." *Ones' complement* is shorthand for "diminished radix complement in radix 2."

Rule	Severity	Likelihood	Remediation Cost	Priority	Level
INT31-C	High	Probable	High	P6	L2

Related Vulnerabilities

CVE-2009-1376 results from a violation of this rule. In version 2.5.5 of Pidgin, a `size_t` offset is set to the value of a 64-bit unsigned integer, which can lead to truncation [xorl 2009] on platforms where a `size_t` is implemented as a 32-bit unsigned integer. An attacker can execute arbitrary code by carefully choosing this value and causing a buffer overflow.

Related Guidelines

ISO/IEC TR 24772:2013	Numeric Conversion Errors [FLC]
MISRA C:2012	Rule 10.1 (required) Rule 10.3 (required) Rule 10.4 (required) Rule 10.6 (required) Rule 10.7 (required)
MITRE CWE	CWE-192, Integer Coercion Error CWE-197, Numeric Truncation Error CWE-681, Incorrect Conversion between Numeric Types

Bibliography

[Dowd 2006]	Chapter 6, "C Language Issues" ("Type Conversions," pp. 223–270)
[ISO/IEC 9899:2011]	6.3.1.3, "Signed and Unsigned Integers"
[Jones 2008]	
[Seacord 2013b]	Chapter 5, "Integer Security"
[Viega 2005]	Section 5.2.9, "Truncation Error" Section 5.2.10, "Sign Extension Error" Section 5.2.11, "Signed to Unsigned Conversion Error" Section 5.2.12, "Unsigned to Signed Conversion Error"
[Warren 2002]	Chapter 2, "Basics"
[xorl 2009]	"CVE-2009-1376: Pidgin MSN SLP Integer Truncation"

■ INT32-C. Ensure that operations on signed integers do not result in overflow

Signed integer overflow is undefined behavior 36 (see Appendix B). Consequently, implementations have considerable latitude in how they deal with signed integer overflow (see "MSC15-C. Do not depend on undefined behavior"). An implementation that defines signed integer types as being modulo, for example, need not detect integer overflow. Implementations may also trap on signed arithmetic overflows, or simply assume that overflows will never happen and generate object code accordingly. It is also possible for the same conforming implementation to emit code that exhibits different behavior in different contexts. For example, an implementation may determine that a signed integer loop control variable declared in a local scope cannot overflow and may emit efficient code on the basis of that determination, while the same implementation may determine that a global variable used in a similar context will wrap.

For these reasons, it is important to ensure that operations on signed integers do not result in overflow. Of particular importance are operations on signed integer values that originate from a **tainted source** and are used as

- Integer operands of any pointer arithmetic, including array indexing;
- The assignment expression for the declaration of a variable length array;
- The postfix expression preceding square brackets [] or the expression in square brackets [] of a subscripted designation of an element of an array object; and
- Function arguments of type size_t or rsize_t (for example, an argument to a memory allocation function).

Integer operations will overflow if the resulting value cannot be represented by the underlying representation of the integer. Table 4–2 indicates which operations can result in overflow.

The following sections examine specific operations that are susceptible to integer overflow. When operating on integer types with less precision than int, integer promotions are applied. The usual arithmetic conversions may also be applied to (implicitly) convert operands to equivalent types before arithmetic operations are performed. Programmers should understand integer conversion rules before trying to implement secure arithmetic operations (see "INT02-C. Understand integer conversion rules").

Table 4–2. Operations That Can Result in Overflow

Operator	Overflow	Operator	Overflow	Operator	Overflow	Operator	Overflow
+	Yes	-=	Yes	<<	Yes	<	No
-	Yes	*=	Yes	>>	No	>	No
*	Yes	/=	Yes	&	No	>=	No
/	Yes	%=	Yes	|	No	<=	No
%	Yes	<<=	Yes	^	No	==	No
++	Yes	>>=	No	~	No	!=	No
--	Yes	&=	No	!	No	&&	No
=	No	|=	No	un +	No	||	No
+=	Yes	^=	No	un -	Yes	?:	No

The C Standard defines the behavior of compound arithmetic functions such as `atomic_fetch_add()` on atomic signed integer types to use two's complement representation with silent wraparound on overflow; there are no undefined results. Although defined, these results may be unexpected and therefore carry similar risks to unsigned integer wrapping (see "INT30-C. Ensure that unsigned integer operations do not wrap"). Consequently, signed integer overflow of atomic integer types should also be prevented or detected.

Addition

Addition is between two operands of arithmetic type or between a pointer to an object type and an integer type. This rule only applies to addition between two operands of arithmetic type (see "ARR37-C. Do not add or subtract an integer to a pointer to a non-array object" and "ARR30-C. Do not form or use out-of-bounds pointers or array subscripts").

Incrementing is equivalent to adding 1.

Noncompliant Code Example

This noncompliant code example can result in a signed integer overflow during the addition of the signed operands `si_a` and `si_b`:

```
void func(signed int si_a, signed int si_b) {
  signed int sum = si_a + si_b;
  /* ... */
}
```

Compliant Solution

This compliant solution ensures that the addition operation cannot overflow, regardless of representation:

```c
#include <limits.h>

void f(signed int si_a, signed int si_b) {
  signed int sum;
  if (((si_b > 0) && (si_a > (INT_MAX - si_b))) ||
      ((si_b < 0) && (si_a < (INT_MIN - si_b)))) {
    /* Handle error */
  } else {
    sum = si_a + si_b;
  }
  /* ... */
}
```

Subtraction

Subtraction is between two operands of arithmetic type, two pointers to qualified or unqualified versions of compatible object types, or a pointer to an object type and an integer type. This rule applies only to subtraction between two operands of arithmetic type (see "ARR36-C. Do not subtract or compare two pointers that do not refer to the same array"; "ARR37-C. Do not add or subtract an integer to a pointer to a non-array object"; and "ARR30-C. Do not form or use out-of-bounds pointers or array subscripts" for information about pointer subtraction).

Decrementing is equivalent to subtracting 1.

Noncompliant Code Example

This noncompliant code example can result in a signed integer overflow during the subtraction of the signed operands si_a and si_b:

```c
void func(signed int si_a, signed int si_b) {
  signed int diff = si_a - si_b;
  /* ... */
}
```

Compliant Solution

This compliant solution tests the operands of the subtraction to guarantee there is no possibility of signed overflow, regardless of representation:

```
#include <limits.h>

void func(signed int si_a, signed int si_b) {
  signed int diff;
  if ((si_b > 0 && si_a < INT_MIN + si_b) ||
      (si_b < 0 && si_a > INT_MAX + si_b)) {
    /* Handle error */
  } else {
    diff = si_a - si_b;
  }
  /* ... */
}
```

Multiplication

Multiplication is between two operands of arithmetic type.

Noncompliant Code Example

This noncompliant code example can result in a signed integer overflow during the multiplication of the signed operands si_a and si_b:

```
void func(signed int si_a, signed int si_b) {
  signed int result = si_a * si_b;
  /* ... */
}
```

Compliant Solution

The product of two operands can always be represented using twice the number of bits than exist in the precision of the larger of the two operands. This compliant solution eliminates signed overflow on systems where long long is at least twice the precision of int:

```
#include <stddef.h>
#include <assert.h>
#include <limits.h>
#include <inttypes.h>

extern size_t popcount(uintmax_t);
#define PRECISION(umax_value) popcount(umax_value)

void func(signed int si_a, signed int si_b) {
  signed int result;
  signed long long tmp;
  assert(PRECISION(ULLONG_MAX) >= 2 * PRECISION(UINT_MAX));
```

```
  tmp = (signed long long)si_a * (signed long long)si_b;
  /*
   * If the product cannot be represented as a 32-bit integer,
   * handle as an error condition.
   */
  if ((tmp > INT_MAX) || (tmp < INT_MIN)) {
    /* Handle error */
  } else {
    result = (int)tmp;
  }
  /* ... */
}
```

The assertion fails if long long has less than twice the precision of int. The PRECISION() macro and popcount() function provide the correct precision for any integer type (see "INT35-C. Use correct integer precisions").

Compliant Solution

The following portable compliant solution can be used with any conforming implementation, including those that do not have an integer type that is at least twice the precision of int:

```
#include <limits.h>

void func(signed int si_a, signed int si_b) {
  signed int result;
  if (si_a > 0) {  /* si_a is positive */
    if (si_b > 0) {  /* si_a and si_b are positive */
      if (si_a > (INT_MAX / si_b)) {
        /* Handle error */
      }
    } else { /* si_a positive, si_b nonpositive */
      if (si_b < (INT_MIN / si_a)) {
        /* Handle error */
      }
    } /* si_a positive, si_b nonpositive */
  } else { /* si_a is nonpositive */
    if (si_b > 0) { /* si_a is nonpositive, si_b is positive */
      if (si_a < (INT_MIN / si_b)) {
        /* Handle error */
      }
    } else { /* si_a and si_b are nonpositive */
      if ( (si_a != 0) && (si_b < (INT_MAX / si_a))) {
        /* Handle error */
      }
    } /* End if si_a and si_b are nonpositive */
```

```
  } /* End if si_a is nonpositive */

  result = si_a * si_b;
}
```

Division

Division is between two operands of arithmetic type. Overflow can occur during two's complement signed integer division when the dividend is equal to the minimum (negative) value for the signed integer type and the divisor is equal to -1. Division operations are also susceptible to divide-by-zero errors (see "INT33-C. Ensure that division and remainder operations do not result in divide-by-zero errors").

Noncompliant Code Example

This noncompliant code example prevents divide-by-zero errors in compliance with "INT33-C. Ensure that division and remainder operations do not result in divide-by-zero errors" but does not prevent a signed integer overflow error in two's complement.

```
void func(signed long s_a, signed long s_b) {
  signed long result;
  if (s_b == 0) {
    /* Handle error */
  } else {
    result = s_a / s_b;
  }
  /* ... */
}
```

Compliant Solution

This compliant solution eliminates the possibility of divide-by-zero errors or signed overflow:

```
#include <limits.h>

void func(signed long s_a, signed long s_b) {
  signed long result;
  if ((s_b == 0) || ((s_a == LONG_MIN) && (s_b == -1))) {
    /* Handle error */
  } else {
    result = s_a / s_b;
  }
  /* ... */
}
```

Remainder

The remainder operator provides the remainder when two operands of integer type are divided. Because many platforms implement remainder and division in the same instruction, the remainder operator is also susceptible to arithmetic overflow and division by 0 (see "INT33-C. Ensure that division and remainder operations do not result in divide-by-zero errors").

Noncompliant Code Example

Many hardware architectures implement remainder as part of the division operator, which can overflow. Overflow can occur during a remainder operation when the dividend is equal to the minimum (negative) value for the signed integer type and the divisor is equal to -1. This occurs even though the result of such a remainder operation is mathematically 0. This noncompliant code example prevents divide-by-zero errors in compliance with "INT33-C. Ensure that division and remainder operations do not result in divide-by-zero errors" but does not prevent integer overflow:

```
void func(signed long s_a, signed long s_b) {
  signed long result;
  if (s_b == 0) {
    /* Handle error */
  } else {
    result = s_a % s_b;
  }
  /* ... */
}
```

Compliant Solution

This compliant solution also tests the remainder operands to guarantee there is no possibility of an overflow:

```
#include <limits.h>

void func(signed long s_a, signed long s_b) {
  signed long result;
  if ((s_b == 0 ) || ((s_a == LONG_MIN) && (s_b == -1))) {
    /* Handle error */
  } else {
    result = s_a % s_b;
  }

  /* ... */
}
```

Left-Shift Operator

The left-shift operator takes two integer operands. The result of E1 << E2 is E1 left-shifted E2 bit positions; vacated bits are filled with zeros.

The C Standard, 6.5.7 paragraph 4 [ISO/IEC 9899:2011], states

> If E1 has a signed type and nonnegative value, and E1 × 2^{E2} is representable in the result type, then that is the resulting value; otherwise, the behavior is undefined.

In almost every case, an attempt to shift by a negative number of bits or by more bits than exist in the operand indicates a logic error. These issues are covered by "INT34-C. Do not shift an expression by a negative number of bits or by greater than or equal to the number of bits that exist in the operand."

Noncompliant Code Example

This noncompliant code example performs a left shift after verifying that the number being shifted is not negative, and the number of bits to shift is valid. The PRECISION() macro and popcount() function provide the correct precision for any integer type (see "INT35-C. Use correct integer precisions"). However, because this code does no overflow check, it can result in an unrepresentable value.

```
#include <limits.h>
#include <stddef.h>
#include <inttypes.h>

extern size_t popcount(uintmax_t);
#define PRECISION(umax_value) popcount(umax_value)

void func(signed long si_a, signed long si_b) {
  signed long result;
  if ((si_a < 0) || (si_b < 0) ||
      (si_b >= PRECISION(ULONG_MAX))) {
    /* Handle error */
  } else {
    result = si_a << si_b;
  }
  /* ... */
}
```

Compliant Solution

This compliant solution eliminates the possibility of overflow resulting from a left-shift operation:

```
#include <limits.h>
#include <stddef.h>
```

```
#include <inttypes.h>

extern size_t popcount(uintmax_t);
#define PRECISION(umax_value) popcount(umax_value)

void func(signed long si_a, signed long si_b) {
  signed long result;
  if ((si_a < 0) || (si_b < 0) ||
      (si_b >= PRECISION(ULONG_MAX)) ||
      (si_a > (LONG_MAX >> si_b))) {
    /* Handle error */
  } else {
    result = si_a << si_b;
  }
  /* ... */
}
```

Unary Negation

The unary negation operator takes an operand of arithmetic type. Overflow can occur during two's complement unary negation when the operand is equal to the minimum (negative) value for the signed integer type.

Noncompliant Code Example

This noncompliant code example can result in a signed integer overflow during the unary negation of the signed operand s_a:

```
void func(signed long s_a) {
  signed long result = -s_a;
  /* ... */
}
```

Compliant Solution

This compliant solution tests the negation operation to guarantee there is no possibility of signed overflow:

```
#include <limits.h>

void func(signed long s_a) {
  signed long result;
  if (s_a == LONG_MIN) {
    /* Handle error */
  } else {
    result = -s_a;
  }
  /* ... */
}
```

Risk Assessment

Integer overflow can lead to buffer overflows and the execution of arbitrary code by an attacker.

Rule	Severity	Likelihood	Remediation Cost	Priority	Level
INT32-C	High	Likely	High	P9	L2

Related Guidelines

ISO/IEC TR 24772:2013	Arithmetic Wrap-around Error [FIF]
ISO/IEC TS 17961:2013	Overflowing signed integers [intoflow]
MITRE CWE	CWE-129, Improper Validation of Array Index CWE-190, Integer Overflow or Wraparound

Bibliography

[Dowd 2006]	Chapter 6, "C Language Issues" ("Arithmetic Boundary Conditions," pp. 211–223)
[ISO/IEC 9899:2011]	6.5.5, "Multiplicative Operators"
[Seacord 2013b]	Chapter 5, "Integer Security"
[Viega 2005]	Section 5.2.7, "Integer Overflow"
[Warren 2002]	Chapter 2, "Basics"

■ INT33-C. Ensure that division and remainder operations do not result in divide-by-zero errors

Division and remainder operations result in undefined behavior if the value of the second operand of the / or % operator is zero (see undefined behavior 45 in Appendix B). Ensure that division and remainder operations do not result in divide-by-zero errors.

Division

The result of the / operator is the quotient from the division of the first arithmetic operand by the second arithmetic operand. Division operations are susceptible to divide-by-zero errors. Overflow can also occur during two's complement signed integer division when the dividend is equal to the minimum (most negative) value for the signed integer type and the divisor is equal to –1 (see "INT32-C. Ensure that operations on signed integers do not result in overflow").

Noncompliant Code Example

This noncompliant code example prevents signed integer overflow in compliance with "INT32-C. Ensure that operations on signed integers do not result in overflow" but fails to prevent a divide-by-zero error during the division of the signed operands s_a and s_b.

```
#include <limits.h>

void func(signed long s_a, signed long s_b) {
  signed long result;
  if ((s_a == LONG_MIN) && (s_b == -1)) {
    /* Handle error */
  } else {
    result = s_a / s_b;
  }
  /* ... */
}
```

Compliant Solution

This compliant solution tests the division operation to guarantee there is no possibility of divide-by-zero errors or signed overflow:

```
#include <limits.h>

void func(signed long s_a, signed long s_b) {
  signed long result;
  if ((s_b == 0) || ((s_a == LONG_MIN) && (s_b == -1))) {
    /* Handle error */
  } else {
    result = s_a / s_b;
  }
  /* ... */
}
```

Remainder

The remainder operator provides the remainder when two operands of integer type are divided.

Noncompliant Code Example

This noncompliant code example prevents signed integer overflow in compliance with "INT32-C. Ensure that operations on signed integers do not result in overflow" but fails to prevent a divide-by-zero error during the remainder operation on the signed operands s_a and s_b:

```
#include <limits.h>

void func(signed long s_a, signed long s_b) {
  signed long result;
  if ((s_a == LONG_MIN) && (s_b == -1)) {
    /* Handle error */
  } else {
    result = s_a % s_b;
  }
  /* ... */
}
```

Compliant Solution

This compliant solution tests the remainder operand to guarantee there is no possibility of a divide-by-zero error or an overflow error:

```
#include <limits.h>

void func(signed long s_a, signed long s_b) {
  signed long result;
  if ((s_b == 0 ) || ((s_a == LONG_MIN) && (s_b == -1))) {
    /* Handle error */
  } else {
    result = s_a % s_b;
  }
  /* ... */
}
```

Risk Assessment

A divide-by-zero error can result in abnormal program termination and denial of service.

Rule	Severity	Likelihood	Remediation Cost	Priority	Level
INT33-C	Low	Likely	Medium	P6	L2

Related Guidelines

ISO/IEC TS 17961:2013	Integer division errors [diverr]
MITRE CWE	CWE-369, Divide By Zero

Bibliography

[Seacord 2013b]	Chapter 5, "Integer Security"
[Warren 2002]	Chapter 2, "Basics"

■ INT34-C. Do not shift an expression by a negative number of bits or by greater than or equal to the number of bits that exist in the operand

Bitwise shifts include left-shift operations of the form *shift-expression << additive-expression* and right-shift operations of the form *shift-expression >> additive-expression*. The standard integer promotions are first performed on the operands, each of which has an integer type. The type of the result is that of the promoted left operand. If the value of the right operand is negative or is greater than or equal to the width of the promoted left operand, the behavior is undefined (see undefined behavior 51 in Appendix B.)

Do not shift an expression by a negative number of bits or by a number greater than or equal to the *precision* of the promoted left operand. The precision of an integer type is the number of bits it uses to represent values, excluding any sign and padding bits. For unsigned integer types the width and the precision are the same, whereas for signed integer types the width is one greater than the precision. This rule uses precision instead of width because, in almost every case, an attempt to shift by a number of bits greater than or equal to the precision of the operand indicates a bug (logic error). A logic error is different from overflow, in which there is simply a representational deficiency. In general, shifts should only be performed on unsigned operands (see "INT13-C. Use bitwise operators only on unsigned operands").

Noncompliant Code Example (Left Shift, Unsigned Type)

The result of E1 << E2 is E1 left-shifted E2 bit positions; vacated bits are filled with zeros. Figure 4–1 illustrates the left-shift operation.

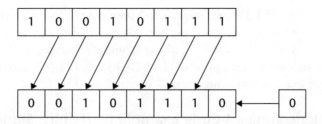

Figure 4–1. Left-shift operation

According to the C Standard, if E1 has an unsigned type, the value of the result is E1 * 2^{E2}, reduced modulo 1 more than the maximum value representable in the result type.

This noncompliant code example fails to ensure that the right operand is less than the precision of the promoted left operand:

```
void func(unsigned int ui_a, unsigned int ui_b) {
  unsigned int uresult = ui_a << ui_b;
  /* ... */
}
```

Compliant Solution (Left Shift, Unsigned Type)

This compliant solution eliminates the possibility of shifting by greater than or equal to the number of bits that exist in the precision of the left operand:

```
#include <limits.h>
#include <stddef.h>
#include <inttypes.h>

extern size_t popcount(uintmax_t);
#define PRECISION(x) popcount(x)

void func(unsigned int ui_a, unsigned int ui_b) {
  unsigned int uresult = 0;
  if (ui_b >= PRECISION(UINT_MAX)) {
    /* Handle error */
  } else {
    uresult = ui_a << ui_b;
  }

  /* ... */
}
```

The PRECISION() macro and popcount() function provide the correct precision for any integer type (see "INT35-C. Use correct integer precisions").

Modulo behavior resulting from left-shifting an unsigned integer type is permitted by exception INT30-EX3 to "INT30-C. Ensure that unsigned integer operations do not wrap."

Noncompliant Code Example (Left Shift, Signed Type)

The result of E1 << E2 is E1 left-shifted E2 bit positions; vacated bits are filled with zeros. If E1 has a signed type and nonnegative value, and E1 * 2^{E2} is representable in the result type, then that is the resulting value; otherwise, the behavior is undefined.

This noncompliant code example fails to ensure that left and right operands have nonnegative values and that the right operand is less than the precision of the promoted left operand. This example does check for signed integer overflow in compliance with "INT32-C. Ensure that operations on signed integers do not result in overflow."

```
#include <limits.h>
#include <stddef.h>
#include <inttypes.h>

void func(signed long si_a, signed long si_b) {
  signed long result;
  if (si_a > (LONG_MAX >> si_b)) {
    /* Handle error */
  } else {
    result = si_a << si_b;
  }
  /* ... */
}
```

Shift operators and other bitwise operators should be used only with unsigned integer operands in accordance with "INT13-C. Use bitwise operators only on unsigned operands."

Compliant Solution (Left Shift, Signed Type)

In addition to the check for overflow, this compliant solution ensures that both the left and right operands have nonnegative values and that the right operand is less than the precision of the promoted left operand:

```
#include <limits.h>
#include <stddef.h>
#include <inttypes.h>
```

```
extern size_t popcount(uintmax_t);
#define PRECISION(x) popcount(x)

void func(signed long si_a, signed long si_b) {
  signed long result;
  if ((si_a < 0) || (si_b < 0) ||
      (si_b >= PRECISION(ULONG_MAX)) ||
      (si_a > (LONG_MAX >> si_b))) {
    /* Handle error */
  } else {
    result = si_a << si_b;
  }
  /* ... */
}
```

Noncompliant Code Example (Right Shift)

The result of E1 >> E2 is E1 right-shifted E2 bit positions. If E1 has an unsigned type or if E1 has a signed type and a nonnegative value, the value of the result is the integral part of the quotient of E1 / 2^{E2}. If E1 has a signed type and a negative value, the resulting value is implementation-defined and can be either an arithmetic (signed) shift, as shown in Figure 4–2, or a logical (unsigned) shift, as shown in Figure 4–3.

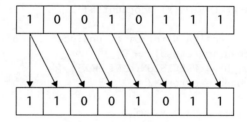

Figure 4–2. Arithmetic (signed) shift

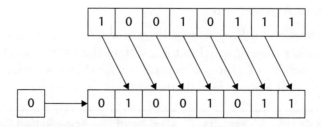

Figure 4–3. Logical (unsigned) shift

This noncompliant code example fails to test whether the right operand is greater than or equal to the precision of the promoted left operand, allowing undefined behavior:

```c
void func(unsigned int ui_a, unsigned int ui_b) {
  unsigned int uresult = ui_a >> ui_b;
  /* ... */
}
```

When working with signed operands, making assumptions about whether a right shift is implemented as an arithmetic (signed) shift or a logical (unsigned) shift can also lead to vulnerabilities (see "INT13-C. Use bitwise operators only on unsigned operands").

Compliant Solution (Right Shift)

This compliant solution eliminates the possibility of shifting by greater than or equal to the number of bits that exist in the precision of the left operand:

```c
#include <limits.h>
#include <stddef.h>
#include <inttypes.h>

extern size_t popcount(uintmax_t);
#define PRECISION(x) popcount(x)

void func(unsigned int ui_a, unsigned int ui_b) {
  unsigned int uresult = 0;
  if (ui_b >= PRECISION(UINT_MAX)) {
    /* Handle error */
  } else {
    uresult = ui_a >> ui_b;
  }
  /* ... */
}
```

Risk Assessment

Although shifting a negative number of bits or shifting a number of bits greater than or equal to the width of the promoted left operand is undefined behavior in C, the risk is generally low because processors frequently reduce the shift amount modulo the width of the type.

Rule	Severity	Likelihood	Remediation Cost	Priority	Level
INT34-C	Low	Unlikely	Medium	P2	L3

Related Guidelines

ISO/IEC TR 24772:2013	Arithmetic Wrap-around Error [FIF]

Bibliography

[C99 Rationale 2003]	6.5.7, "Bitwise Shift Operators"
[Dowd 2006]	Chapter 6, "C Language Issues"
[Seacord 2013b]	Chapter 5, "Integer Security"
[Viega 2005]	Section 5.2.7, "Integer Overflow"

■ INT35-C. Use correct integer precisions

Integer types in C have both a *size* and a *precision*. The size indicates the number of bytes used by an object and can be retrieved for any object or type using the `sizeof` operator. The precision of an integer type is the number of bits it uses to represent values, excluding any sign and padding bits.

Padding bits contribute to the integer's size but not to its precision. Consequently, inferring the precision of an integer type from its size may result in too large a value, which can then lead to incorrect assumptions about the numeric range of these types. Programmers should use correct integer precisions in their code, and in particular, should not use the `sizeof` operator to compute the precision of an integer type on architectures that use padding bits or in **strictly conforming** (that is, portable) programs.

Noncompliant Code Example

This noncompliant code example illustrates a function that produces 2 raised to the power of the function argument. To prevent undefined behavior in compliance with "INT34-C. Do not shift an expression by a negative number of bits or by greater than or equal to the number of bits that exist in the operand," the function ensures that the argument is less than the number of bits used to store a value of type `unsigned int`.

```
#include <limits.h>

unsigned int pow2(unsigned int exp) {
  if (exp >= sizeof(unsigned int) * CHAR_BIT) {
    /* Handle error */
  }
  return 1 << exp;
}
```

However, if this code runs on a platform where unsigned int has one or more padding bits, it can still result in values for exp that are too large. For example, a platform that stores unsigned int in 64 bits, but uses only 48 bits to represent the value, could perform a left shift on an invalid value of 56.

Compliant Solution

This compliant solution uses a popcount() function, which counts the number of bits set on any unsigned integer, allowing this code to determine the precision of any integer type, signed or unsigned.

```
#include <stddef.h>
#include <stdint.h>

/* Returns the number of set bits */
size_t popcount(uintmax_t num) {
  size_t precision = 0;
  while (num != 0) {
    if (num % 2 == 1) {
      precision++;
    }
    num >>= 1;
  }
  return precision;
}
#define PRECISION(umax_value) popcount(umax_value)
```

Implementations can replace the PRECISION() macro with a type-generic macro that returns an integer constant expression that is the precision of the specified type for that implementation. This return value can then be used anywhere an integer constant expression can be used, such as in a static assertion (see "DCL03-C. Use a static assertion to test the value of a constant expression"). The following type-generic macro, for example, might be used for a specific implementation targeting the 32-bit x86 architecture:

```
#define PRECISION(value)  _Generic(value, \
  unsigned char : 8, \
  unsigned short: 16, \
  unsigned int : 32, \
  unsigned long : 32, \
  unsigned long long : 64, \
  signed char : 7, \
  signed short : 15, \
  signed int : 31, \
  signed long : 31, \
  signed long long : 63)
```

The revised version of the pow2() function uses the PRECISION() macro to determine the precision of the unsigned type:

```
#include <stddef.h>
#include <stdint.h>
#include <limits.h>

extern size_t popcount(uintmax_t);
#define PRECISION(umax_value) popcount(umax_value)

unsigned int pow2(unsigned int exp) {
  if (exp >= PRECISION(UINT_MAX)) {
    /* Handle error */
  }
  return 1 << exp;
}
```

Risk Assessment

Mistaking an integer's size for its precision can permit invalid precision arguments to operations such as bitwise shifts, resulting in undefined behavior.

Rule	Severity	Likelihood	Remediation Cost	Priority	Level
INT35-C	Low	Unlikely	Medium	P2	L3

Bibliography

[C99 Rationale 2003]	6.5.7, "Bitwise Shift Operators"
[Dowd 2006]	Chapter 6, "C Language Issues"

■ INT36-C. Converting a pointer to integer or integer to pointer

Although programmers often use integers and pointers interchangeably in C, pointer-to-integer and integer-to-pointer conversions are implementation-defined.

Conversions between integers and pointers can have undesired consequences depending on the implementation. According to the C Standard, 6.3.2.3 [ISO/IEC 9899:2011],

An integer may be converted to any pointer type. Except as previously specified, the result is implementation-defined, might not be correctly aligned, might not point to an entity of the referenced type, and might be a trap representation.

Any pointer type may be converted to an integer type. Except as previously specified, the result is implementation-defined. If the result cannot be represented in the integer type, the behavior is undefined. The result need not be in the range of values of any integer type.

Do not convert an integer type to a pointer type if the resulting pointer is incorrectly aligned, does not point to an entity of the referenced type, or is a trap representation.

Do not convert a pointer type to an integer type if the result cannot be represented in the integer type (see undefined behavior 24 in Appendix B).

The mapping between pointers and integers must be consistent with the addressing structure of the execution environment. Issues may arise, for example, on architectures that have a segmented memory model.

Noncompliant Code Example

The size of a pointer can be greater than the size of an integer, such as in an implementation where pointers are 64 bits and unsigned integers are 32 bits. This code example is noncompliant on such implementations because the result of converting the 64-bit `ptr` cannot be represented in the 32-bit integer type:

```
void f(void) {
  char *ptr;
  /* ... */
  unsigned int number = (unsigned int)ptr;
  /* ... */
}
```

Compliant Solution

Any **valid pointer** to void can be converted to `intptr_t` or `uintptr_t` and back with no change in value (see INT36-EX2). The C Standard guarantees that a pointer to void may be converted to or from a pointer to any object type and back again and that the result must compare equal to the original pointer. Consequently, converting directly from a `char *` pointer to a `uintptr_t`, as in this compliant solution, is allowed on implementations that support the `uintptr_t` type.

```
#include <stdint.h>

void f(void) {
  char *ptr;
  /* ... */
  uintptr_t number = (uintptr_t)ptr;
  /* ... */
}
```

Noncompliant Code Example

In this noncompliant code example, the pointer `ptr` is converted to an integer value. The high-order 9 bits of the number are used to hold a flag value, and the result is converted back into a pointer. This example is noncompliant on an implementation where pointers are 64 bits and unsigned integers are 32 bits because the result of converting the 64-bit `ptr` cannot be represented in the 32-bit integer type.

```
void func(unsigned int flag) {
  char *ptr;
  /* ... */
  unsigned int number = (unsigned int)ptr;
  number = (number & 0x7fffff) | (flag << 23);
  ptr = (char *)number;
}
```

A similar scheme was used in early versions of Emacs, limiting its portability and preventing the ability to edit files larger than 8MB.

Compliant Solution

This compliant solution uses a `struct` to provide storage for both the pointer and the flag value. This solution is portable to machines of different word sizes, both smaller and larger than 32 bits, working even when pointers cannot be represented in any integer type.

```
struct ptrflag {
  char *pointer;
  unsigned int flag : 9;
} ptrflag;

void func(unsigned int flag) {
  char *ptr;
  /* ... */
```

```
    ptrflag.pointer = ptr;
    ptrflag.flag = flag;
}
```

Noncompliant Code Example

It is sometimes necessary to access memory at a specific location, requiring a literal integer to pointer conversion. In this noncompliant code example, a pointer is set directly to an integer constant, where it is unknown whether the result will be as intended:

```
unsigned int *g(void) {
  unsigned int *ptr = 0xdeadbeef;
  /* ... */
  return ptr;
}
```

The result of this assignment is implementation-defined, might not be correctly aligned, might not point to an entity of the referenced type, and might be a trap representation.

Compliant Solution

Adding an explicit cast may help the compiler convert the integer value into a valid pointer. A common technique is to assign the integer to a volatile-qualified object of type intptr_t or uintptr_t and then assign the integer value to the pointer:

```
unsigned int *g(void) {
  volatile uintptr_t iptr = 0xdeadbeef;
  unsigned int *ptr = (unsigned int *)iptr;
  /* ... */
  return ptr;
}
```

Exceptions

INT36-EX1: A null pointer can be converted to an integer; it takes on the value 0. Likewise, the integer value 0 can be converted to a pointer; it becomes the null pointer.

INT36-EX2: Any valid pointer to void can be converted to intptr_t or uintptr_t or their underlying types and back again with no change in value.

Use of underlying types instead of `intptr_t` or `uintptr_t` is discouraged, however, because it limits portability.

```
#include <assert.h>
#include <stdint.h>

void h(void) {
  intptr_t i = (intptr_t)(void *)&i;
  uintptr_t j = (uintptr_t)(void *)&j;

  void *ip = (void *)i;
  void *jp = (void *)j;

  assert(ip == &i);
  assert(jp == &j);
}
```

Risk Assessment

Converting from pointer to integer or vice versa results in code that is not portable and may create unexpected pointers to invalid memory locations.

Rule	Severity	Likelihood	Remediation Cost	Priority	Level
INT36-C	Low	Probable	High	P2	L3

Related Guidelines

ISO/IEC TR 24772:2013	Pointer Casting and Pointer Type Changes [HFC]
ISO/IEC TS 17961:2013	Converting a pointer to integer or integer to pointer [intptrconv]
MITRE CWE	CWE-466, Return of Pointer Value Outside of Expected Range CWE-587, Assignment of a Fixed Address to a Pointer

Bibliography

[ISO/IEC 9899:2011]	6.3.2.3, "Pointers"

Chapter 5

Floating Point (FLP)

Chapter Contents

Risk Assessment Summary

Rule	Severity	Likelihood	Remediation Cost	Priority	Level
FLP30-C	Low	Probable	Low	P6	L2
FLP32-C	Medium	Probable	Medium	P8	L2
FLP34-C	Low	Unlikely	Low	P3	L3
FLP36-C	Low	Unlikely	Medium	P2	L3

■ FLP30-C. Do not use floating-point variables as loop counters

Because floating-point numbers represent real numbers, it is often mistakenly assumed that they can represent any simple fraction exactly. Floating-point numbers are subject to representational limitations just as integers are, and binary floating-point numbers cannot represent all real numbers exactly, even if they can be represented in a small number of decimal digits.

In addition, because floating-point numbers can represent large values, it is often mistakenly assumed that they can represent all significant digits of those values. To gain a large dynamic range, floating-point numbers maintain a fixed number of precision bits (also called the *significand*) and an exponent, which limit the number of significant digits they can represent.

Different implementations have different precision limitations, and to keep code portable, floating-point variables should not be used as loop counters.

Noncompliant Code Example

In this noncompliant code example, a floating-point variable is used as a loop counter. The decimal number 0.1 is a repeating fraction in binary and cannot be exactly represented as a binary floating-point number. Depending on the implementation, the loop may iterate 9 or 10 times.

```
void func(void) {
  for (float x = 0.1f; x <= 1.0f; x += 0.1f) {
    /* Loop may iterate 9 or 10 times */
  }
}
```

For example, when compiled with GCC or Microsoft Visual Studio 2013 and executed on an x86 processor, the loop is evaluated only nine times.

Compliant Solution

In this compliant solution, the loop counter is an integer from which the floating-point value is derived:

```
#include <stddef.h>

void func(void) {
  for (size_t count = 1; count <= 10; ++count) {
    float x = count / 10.0f;
    /* Loop iterates exactly 10 times */
  }
}
```

Noncompliant Code Example

In this noncompliant code example, a floating-point loop counter is incremented by an amount that is too small to change its value given its precision:

```c
void func(void) {
  for (float x = 100000001.0f; x <= 100000010.0f; x += 1.0f) {
    /* Loop may not terminate */
  }
}
```

On many implementations, this produces an infinite loop.

Compliant Solution

In this compliant solution, the loop counter is an integer from which the floating-point value is derived. The variable x is incremented to maintain the same value it held at each iteration of the loop in the noncompliant code example.

```c
void func(void) {
  float x = 100000001.0f;
  for (size_t count = 1; count <= 10; ++count, x += 1.0f) {
    /* Loop iterates exactly 10 times */
  }
}
```

Risk Assessment

The use of floating-point variables as loop counters can result in unexpected behavior.

Rule	Severity	Likelihood	Remediation Cost	Priority	Level
FLP30-C	Low	Probable	Low	P6	L2

Related Guidelines

ISO/IEC TR 24772:2013	Floating-Point Arithmetic [PLF]
MISRA C:2012	Directive 1.1 (required) Rule 14.1 (required)

Bibliography

[Lockheed Martin 2005]	AV Rule 197

■ FLP32-C. Prevent or detect domain and range errors in math functions

The C Standard, 7.12.1 [ISO/IEC 9899:2011], defines three types of errors that relate specifically to math functions in <math.h>. Paragraph 2 states:

> A *domain error* occurs if an input argument is outside the domain over which the mathematical function is defined.

Paragraph 3 states:

> A *pole error* (also known as a singularity or infinitary) occurs if the mathematical function has an exact infinite result as the finite input argument(s) are approached in the limit.

Paragraph 4 states:

> A *range error* occurs if the mathematical result of the function cannot be represented in an object of the specified type, due to extreme magnitude.

An example of a domain error is the square root of a negative number, such as sqrt(-1.0), which has no meaning in real arithmetic. In contrast, 10 raised to the 1-millionth power, pow(10., 1e6), cannot be represented in many floating-point implementations because of the limited range of the type double and consequently constitutes a range error. In both cases, the function will return some value, but the value returned is not the correct result of the computation. An example of a pole error is log(0.0), which results in negative infinity.

Programmers can prevent domain and pole errors by carefully bounds-checking the arguments before calling mathematical functions and taking alternative action if the bounds are violated.

Range errors usually cannot be prevented because they are dependent on the implementation of floating-point numbers as well as on the function being applied. Instead of preventing range errors, programmers should attempt to detect them and take alternative action if a range error occurs.

Table 5–1 lists the double forms of standard mathematical functions, along with checks that should be performed to ensure a proper input domain, and indicates whether they can also result in range or pole errors, as reported by the C Standard. Both float and long double forms of these functions also exist but are omitted from the table for brevity. If a function

Table 5–1. Standard Mathematical Functions

Function	Domain	Range	Pole
acos(x)	-1 <= x && x <= 1	No	No
asin(x)	-1 <= x && x <= 1	Yes	No
atan(x)	None	Yes	No
atan2(y, x)	x != 0 && y != 0	No	No
acosh(x)	x >= 1	Yes	No
asin(x)	None	Yes	No
atanh(x)	-1 < x && x < 1	Yes	Yes
cosh(x), sinh(x)	None	Yes	No
exp(x), exp2(x), expm1(x)	None	Yes	No
ldexp(x, exp)	None	Yes	No
log(x), log10(x), log2(x)	x >= 0	No	Yes
log1p(x)	x > -1	No	Yes
ilogb(x)	x != 0 && !isinf(x) && !isnan(x)	Yes	No
logb(x)	x != 0	Yes	Yes
scalbn(x, n), scalbln(x, n)	None	Yes	No
hypot(x, y)	None	Yes	No
pow(x,y)	x > 0 || (x == 0 && y > 0) || (x < 0 && y is an integer)	Yes	Yes
sqrt(x)	x >= 0	No	No
erf(x)	None	Yes	No
erfc(x)	None	Yes	No
lgamma(x), tgamma(x)	x != 0 && ! (x < 0 && x is an integer)	Yes	Yes
lrint(x), lround(x)	None	Yes	No
fmod(x, y), remainder(x, y), remquo(x, y, quo)	y != 0	Yes	No
nextafter(x, y), nexttoward(x, y)	None	Yes	No
fdim(x,y)	None	Yes	No
fma(x,y,z)	None	Yes	No

has a specific domain over which it is defined, the programmer must check its input values. The programmer must also check for range errors where they might occur. The standard math functions not listed in this table, such as fabs(), have no domain restrictions and cannot result in range or pole errors.

Domain and Pole Checking

The most reliable way to handle domain and pole errors is to prevent them by checking arguments beforehand, as in the following exemplar:

```
double safe_sqrt(double x) {
  if (x < 0) {
    fprintf(stderr, "sqrt requires a nonnegative argument");
    return 0;
  }
  return sqrt (x);
}
```

Range Checking

Programmers usually cannot prevent range errors, so the most reliable way to handle them is to detect when they have occurred and act accordingly.

The exact treatment of error conditions from math functions is tedious. The C Standard, 7.12.1, paragraph 5 [ISO/IEC 9899:2011], defines the following behavior for floating-point overflow:

> A floating result overflows if the magnitude of the mathematical result is finite but so large that the mathematical result cannot be represented without extraordinary roundoff error in an object of the specified type. If a floating result overflows and default rounding is in effect, then the function returns the value of the macro HUGE_VAL, HUGE_VALF, or HUGE_VALL according to the return type, with the same sign as the correct value of the function; if the integer expression math_errhandling & MATH_ERRNO is nonzero, the integer expression errno acquires the value ERANGE; if the integer expression math_errhandling & MATH_ERREXCEPT is nonzero, the "overflow" floating-point exception is raised.

It is preferable not to check for errors by comparing the returned value against HUGE_VAL or 0 for several reasons:

- These are, in general, valid (albeit unlikely) data values.
- Making such tests requires detailed knowledge of the various error returns for each math function.

- Multiple results aside from HUGE_VAL and 0 are possible, and programmers must know which are possible in each case.
- Different versions of the library have varied in their error-return behavior.

Checking for math errors using errno can be unreliable because an implementation might not set errno. For real functions, the programmer determines if the implementation sets errno by checking whether math_errhandling & MATH_ERRNO is nonzero. For complex functions, the C Standard, 7.3.2, paragraph 1, simply states that "an implementation may set errno but is not required to" [ISO/IEC 9899:2011].

The obsolete *System V Interface Definition, Third Edition,* (SVID3) [UNIX 1992] provides more control over the treatment of errors in the math library. The programmer can define a function named matherr() that is invoked if errors occur in a math function. This function can print diagnostics, terminate the execution, or specify the desired return value. The matherr() function has not been adopted by C or POSIX, so it is not generally portable.

The following error-handing template uses C Standard functions for floating-point errors when the C macro math_errhandling is defined and indicates that they should be used; otherwise, it examines errno:

```c
#include <math.h>
#include <fenv.h>
#include <errno.h>

/* ... */
/* Use to call a math function and check errors */
{
  #pragma STDC FENV_ACCESS ON

  if (math_errhandling & MATH_ERREXCEPT) {
    feclearexcept(FE_ALL_EXCEPT);
  }
  errno = 0;

  /* Call the math function */

  if ((math_errhandling & MATH_ERRNO) && errno != 0) {
    /* Handle range error */
  } else if ((math_errhandling & MATH_ERREXCEPT) &&
             fetestexcept(FE_INVALID | FE_DIVBYZERO |
                          FE_OVERFLOW | FE_UNDERFLOW) != 0) {
    /* Handle range error */
  }
}
```

See "FLP03-C. Detect and handle floating-point errors" for more details on how to detect floating-point errors.

Subnormal Numbers

A subnormal number is a nonzero number that does not use all of its precision bits [IEEE 754 2008]. They can be used to represent values that are closer to 0 than the smallest normal number (one that uses all of its precision bits). However, the `asin()`, `asinh()`, `atan()`, `atanh()`, and `erf()` functions may produce range errors specifically when passed a subnormal number. When evaluated with a subnormal number, these functions can produce an inexact, subnormal value, which is an underflow error. The C Standard, 7.12.1, paragraph 6 [ISO/IEC 9899:2011], defines the following behavior for floating-point underflow:

> The result underflows if the magnitude of the mathematical result is so small that the mathematical result cannot be represented, without extraordinary roundoff error, in an object of the specified type. If the result underflows, the function returns an implementation-defined value whose magnitude is no greater than the smallest normalized positive number in the specified type; if the integer expression `math_errhandling & MATH_ERRNO` is nonzero, whether `errno` acquires the value `ERANGE` is implementation-defined; if the integer expression `math_errhandling & MATH_ERREXCEPT` is nonzero, whether the "underflow" floating-point exception is raised is implementation-defined.

Implementations that support floating-point arithmetic but do not support subnormal numbers, such as IBM S/360 hex floating-point or nonconforming IEEE-754 implementations that skip subnormals (or support them by flushing them to zero), can return a range error when calling one of the following families of functions with the following arguments:

- `fmod((min+subnorm), min)`
- `remainder((min+subnorm), min)`
- `remquo((min+subnorm), min, quo)`

where `min` is the minimum value for the corresponding floating-point type and `subnorm` is a subnormal value.

If Annex F is supported and subnormal results are supported, the returned value is exact and a range error cannot occur. The C Standard, F.10.7.1 [ISO/IEC 9899:2011], specifies the following for the `fmod()`, `remainder()`, and `remquo()` functions:

> When subnormal results are supported, the returned value is exact and is independent of the current rounding direction mode.

Annex F, subclause F.10.7.2, paragraph 2, and subclause F.10.7.3, paragraph 2, of the C Standard identify when subnormal results are supported.

Noncompliant Code Example (sqrt())

This noncompliant code example determines the square root of x:

```
#include <math.h>

void func(double x) {
  double result;
  result = sqrt(x);
}
```

However, this code may produce a domain error if x is negative.

Compliant Solution (sqrt())

Because this function has domain errors but no range errors, bounds checking can be used to prevent domain errors:

```
#include <math.h>

void func(double x) {
  double result;

  if (isless(x, 0.0)) {
    /* Handle domain error */
  }

  result = sqrt(x);
}
```

Noncompliant Code Example (sinh(), Range Errors)

This noncompliant code example determines the hyperbolic sine of x:

```
#include <math.h>

void func(double x) {
  double result;
  result = sinh(x);
}
```

This code may produce a range error if x has a very large magnitude.

Compliant Solution (`sinh()`, Range Errors)

Because this function has no domain errors but may have range errors, the programmer must detect a range error and act accordingly:

```
#include <math.h>
#include <fenv.h>
#include <errno.h>

void func(double x) {
  double result;
  {
    #pragma STDC FENV_ACCESS ON
    if (math_errhandling & MATH_ERREXCEPT) {
      feclearexcept(FE_ALL_EXCEPT);
    }
    errno = 0;

    result = sinh(x);

    if ((math_errhandling & MATH_ERRNO) && errno != 0) {
      /* Handle range error */
    } else if ((math_errhandling & MATH_ERREXCEPT) &&
                 fetestexcept(FE_INVALID | FE_DIVBYZERO |
                                 FE_OVERFLOW | FE_UNDERFLOW) != 0) {
      /* Handle range error */
    }
  }

  /* Use result... */
}
```

Noncompliant Code Example (`pow()`)

This noncompliant code example raises x to the power of y:

```
#include <math.h>

void func(double x, double y) {
  double result;
  result = pow(x, y);
}
```

This code may produce a domain error if x is negative and y is not an integer value or if x is 0 and y is 0. A domain error or pole error may occur if x is 0 and y is negative, and a range error may occur if the result cannot be represented as a double.

Compliant Solution (pow())

Because the pow() function can produce domain errors, pole errors, and range errors, the programmer must first check that x and y lie within the proper domain and do not generate a pole error and then detect whether a range error occurs and act accordingly:

```c
#include <math.h>
#include <fenv.h>
#include <errno.h>

void func(double x, double y) {
  double result;

  if (((x == 0.0f) && islessequal(y, 0.0)) || isless(x, 0.0)) {
    /* Handle domain or pole error */
  }

  {
    #pragma STDC FENV_ACCESS ON
    if (math_errhandling & MATH_ERREXCEPT) {
      feclearexcept(FE_ALL_EXCEPT);
    }
    errno = 0;

    result = pow(x, y);

    if ((math_errhandling & MATH_ERRNO) && errno != 0) {
      /* Handle range error */
    } else if ((math_errhandling & MATH_ERREXCEPT) &&
                fetestexcept(FE_INVALID | FE_DIVBYZERO |
                             FE_OVERFLOW | FE_UNDERFLOW) != 0) {
      /* Handle range error */
    }
  }

  /* Use result... */
}
```

Noncompliant Code Example (asin(), Subnormal Number)

This noncompliant code example determines the inverse sine of x:

```c
#include <math.h>

void func(float x) {
  float result = asin(x);
  /* ... */
}
```

Compliant Solution (`asin()`, Subnormal Number)

Because this function has no domain errors but may have range errors, the programmer must detect a range error and act accordingly:

```c
#include <math.h>
#include <fenv.h>
#include <errno.h>

void func(float x) {
  float result;

  {
    #pragma STDC FENV_ACCESS ON
    if (math_errhandling & MATH_ERREXCEPT) {
      feclearexcept(FE_ALL_EXCEPT);
    }
    errno = 0;

    result = asin(x);

    if ((math_errhandling & MATH_ERRNO) && errno != 0) {
      /* Handle range error */
    } else if ((math_errhandling & MATH_ERREXCEPT) &&
               fetestexcept(FE_INVALID | FE_DIVBYZERO |
                            FE_OVERFLOW | FE_UNDERFLOW) != 0) {
      /* Handle range error */
    }
  }

  /* Use result... */
}
```

Risk Assessment

Failure to prevent or detect domain and range errors in math functions may cause unexpected results.

Rule	Severity	Likelihood	Remediation Cost	Priority	Level
FLP32-C	Medium	Probable	Medium	P8	L2

Related Guidelines

MITRE CWE	CWE-682, Incorrect Calculation

Bibliography

[IEEE 754 2008]	
[ISO/IEC 9899:2011]	7.3.2, "Conventions"
	7.12.1, "Treatment of Error Conditions"
	F.10.7, "Remainder Functions"
[Plum 1985]	Rule 2-2
[Plum 1989]	Topic 2.10, "conv—Conversions and Overflow"
[UNIX 1992]	*System V Interface Definition, Second Edition* (SVID3)

■ FLP34-C. Ensure that floating-point conversions are within range of the new type

If a floating-point value is to be converted to a floating-point value of a smaller range and precision or to an integer type, or if an integer type is to be converted to a floating-point type, the value must be representable in the destination type. The C Standard, 6.3.1.4, paragraph 1 [ISO/IEC 9899:2011], says,

> When a finite value of real floating type is converted to an integer type other than _Bool, the fractional part is discarded (i.e., the value is truncated toward zero). If the value of the integral part cannot be represented by the integer type, the behavior is undefined.

Paragraph 2 of the same subclause says,

> When a value of integer type is converted to a real floating type, if the value being converted can be represented exactly in the new type, it is unchanged. If the value being converted is in the range of values that can be represented but cannot be represented exactly, the result is either the nearest higher or nearest lower representable value, chosen in an implementation-defined manner. If the value being converted is outside the range of values that can be represented, the behavior is undefined.

And subclause 6.3.1.5, paragraph 1, says,

> When a value of real floating type is converted to a real floating type, if the value being converted can be represented exactly in the new type, it is unchanged. If the value being converted is in the range of values that can be represented but cannot be represented exactly, the result is either

the nearest higher or nearest lower representable value, chosen in an implementation-defined manner. If the value being converted is outside the range of values that can be represented, the behavior is undefined.

See undefined behaviors 17 and 18 in Appendix B.

This rule does not apply to demotions of floating-point types on implementations that support signed infinity, such as IEEE 754, as all values are within range.

Noncompliant Code Example (float to int)

This noncompliant code example leads to undefined behavior if the integral part of f_a cannot be represented as an integer:

```
void func(float f_a) {
  int i_a;

  /* Undefined if the integral part of f_a >= INT_MAX */
  i_a = f_a;
}
```

Compliant Solution (float to int)

This compliant solution ensures that the range of values of type float is greater than that of an int, as is the case in most implementations.

```
#include <limits.h>
#include <float.h>
#include <assert.h>

void func(float f_a) {
  int i_a;

  static_assert(
    (double)INT_MAX < (double)FLT_MAX),
    "not all int values can be represented as float"
  );
  i_a = f_a;
}
```

Noncompliant Code Example (Narrowing Conversion)

This noncompliant code example attempts to perform conversions that may result in truncating values outside the range of the destination types:

```
void func(double d_a, long double big_d) {
  double d_b = (float)big_d;
  float f_a = (float)d_a;
  float f_b = (float)big_d;
}
```

As a result of these conversions, it is possible that d_a is outside the range of values that can be represented by a float or that big_d is outside the range of values that can be represented as either a float or a double. If this is the case, the result is undefined on implementations that do not support Annex F, "IEC 60559 Floating-Point Arithmetic."

Compliant Solution (Narrowing Conversion)

This compliant solution checks whether the values to be stored can be represented in the new type:

```
#include <float.h>

void func(double d_a, long double big_d) {
  double d_b;
  float f_a;
  float f_b;

  if (isgreater(d_a, FLT_MAX) || isless(d_a, -FLT_MAX)) {
    /* Handle error */
  } else {
    f_a = (float)d_a;
  }
  if (isgreater(big_d, FLT_MAX) || isless(big_d, -FLT_MAX)) {
    /* Handle error */
  } else {
    f_b = (float)big_d;
  }
  if (isgreater(big_d, DBL_MAX) || isless(big_d, -DBL_MAX)) {
    /* Handle error */
  } else {
    d_b = (double)big_d;
  }
}
```

Risk Assessment

Converting a floating-point value to a floating-point value of a smaller range and precision or to an integer type, or converting an integer type to a floating-point type, can result in a value that is not representable in the destination type and is undefined behavior on implementations that do not support Annex F.

Rule	Severity	Likelihood	Remediation Cost	Priority	Level
FLP34-C	Low	Unlikely	Low	P3	L3

Related Guidelines

ISO/IEC TR 24772:2013	Numeric Conversion Errors [FLC]
MITRE CWE	CWE-681, Incorrect Conversion between Numeric Types

Bibliography

[IEEE 754 2008]	
[ISO/IEC 9899:2011]	6.3.1.4, "Real Floating and Integer" 6.3.1.5, "Real Floating Types"

▪ FLP36-C. Preserve precision when converting integral values to floating-point type

Narrower arithmetic types can be cast to wider types without any effect on the magnitude of numeric values. However, whereas integer types represent exact values, floating-point types have limited precision. The C Standard, 6.3.1.4, paragraph 2 [ISO/IEC 9899:2011], states:

> When a value of integer type is converted to a real floating type, if the value being converted can be represented exactly in the new type, it is unchanged. If the value being converted is in the range of values that can be represented but cannot be represented exactly, the result is either the nearest higher or nearest lower representable value, chosen in an implementation-defined manner. If the value being converted is outside the range of values that can be represented, the behavior is undefined. Results of some implicit conversions may be represented in greater range and precision than that required by the new type (see 6.3.1.8 and 6.8.6.4).

Conversion from integral types to floating-point types without sufficient precision can lead to loss of precision (loss of least significant bits). No run-time exception occurs despite the loss.

Noncompliant Code Example

In this noncompliant example, a large value of type long int is converted to a value of type float without ensuring it is representable in the type:

```c
#include <stdio.h>

int main(void) {
  long int big = 1234567890;
  float approx = big;
  printf("%d\n", (big - (long int)approx));
  return 0;
}
```

For most floating-point hardware, the value closest to 1234567890 that is representable in type float is 1234567844; consequently, this program prints the value –46.

Compliant Solution

This compliant solution replaces the type float with a double. Furthermore, it uses an assertion to guarantee that the double type can represent any long int without loss of precision (see "INT35-C. Use correct integer precisions" and "MSC11-C. Incorporate diagnostic tests using assertions").

```c
#include <assert.h>
#include <stdio.h>
#include <float.h>
#include <limits.h>
#include <math.h>
#include <stdint.h>

extern size_t popcount(uintmax_t); /* See INT35-C */
#define PRECISION(umax_value) popcount(umax_value)

int main(void) {
  assert(PRECISION(LONG_MAX) <= DBL_MANT_DIG * log2(DBL_MANT_DIG));
  long int big = 1234567890;
  double approx = big;
  printf("%d\n", (big - (long int)approx));
  return 0;
}
```

On the same implementation, this program prints 0, implying that the integer value 1234567890 is representable in type double without change.

Risk Assessment

Conversion from integral types to floating-point types without sufficient precision can lead to loss of precision (loss of least significant bits).

Rule	Severity	Likelihood	Remediation Cost	Priority	Level
FLP36-C	Low	Unlikely	Medium	P2	L3

Bibliography

| [ISO/IEC 9899:2011] | 6.3.1.4, "Real Floating and Integer" |

Chapter 6

Arrays (ARR)

Chapter Contents

Risk Assessment Summary

Rule	Severity	Likelihood	Remediation Cost	Priority	Level
ARR30-C	High	Likely	High	P9	L2
ARR32-C	High	Probable	High	P6	L2
ARR36-C	Medium	Probable	Medium	P8	L2
ARR37-C	Medium	Probable	Medium	P8	L2

continues

Rule	Severity	Likelihood	Remediation Cost	Priority	Level
ARR38-C	High	Likely	Medium	P18	L1
ARR39-C	High	Probable	High	P6	L2

■ ARR30-C. Do not form or use out-of-bounds pointers or array subscripts

The C Standard identifies four distinct situations in which undefined behavior can arise as a result of **invalid pointer** operations:

- Addition or subtraction of a pointer into, or just beyond, an array object and an integer type produces a result that does not point into, or just beyond, the same array object (see undefined behavior 46 in Appendix B).
- Addition or subtraction of a pointer into, or just beyond, an array object and an integer type produces a result that points just beyond the array object and is used as the operand of a unary * operator that is evaluated (see undefined behavior 47 in Appendix B).
- An array subscript is out of range, even if an object is apparently accessible with the given subscript, for example, in the lvalue expression a[1][7] given the declaration int a[4][5] (see undefined behavior 49 in Appendix B).
- An attempt is made to access, or generate a pointer to just past, a flexible array member of a structure when the referenced object provides no elements for that array (see undefined behavior 62 in Appendix B).

Noncompliant Code Example (Forming Out-of-Bounds Pointer)

In this noncompliant code example, the function f() attempts to validate the index before using it as an offset to the statically allocated table of integers. However, the function fails to reject negative index values. When index is less than zero, the behavior of the addition expression in the return statement of the function is undefined behavior 46. On some implementations, the addition alone can trigger a hardware trap. On other implementations, the addition may produce a result that, when dereferenced, triggers a hardware trap. Other implementations still may produce a dereferenceable pointer that points to an object distinct from table. Using such a pointer to access the object may lead to information exposure or cause the wrong object to be modified.

```
enum { TABLESIZE = 100 };

static int table[TABLESIZE];

int *f(int index) {
  if (index < TABLESIZE) {
    return table + index;
  }
  return NULL;
}
```

Compliant Solution

One compliant solution is to detect and reject invalid values of index if using them in pointer arithmetic would result in an invalid pointer:

```
enum { TABLESIZE = 100 };

static int table[TABLESIZE];

int *f(int index) {
  if (index >= 0 && index < TABLESIZE) {
    return table + index;
  }
  return NULL;
}
```

Compliant Solution

Another slightly simpler and potentially more efficient compliant solution is to use an unsigned type to avoid having to check for negative values while still rejecting out-of-bounds positive values of index:

```
#include <stddef.h>

enum { TABLESIZE = 100 };

static int table[TABLESIZE];

int *f(size_t index) {
  if (index < TABLESIZE) {
    return table + index;
  }
  return NULL;
}
```

Noncompliant Code Example (Dereferencing Past-the-End Pointer)

This noncompliant code example shows the flawed logic in the Windows Distributed Component Object Model (DCOM) Remote Procedure Call (RPC) interface that was exploited by the W32.Blaster.Worm. The error is that the `while` loop in the `GetMachineName()` function (used to extract the host name from a longer string) is not sufficiently bounded. When the character array pointed to by `pwszTemp` does not contain the backslash character among the first `MAX_COMPUTERNAME_LENGTH_FQDN + 1` elements, the final valid iteration of the loop will dereference past the end pointer, resulting in exploitable undefined behavior 47. In this case, the actual exploit allowed the attacker to inject executable code into a running program. Economic damage from the Blaster worm has been estimated to be at least $525 million [Pethia 2003].

For a discussion of this programming error in the Common Weakness Enumeration database, see CWE-119, "Improper Restriction of Operations within the Bounds of a Memory Buffer," and CWE-121, "Stack-based Buffer Overflow" [MITRE 2013].

```
error_status_t _RemoteActivation(
    /* ... */, WCHAR *pwszObjectName, ... ) {
  *phr = GetServerPath(
            pwszObjectName, &pwszObjectName);
  /* ... */
}

HRESULT GetServerPath(
  WCHAR *pwszPath, WCHAR **pwszServerPath ){
  WCHAR *pwszFinalPath = pwszPath;
  WCHAR wszMachineName[MAX_COMPUTERNAME_LENGTH_FQDN+1];
  hr = GetMachineName(pwszPath, wszMachineName);
  *pwszServerPath = pwszFinalPath;
}

HRESULT GetMachineName(
  WCHAR *pwszPath,
  WCHAR wszMachineName[MAX_COMPUTERNAME_LENGTH_FQDN+1])
{
  pwszServerName = wszMachineName;
  LPWSTR pwszTemp = pwszPath + 2;
  while (*pwszTemp != L'\\')
    *pwszServerName++ = *pwszTemp++;
  /* ... */
}
```

Compliant Solution

In this compliant solution, the `while` loop in the `GetMachineName()` function is bounded so that the loop terminates when a backslash character is found, the null-termination wide character (`L'\0'`) is discovered, or the end of the buffer is reached. This code does not result in a buffer overflow even if no backslash character is found in `wszMachineName`.

```
HRESULT GetMachineName(
  wchar_t *pwszPath,
  wchar_t wszMachineName[MAX_COMPUTERNAME_LENGTH_FQDN+1])
{
  wchar_t *pwszServerName = wszMachineName;
  wchar_t *pwszTemp = pwszPath + 2;
  wchar_t *end_addr
    = pwszServerName + MAX_COMPUTERNAME_LENGTH_FQDN;
  while ( (*pwszTemp != L'\\')
    && ((*pwszTemp != L'\0'))
    && (pwszServerName < end_addr) )
  {
    *pwszServerName++ = *pwszTemp++;
  }

  /* ... */
}
```

This compliant solution is for illustrative purposes and is not necessarily the solution implemented by Microsoft. This particular solution may not be correct because there is no guarantee that a backslash is found.

Noncompliant Code Example (Using Past-the-End Index)

Similar to the dereferencing-past-the-end-pointer error, the function `insert_in_table()` in this noncompliant code example uses an otherwise valid index to attempt to store a value in an element just past the end of an array.

First, the function incorrectly validates the index `pos` against the size of the buffer. When `pos` is initially equal to `size`, the function attempts to store `value` in a memory location just past the end of the buffer.

Second, when the index is greater than `size`, the function modifies `size` before growing the size of the buffer. If the call to `realloc()` fails to increase the size of the buffer, the next call to the function with a value of `pos` equal to or greater than the original value of `size` will again attempt to store `value` in a memory location just past the end of the buffer or beyond.

Third, the function violates "INT30-C. Ensure that unsigned integer operations do not wrap," which could lead to wrapping when 1 is added to pos or when size is multiplied by the size of int.

For a discussion of this programming error in the Common Weakness Enumeration database, see CWE-122, "Heap-based Buffer Overflow," and CWE-129, "Improper Validation of Array Index" [MITRE 2013].

```c
#include <stdlib.h>

static int *table = NULL;
static size_t size = 0;

int insert_in_table(size_t pos, int value) {
  if (size < pos) {
    int *tmp;
    size = pos + 1;
    tmp = (int *)realloc(table, sizeof(*table) * size);
    if (tmp == NULL) {
      return -1; /* Failure */
    }
    table = tmp;
  }

  table[pos] = value;
  return 0;
}
```

Compliant Solution

This compliant solution correctly validates the index pos by using the <= relational operator, ensures the multiplication will not overflow, and avoids modifying size until it has verified that the call to realloc() was successful:

```c
#include <stdint.h>
#include <stdlib.h>

static int *table = NULL;
static size_t size = 0;

int insert_in_table(size_t pos, int value) {
  if (size <= pos) {
    int *tmp;
    if ((pos + 1) > SIZE_MAX / sizeof(*table)) {
      return -1;
    }
```

```
    tmp = (int *)realloc(table, sizeof(*table) * (pos + 1));
    if (tmp == NULL) {
      return -1;
    }
    /* Modify size only after realloc() succeeds */
    size = pos + 1;
    table = tmp;
  }

  table[pos] = value;
  return 0;
}
```

Noncompliant Code Example (Apparently Accessible Out-of-Range Index)

This noncompliant code example declares matrix to consist of 7 rows and 5 columns in row-major order. The function init_matrix iterates over all 35 elements in an attempt to initialize each to the value given by the function argument x. However, because multidimensional arrays are declared in C in row-major order, the function iterates over the elements in column-major order, and when the value of j reaches the value COLS during the first iteration of the outer loop, the function attempts to access element matrix[0][5]. Because the type of matrix is int[7][5], the j subscript is out of range, and the access has undefined behavior (see undefined behavior 49 in Appendix B).

```
#include <stddef.h>

#define COLS 5
#define ROWS 7
static int matrix[ROWS][COLS];

void init_matrix(int x) {
  for (size_t i = 0; i < COLS; i++) {
    for (size_t j = 0; j < ROWS; j++) {
      matrix[i][j] = x;
    }
  }
}
```

Compliant Solution

This compliant solution avoids using out-of-range indices by initializing matrix elements in the same row-major order as multidimensional objects are declared in C:

```
#include <stddef.h>
```

```
#define COLS 5
#define ROWS 7
static int matrix[ROWS][COLS];

void init_matrix(int x) {
  for (size_t i = 0; i < ROWS; i++) {
    for (size_t j = 0; j < COLS; j++) {
      matrix[i][j] = x;
    }
  }
}
```

Noncompliant Code Example (Pointer Past Flexible Array Member)

In this noncompliant code example, the function find() attempts to iterate over the elements of the flexible array member buf, starting with the second element. However, because function g() does not allocate any storage for the member, the expression first++ in find() attempts to form a pointer just past the end of buf when there are no elements. This attempt is undefined behavior (see undefined behavior 62 in Appendix B; also see "MSC21-C. Use robust loop termination conditions" for more information).

```
#include <stdlib.h>

struct S {
  size_t len;
  char buf[]; /* Flexible array member */
};

const char *find(const struct S *s, int c) {
  const char *first = s->buf;
  const char *last = s->buf + s->len;

  while (first++ != last) { /* Undefined behavior */
    if (*first == (unsigned char)c) {
      return first;
    }
  }
  return NULL;
}

void g(void) {
  struct S *s = (struct S *)malloc(sizeof(struct S));
  if (s == NULL) {
```

```
      /* Handle error */
  }
  s->len = 0;
  find(s, 'a');
}
```

Compliant Solution

This compliant solution avoids incrementing the pointer unless a value past the pointer's current value is known to exist:

```
#include <stdlib.h>

struct S {
  size_t len;
  char buf[]; /* Flexible array member */
};

const char *find(const struct S *s, int c) {
  const char *first = s->buf;
  const char *last = s->buf + s->len;

  while (first != last) { /* Avoid incrementing here */
    if (*++first == (unsigned char)c) {
      return first;
    }
  }
  return NULL;
}

void g(void) {
  struct S *s = (struct S *)malloc(sizeof(struct S));
  if (s == NULL) {
    /* handle error */
  }
  s->len = 0;
  find(s, 'a');
}
```

Noncompliant Code Example (Null Pointer Arithmetic)

This noncompliant code example is similar to an Adobe Flash Player vulnerability that was first exploited in 2008. This code allocates a block of memory and initializes it with some data. The data does not belong at the beginning of the block, which is left uninitialized. Instead, it is placed offset bytes within the block. The function ensures that the data fits within the allocated block.

```
#include <string.h>
#include <stdlib.h>

char *init_block(size_t block_size, size_t offset,
                 char *data, size_t data_size) {
  char *buffer = malloc(block_size);
  if (data_size > block_size ||
      block_size - data_size > offset) {
    /* Data won't fit in buffer, handle error */
  }
  memcpy(buffer + offset, data, data_size);
  return buffer;
}
```

This function fails to check if the allocation succeeds, which is a violation of "ERR33-C. Detect and handle standard library errors." If the allocation fails, then malloc() returns a null pointer. The null pointer is added to offset and passed as the destination argument to memcpy(). Because a null pointer does not point to a valid object, the result of the pointer arithmetic is undefined behavior (see undefined behavior 46 in Appendix B).

An attacker who can supply the arguments to this function can exploit it to execute arbitrary code. This can be accomplished by providing an overly large value for block_size, which causes malloc() to fail and return a null pointer. The offset argument will then serve as the destination address to the call to memcpy(). The attacker can specify the data and data_size arguments to provide the address and length of the address, respectively, that the attacker wishes to write into the memory referenced by offset. The overall result is that the call to memcpy() can be exploited by an attacker to overwrite an arbitrary memory location with an attacker-supplied address, typically resulting in arbitrary code execution.

Compliant Solution (Null Pointer Arithmetic)

This compliant solution ensures that the call to malloc() succeeds:

```
#include <string.h>
#include <stdlib.h>

char *init_block(size_t block_size, size_t offset,
                 char *data, size_t data_size) {
  char *buffer = malloc(block_size);
```

```
  if (NULL == buffer) {
    /* Handle error */
  }
  if (data_size > block_size || block_size - data_size > offset) {
    /* Data won't fit in buffer, handle error */
  }
  memcpy(buffer + offset, data, data_size);
  return buffer;
}
```

Risk Assessment

Writing to out-of-range pointers or array subscripts can result in a buffer overflow and the execution of arbitrary code with the permissions of the vulnerable process. Reading from out-of-range pointers or array subscripts can result in unintended information disclosure.

Rule	Severity	Likelihood	Remediation Cost	Priority	Level
ARR30-C	High	Likely	High	P9	L2

Related Vulnerabilities

CVE-2008-1517 results from a violation of this rule. Before Mac OS X version 10.5.7, the XNU kernel accessed an array at an unverified user-input index, allowing an attacker to execute arbitrary code by passing an index greater than the length of the array and therefore accessing outside memory [xorl 2009].

Related Guidelines

ISO/IEC TR 24772:2013	Arithmetic Wrap-around Error [FIF]
	Unchecked Array Indexing [XYZ]
ISO/IEC TS 17961:2013	Forming or using out-of-bounds pointers or array subscripts [invptr]
MITRE CWE	CWE-119, Improper Restriction of Operations within the Bounds of a Memory Buffer
	CWE-122, Heap-based Buffer Overflow
	CWE-129, Improper Validation of Array Index
	CWE-788, Access of Memory Location after End of Buffer

Bibliography

[Finlay 2003]	
[Microsoft 2003]	
[Pethia 2003]	
[Seacord 2013b]	Chapter 1, "Running with Scissors"
[Viega 2005]	Section 5.2.13, "Unchecked Array Indexing"
[xorl 2009]	"CVE-2008-1517: Apple Mac OS X (XNU) Missing Array Index Validation"

■ ARR32-C. Ensure size arguments for variable length arrays are in a valid range

Variable length arrays (VLAs), a conditionally supported language feature, are essentially the same as traditional C arrays except that they are declared with a size that is not a constant integer expression and can be declared only at block scope or function prototype scope and no linkage. When supported, a variable length array can be declared,

```
{ /* Block scope */
  char vla[size];
}
```

where the integer expression `size` and the declaration of `vla` are both evaluated at runtime. If the size argument supplied to a variable length array is not a positive integer value, the behavior is undefined (see undefined behavior 75 in Appendix B). Additionally, if the magnitude of the argument is excessive, the program may behave in an unexpected way. An attacker may be able to leverage this behavior to overwrite critical program data [Griffiths 2006]. The programmer must ensure that size arguments to variable length arrays, especially those derived from **untrusted data**, are in a valid range.

Because variable length arrays are a conditionally supported feature of C11, their use in portable code should be guarded by testing the value of the macro __STDC_NO_VLA__. Implementations that do not support variable length arrays indicate so by setting __STDC_NO_VLA__ to the integer constant 1.

Noncompliant Code Example

In this noncompliant code example, a variable length array of size size is declared. The size is declared as size_t in compliance with "INT01-C. Use rsize_t or size_t for all integer values representing the size of an object."

```
#include <stddef.h>

void func(size_t size) {
  int vla[size];
  /* ... */
}
```

However, the value of size may be zero or excessive, potentially giving rise to a security vulnerability.

Compliant Solution

This compliant solution ensures the size argument used to allocate vla is in a valid range (between 1 and a programmer-defined maximum); otherwise, it uses an algorithm that relies on dynamic memory allocation:

```
#include <stdlib.h>

enum { MAX_ARRAY = 1024 };
extern void do_work(int *array, size_t size);

void func(size_t size) {
  if (0 < size && size < MAX_ARRAY) {
    int vla[size];
    do_work(vla, size);
  } else {
    int *array = (int *)malloc(size * sizeof(int));
    if (array == NULL) {
      /* Handle error */
    }
    do_work(array, size);
    free(array);
  }
}
```

Risk Assessment

Failure to properly specify the size of a variable length array may allow arbitrary code execution or result in stack exhaustion.

Rule	Severity	Likelihood	Remediation Cost	Priority	Level
ARR32-C	High	Probable	High	P6	L2

Related Guidelines

ISO/IEC TR 24772:2013	Unchecked Array Indexing [XYZ]
ISO/IEC TS 17961:2013	Tainted, potentially mutilated, or out-of-domain integer values are used in a restricted sink [taintsink]

Bibliography

[Griffiths 2006]

■ ARR36-C. Do not subtract or compare two pointers that do not refer to the same array

When two pointers are subtracted, both must point to elements of the same array object or just past the last element of the array object (C Standard, 6.5.6 [ISO/IEC 9899:2011]); the result is the difference of the subscripts of the two array elements. Otherwise, the operation has undefined behavior (see undefined behavior 48 in Appendix B).

Similarly, comparing pointers using the relational operators <, <=, >=, and > gives the positions of the pointers relative to each other. Subtracting or comparing pointers that do not refer to the same array is undefined behavior (see undefined behaviors 48 and 53 in Appendix B).

Comparing pointers using the equality operators == and != has well-defined semantics regardless of whether or not either of the pointers is null, points into the same object, or points one past the last element of an array object or function.

Noncompliant Code Example

In this noncompliant code example, pointer subtraction is used to determine how many free elements are left in the nums array:

```
#include <stddef.h>

enum { SIZE = 32 };
```

```
void func(void) {
  int nums[SIZE];
  int end;
  int *next_num_ptr = nums;
  size_t free_elements;

  /* Increment next_num_ptr as array fills */

  free_elements = &end - next_num_ptr;
}
```

This program incorrectly assumes that the nums array is adjacent to the end variable in memory. A compiler is permitted to insert padding bits between these two variables, or even reorder them in memory.

Compliant Solution

In this compliant solution, the number of free elements is computed by subtracting next_num_ptr from the address of the pointer past the nums array. While this pointer may not be dereferenced, it may be used in pointer arithmetic.

```
#include <stddef.h>

enum { SIZE = 32 };

void func(void) {
  int nums[SIZE];
  int *next_num_ptr = nums;
  size_t free_elements;

  /* Increment next_num_ptr as array fills */

  free_elements = &(nums[SIZE]) - next_num_ptr;
}
```

Exceptions

ARR36-EX1: Comparing two pointers to distinct members of the same struct object is allowed. Pointers to structure members declared later in the structure compare greater than pointers to members declared earlier in the structure.

Risk Assessment

Rule	Severity	Likelihood	Remediation Cost	Priority	Level
ARR36-C	Medium	Probable	Medium	P8	L2

Related Guidelines

ISO/IEC TS 17961:2013	Subtracting or comparing two pointers that do not refer to the same array [ptrobj]
MITRE CWE	CWE-469, Use of Pointer Subtraction to Determine Size

Bibliography

[Banahan 2003]	Section 5.3, "Pointers" Section 5.7, "Expressions Involving Pointers"
[ISO/IEC 9899:2011]	6.5.6, "Additive Operators"

■ ARR37-C. Do not add or subtract an integer to a pointer to a non-array object

Pointer arithmetic must be performed only on pointers that reference elements of array objects. The C Standard, 6.5.6 [ISO/IEC 9899:2011], states the following about pointer arithmetic:

> When an expression that has integer type is added to or subtracted from a pointer, the result has the type of the pointer operand. If the pointer operand points to an element of an array object, and the array is large enough, the result points to an element offset from the original element such that the difference of the subscripts of the resulting and original array elements equals the integer expression.

Noncompliant Code Example

This noncompliant code example attempts to access structure members using pointer arithmetic. This practice is dangerous because structure members are not guaranteed to be contiguous.

```
struct numbers {
  short num_a, num_b, num_c;
};

int sum_numbers(const struct numbers *numb){
  int total = 0;
  const short *numb_ptr;

  for (numb_ptr = &numb->num_a;
       numb_ptr <= &numb->num_c;
       numb_ptr++) {
    total += *numb_ptr;
  }

  return total;
}

int main(void) {
  struct numbers my_numbers = { 1, 2, 3 };
  sum_numbers(&my_numbers);
  return 0;
}
```

Compliant Solution

It is possible to use the -> operator to dereference each structure member:

```
total = numb->num_a + numb->num_b + numb->num_c;
```

However, this solution results in code that is hard to write and hard to maintain (especially if there are many more structure members), which is exactly what the author of the noncompliant code example was likely trying to avoid.

Compliant Solution

A better solution is to define the structure to contain an array member to store the numbers in an array rather than a structure, as in this compliant solution:

```
#include <stddef.h>

struct numbers {
  short a[3];
};

int sum_numbers(const short *numb, size_t dim) {
  int total = 0;
```

```
  for (size_t i = 0; i < dim; ++i) {
    total += numb[i];
  }

  return total;
}

int main(void) {
  struct numbers my_numbers = { .a[0]= 1, .a[1]= 2, .a[2]= 3 };
  sum_numbers(
    my_numbers.a,
    sizeof(my_numbers.a)/sizeof(my_numbers.a[0])
  );
  return 0;
}
```

Array elements are guaranteed to be contiguous in memory, so this solution is portable.

Exceptions

ARR37-EX1: Any non-array object in memory can be considered an array consisting of a single element. Adding one to a pointer to such an object yields a pointer one element past the end of the array, and subtracting one from that pointer yields the original pointer. This allows for code such as the following:

```
#include <stdlib.h>
#include <string.h>

struct s {
  char *c_str;
  /* Other members */
};

struct s *create_s(const char *c_str) {
  struct s *ret;
  size_t len = strlen(c_str) + 1;

  ret = (struct s *)malloc(sizeof(struct s) + len);
  if (ret != NULL) {
    ret->c_str = (char *)(ret + 1);
    memcpy(ret + 1, c_str, len);
  }
  return ret;
}
```

A more general and safer solution to this problem is to use a flexible array member that guarantees that the array that follows the structure is properly aligned by inserting padding, if necessary, between it and the member that immediately precedes it.

Risk Assessment

Rule	Severity	Likelihood	Remediation Cost	Priority	Level
ARR37-C	Medium	Probable	Medium	P8	L2

Related Guidelines

MITRE CWE	CWE-469, Use of Pointer Subtraction to Determine Size

Bibliography

[Banahan 2003]	Section 5.3, "Pointers" Section 5.7, "Expressions Involving Pointers"
[ISO/IEC 9899:2011]	6.5.6, "Additive Operators"

■ ARR38-C. Guarantee that library functions do not form invalid pointers

C library functions that make changes to arrays or objects take at least two arguments: a pointer to the array or object and an integer indicating the number of elements or bytes to be manipulated. Supplying improper arguments to such a function might cause the function to form a pointer that does not point into or just past the end of the object, resulting in undefined behavior.

Annex J of the C Standard [ISO/IEC 9899:2011] states that it is undefined behavior if the "pointer passed to a library function array parameter does not have a value such that all address computations and object accesses are valid" (see undefined behavior 109 in Appendix B).

In the following code,

```
int arr[5];
int *p = arr;

unsigned char *p2 = (unsigned char *)arr;
unsigned char *p3 = arr + 2;
void *p4 = arr;
```

the element count of the pointer p is sizeof(arr) / sizeof(arr[0]); that is, 5. The element count of the pointer p2 is sizeof(arr); that is, 20, on implementations where sizeof(int) == 4. The element count of the pointer p3 is 12 on implementations where sizeof(int) == 4, because p3 points two elements past the start of the array arr. The element count of p4 is treated as though it were unsigned char * instead of void *, so it is the same as p2.

Pointer + Integer

The standard library functions listed in Table 6–1 take a pointer argument and a size argument, with the constraint that the pointer must point to a valid memory object of at least the number of elements indicated by the size argument.

For calls that take a pointer and an integer size, the given size should not be greater than the element count of the pointer.

Noncompliant Code Example (Element Count)

In this noncompliant code example, the incorrect element count is used in a call to wmemcpy(). The sizeof operator returns the size expressed in bytes, but wmemcpy() uses an element count based on wchar_t *.

```
#include <string.h>
#include <wchar.h>

static const char str[] = "Hello world";
static const wchar_t w_str[] = L"Hello world";
void func(void) {
  char buffer[32];
  wchar_t w_buffer[32];
  memcpy(buffer, str, sizeof(str)); /* Compliant */
  wmemcpy(w_buffer, w_str, sizeof(w_str)); /* Noncompliant */
}
```

Table 6–1. Library Functions That Take a Pointer and an Integer

fgets()	fgetws()	mbstowcs()[1]	wcstombs()[1]
mbrtoc16()[2]	mbrtoc32()[2]	mbsrtowcs()[1]	wcsrtombs()[1]
mbtowc()[2]	mbrtowc()[1]	mblen()	mbrlen()
memchr()	wmemchr()	memset()	wmemset()
strftime()	wcsftime()	strxfrm()[1]	wcsxfrm()[1]
strncat()[2]	wcsncat()[2]	snprintf()	vsnprintf()
swprintf()	vswprintf()	setvbuf()	tmpnam_s()
snprintf_s()	sprintf_s()	vsnprintf_s()	vsprintf_s()
gets_s()	getenv_s()	wctomb_s()	mbstowcs_s()[3]
wcstombs_s()[3]	memcpy_s()[3]	memmove_s()[3]	strncpy_s()[3]
strncat_s()[3]	strtok_s()[2]	strerror_s()	strnlen_s()
asctime_s()	ctime_s()	snwprintf_s()	swprintf_s()
vsnwprintf_s()	vswprintf_s()	wcsncpy_s()[3]	wmemcpy_s()[3]
wmemmove_s()[3]	wcsncat_s()[3]	wcstok_s()[2]	wcsnlen_s()
wcrtomb_s()	mbsrtowcs_s()[3]	wcsrtombs_s()[3]	memset_s()[4]

1. Takes two pointers and an integer, but the integer specifies the element count only of the output buffer, not of the input buffer.
2. Takes two pointers and an integer, but the integer specifies the element count only of the input buffer, not of the output buffer.
3. Takes two pointers and two integers; each integer corresponds to the element count of one of the pointers.
4. Takes a pointer and two size-related integers; the first size-related integer parameter specifies the number of bytes available in the buffer; the second size-related integer parameter specifies the number of bytes to write within the buffer.

Compliant Solution (Element Count)

When using functions that operate on pointed-to regions, programmers must always express the integer size in terms of the element count expected by the function. For example, memcpy() expects the element count expressed in terms of void *, but wmemcpy() expects the element count expressed in terms of wchar_t *. Instead of the sizeof operator, functions that return the number of elements in the string are called, which matches the expected element count for the copy functions. In the case of this compliant solution, where the argument is an array A of type T, the expression sizeof(A) / sizeof(T), or equivalently sizeof(A) / sizeof(*A), can be used to compute the number of elements in the array.

```
#include <string.h>
#include <wchar.h>

static const char str[] = "Hello world";
static const wchar_t w_str[] = L"Hello world";
void func(void) {
  char buffer[32];
  wchar_t w_buffer[32];
  memcpy(buffer, str, strlen(str) + 1);
  wmemcpy(w_buffer, w_str, wcslen(w_str) + 1);
}
```

Noncompliant Code Example (Pointer + Integer)

This noncompliant code example assigns a value greater than the number of bytes of available memory to n, which is then passed to memset():

```
#include <stdlib.h>
#include <string.h>

void f1(size_t nchars) {
  char *p = (char *)malloc(nchars);
  /* ... */
  const size_t n = nchars + 1;
  /* ... */
  memset(p, 0, n);
}
```

Compliant Solution (Pointer + Integer)

This compliant solution ensures that the value of n is not greater than the number of bytes of the dynamic memory pointed to by the pointer p:

```
#include <stdlib.h>
#include <string.h>

void f1(size_t nchars) {
  char *p = (char *)malloc(nchars);
  /* ... */
  const size_t n = nchars;
```

```
/* ... */
  memset(p, 0, n);
}
```

Noncompliant Code Example (Pointer + Integer)

In this noncompliant code example, the element count of the array a is ARR_SIZE elements. Because `memset()` expects a byte count, the size of the array is scaled incorrectly by `sizeof(int)` instead of `sizeof(long)`, which can form an invalid pointer on architectures where `sizeof(int) != sizeof(long)`.

```
#include <string.h>

void f2(void) {
  const size_t ARR_SIZE = 4;
  long a[ARR_SIZE];
  const size_t n = sizeof(int) * ARR_SIZE;
  void *p = a;

  memset(p, 0, n);
}
```

Compliant Solution (Pointer + Integer)

In this compliant solution, the element count required by `memset()` is properly calculated without resorting to scaling:

```
#include <string.h>

void f2(void) {
  const size_t ARR_SIZE = 4;
  long a[ARR_SIZE];
  const size_t n = sizeof(a);
  void *p = a;

  memset(p, 0, n);
}
```

Two Pointers + One Integer

The standard library functions listed in Table 6–2 take two pointer arguments and a size argument, with the constraint that both pointers must point to valid memory objects of at least the number of elements indicated by the size argument.

For calls that take two pointers and an integer size, the given size should not be greater than the element count of either pointer.

Table 6–2. Library Functions That Take Two Pointers and an Integer

memcpy()	wmemcpy()	memmove()	wmemmove()
strncpy()	wcsncpy()	memcmp()	wmemcmp()
strncmp()	wcsncmp()	strcpy_s()	wcscpy_s()
strcat_s()	wcscat_s()		

Noncompliant Code Example (Two Pointers + One Integer)

This code example is noncompliant because the value of n is incorrectly computed, allowing a possible write past the end of the object referenced by p:

```
#include <string.h>

void f4(char p[], const char *q) {
  const size_t n = sizeof(p);
  memcpy(p, q, n);
}
```

This example also violates "ARR01-C. Do not apply the sizeof operator to a pointer when taking the size of an array."

Compliant Solution (Two Pointers + One Integer)

This compliant solution ensures that n is equal to the size of the character array:

```
#include <string.h>

void f4(char p[], const char *q, size_t n) {
  memcpy(p, q, n);
}
```

One Pointer + Two Integers

The standard library functions listed in Table 6–3 take a pointer argument and two size arguments, with the constraint that the pointer must point to a valid memory object containing at least as many bytes as the product of the two size arguments.

For calls that take a pointer and two integers, one integer represents the number of bytes required for an individual object, and a second integer

Table 6–3. Library Functions That Take a Pointer and Two Integers

bsearch()	bsearch_s()	qsort()	qsort_s()
fread()	fwrite()		

represents the number of elements in the array. The resulting product of the two integers should not be greater than the element count of the pointer were it expressed as an unsigned char *.

Noncompliant Code Example (One Pointer + Two Integers)

This noncompliant code example allocates a variable number of objects of type struct obj. The function checks that num_objs is small enough to prevent wrapping, in compliance with "INT30-C. Ensure that unsigned integer operations do not wrap." The size of struct obj is assumed to be 16 bytes to account for padding to achieve the assumed alignment of long long. However, the padding typically depends on the target architecture, so this object size may be incorrect, resulting in an incorrect element count.

```
#include <stdint.h>
#include <stdio.h>

struct obj {
  char c;
  long long i;
};

void func(FILE *f, struct obj *objs, size_t num_objs) {
  const size_t obj_size = 16;
  if (num_objs > (SIZE_MAX / obj_size) ||
      num_objs != fwrite(objs, obj_size, num_objs, f)) {
    /* Handle error */
  }
}
```

Compliant Solution (One Pointer + Two Integers)

This compliant solution uses the sizeof operator to correctly provide the object size and num_objs to provide the element count:

```
#include <stdint.h>
#include <stdio.h>

struct obj {
```

```
  char c;
  long long i;
};

void func(FILE *f, struct obj *objs, size_t num_objs) {
  const size_t obj_size = sizeof *objs;
  if (num_objs > (SIZE_MAX / obj_size) ||
      num_objs != fwrite(objs, obj_size, num_objs, f)) {
    /* Handle error */
  }
}
```

Noncompliant Code Example (One Pointer + Two Integers)

In this noncompliant code example, the function f() calls fread() to read nitems of type wchar_t, each size bytes in size, into an array of BUFFER_SIZE elements, wbuf. However, the expression used to compute the value of nitems fails to account for the fact that, unlike the size of char, the size of wchar_t may be greater than 1. Consequently, fread() could attempt to form pointers past the end of wbuf and use them to assign values to nonexistent elements of the array. Such an attempt is undefined behavior (see undefined behavior 109 in Appendix B). A likely consequence of this undefined behavior is a buffer overflow. For a discussion of this programming error in the Common Weakness Enumeration database, see CWE-121, "Stack-based Buffer Overflow," and CWE-805, "Buffer Access with Incorrect Length Value" [MITRE 2013].

```
#include <stddef.h>
#include <stdio.h>

void f(FILE *file) {
  enum { BUFFER_SIZE = 1024 };
  wchar_t wbuf[BUFFER_SIZE];

  const size_t size = sizeof(*wbuf);
  const size_t nitems = sizeof(wbuf);

  size_t nread = fread(wbuf, size, nitems, file);
  /* ... */
}
```

Compliant Solution (One Pointer + Two Integers)

This compliant solution correctly computes the maximum number of items for fread() to read from the file:

```
#include <stddef.h>
#include <stdio.h>

void f(FILE *file) {
  enum { BUFFER_SIZE = 1024 };
  wchar_t wbuf[BUFFER_SIZE];

  const size_t size = sizeof(*wbuf);
  const size_t nitems = sizeof(wbuf) / size;

  size_t nread = fread(wbuf, size, nitems, file);
  /* ... */
}
```

Risk Assessment

Depending on the library function called, an attacker may be able to use a heap or stack overflow vulnerability to run arbitrary code.

Rule	Severity	Likelihood	Remediation Cost	Priority	Level
ARR38-C	High	Likely	Medium	P18	L1

Related Guidelines

ISO/IEC TS 17961:2013	Forming invalid pointers by library functions [libptr]
ISO/IEC TR 24772:2013	Buffer Boundary Violation (Buffer Overflow) [HCB] Unchecked Array Copying [XYW]
MITRE CWE	CWE-119, Improper Restriction of Operations within the Bounds of a Memory Buffer CWE-121, Stack-based Buffer Overflow CWE-805, Buffer Access with Incorrect Length Value

Bibliography

[ISO/IEC TS 17961:2013]

■ ARR39-C. Do not add or subtract a scaled integer to a pointer

Pointer arithmetic is appropriate only when the pointer argument refers to an array (see "ARR37-C. Do not add or subtract an integer to a pointer to a non-array object"), including an array of bytes. When performing pointer arithmetic, the size of the value to add to or subtract from a pointer is automatically scaled to the size of the type of the referenced array object. Adding or subtracting a scaled integer value to or from a pointer is invalid because it may yield a pointer that does not point to an element within or one past the end of the array (see "ARR30-C. Do not form or use out-of-bounds pointers or array subscripts").

Adding a pointer to an array of a type other than character to the result of the `sizeof` operator or `offsetof` macro, which return a size and an offset, respectively, violates this rule. However, adding an array pointer to the number of array elements, for example, by using the `arr[sizeof(arr)/sizeof(arr[0])])` idiom, is allowed provided that `arr` refers to an array and not a pointer.

Noncompliant Code Example

In this noncompliant code example, `sizeof (buf)` is added to the array `buf`. This example is noncompliant because `sizeof (buf)` is scaled by `int` and then scaled again when added to `buf`.

```
enum { INTBUFSIZE = 80 };

extern int getdata(void);
int buf[INTBUFSIZE];

void func(void) {
  int *buf_ptr = buf;

  while (buf_ptr < (buf + sizeof(buf))) {
    *buf_ptr++ = getdata();
  }
}
```

Compliant Solution

This compliant solution uses an unscaled integer to obtain a pointer to the end of the array:

```
enum { INTBUFSIZE = 80 };

extern int getdata(void);
int buf[INTBUFSIZE];

void func(void) {
  int *buf_ptr = buf;

  while (buf_ptr < (buf + INTBUFSIZE)) {
    *buf_ptr++ = getdata();
  }
}
```

Noncompliant Code Example

In this noncompliant code example, skip is added to the pointer s. However, skip represents the byte offset of ull_b in struct big. When added to s, skip is scaled by the size of struct big.

```
#include <string.h>
#include <stdlib.h>
#include <stddef.h>

struct big {
  unsigned long long ull_a;
  unsigned long long ull_b;
  unsigned long long ull_c;
  int si_e;
  int si_f;
};

void func(void) {
  size_t skip = offsetof(struct big, ull_b);
  struct big *s = (struct big *)malloc(sizeof(struct big));
  if (s == NULL) {
    /* Handle malloc error */
  }

  memset(s + skip, 0, sizeof(struct big) - skip);
  /* ... */
  free(s);
  s = NULL;
}
```

Compliant Solution

This compliant solution uses an `unsigned char *` to calculate the offset instead of using a `struct big *`, which would result in scaled arithmetic:

```
#include <string.h>
#include <stdlib.h>
#include <stddef.h>

struct big {
  unsigned long long ull_a;
  unsigned long long ull_b;
  unsigned long long ull_c;
  int si_d;
  int si_e;
};

void func(void) {
  size_t skip = offsetof(struct big, ull_b);
  unsigned char *ptr = (unsigned char *)malloc(
    sizeof(struct big)
  );
  if (ptr == NULL) {
    /* Handle malloc() error */
  }

  memset(ptr + skip, 0, sizeof(struct big) - skip);
  /* ... */
  free(ptr);
  ptr = NULL;
}
```

Noncompliant Code Example

In this noncompliant code example, `wcslen(error_msg) * sizeof(wchar_t)` bytes are scaled by the size of `wchar_t` when added to `error_msg`:

```
#include <wchar.h>
#include <stdio.h>

enum { WCHAR_BUF = 128 };
```

```
void func(void) {
  wchar_t error_msg[WCHAR_BUF];

  wcscpy(error_msg, L"Error: ");
  fgetws(error_msg + wcslen(error_msg) * sizeof(wchar_t),
         WCHAR_BUF - 7, stdin);
  /* ... */
}
```

Compliant Solution

This compliant solution does not scale the length of the string; wcslen() returns the number of characters, and the addition to error_msg is scaled:

```
#include <wchar.h>
#include <stdio.h>

enum { WCHAR_BUF = 128 };
const wchar_t ERROR_PREFIX[7] = L"Error: ";

void func(void) {
  const size_t prefix_len = wcslen(ERROR_PREFIX);
  wchar_t error_msg[WCHAR_BUF];

  wcscpy(error_msg, ERROR_PREFIX);
  fgetws(error_msg + prefix_len,
         WCHAR_BUF - prefix_len, stdin);
  /* ... */
}
```

Risk Assessment

Failure to understand and properly use pointer arithmetic can allow an attacker to execute arbitrary code.

Rule	Severity	Likelihood	Remediation Cost	Priority	Level
ARR39-C	High	Probable	High	P6	L2

Related Guidelines

ISO/IEC TR 24772:2013	Pointer Casting and Pointer Type Changes [HFC] Pointer Arithmetic [RVG]
MISRA C:2012	Rule 18.1 (required) Rule 18.2 (required) Rule 18.3 (required) Rule 18.4 (advisory)
MITRE CWE	CWE 468, Incorrect Pointer Scaling

Bibliography

[Dowd 2006]	Chapter 6, "C Language Issues"
[Murenin 2007]	

Chapter 7

Characters and Strings (STR)

Chapter Contents

Risk Assessment Summary

Rule	Severity	Likelihood	Remediation Cost	Priority	Level
STR30-C	Low	Likely	Low	P9	L2
STR31-C	High	Likely	Medium	P18	L1

continues

201

Rule	Severity	Likelihood	Remediation Cost	Priority	Level
STR32-C	High	Probable	Medium	P12	L1
STR34-C	Medium	Probable	Medium	P8	L2
STR37-C	Low	Unlikely	Low	P3	L3
STR38-C	High	Likely	Low	P27	L1

■ STR30-C. Do not attempt to modify string literals

According to the C Standard, 6.4.5, paragraph 3 [ISO/IEC 9899:2011]:

> A *character string literal* is a sequence of zero or more multibyte characters enclosed in double-quotes, as in "xyz". A *UTF–8 string literal* is the same, except prefixed by u8. A *wide string literal* is the same, except prefixed by the letter L, u, or U.

At compile time, string literals are used to create an array of static storage duration of sufficient length to contain the character sequence and a terminating null character. String literals are usually referred to by a pointer to (or array of) characters. Ideally, they should be assigned only to pointers to (or arrays of) const char or const wchar_t. It is unspecified whether these arrays of string literals are distinct from each other. The behavior is undefined if a program attempts to modify any portion of a string literal. Modifying a string literal frequently results in an access violation because string literals are typically stored in read-only memory (see undefined behavior 33 in Appendix B.)

Avoid assigning a string literal to a pointer to non-const, or casting a string literal to a pointer to non-const. For the purposes of this rule, a pointer to (or array of) const characters must be treated as a string literal. Similarly, the returned value of the following library functions must be treated as a string literal if the first argument is a string literal:

- strpbrk(), strchr(), strrchr(), strstr()
- wcspbrk(), wcschr(), wcsrchr(), wcsstr()
- memchr(), wmemchr()

This rule is a specific instance of "EXP40-C. Do not modify constant objects."

Noncompliant Code Example

In this noncompliant code example, the `char` pointer p is initialized to the address of a string literal. Attempting to modify the string literal is undefined behavior:

```
char *p = "string literal";
p[0] = 'S';
```

Compliant Solution

As an array initializer, a string literal specifies the initial values of characters in an array as well as the size of the array (see "STR11-C. Do not specify the bound of a character array initialized with a string literal"). This code creates a copy of the string literal in the space allocated to the character array a. The string stored in a can be modified safely.

```
char a[] = "string literal";
a[0] = 'S';
```

Noncompliant Code Example (POSIX)

In this noncompliant code example, a string literal is passed to the (pointer to non-`const`) parameter of the POSIX function `mkstemp()`, which then modifies the characters of the string literal:

```
#include <stdlib.h>

void func(void) {
  mkstemp("/tmp/edXXXXXX");
}
```

The behavior of `mkstemp()` is described in more detail in "FIO21-C. Do not create temporary files in shared directories."

Compliant Solution (POSIX)

This compliant solution uses a named array instead of passing a string literal:

```
#include <stdlib.h>

void func(void) {
  static char fname[] = "/tmp/edXXXXXX";
  mkstemp(fname);
}
```

Noncompliant Code Example (Result of `strrchr()`)

In this noncompliant example, the `char *` result of the `strrchr()` function is used to modify the object pointed to by `pathname`. Because the argument to `strrchr()` points to a string literal, the effects of the modification are undefined.

```
#include <stdio.h>
#include <string.h>

const char *get_dirname(const char *pathname) {
  char *slash;
  slash = strrchr(pathname, '/');
  if (slash) {
    *slash = '\0'; /* Undefined behavior */
  }
  return pathname;
}

int main(void) {
  puts(get_dirname(__FILE__));
  return 0;
}
```

Compliant Solution (Result of `strrchr()`)

This compliant solution avoids modifying a `const` object, even if it is possible to obtain a non-`const` pointer to such an object by calling a standard C library function, such as `strrchr()`. To reduce the risk to callers of `get_dirname()`, a buffer and length for the directory name are passed into the function. It is insufficient to change `pathname` to require a `char *` instead of a `const char *` because conforming compilers are not required to diagnose passing a string literal to a function accepting a `char *`.

```
#include <stddef.h>
#include <stdio.h>
#include <string.h>

char *get_dirname(const char *pathname, char *dirname, size_t size) {
  const char *slash;
  slash = strrchr(pathname, '/');
  if (slash) {
    ptrdiff_t slash_idx = slash - pathname;
    if ((size_t)slash_idx < size) {
      memcpy(dirname, pathname, slash_idx);
      dirname[slash_idx] = '\0';
```

```
      return dirname;
    }
  }
  return 0;
}

int main(void) {
  char dirname[260];
  if (get_dirname(__FILE__, dirname, sizeof(dirname))) {
    puts(dirname);
  }
  return 0;
}
```

Risk Assessment

Modifying string literals can lead to abnormal program termination and possibly **denial-of-service attacks**.

Rule	Severity	Likelihood	Remediation Cost	Priority	Level
STR30-C	Low	Likely	Low	P9	L2

Related Guidelines

ISO/IEC TS 17961:2013	Modifying string literals [strmod]

Bibliography

[ISO/IEC 9899:2011]	6.4.5, "String Literals"
[Plum 1991]	Topic 1.26, "Strings—String Literals"
[Summit 1995]	comp.lang.c FAQ List, Question 1.32

■ STR31-C. Guarantee that storage for strings has sufficient space for character data and the null terminator

Copying data to a buffer that is not large enough to hold that data results in a buffer overflow. Buffer overflows occur frequently when manipulating strings [Seacord 2013b]. To prevent such errors, either limit copies through truncation or, preferably, ensure that the destination is of sufficient size to hold the character data to be copied and the null-termination character (see "STR03-C. Do not inadvertently truncate a string").

When strings live on the heap, this rule is a specific instance of "MEM35-C. Allocate sufficient memory for an object." Because strings are represented as arrays of characters, this rule is related to both "ARR30-C. Do not form or use out-of-bounds pointers or array subscripts" and "ARR38-C. Guarantee that library functions do not form invalid pointers."

Noncompliant Code Example (Off-by-One Error)

This noncompliant code example demonstrates an *off-by-one* error [Dowd 2006]. The loop copies data from src to dest. However, because the loop does not account for the null-termination character, it may be incorrectly written 1 byte past the end of dest.

```
#include <stddef.h>

enum { ARRAY_SIZE = 32 };

void func(void) {
  char dest[ARRAY_SIZE];
  char src[ARRAY_SIZE];
  size_t i;

  for (i = 0; src[i] && (i < sizeof(dest)); ++i) {
    dest[i] = src[i];
  }
  dest[i] = '\0';
}
```

Compliant Solution (Off-by-One Error)

In this compliant solution, the loop termination condition is modified to account for the null-termination character that is appended to dest:

```
#include <stddef.h>

enum { ARRAY_SIZE = 32 };

void func(void) {
  char dest[ARRAY_SIZE];
  char src[ARRAY_SIZE];
  size_t i;
```

```
  for (i = 0; src[i] && (i < sizeof(dest) - 1); ++i) {
    dest[i] = src[i];
  }
  dest[i] = '\0';
}
```

Noncompliant Code Example (gets())

The gets() function, which was deprecated in the C99 Technical Corrigendum 3 and removed from C11, is inherently unsafe and should never be used because it provides no way to control how much data is read into a buffer from stdin. This noncompliant code example assumes that gets() will not read more than BUFFER_SIZE - 1 characters from stdin. This is an invalid assumption, and the resulting operation can result in a buffer overflow.

The gets() function reads characters from stdin into a destination array until end-of-file is encountered or a new-line character is read. Any new-line character is discarded, and a null character is written immediately after the last character read into the array.

```
#include <stdio.h>

#define BUFFER_SIZE 1024

void func(void) {
  char buf[BUFFER_SIZE];
  if (gets(buf) == NULL) {
    /* Handle error */
  }
}
```

See also "MSC24-C. Do not use deprecated or obsolescent functions."

Compliant Solution (fgets())

The fgets() function reads, at most, one less than the specified number of characters from a stream into an array. This solution is compliant because the number of characters copied from stdin to buf cannot exceed the allocated memory:

```
#include <stdio.h>
#include <string.h>

enum { BUFFERSIZE = 32 };
```

```
void func(void) {
  char buf[BUFFERSIZE];
  int ch;

  if (fgets(buf, sizeof(buf), stdin)) {
    /* fgets() succeeded; scan for new-line character */
    char *p = strchr(buf, '\n');
    if (p) {
      *p = '\0';
    } else {
      /* New-line not found; flush stdin to end of line */
      while ((ch = getchar()) != '\n' && ch != EOF)
        ;
      if (ch == EOF && !feof(stdin) && !ferror(stdin)) {
        /* Character resembles EOF; handle error */
      }
    }
  } else {
    /* fgets() failed; handle error */
  }
}
```

The fgets() function is not a strict replacement for the gets() function because fgets() retains the new-line character (if read) and may also return a partial line. It is possible to use fgets() to safely process input lines too long to store in the destination array, but this is not recommended for performance reasons. Consider using one of the following compliant solutions when replacing gets().

Compliant Solution (gets_s())

The gets_s() function reads, at most, one less than the number of characters specified from the stream pointed to by stdin into an array.

The C Standard, Annex K [ISO/IEC 9899:2011], states:

> No additional characters are read after a new-line character (which is discarded) or after end-of-file. The discarded new-line character does not count towards number of characters read. A null character is written immediately after the last character read into the array.

If end-of-file is encountered and no characters have been read into the destination array, or if a read error occurs during the operation, then the first character in the destination array is set to the null character and the other elements of the array take unspecified values:

```
#define __STDC_WANT_LIB_EXT1__ 1
#include <stdio.h>

enum { BUFFERSIZE = 32 };

void func(void) {
  char buf[BUFFERSIZE];

  if (gets_s(buf, sizeof(buf)) == NULL) {
    /* Handle error */
  }
}
```

Compliant Solution (getline(), POSIX)

The getline() function is similar to the fgets() function but can dynamically allocate memory for the input buffer. If passed a null pointer, getline() dynamically allocates a buffer of sufficient size to hold the input. If passed a pointer to dynamically allocated storage that is too small to hold the contents of the string, the getline() function resizes the buffer, using realloc(), rather than truncating the input. If successful, the getline() function returns the number of characters read, which can be used to determine if the input has any null characters before the new-line. The getline() function works only with dynamically allocated buffers. Allocated memory must be explicitly deallocated by the caller to avoid memory leaks (see "MEM31-C. Free dynamically allocated memory when no longer needed").

```
#include <stdio.h>
#include <stdlib.h>
#include <string.h>

void func(void) {
  int ch;
  size_t buffer_size = 32;
  char *buffer = malloc(buffer_size);

  if (!buffer) {
    /* Handle error */
    return;
  }

  if ((ssize_t size = getline(&buffer, &buffer_size, stdin))
        == -1) {
    /* Handle error */
  } else {
    char *p = strchr(buffer, '\n');
```

```
      if (p) {
        *p = '\0';
      } else {
        /* New-line not found; flush stdin to end of line */
        while ((ch = getchar()) != '\n' && ch != EOF)
          ;
        if (ch == EOF && !feof(stdin) && !ferror(stdin)) {
          /* Character resembles EOF; handle error */
        }
      }
    }
    free (buffer);
}
```

Note that the `getline()` function uses an **in-band error indicator**, in violation of "ERR02-C. Avoid in-band error indicators."

Noncompliant Code Example (`getchar()`)

Reading one character at a time provides more flexibility in controlling behavior, though with additional performance overhead. This noncompliant code example uses the `getchar()` function to read one character at a time from `stdin` instead of reading the entire line at once. The `stdin` stream is read until end-of-file is encountered or a new-line character is read. Any new-line character is discarded, and a null character is written immediately after the last character read into the array. Similar to the noncompliant code example that invokes `gets()`, there are no guarantees that this code will not result in a buffer overflow.

```
#include <stdio.h>

enum { BUFFERSIZE = 32 };

void func(void) {
  char buf[BUFFERSIZE];
  char *p;
  int ch;
  p = buf;
  while ((ch = getchar()) != '\n' && ch != EOF) {
    *p++ = (char)ch;
  }
  *p++ = 0;
  if (ch == EOF) {
      /* Handle EOF or error */
  }
}
```

After the loop ends, if ch == EOF, the loop has read through to the end of the stream without encountering a new-line character, or a read error occurred before the loop encountered a new-line character. To conform to "FIO34-C. Distinguish between characters read from a file and EOF or WEOF," the error-handling code must verify that an end-of-file or error has occurred by calling feof() and ferror().

Compliant Solution (getchar())

In this compliant solution, characters are no longer copied to buf once index == BUFFERSIZE - 1, leaving room to null-terminate the string. The loop continues to read characters until the end of the line, the end of the file, or an error is encountered. When chars_read > index, the input string has been truncated.

```
#include <stdio.h>

enum { BUFFERSIZE = 32 };
void func(void) {
  char buf[BUFFERSIZE];
  int ch;
  size_t index = 0;
  size_t chars_read = 0;

  while ((ch = getchar()) != '\n' && ch != EOF) {
    if (index < sizeof(buf) - 1) {
      buf[index++] = (char)ch;
    }
    chars_read++;
  }
  buf[index] = '\0';  /* Terminate string */
  if (ch == EOF) {
    /* Handle EOF or error */
  }
  if (chars_read > index) {
    /* Handle truncation */
  }
}
```

Noncompliant Code Example (fscanf())

In this noncompliant example, the call to fscanf() can result in a write outside the character array buf:

```
#include <stdio.h>
```

```
enum { BUF_LENGTH = 1024 };

void get_data(void) {
  char buf[BUF_LENGTH];
  if (1 != fscanf(stdin, "%s", buf)) {
    /* Handle error */
  }

  /* Rest of function */
}
```

Compliant Solution (fscanf())

In this compliant solution, the call to fscanf() is constrained not to overflow buf:

```
#include <stdio.h>

enum { BUF_LENGTH = 1024 };

void get_data(void) {
  char buf[BUF_LENGTH];
  if (1 != fscanf(stdin, "%1023s", buf)) {
    /* Handle error */
  }

  /* Rest of function */
}
```

Noncompliant Code Example (argv)

In a **hosted environment**, arguments read from the command line are stored in process memory. The function main(), called at program startup, is typically declared as follows when the program accepts command-line arguments:

```
int main(int argc, char *argv[]) { /* ... */ }
```

Command-line arguments are passed to main() as pointers to strings in the array members argv[0] through argv[argc - 1]. If the value of argc is greater than 0, the string pointed to by argv[0] is, by convention, the program name. If the value of argc is greater than 1, the strings referenced by argv[1] through argv[argc - 1] are the program arguments.

Vulnerabilities can occur when inadequate space is allocated to copy a command-line argument or other program input. In this noncompliant code example, an attacker can manipulate the contents of argv[0] to cause a buffer overflow:

```
#include <string.h>

int main(int argc, char *argv[]) {
  /* Ensure argv[0] is not null */
  const char *const name = (argc && argv[0]) ? argv[0] : "";
  char prog_name[128];
  strcpy(prog_name, name);

  return 0;
}
```

Compliant Solution (argv)

The strlen() function can be used to determine the length of the strings ref-erenced by argv[0] through argv[argc - 1] so that adequate memory can be dynamically allocated.

```
#include <stdlib.h>
#include <string.h>

int main(int argc, char *argv[]) {
  /* Ensure argv[0] is not null */
  const char *const name = (argc && argv[0]) ? argv[0] : "";
  char *prog_name = (char *)malloc(strlen(name) + 1);
  if (prog_name != NULL) {
    strcpy(prog_name, name);
  } else {
    /* Handle error */
  }
  free(prog_name);
  return 0;
}
```

Remember to add a byte to the destination string size to accommodate the null-termination character.

Compliant Solution (argv)

The strcpy_s() function provides additional safeguards, including accepting the size of the destination buffer as an additional argument (see "STR07-C. Use the bounds-checking interfaces for remediation of existing string manip-ulation code").

```
#define __STDC_WANT_LIB_EXT1__ 1
#include <stdlib.h>
#include <string.h>
```

```
int main(int argc, char *argv[]) {
  /* Ensure argv[0] is not null */
  const char *const name = (argc && argv[0]) ? argv[0] : "";
  char *prog_name;
  size_t prog_size;

  prog_size = strlen(name) + 1;
  prog_name = (char *)malloc(prog_size);

  if (prog_name != NULL) {
    if (strcpy_s(prog_name, prog_size, name)) {
      /* Handle  error */
    }
  } else {
    /* Handle error */
  }
  /* ... */
  free(prog_name);
  return 0;
}
```

The `strcpy_s()` function can be used to copy data to or from dynamically allocated memory or a statically allocated array. If insufficient space is available, `strcpy_s()` returns an error.

Compliant Solution (`argv`)

If an argument will not be modified or concatenated, there is no reason to make a copy of the string. Not copying a string is the best way to prevent a buffer overflow and is also the most efficient solution. Care must be taken to avoid assuming that `argv[0]` is non-null.

```
int main(int argc, char *argv[]) {
  /* Be prepared for argv[0] to be null */
  const char * const prog_name = (argc && argv[0]) ? argv[0] : "";
  /* ... */
  return 0;
}
```

Noncompliant Code Example (`getenv()`)

According to the C Standard, 7.22.4.6, paragraph 2 [ISO/IEC 9899:2011]:

> The `getenv` function searches an environment list, provided by the host environment, for a string that matches the string pointed to by `name`. The set

of environment names and the method for altering the environment list are implementation-defined.

Environment variables can be arbitrarily large, and copying them into fixed-length arrays without first determining the size and allocating adequate storage can result in a buffer overflow.

```
#include <stdlib.h>
#include <string.h>

void func(void) {
  char buff[256];
  char *editor = getenv("EDITOR");
  if (editor == NULL) {
    /* EDITOR environment variable not set */
  } else {
    strcpy(buff, editor);
  }
}
```

Compliant Solution (getenv())

Environmental variables are loaded into process memory when the program is loaded. As a result, the length of these strings can be determined by calling the strlen() function, and the resulting length can be used to allocate adequate dynamic memory:

```
#include <stdlib.h>
#include <string.h>

void func(void) {
  char *buff;
  char *editor = getenv("EDITOR");
  if (editor == NULL) {
    /* EDITOR environment variable not set */
  } else {
    size_t len = strlen(editor) + 1;
    buff = (char *)malloc(len);
    if (buff == NULL) {
      /* Handle error */
    }
    memcpy(buff, editor, len);
    free(buff);
  }
}
```

Noncompliant Code Example (`sprintf()`)

In this noncompliant code example, name refers to an external string; it could have originated from user input, from the file system, or from the network. The program constructs a file name from the string in preparation for opening the file.

```
#include <stdio.h>

void func(const char *name) {
  char filename[128];
  sprintf(filename, "%s.txt", name);
}
```

Because the sprintf() function makes no guarantees regarding the length of the generated string, a sufficiently long string in name could generate a buffer overflow.

Compliant Solution (`sprintf()`)

The buffer overflow in the preceding noncompliant example can be prevented by adding a precision to the %s conversion specification. If the precision is specified, no more than that many bytes are written. The precision 123 in this compliant solution ensures that filename can contain the first 123 characters of name, the .txt extension, and the null terminator.

```
#include <stdio.h>

void func(const char *name) {
  char filename[128];
  sprintf(filename, "%.123s.txt", name);
}
```

Compliant Solution (`snprintf()`)

A more general solution is to use the snprintf() function:

```
#include <stdio.h>

void func(const char *name) {
  char filename[128];
  snprintf(filename, sizeof(filename), "%s.txt", name);
}
```

Risk Assessment

Copying string data to a buffer that is too small to hold that data results in a buffer overflow. Attackers can exploit this condition to execute arbitrary code with the permissions of the vulnerable process.

Rule	Severity	Likelihood	Remediation Cost	Priority	Level
STR31-C	High	Likely	Medium	P18	L1

Related Vulnerabilities

CVE-2009-1252 results from a violation of this rule. The Network Time Protocol daemon (NTPd), before versions 4.2.4p7 and 4.2.5p74, contained calls to `sprintf` that allow an attacker to execute arbitrary code by overflowing a character array [xorl 2009].

CVE-2009-0587 results from a violation of this rule. Before version 2.24.5, Evolution Data Server performed unchecked arithmetic operations on the length of a user-input string and used the value to allocate space for a new buffer. An attacker could thereby execute arbitrary code by inputting a long string, resulting in incorrect allocation and buffer overflow [xorl 2009].

Related Guidelines

ISO/IEC TR 24772:2013	String Termination [CJM] Buffer Boundary Violation (Buffer Overflow) [HCB] Unchecked Array Copying [XYW]
ISO/IEC TS 17961:2013	Using a tainted value to write to an object using a formatted input or output function [taintformatio] Tainted strings are passed to a string copying function [taintstrcpy]
MITRE CWE	CWE-119, Improper Restriction of Operations within the Bounds of a Memory Buffer CWE-120, Buffer Copy without Checking Size of Input ("Classic Buffer Overflow") CWE-193, Off-by-one Error

Bibliography

[Dowd 2006]	Chapter 7, "Program Building Blocks" ("Loop Constructs," pp. 327–336)
[Drepper 2006]	Section 2.1.1, "Respecting Memory Bounds"
[ISO/IEC 9899:2011]	K.3.5.4.1, "The gets_s Function"
[Lai 2006]	
[NIST 2006]	SAMATE Reference Dataset Test Case ID 000-000-088
[Seacord 2013b]	Chapter 2, "Strings"
[xorl 2009]	FreeBSD-SA-09:11: NTPd Remote Stack Based Buffer Overflows

■ STR32-C. Do not pass a non-null-terminated character sequence to a library function that expects a string

Many library functions accept a string or wide string argument with the constraint that the string they receive is properly null-terminated. Passing a character sequence or wide character sequence that is not null-terminated to such a function can result in accessing memory that is outside the bounds of the object. Do not pass a character sequence or wide character sequence that is not null-terminated to a library function that expects a string or wide string argument.

Noncompliant Code Example

This code example is noncompliant because the character sequence c_str will not be null-terminated when passed as an argument to printf() (see "STR11-C. Do not specify the bound of a character array initialized with a string literal" on how to properly initialize character arrays).

```c
#include <stdio.h>

void func(void) {
  char c_str[3] = "abc";
  printf("%s\n", c_str);
}
```

Compliant Solution

This compliant solution does not specify the bound of the character array in the array declaration. If the array bound is omitted, the compiler allocates sufficient storage to store the entire string literal, including the terminating null character.

```
#include <stdio.h>

void func(void) {
  char c_str[] = "abc";
  printf("%s\n", c_str);
}
```

Noncompliant Code Example

This code example is noncompliant because the wide character sequence cur_msg will not be null-terminated when passed to wcslen(). This will occur if lessen_memory_usage() is invoked while cur_msg_size still has its initial value of 1024.

```
#include <stdlib.h>
#include <wchar.h>

wchar_t *cur_msg = NULL;
size_t cur_msg_size = 1024;
size_t cur_msg_len = 0;

void lessen_memory_usage(void) {
  wchar_t *temp;
  size_t temp_size;

  /* ... */

  if (cur_msg != NULL) {
    temp_size = cur_msg_size / 2 + 1;
    temp = realloc(cur_msg, temp_size * sizeof(wchar_t));
    /* temp and cur_msg may no longer be null-terminated */
    if (temp == NULL) {
      /* Handle error */
    }

    cur_msg = temp;
    cur_msg_size = temp_size;
    cur_msg_len = wcslen(cur_msg);
  }
}
```

Compliant Solution

In this compliant solution, `cur_msg` will always be null-terminated when passed to `wcslen()`.

```
#include <stdlib.h>
#include <wchar.h>

wchar_t *cur_msg = NULL;
size_t cur_msg_size = 1024;
size_t cur_msg_len = 0;

void lessen_memory_usage(void) {
  wchar_t *temp;
  size_t temp_size;

  /* ... */

  if (cur_msg != NULL) {
    temp_size = cur_msg_size / 2 + 1;
    temp = realloc(cur_msg, temp_size * sizeof(wchar_t));
    /* temp and cur_msg may no longer be null-terminated */
    if (temp == NULL) {
      /* Handle error */
    }

    cur_msg = temp;
    /* Properly null-terminate cur_msg */
    cur_msg[temp_size - 1] = L'\0';
    cur_msg_size = temp_size;
    cur_msg_len = wcslen(cur_msg);
  }
}
```

Noncompliant Code Example (`strncpy()`)

Although the `strncpy()` function takes a string as input, it does not guarantee that the resulting value is still null-terminated. In the following noncompliant code example, if no null character is contained in the first n characters of the source array, the result will not be null-terminated. Passing a non-null-terminated character sequence to `strlen()` is undefined behavior.

```
#include <string.h>

enum { STR_SIZE = 32 };
```

```
size_t func(const char *source) {
  char c_str[STR_SIZE];

  c_str[sizeof(c_str) - 1] = '\0';
  strncpy(c_str, source, sizeof(c_str));
  return strlen(c_str);
}
```

Compliant Solution (Truncation)

This compliant solution is correct if the programmer's intent is to truncate the string:

```
#include <string.h>

enum { STR_SIZE = 32 };

size_t func(const char *source) {
  char c_str[STR_SIZE];

  strncpy(c_str, source, sizeof(c_str) - 1);
  str[sizeof(c_str) - 1] = '\0';
  return strlen(c_str);
}
```

Compliant Solution (Truncation, strncpy_s())

The C Standard, Annex K strncpy_s() function can also be used to copy with truncation. The strncpy_s() function copies up to n characters from the source array to a destination array. If no null character was copied from the source array, then the nth position in the destination array is set to a null character, guaranteeing that the resulting string is null-terminated.

```
#define __STDC_WANT_LIB_EXT1__ 1
#include <string.h>

enum { STR_SIZE = 32 };

size_t func(const char *source) {
  char a[STR_SIZE];

  if (source) {
    errno_t err = strncpy_s(
      a, sizeof(a), source, strlen(source)
    );
    if (err != 0) {
```

```
      /* Handle error */
    }
  } else {
    /* Handle null pointer */
  }
  return strlen_s(s, sizeof(a));
}
```

Compliant Solution (Copy without Truncation)

If the programmer's intent is to copy without truncation, this compliant solution copies the data and guarantees that the resulting array is null-terminated. If the string cannot be copied, it is handled as an error condition.

```
#include <string.h>

enum { STR_SIZE = 32 };

size_t func(const char *source) {
  char c_str[STR_SIZE];

  if (source) {
    if (strlen(source) < sizeof(c_str)) {
      strcpy(c_str, source);
    } else {
      /* Handle string-too-large */
    }
  } else {
    /* Handle null pointer */
  }
  return strlen(c_str);
}
```

Risk Assessment

Failure to properly null-terminate a character sequence that is passed to a library function that expects a string can result in buffer overflows and the execution of arbitrary code with the permissions of the vulnerable process. Null-termination errors can also result in unintended information disclosure.

Rule	Severity	Likelihood	Remediation Cost	Priority	Level
STR32-C	High	Probable	Medium	P12	L1

Related Guidelines

ISO/IEC TR 24772:2013	String Termination [CMJ]
ISO/IEC TS 17961:2013	Passing a non-null-terminated character sequence to a library function that expects a string [strmod]
MITRE CWE	CWE-119, Improper Restriction of Operations within the Bounds of a Memory Buffer CWE-170, Improper Null Termination

Bibliography

[Seacord 2013b]	Chapter 2, "Strings"
[Viega 2005]	Section 5.2.14, "Miscalculated NULL Termination"

■ STR34-C. Cast characters to unsigned char before converting to larger integer sizes

Signed character data must be converted to unsigned char before being assigned or converted to a larger signed type. This rule applies to both signed char and (plain) char characters on implementations where char is defined to have the same range, representation, and behavior as signed char. However, this rule is applicable only in cases where the character data may contain values that can be interpreted as negative numbers. For example, if the char type is represented by a two's complement 8-bit value, any character value greater than +127 is interpreted as a negative value.

This rule is a generalization of "STR37-C. Arguments to character handling functions must be representable as an unsigned char."

Noncompliant Code Example

This noncompliant code example is taken from a vulnerability in bash versions 1.14.6 and earlier that led to the release of CERT Advisory CA-1996-22. This vulnerability resulted from the sign extension of character data referenced by the c_str pointer in the yy_string_get() function in the parse.y module of the bash source code.

```
static int yy_string_get(void) {
  register char *c_str;
  register int c;

  c_str = bash_input.location.string;
  c = EOF;

  /* If the string doesn't exist or is empty, EOF found */
  if (c_str && *c_str) {
    c = *c_str++;
    bash_input.location.string = c_str;
  }
  return (c);
}
```

The c_str variable is used to traverse the character string containing the command line to be parsed. As characters are retrieved from this pointer, they are stored in a variable of type int. For implementations in which the char type is defined to have the same range, representation, and behavior as signed char, this value is sign-extended when assigned to the int variable. For character code 255 decimal (–1 in two's complement form), this sign extension results in the value –1 being assigned to the integer, which is indistinguishable from EOF.

Noncompliant Code Example

This problem can be repaired by explicitly declaring the c_str variable as unsigned char:

```
static int yy_string_get(void) {
  register unsigned char *c_str;
  register int c;

  c_str = bash_input.location.string;
  c = EOF;

  /* If the string doesn't exist or is empty, EOF found */
  if (c_str && *c_str) {
    c = *c_str++;
    bash_input.location.string = c_str;
  }
  return (c);
}
```

This example, however, violates "STR04-C. Use plain char for characters in the basic character set."

Compliant Solution

In this compliant solution, the result of the expression *c_str++ is cast to unsigned char before assignment to the int variable c:

```
static int yy_string_get(void) {
  register char *c_str;
  register int c;

  c_str = bash_input.location.string;
  c = EOF;

  /* If the string doesn't exist or is empty, EOF found */
  if (c_str && *c_str) {
    /* Cast to unsigned type */
    c = (unsigned char)*c_str++;

    bash_input.location.string = c_str;
  }
  return (c);
}
```

Noncompliant Code Example

In this noncompliant code example, the cast of *s to unsigned int can result in a value in excess of UCHAR_MAX because of integer promotions, a violation of "ARR30-C. Do not form or use out-of-bounds pointers or array subscripts":

```
#include <limits.h>
#include <stddef.h>

static const char table[UCHAR_MAX] = { 'a' /* ... */ };

ptrdiff_t first_not_in_table(const char *c_str) {
  for (const char *s = c_str; *s; ++s) {
    if (table[(unsigned int)*s] != *s) {
      return s - c_str;
    }
  }
  return -1;
}
```

Compliant Solution

This compliant solution casts the value of type char to unsigned char before the implicit promotion to a larger type:

```
#include <limits.h>
#include <stddef.h>

static const char table[UCHAR_MAX] = { 'a' /* ... */ };

ptrdiff_t first_not_in_table(const char *c_str) {
  for (const char *s = c_str; *s; ++s) {
    if (table[(unsigned char)*s] != *s) {
      return s - c_str;
    }
  }
  return -1;
}
```

Risk Assessment

Conversion of character data resulting in a value in excess of UCHAR_MAX is an often-missed error that can result in a disturbingly broad range of potentially severe vulnerabilities.

Rule	Severity	Likelihood	Remediation Cost	Priority	Level
STR34-C	Medium	Probable	Medium	P8	L2

Related Vulnerabilities

CVE-2009-0887 results from a violation of this rule. In Linux PAM (up to version 1.0.3), the libpam implementation of strtok() casts a (potentially signed) character to an integer for use as an index to an array. An attacker can exploit this vulnerability by inputting a string with non-ASCII characters, causing the cast to result in a negative index and accessing memory outside of the array [xorl 2009].

Related Guidelines

ISO/IEC TS 17961:2013	Conversion of signed characters to wider integer types before a check for EOF [signconv]
MISRA-C	Rule 10.1 through Rule 10.4 (required)
MITRE CWE	CWE-704, Incorrect Type Conversion or Cast

Bibliography

[xorl 2009]	CVE-2009-0887: Linux-PAM Signedness Issue

■ STR37-C. Arguments to character handling functions must be representable as an unsigned char

According to the C Standard, 7.4 [ISO/IEC 9899:2011],

> The header <ctype.h> declares several functions useful for classifying and mapping characters. In all cases the argument is an int, the value of which shall be representable as an unsigned char or shall equal the value of the macro EOF. If the argument has any other value, the behavior is undefined.

See also undefined behavior 113 in Appendix B.

This rule is applicable only to code that runs on platforms where the char data type is defined to have the same range, representation, and behavior as signed char. Table 7–1 lists the character classification functions that this rule addresses.

This rule is a specific instance of "STR34-C. Cast characters to unsigned char before converting to larger integer sizes."

Noncompliant Code Example

On implementations where plain char is signed, this code example is noncompliant because the parameter to isspace(), *t, is defined as a const char *, and this value might not be representable as an unsigned char:

```
#include <ctype.h>
#include <string.h>

size_t count_preceding_whitespace(const char *s) {
  const char *t = s;
  size_t length = strlen(s) + 1;
  while (isspace(*t) && (t - s < length)) {
    ++t;
  }
  return t - s;
}
```

Table 7–1. Character Classification Functions

isalnum()	isalpha()	isascii()[XSI]	isblank()
iscntrl()	isdigit()	isgraph()	islower()
isprint()	ispunct()	isspace()	isupper()
isxdigit()	toascii()[XSI]	toupper()	tolower()

XSI denotes an X/Open System Interfaces Extension to ISO/IEC 9945—POSIX. These functions are not defined by the C Standard.

The argument to isspace() must be EOF or representable as an unsigned char; otherwise, the result is undefined.

Compliant Solution

This compliant solution casts the character to unsigned char before passing it as an argument to the isspace() function:

```
#include <ctype.h>
#include <string.h>

size_t count_preceding_whitespace(const char *s) {
  const char *t = s;
  size_t length = strlen(s) + 1;
  while (isspace((unsigned char)*t) && (t - s < length)) {
    ++t;
  }
  return t - s;
}
```

Risk Assessment

Passing values that cannot be represented as an unsigned char to character handling functions is undefined behavior.

Rule	Severity	Likelihood	Remediation Cost	Priority	Level
STR37-C	Low	Unlikely	Low	P3	L3

Related Guidelines

ISO/IEC TS 17961:2013	Passing arguments to character-handling functions that are not representable as unsigned char [chrsgnext]
MITRE CWE	CWE-704, Incorrect Type Conversion or Cast CWE-686, Function Call with Incorrect Argument Type

Bibliography

[ISO/IEC 9899:2011]	7.4, "Character Handling <ctype.h>"
[Kettlewell 2002]	Section 1.1, "<ctype.h> and Characters Types"

■ STR38-C. Do not confuse narrow and wide character strings and functions

Passing narrow string arguments to wide string functions or wide string arguments to narrow string functions can lead to unexpected and undefined behavior. Scaling problems are likely (see "ARR39-C. Do not add or subtract a scaled integer to a pointer") because of the difference in size between wide and narrow characters. Because wide strings are terminated by a null wide character and can contain null bytes, determining the length is also problematic.

Because wchar_t and char are distinct types, many compilers will produce a warning diagnostic if an inappropriate function is used (see "MSC00-C. Compile cleanly at high warning levels").

Noncompliant Code Example (Wide Strings with Narrow String Functions)

This noncompliant code example incorrectly uses the strncpy() function in an attempt to copy up to 10 wide characters. However, because wide characters can contain null bytes, the copy operation may end earlier than anticipated, resulting in the truncation of the wide string.

```
#include <stddef.h>
#include <string.h>

void func(void) {
  wchar_t wide_str1[]  = L"0123456789";
  wchar_t wide_str2[]  = L"0000000000";

  strncpy(wide_str2, wide_str1, 10);
}
```

Noncompliant Code Example (Narrow Strings with Wide String Functions)

This noncompliant code example incorrectly invokes the wcsncpy() function to copy up to 10 wide characters from narrow_str1 to narrow_str2. Because narrow_str2 is a narrow string, it has insufficient memory to store the result of the copy and the copy will result in a buffer overflow.

```
#include <wchar.h>

void func(void) {
  char narrow_str1[] = "01234567890123456789";
```

```
  char narrow_str2[] = "0000000000";

  wcsncpy(narrow_str2, narrow_str1, 10);
}
```

Compliant Solution

This compliant solution uses the proper-width functions. Using wcsncpy() for wide character strings and strncpy() for narrow character strings ensures that data is not truncated and buffer overflow does not occur.

```
#include <string.h>
#include <wchar.h>

void func(void) {
  wchar_t wide_str1[] = L"0123456789";
  wchar_t wide_str2[] = L"0000000000";
  wcsncpy(wide_str2, wide_str1, 10);

  char narrow_str1[] = "0123456789";
  char narrow_str2[] = "0000000000";
  strncpy(narrow_str2, narrow_str1, 10);
}
```

Noncompliant Code Example (strlen())

In this noncompliant code example, the strlen() function is used to determine the size of a wide character string:

```
#include <stdlib.h>
#include <string.h>

void func(void) {
  wchar_t wide_str1[] = L"0123456789";
  wchar_t *wide_str2 = (wchar_t*)malloc(strlen(wide_str1) + 1);
  if (wide_str2 == NULL) {
    /* Handle error */
  }
  /* ... */
  free(wide_str2);
  wide_str2 = NULL;
}
```

The strlen() function determines the number of characters that precede the terminating null character. However, wide characters can contain null bytes, particularly when expressing characters from the ASCII character set, as in this example. As a result, the `strlen()` function will return the number of bytes preceding the first null byte in the wide string.

Compliant Solution

This compliant solution correctly calculates the number of bytes required to contain a copy of the wide string, including the terminating null wide character:

```c
#include <stdlib.h>
#include <wchar.h>

void func(void) {
  wchar_t wide_str1[] = L"0123456789";
  wchar_t *wide_str2 = (wchar_t *)malloc(
    (wcslen(wide_str1) + 1) * sizeof(wchar_t));
  if (wide_str2 == NULL) {
    /* Handle error */
  }
  /* ... */

  free(wide_str2);
  wide_str2 = NULL;
}
```

Risk Assessment

Confusing narrow and wide character strings can result in buffer overflows, data truncation, and other defects.

Rule	Severity	Likelihood	Remediation Cost	Priority	Level
STR38-C	High	Likely	Low	P27	L1

Bibliography

[ISO/IEC 9899:2011]   7.24.2.4, "The `strncpy` Function"
7.29.4.2.2, "The `wcsncpy` Function"

Chapter 8

Memory Management (MEM)

Chapter Contents

Risk Assessment Summary

Rule	Severity	Likelihood	Remediation Cost	Priority	Level
MEM30-C	High	Likely	Medium	P18	L1
MEM31-C	High	Probable	Medium	P12	L1
MEM33-C	Low	Unlikely	Low	P3	L3
MEM34-C	High	Likely	Medium	P18	L1
MEM35-C	High	Probable	High	P6	L2
MEM36-C	Low	Probable	High	P2	L3

■ MEM30-C. Do not access freed memory

Evaluating pointers into memory that have been deallocated by a memory management function, including dereferencing, acting as an operand of an arithmetic operation, type casting, or using the pointer as the right-hand side of an assignment, is undefined behavior. Pointers to memory that have been deallocated are referred to as **dangling pointers**. Accessing a dangling pointer can result in exploitable vulnerabilities.

According to the C Standard, using the value of a pointer that refers to space deallocated by a call to the `free()` or `realloc()` function is undefined behavior (see undefined behavior 177 in Appendix B).

Reading a pointer to deallocated memory is undefined behavior because the pointer value is indeterminate and might be a trap representation. Fetching a trap representation might perform a hardware trap (but is not required to).

It is at the memory manager's discretion when to reallocate or recycle the freed memory. When memory is freed, all pointers into it become invalid, and its contents might either be returned to the operating system, making the freed space inaccessible, or remain intact and accessible. As a result, the data at the freed location can appear to be valid but change unexpectedly. Consequently, memory must not be written to or read from once it is freed.

Noncompliant Code Example

This example from Brian Kernighan and Dennis Ritchie [Kernighan 1988] shows both the incorrect and correct techniques for freeing the memory associated with a linked list. In their (intentionally) incorrect example, p is freed before p->next is executed so that p->next reads memory that has already been freed.

```
#include <stdlib.h>

struct node {
  int value;
  struct node *next;
};

void free_list(struct node *head) {
  for (struct node *p = head; p != NULL; p = p->next) {
    free(p);
  }
}
```

Compliant Solution

Kernighan and Ritchie correct this error by storing a reference to p->next in q before freeing p:

```c
#include <stdlib.h>

struct node {
  int value;
  struct node *next;
};

void free_list(struct node *head) {
  struct node *q;
  for (struct node *p = head; p != NULL; p = q) {
    q = p->next;
    free(p);
  }
}
```

Noncompliant Code Example

In this noncompliant code example, buf is written to after it has been freed. Write-after-free vulnerabilities can be exploited to run arbitrary code with the permissions of the vulnerable process and are seldom this obvious. Typically, allocations and frees are far removed, making it difficult to recognize and diagnose these problems.

```c
#include <stdlib.h>
#include <string.h>

int main(int argc, char *argv[]) {
  char *return_val = 0;
  const size_t bufsize = strlen(argv[0]) + 1;
  char *buf = (char *)malloc(bufsize);
  if (!buf) {
    return EXIT_FAILURE;
  }
  /* ... */
  free(buf);
  /* ... */
  strcpy(buf, argv[0]);
  /* ... */
  return EXIT_SUCCESS;
}
```

Compliant Solution

In this compliant solution, the memory is not freed until after its final use:

```c
#include <stdlib.h>
#include <string.h>

int main(int argc, char *argv[]) {
  char *return_val = 0;
  const size_t bufsize = strlen(argv[0]) + 1;
  char *buf = (char *)malloc(bufsize);
  if (!buf) {
    return EXIT_FAILURE;
  }
  /* ... */
  strcpy(buf, argv[0]);
  /* ... */
  free(buf);
  return EXIT_SUCCESS;
}
```

Noncompliant Code Example

In this noncompliant example, `realloc()` may free `c_str1` when it returns a null pointer, resulting in `c_str1` being freed twice. The C Standards Committee's proposed response to Defect Report #400 (http://www.open-std.org/jtc1/sc22/wg14/www/docs/summary.htm) makes it implementation-defined whether or not the old object is deallocated when `size` is zero and memory for the new object is not allocated. The current implementation of `realloc()` in the GNU C Library and Microsoft Visual Studio's C Runtime Library will free `c_str1` and return a null pointer for zero byte allocations. Freeing a pointer twice can result in a potentially exploitable vulnerability commonly referred to as a **double-free vulnerability** [Seacord 2013b].

```c
#include <stdlib.h>

void f(char *c_str1, size_t size) {
  char *c_str2 = (char *)realloc(c_str1, size);
  if (c_str2 == NULL) {
    free(c_str1);
  }
}
```

Compliant Solution

This compliant solution does not pass a size argument of zero to the `realloc()` function, eliminating the possibility of `c_str1` being freed twice:

```
#include <stdlib.h>

void f(char *c_str1, size_t size) {
  if (size != 0) {
    char *c_str2 = (char *)realloc(c_str1, size);
    if (c_str2 == NULL) {
      free(c_str1);
    }
  }
  else {
    free(c_str1);
  }

}
```

If the intent of calling f() is to reduce the size of the object, then doing nothing when the size is zero would be unexpected; instead, this compliant solution frees the object.

Noncompliant Code Example

In this noncompliant example (CVE-2009-1364) from libwmf version 0.2.8.4, the return value of gdRealloc (a simple wrapper around realloc() that reallocates space pointed to by im->clip->list) is set to more. However, the value of im->clip->list is used directly afterwards in the code, and the C Standard specifies that if realloc() moves the area pointed to, then the original block is freed. An attacker can then execute arbitrary code by forcing a reallocation (with a sufficient im->clip->count) and accessing freed memory [xorl 2009].

```
void gdClipSetAdd(gdImagePtr im, gdClipRectanglePtr rect) {
  gdClipRectanglePtr more;
  if (im->clip == 0) {
  /* ... */
  }
  if (im->clip->count == im->clip->max) {
    more = gdRealloc (im->clip->list,(im->clip->max + 8) *
                      sizeof (gdClipRectangle));
    /*
     * If the realloc fails, then we have not lost the
     * im->clip->list value.
     */
    if (more == 0) return;
    im->clip->max += 8;
  }
  im->clip->list[im->clip->count] = *rect;
  im->clip->count++;
```

Compliant Solution

This compliant solution simply reassigns `im->clip->list` to the value of `more` after the call to `realloc()`:

```
void gdClipSetAdd(gdImagePtr im,gdClipRectanglePtr rect) {
  gdClipRectanglePtr more;
  if (im->clip == 0) {
    /* ... */
  }
  if (im->clip->count == im->clip->max) {
    more = gdRealloc (im->clip->list,(im->clip->max + 8) *
                      sizeof (gdClipRectangle));
    if (more == 0) return;
    im->clip->max += 8;
    im->clip->list = more;
  }
  im->clip->list[im->clip->count] = *rect;
  im->clip->count++;
```

Risk Assessment

Reading memory that has already been freed can lead to abnormal program termination and denial-of-service attacks. Writing memory that has already been freed can additionally lead to the execution of arbitrary code with the permissions of the vulnerable process.

Freeing memory multiple times has similar consequences to accessing memory after it is freed. Reading a pointer to deallocated memory is undefined behavior because the pointer value is indeterminate and might be a trap representation. When reading from or writing to freed memory does not cause a trap, it may corrupt the underlying data structures that manage the heap in a manner that can be exploited to execute arbitrary code. Alternatively, writing to memory after it has been freed might modify memory that has been reallocated.

Programmers should be wary when freeing memory in a loop or conditional statement; if coded incorrectly, these constructs can lead to double-free vulnerabilities. It is also a common error to misuse the `realloc()` function in a manner that results in double-free vulnerabilities (see "MEM04-C. Beware of zero-length allocations").

Rule	Severity	Likelihood	Remediation Cost	Priority	Level
MEM30-C	High	Likely	Medium	P18	L1

Related Vulnerabilities

VU#623332 describes a double-free vulnerability in the MIT Kerberos 5 function `krb5_recvauth()`.

Related Guidelines

ISO/IEC TR 24772:2013	Dangling References to Stack Frames [DCM] Dangling Reference to Heap [XYK]
ISO/IEC TS 17961:2013	Accessing freed memory [accfree] Freeing memory multiple times [dblfree]
MISRA C:2012	Rule 18.6 (required)
MITRE CWE	CWE-415, Double Free CWE-416, Use After Free

Bibliography

[ISO/IEC 9899:2011]	7.22.3, "Memory Management Functions"
[Kernighan 1988]	Section 7.8.5, "Storage Management"
[MIT 2005]	
[OWASP Freed Memory]	
[Seacord 2013b]	Chapter 4, "Dynamic Memory Management"
[Viega 2005]	Section 5.2.19, "Using Freed Memory"
[VU#623332]	
[xorl 2009]	CVE-2009-1364: LibWMF Pointer Use after `free()`

■ MEM31-C. Free dynamically allocated memory when no longer needed

Before the lifetime of the last pointer that stores the return value of a call to a standard memory allocation function has ended, it must be matched by a call to `free()` with that pointer value.

Noncompliant Code Example

In this noncompliant example, the object allocated by the call to `malloc()` is not freed before the end of the lifetime of the last pointer `text_buffer` referring to the object:

```c
#include <stdlib.h>

enum { BUFFER_SIZE = 32 };

int f(void) {
  char *text_buffer = (char *)malloc(BUFFER_SIZE);
  if (text_buffer == NULL) {
    return -1;
  }
  return 0;
}
```

Compliant Solution

In this compliant solution, the pointer is deallocated with a call to `free()`:

```c
#include <stdlib.h>

enum { BUFFER_SIZE = 32 };

int f(void) {
  char *text_buffer = (char *)malloc(BUFFER_SIZE);
  if (text_buffer == NULL) {
    return -1;
  }

  free(text_buffer);
  return 0;
}
```

Exceptions

MEM31-EX1: Allocated memory does not need to be freed if it is assigned to a pointer with static storage duration whose lifetime is the entire execution of a program. The following code example illustrates a pointer that stores the return value from `malloc()` in a `static` variable:

```c
#include <stdlib.h>

enum { BUFFER_SIZE = 32 };
```

```
int f(void) {
  static char *text_buffer = NULL;
  if (text_buffer == NULL) {
    text_buffer = (char *)malloc(BUFFER_SIZE);
    if (text_buffer == NULL) {
      return -1;
    }
  }
  return 0;
}
```

Risk Assessment

Failing to free memory can result in the exhaustion of system memory resources, which can lead to a denial-of-service attack.

Rule	Severity	Likelihood	Remediation Cost	Priority	Level
MEM31-C	High	Probable	Medium	P12	L2

Related Guidelines

ISO/IEC TR 24772:2013	Memory Leak [XYL]
ISO/IEC TS 17961:2013	Failing to close files or free dynamic memory when they are no longer needed [fileclose]
MITRE CWE	CWE-401, Improper Release of Memory Before Removing Last Reference ("Memory Leak")

Bibliography

[ISO/IEC 9899:2011]	7.22.3, "Memory Management Functions"

■ MEM33-C. Allocate and copy structures containing a flexible array member dynamically

The C Standard, 6.7.2.1, paragraph 18 [ISO/IEC 9899:2011], says:

> As a special case, the last element of a structure with more than one named member may have an incomplete array type; this is called a *flexible array member*. In most situations, the flexible array member is ignored.

In particular, the size of the structure is as if the flexible array member were omitted except that it may have more trailing padding than the omission would imply.

The following is an example of a structure that contains a flexible array member:

```
struct flex_array_struct {
  int num;
  int data[];
};
```

This definition means that when computing the size of such a structure, only the first member, num, is considered. Unless the appropriate size of the flexible array member has been explicitly added when allocating storage for an object of the struct, the result of accessing the member data of a variable of nonpointer type struct flex_array_struct is undefined. "DCL38-C. Use the correct syntax when declaring a flexible array member" describes the correct way to declare a struct with a flexible array member.

To avoid the potential for undefined behavior, structures that contain a flexible array member should always be allocated dynamically. Structures with a flexible array member must

- Have dynamic storage duration (be allocated via malloc() or another dynamic allocation function)
- Be dynamically copied using memcpy() or a similar function and not by assignment
- When used as an argument to a function, be passed by pointer and not copied by value

Noncompliant Code Example (Storage Duration)

This noncompliant code example uses automatic storage for a structure containing a flexible array member:

```
#include <stddef.h>

struct flex_array_struct {
  size_t num;
  int data[];
};
```

```
void func(void) {
  struct flex_array_struct flex_struct;
  size_t array_size = 4;

  /* Initialize structure */
  flex_struct.num = array_size;

  for (size_t i = 0; i < array_size; ++i) {
    flex_struct.data[i] = 0;
  }
}
```

Because the memory for `flex_struct` is reserved on the stack, no space is reserved for the `data` member. Accessing the `data` member is undefined behavior.

Compliant Solution (Storage Duration)

This compliant solution dynamically allocates storage for `flex_array_struct`:

```
#include <stdlib.h>

struct flex_array_struct {
  size_t num;
  int data[];
};

void func(void) {
  struct flex_array_struct *flex_struct;
  size_t array_size = 4;

  /* Dynamically allocate memory for the struct */
  flex_struct = (struct flex_array_struct *)malloc(
    sizeof(struct flex_array_struct)
    + sizeof(int) * array_size);
  if (flex_struct == NULL) {
    /* Handle error */
  }

  /* Initialize structure */
  flex_struct->num = array_size;

  for (size_t i = 0; i < array_size; ++i) {
    flex_struct->data[i] = 0;
  }
}
```

Noncompliant Code Example (Copying)

This noncompliant code example attempts to copy an instance of a structure containing a flexible array member (struct flex_array_struct) by assignment:

```
#include <stddef.h>

struct flex_array_struct {
  size_t num;
  int data[];
};

void func(struct flex_array_struct *struct_a,
          struct flex_array_struct *struct_b) {
  *struct_b = *struct_a;
}
```

When the structure is copied, the size of the flexible array member is not considered and only the first member of the structure, num, is copied, leaving the array contents untouched.

Compliant Solution (Copying)

This compliant solution uses memcpy() to properly copy the content of struct_a into struct_b:

```
#include <string.h>

struct flex_array_struct {
  size_t num;
  int data[];
};

void func(struct flex_array_struct *struct_a,
          struct flex_array_struct *struct_b) {
  if (struct_a->num > struct_b->num) {
    /* Insufficient space; handle error */
    return;
  }
  memcpy(struct_b, struct_a,
         sizeof(struct flex_array_struct) + (sizeof(int)
           * struct_a->num));
}
```

Noncompliant Code Example (Function Arguments)

In this noncompliant code example, the flexible array structure is passed by value to a function that prints the array elements:

```
#include <stdio.h>
#include <stdlib.h>

struct flex_array_struct {
  size_t num;
  int data[];
};

void print_array(struct flex_array_struct struct_p) {
  puts("Array is: ");
  for (size_t i = 0; i < struct_p.num; ++i) {
    printf("%d ", struct_p.data[i]);
  }
  putchar('\n');
}

void func(void) {
  struct flex_array_struct *struct_p;
  size_t array_size = 4;

  /* Space is allocated for the struct and initialized */
  struct_p = (struct flex_array_struct *)malloc(
    sizeof(struct flex_array_struct)
    + sizeof(int) * array_size);
  if (struct_p == NULL) {
    /* Handle error */
  }
  struct_p->num = array_size;

  for (size_t i = 0; i < array_size; ++i) {
    struct_p->data[i] = i;
  }
  print_array(*struct_p);
}
```

Because the argument is passed by value, the size of the flexible array member is not considered when the structure is copied, and only the first member of the structure, num, is copied.

Compliant Solution (Function Arguments)

In this compliant solution, the structure is passed by reference and not by value:

```
#include <stdio.h>
#include <stdlib.h>

struct flex_array_struct {
  size_t num;
```

```
    int data[];
};

void print_array(struct flex_array_struct *struct_p) {
  puts("Array is: ");
  for (size_t i = 0; i < struct_p->num; ++i) {
    printf("%d ", struct_p->data[i]);
  }
  putchar('\n');
}

void func(void) {
  struct flex_array_struct *struct_p;
  size_t array_size = 4;

  /* Space is allocated for the struct and initialized... */

  print_array(struct_p);
}
```

Risk Assessment

Failure to use structures with a flexible array member correctly can result in undefined behavior.

Rule	Severity	Likelihood	Remediation Cost	Priority	Level
MEM33-C	Low	Unlikely	Low	P3	L3

Bibliography

[ISO/IEC 9899:2011]	6.7.2.1, "Structure and Union Specifiers"
[ISO/IEC JTC1/SC22/WG14 N791]	Solving the Struct Hack Problem

■ MEM34-C. Only free memory allocated dynamically

The C Standard, Annex J [ISO/IEC 9899:2011], states that the behavior of a program is undefined when

> The pointer argument to the free or realloc function does not match a pointer earlier returned by a memory management function, or the space has been deallocated by a call to free or realloc.

See also undefined behavior 179 in Appendix B.

Freeing memory that is not allocated dynamically can result in heap corruption and other serious errors. Do not call `free()` on a pointer other than one returned by a standard memory allocation function, such as `malloc()`, `calloc()`, `realloc()`, or `aligned_alloc()`.

A similar situation arises when `realloc()` is supplied a pointer to non-dynamically allocated memory. The `realloc()` function is used to resize a block of dynamic memory. If `realloc()` is supplied a pointer to memory not allocated by a standard memory allocation function, the behavior is undefined. One consequence is that the program may terminate abnormally.

This rule does not apply to null pointers. The C Standard guarantees that if `free()` is passed a null pointer, no action occurs.

Noncompliant Code Example

This noncompliant code example sets `c_str` to reference either dynamically allocated memory or a statically allocated string literal depending on the value of `argc`. In either case, `c_str` is passed as an argument to `free()`. If anything other than dynamically allocated memory is referenced by `c_str`, the call to `free(c_str)` is erroneous.

```
#include <stdlib.h>
#include <string.h>
#include <stdio.h>

enum { MAX_ALLOCATION = 1000 };

int main(int argc, const char *argv[]) {
  char *c_str = NULL;
  size_t len;

  if (argc == 2) {
    len = strlen(argv[1]) + 1;
    if (len > MAX_ALLOCATION) {
      /* Handle error */
    }
    c_str = (char *)malloc(len);
    if (c_str == NULL) {
      /* Handle error */
    }
    strcpy(c_str, argv[1]);
  } else {
    c_str = "usage: $>a.exe [string]";
    printf("%s\n", c_str);
  }
```

```
    free(c_str);
    return 0;
}
```

Compliant Solution

This compliant solution eliminates the possibility of `c_str` referencing memory that is not allocated dynamically when passed to `free()`:

```c
#include <stdlib.h>
#include <string.h>
#include <stdio.h>

enum { MAX_ALLOCATION = 1000 };

int main(int argc, const char *argv[]) {
  char *c_str = NULL;
  size_t len;

  if (argc == 2) {
    len = strlen(argv[1]) + 1;
    if (len > MAX_ALLOCATION) {
      /* Handle error */
    }
    c_str = (char *)malloc(len);
    if (c_str == NULL) {
      /* Handle error */
    }
    strcpy(c_str, argv[1]);
  } else {
    printf("%s\n", "usage: $>a.exe [string]");
    return EXIT_FAILURE;
  }
  free(c_str);
  return 0;
}
```

Noncompliant Code Example (`realloc()`)

In this noncompliant example, the pointer parameter to `realloc()`, buf, does not refer to dynamically allocated memory:

```c
#include <stdlib.h>

enum { BUFSIZE = 256 };

void f(void) {
  char buf[BUFSIZE];
```

```
      char *p = (char *)realloc(buf, 2 * BUFSIZE);
      if (p == NULL) {
        /* Handle error */
      }
    }
```

Compliant Solution (realloc())

In this compliant solution, buf refers to dynamically allocated memory:

```
#include <stdlib.h>

enum { BUFSIZE = 256 };

void f(void) {
  char *buf = (char *)malloc(BUFSIZE * sizeof(char));
  char *p = (char *)realloc(buf, 2 * BUFSIZE);
  if (p == NULL) {
    /* Handle error */
  }
}
```

Note that realloc() will behave properly even if malloc() failed, because when given a null pointer, realloc() behaves like a call to malloc().

Risk Assessment

The consequences of this error depend on the implementation, but they range from nothing to arbitrary code execution if that memory is reused by malloc().

Rule	Severity	Likelihood	Remediation Cost	Priority	Level
MEM34-C	High	Likely	Medium	P18	L1

Related Guidelines

ISO/IEC TS 17961:2013	Reallocating or freeing memory that was not dynamically allocated [xfree]
MITRE CWE	CWE-590, Free of Memory Not on the Heap

Bibliography

[ISO/IEC 9899:2011]	J.2, "Undefined Behavior"
[Seacord 2013b]	Chapter 4, "Dynamic Memory Management"

■ MEM35-C. Allocate sufficient memory for an object

The types of integer expressions used as size arguments to malloc(), calloc(), realloc(), or aligned_alloc() must have sufficient range to represent the size of the objects to be stored. If size arguments are incorrect or can be manipulated by an attacker, then a buffer overflow may occur. Incorrect size arguments, inadequate range checking, integer overflow, or truncation can result in the allocation of an inadequately sized buffer.

Typically, the amount of memory to allocate will be the size of the type of object to allocate. When allocating space for an array, the size of the object will be multiplied by the bounds of the array. When allocating space for a structure containing a flexible array member, the size of the array member must be added to the size of the structure (see "MEM33-C. Allocate and copy structures containing a flexible array member dynamically"). Use the correct type of the object when computing the size of memory to allocate.

"STR31-C. Guarantee that storage for strings has sufficient space for character data and the null terminator" is a specific instance of this rule.

Noncompliant Code Example (Integer)

In this noncompliant code example, an array of long is allocated and assigned to p. The code checks for unsigned integer overflow in compliance with "INT32-C. Ensure that operations on signed integers do not result in overflow" and also ensures that len is not equal to zero (see "MEM04-C. Beware of zero-length allocations"). However, because sizeof(int) is used to compute the size and not sizeof(long), an insufficient amount of memory can be allocated on implementations where sizeof(long) is larger than sizeof(int).

```
#include <stdint.h>
#include <stdlib.h>

void function(size_t len) {
  long *p;
  if (len == 0 || len > SIZE_MAX / sizeof(long)) {
    /* Handle overflow */
  }
  p = (long *)malloc(len * sizeof(int));
  if (p == NULL) {
    /* Handle error */
  }
  free(p);
}
```

Compliant Solution (Integer)

This compliant solution uses sizeof(long) to correctly size the memory allocation:

```
#include <stdint.h>
#include <stdlib.h>

void function(size_t len) {
  long *p;
  if (len == 0 || len > SIZE_MAX / sizeof(long)) {
    /* Handle overflow */
  }
  p = (long *)malloc(len * sizeof(long));
  if (p == NULL) {
    /* Handle error */
  }
  free(p);
}
```

Compliant Solution (Integer)

Alternatively, sizeof(*p) can be used to properly size the allocation:

```
#include <stdint.h>
#include <stdlib.h>

void function(size_t len) {
  long *p;
  if (len == 0 || len > SIZE_MAX / sizeof(*p)) {
    /* Handle overflow */
  }
  p = (long *)malloc(len * sizeof(*p));
  if (p == NULL) {
    /* Handle error */
  }
  free(p);
}
```

Noncompliant Code Example (Pointer)

In this noncompliant code example, inadequate space is allocated for a struct tm object because the size of the pointer is being used to determine the size of the pointed-to object:

```
#include <stdlib.h>
#include <time.h>
```

```
struct tm *make_tm(int year, int mon, int day, int hour,
                   int min, int sec) {
  struct tm *tmb;
  tmb = (struct tm *)malloc(sizeof(tmb));
  if (tmb == NULL) {
    return NULL;
  }
  *tmb = (struct tm) {
    .tm_sec = sec, .tm_min = min, .tm_hour = hour,
    .tm_mday = day, .tm_mon = mon, .tm_year = year
  };
  return tmb;
}
```

Compliant Solution (Pointer)

In this compliant solution, the correct amount of memory is allocated for the struct tm object. When allocating space for a single object, passing the dereferenced pointer type to the sizeof operator is a simple way to allocate sufficient memory. Because the sizeof operator does not evaluate its operand, dereferencing an uninitialized or null pointer in this context is well-defined behavior.

```
#include <stdlib.h>
#include <time.h>

struct tm *make_tm(int year, int mon, int day, int hour,
                   int min, int sec) {
  struct tm *tmb;
  tmb = (struct tm *)malloc(sizeof(*tmb));
  if (tmb == NULL) {
    return NULL;
  }
  *tmb = (struct tm) {
    .tm_sec = sec, .tm_min = min, .tm_hour = hour,
    .tm_mday = day, .tm_mon = mon, .tm_year = year
  };
  return tmb;
}
```

Risk Assessment

Providing invalid size arguments to memory allocation functions can lead to buffer overflows and the execution of arbitrary code with the permissions of the vulnerable process.

Rule	Severity	Likelihood	Remediation Cost	Priority	Level
MEM35-C	High	Probable	High	P6	L2

Related Guidelines

ISO/IEC TR 24772:2013	Buffer Boundary Violation (Buffer Overflow) [HCB]
ISO/IEC TS 17961:2013	Taking the size of a pointer to determine the size of the pointed-to type [sizeofptr]
MITRE CWE	CWE-131, Incorrect Calculation of Buffer Size CWE-190, Integer Overflow or Wraparound CWE-467, Use of sizeof() on a Pointer Type

Bibliography

[Coverity 2007]	
[Drepper 2006]	Section 2.1.1, "Respecting Memory Bounds"
[Seacord 2013b]	Chapter 4, "Dynamic Memory Management" Chapter 5, "Integer Security"
[Viega 2005]	Section 5.6.8, "Use of sizeof() on a Pointer Type"
[xorl 2009]	CVE-2009-0587: Evolution Data Server Base64 Integer Overflows

■ MEM36-C. Do not modify the alignment of objects by calling realloc()

Do not invoke realloc() to modify the size of allocated objects that have stricter alignment requirements than those guaranteed by malloc(). Storage allocated by a call to the standard aligned_alloc() function, for example, can have stricter than normal alignment requirements. The C Standard requires only that a pointer returned by realloc() be suitably aligned so that it may be assigned to a pointer to any type of object with a fundamental alignment requirement.

Noncompliant Code Example

This noncompliant code example returns a pointer to allocated memory that has been aligned to a 4096-byte boundary. If the `resize` argument to the `realloc()` function is larger than the object referenced by `ptr`, then `realloc()` will allocate new memory that is suitably aligned so that it may be assigned to a pointer to any type of object with a fundamental alignment requirement but may not preserve the stricter alignment of the original object.

```
#include <stdlib.h>

void func(void) {
  size_t resize = 1024;
  size_t alignment = 1 << 12;
  int *ptr;
  int *ptr1;

  if (NULL == (ptr = (int *)aligned_alloc(alignment, sizeof(int)))) {
    /* Handle error */
  }

  if (NULL == (ptr1 = (int *)realloc(ptr, resize))) {
    /* Handle error */
  }
}
```

Compliant Solution

This compliant solution allocates `resize` bytes of new memory with the same alignment as the old memory, copies the original memory content, and then frees the old memory. This solution has **implementation-defined behavior** because it depends on whether extended alignments in excess of `_Alignof (max_align_t)` are supported and the contexts in which they are supported. If not supported, the behavior of this compliant solution is undefined.

```
#include <stdlib.h>
#include <string.h>

void func(void) {
  size_t resize = 1024;
  size_t alignment = 1 << 12;
  int *ptr;
  int *ptr1;
```

```
    if (NULL == (ptr = (int *)aligned_alloc(alignment,
                                         sizeof(int)))) {
      /* Handle error */
    }

    if (NULL == (ptr1 = (int *)aligned_alloc(alignment,
                                           resize))) {
      /* Handle error */
    }

    if (NULL == (memcpy(ptr1, ptr, sizeof(int)))) {
      /* Handle error */
    }

    free(ptr);
}
```

Compliant Solution (Windows)

Windows defines the _aligned_malloc() function to allocate memory on a specified alignment boundary. The _aligned_realloc() function [MSDN] can be used to change the size of this memory. This compliant solution demonstrates one such usage:

```
#include <malloc.h>

void func(void) {
  size_t alignment = 1 << 12;
  int *ptr;
  int *ptr1;

  /* Original allocation */
  if (NULL == (ptr = (int *)_aligned_malloc(sizeof(int),
                                        alignment))) {
    /* Handle error */
  }

  /* Reallocation */
  if (NULL == (ptr1 = (int *)_aligned_realloc(ptr, 1024,
                                          alignment))) {
    _aligned_free(ptr);
    /* Handle error */
  }

  _aligned_free(ptr1);
}
```

Note that the size and alignment arguments for _aligned_malloc() are provided in reverse order of the C Standard aligned_alloc() function.

Risk Assessment

Improper alignment can lead to arbitrary memory locations being accessed and written to.

Recommendation	Severity	Likelihood	Remediation Cost	Priority	Level
MEM36-C	Low	Probable	High	P2	L3

Bibliography

[ISO/IEC 9899:2011]	7.22.3.1, "The aligned_alloc Function"
[MSDN]	_aligned_malloc()

Chapter 9

Input/Output (FIO)

Chapter Contents

continues

Rule	Page
FIO46-C. Do not access a closed file	298
FIO47-C. Use valid format strings	299

Risk Assessment Summary

Rule	Severity	Likelihood	Remediation Cost	Priority	Level
FIO30-C	High	Likely	Medium	P18	L1
FIO31-C	Medium	Probable	High	P4	L3
FIO32-C	Medium	Unlikely	Medium	P4	L3
FIO34-C	High	Probable	Medium	P12	L1
FIO37-C	High	Probable	Medium	P12	L1
FIO38-C	Low	Probable	Medium	P4	L3
FIO39-C	Low	Likely	Medium	P6	L2
FIO40-C	Low	Probable	Medium	P4	L3
FIO41-C	Low	Unlikely	Medium	P2	L3
FIO42-C	Medium	Unlikely	Medium	P4	L3
FIO44-C	Medium	Unlikely	Medium	P4	L3
FIO45-C	High	Probable	High	P6	L2
FIO46-C	Medium	Unlikely	Medium	P4	L3
FIO47-C	High	Unlikely	Medium	P6	L2

■ FIO30-C. Exclude user input from format strings

Never call a formatted I/O function with a format string containing a tainted value. An attacker who can fully or partially control the contents of a format string can crash a vulnerable process, view the contents of the stack, view memory content, or write to an arbitrary memory location. Consequently, the attacker can execute arbitrary code with the permissions of the vulnerable process [Seacord 2013b]. Formatted output functions are particularly dangerous because many programmers are unaware of their capabilities. For example, formatted output functions can be used to write an integer value to a specified address using the %n conversion specifier.

Noncompliant Code Example

The incorrect_password() function in this noncompliant code example is called during identification and authentication to display an error message if the specified user is not found or the password is incorrect. The function accepts the name of the user as a string referenced by user. This is an exemplar of untrusted data that originates from an unauthenticated user. The function constructs an error message that is then output to stderr using the C Standard fprintf() function.

```c
#include <stdio.h>
#include <stdlib.h>
#include <string.h>

void incorrect_password(const char *user) {
  int ret;
  /* User names are restricted to 256 or fewer characters */
  static const char msg_format[] = "%s cannot be authenticated.\n";
  size_t len = strlen(user) + sizeof(msg_format);
  char *msg = (char *)malloc(len);
  if (msg == NULL) {
    /* Handle error */
  }
  ret = snprintf(msg, len, msg_format, user);
  if (ret < 0) {
    /* Handle error */
  } else if (ret >= len) {
    /* Handle truncated output */
  }
  fprintf(stderr, msg);
  free(msg);
}
```

The incorrect_password() function calculates the size of the message, allocates dynamic storage, and then constructs the message in the allocated memory using the snprintf() function. The addition operations are not checked for integer overflow because the string referenced by user is known to have a length of 256 or less. Because the %s characters are replaced by the string referenced by user in the call to snprintf(), the resulting string needs 1 byte less than is allocated. The snprintf() function is commonly used for messages that are displayed in multiple locations or messages that are difficult to build. However, the resulting code contains a format-string vulnerability because the `msg` includes untrusted user input and is passed as the format-string argument in the call to `fprintf()`.

Compliant Solution (fputs())

This compliant solution fixes the problem by replacing the `fprintf()` call with a call to `fputs()`, which outputs `msg` directly to `stderr` without evaluating its contents:

```c
#include <stdio.h>
#include <stdlib.h>
#include <string.h>

void incorrect_password(const char *user) {
  int ret;
  /* User names are restricted to 256 or fewer characters */
  static const char msg_format[] = "%s cannot be authenticated.\n";
  size_t len = strlen(user) + sizeof(msg_format);
  char *msg = (char *)malloc(len);
  if (msg == NULL) {
    /* Handle error */
  }
  ret = snprintf(msg, len, msg_format, user);
  if (ret < 0) {
    /* Handle error */
  } else if (ret >= len) {
    /* Handle truncated output */
  }
  fputs(msg, stderr);
  free(msg);
}
```

Compliant Solution (fprintf())

This compliant solution passes the untrusted user input as one of the variadic arguments to `fprintf()` and not as part of the format string, eliminating the possibility of a format-string vulnerability:

```c
#include <stdio.h>

void incorrect_password(const char *user) {
  static const char msg_format[] = "%s cannot be authenticated.\n";
  fprintf(stderr, msg_format, user);
}
```

Noncompliant Code Example (POSIX)

This noncompliant code example is similar to the first noncompliant code example but uses the POSIX function `syslog()` [IEEE Std 1003.1-2013] instead of the `fprintf()` function. The `syslog()` function is also susceptible to format-string vulnerabilities.

```c
#include <stdio.h>
#include <stdlib.h>
#include <string.h>
#include <syslog.h>

void incorrect_password(const char *user) {
  int ret;
  /* User names are restricted to 256 or fewer characters */
  static const char msg_format[] = "%s cannot be authenticated.\n";
  size_t len = strlen(user) + sizeof(msg_format);
  char *msg = (char *)malloc(len);
  if (msg != NULL) {
    /* Handle error */
  }
  ret = snprintf(msg, len, msg_format, user);
  if (ret < 0) {
    /* Handle error */
  } else if (ret >= len) {
    /* Handle truncated output */
  }
  syslog(LOG_INFO, msg);
  free(msg);
}
```

The `syslog()` function first appeared in BSD 4.2 and is supported by Linux and other modern UNIX implementations. It is not available on Windows systems.

Compliant Solution (POSIX)

This compliant solution passes the untrusted user input as one of the variadic arguments to `syslog()` instead of including it in the format string:

```c
#include <syslog.h>

void incorrect_password(const char *user) {
  static const char msg_format[] = "%s cannot be authenticated.\n";
  syslog(LOG_INFO, msg_format, user);
}
```

Risk Assessment

Failing to exclude user input from format specifiers may allow an attacker to crash a vulnerable process, view the contents of the stack, view memory content, or write to an arbitrary memory location and consequently execute arbitrary code with the permissions of the vulnerable process.

Rule	Severity	Likelihood	Remediation Cost	Priority	Level
FIO30-C	High	Likely	Medium	P18	L1

Two examples of format-string vulnerabilities resulting from a violation of this rule include Ettercap and Samba.

In Ettercap v.NG-0.7.2, the `ncurses` user interface suffers from a format-string defect. The `curses_msg()` function in ec_curses.c invokes wdg_scroll_print(), which takes a format string and its parameters and passes it to vw_printw(). The curses_msg() function uses one of its parameters as the format string. This input can include user data, allowing for a format-string vulnerability.

The Samba AFS ACL mapping VFS plug-in fails to properly **sanitize** user-controlled file names that are used in a format specifier supplied to snprintf(). This security flaw becomes exploitable when a user can write to a share that uses Samba's afsacl.so library for setting Windows NT access control lists on files residing on an AFS file system.

Related Guidelines

ISO/IEC TR 24772:2013	Injection [RST]
ISO/IEC TS 17961:2013	Including tainted or out-of-domain input in a format string [usrfmt]
MITRE CWE	CWE-134, Uncontrolled Format String

Bibliography

[IEEE Std 1003.1-2013]	XSH, System Interfaces, syslog
[Seacord 2013b]	Chapter 6, "Formatted Output"
[Viega 2005]	Section 5.2.23, "Format String Problem"

■ FIO31-C. Do not open a file that is already open

Opening a file that is already open has implementation-defined behavior, according to the C Standard, 7.21.3, paragraph 8 [ISO/IEC 9899:2011]:

> Functions that open additional (nontemporary) files require a file name, which is a string. The rules for composing valid file names are implementation-defined. Whether the same file can be simultaneously open multiple times is also implementation-defined.

Some implementations do not allow multiple copies of the same file to be open at the same time. Consequently, portable code cannot depend on what will happen if this rule is violated. Even on implementations that do not outright fail to open an already-opened file, a **TOCTOU** (time-of-check, time-of-use) race condition exists in which the second open could operate on a different file from the first due to the file being moved or deleted (see "FIO45-C. Avoid TOCTOU race conditions while accessing files" for more details on TOCTOU race conditions).

Noncompliant Code Example

This noncompliant code example logs the program's state at runtime:

```c
#include <stdio.h>

void do_stuff(void) {
  FILE *logfile = fopen("log", "a");
  if (logfile == NULL) {
    /* Handle error */
  }

  /* Write logs pertaining to do_stuff() */
  fprintf(logfile, "do_stuff\n");
}

int main(void) {
  FILE *logfile = fopen("log", "a");
  if (logfile == NULL) {
    /* Handle error */
  }

  /* Write logs pertaining to main() */
  fprintf(logfile, "main\n");
```

```
  do_stuff();

  if (fclose(logfile) == EOF) {
    /* Handle error */
  }
  return 0;
}
```

Because the file `log` is opened twice (once in `main()` and again in `do_stuff()`), this program has implementation-defined behavior.

Compliant Solution

In this compliant solution, a reference to the file pointer is passed as an argument to functions that need to perform operations on that file. This reference eliminates the need to open the same file multiple times.

```
#include <stdio.h>

void do_stuff(FILE *logfile) {
  /* Write logs pertaining to do_stuff() */
  fprintf(logfile, "do_stuff\n");
}

int main(void) {
  FILE *logfile = fopen("log", "a");
  if (logfile == NULL) {
    /* Handle error */
  }

  /* Write logs pertaining to main() */
  fprintf(logfile, "main\n");

  do_stuff(logfile);

  if (fclose(logfile) == EOF) {
    /* Handle error */
  }
  return 0;
}
```

Risk Assessment

Simultaneously opening a file multiple times can result in unexpected errors and nonportable behavior.

Rule	Severity	Likelihood	Remediation Cost	Priority	Level
FIO31-C	Medium	Probable	High	P4	L3

Related Guidelines

MITRE CWE	CWE-362, Concurrent Execution using Shared Resource with Improper Synchronization ("Race Condition") CWE-675, Duplicate Operations on Resource

Bibliography

[ISO/IEC 9899:2011]	Subclause 7.21.3, "Files"

■ FIO32-C. Do not perform operations on devices that are only appropriate for files

File names on many operating systems, including Windows and UNIX, may be used to access *special files*, which are actually devices. Reserved Microsoft Windows device names include AUX, CON, PRN, COM1, and LPT1 or paths using the \\.\ device namespace. Device files on UNIX systems are used to apply access rights and to direct operations on the files to the appropriate device drivers.

Performing operations on device files that are intended for ordinary character or binary files can result in crashes and denial-of-service attacks. For example, when Windows attempts to interpret the device name as a file resource, it performs an invalid resource access that usually results in a crash [Howard 2002].

Device files in UNIX can be a security risk when an attacker can access them in an unauthorized way. For example, if attackers can read or write to the /dev/kmem device, they may be able to alter the priority, UID, or other attributes of their process or simply crash the system. Similarly, access to disk devices, tape devices, network devices, and terminals being used by other processes can lead to problems [Garfinkel 1996].

On Linux, it is possible to lock certain applications by attempting to open devices rather than files. Consider the following example:

```
/dev/mouse
/dev/console
/dev/tty0
/dev/zero
```

A Web browser that failed to check for these devices would allow an attacker to create a Web site with image tags such as <IMG src="file:///dev/mouse"> that would lock the user's mouse.

Noncompliant Code Example

In this noncompliant code example, the user can specify a locked device or a FIFO (first-in, first-out) file name, which can cause the program to hang on the call to fopen():

```c
#include <stdio.h>

void func(const char *file_name) {
  FILE *file;
  if ((file = fopen(file_name, "wb")) == NULL) {
    /* Handle error */
  }

  /* Operate on the file */

  if (fclose(file) == EOF) {
    /* Handle error */
  }
}
```

Compliant Solution (POSIX)

POSIX defines the O_NONBLOCK flag to open(), which ensures that delayed operations on a file do not hang the program [IEEE Std 1003.1-2013].

When opening a FIFO with O_RDONLY or O_WRONLY set:

- If O_NONBLOCK is set, an open() for reading-only returns without delay. An open() for writing-only returns an error if no process currently has the file open for reading.

- If O_NONBLOCK is clear, an open() for reading-only blocks the calling thread until a thread opens the file for writing. An open() for writing-only blocks the calling thread until a thread opens the file for reading.

When opening a block special or character special file that supports nonblocking opens:

- If O_NONBLOCK is set, the open() function returns without blocking for the device to be ready or available; subsequent behavior is device-specific.

- If O_NONBLOCK is clear, the open() function blocks the calling thread until the device is ready or available before returning.

Otherwise, the behavior of O_NONBLOCK is unspecified.

Once the file is open, programmers can use the POSIX lstat() and fstat() functions to obtain information about a file and the S_ISREG() macro to determine if the file is a regular file.

Because the behavior of O_NONBLOCK on subsequent calls to read() or write() is unspecified, it is advisable to disable the flag after it has been determined that the file in question is not a special device.

When available (Linux 2.1.126+, FreeBSD, Solaris 10, POSIX.1-2008), the O_NOFOLLOW flag should also be used (see "POS01-C. Check for the existence of links when dealing with files"). When O_NOFOLLOW is not available, symbolic link checks should use the method from "POS35-C. Avoid race conditions while checking for the existence of a symbolic link."

```
#include <sys/types.h>
#include <sys/stat.h>
#include <fcntl.h>
#include <unistd.h>

#ifdef O_NOFOLLOW
  #define OPEN_FLAGS O_NOFOLLOW | O_NONBLOCK
#else
  #define OPEN_FLAGS O_NONBLOCK
#endif

void func(const char *file_name) {
  struct stat orig_st;
  struct stat open_st;
  int fd;
  int flags;

  if ((lstat(file_name, &orig_st) != 0) ||
      (!S_ISREG(orig_st.st_mode))) {
    /* Handle error */
  }
```

```
/* Race window */

fd = open(file_name, OPEN_FLAGS | O_WRONLY);
if (fd == -1) {
  /* Handle error */
}

if (fstat(fd, &open_st) != 0) {
  /* Handle error */
}

if ((orig_st.st_mode != open_st.st_mode) ||
    (orig_st.st_ino  != open_st.st_ino) ||
    (orig_st.st_dev  != open_st.st_dev)) {
  /* The file was tampered with */
}

/*
 * Optional: drop the O_NONBLOCK now that we are sure
 * this is a good file.
 */
if ((flags = fcntl(fd, F_GETFL)) == -1) {
  /* Handle error */
}

if (fcntl(fd, F_SETFL, flags & ~O_NONBLOCK) == -1) {
  /* Handle error */
}

/* Operate on the file */

if (close(fd) == -1) {
  /* Handle error */
}
}
```

This code contains an intractable TOCTOU (time-of-check, time-of-use) race condition under which an attacker can alter the file referenced by file_name following the call to lstat() but before the call to open(). The switch will be discovered after the file is opened, but opening the file cannot be prevented in the case where this action itself causes undesired behavior (see "FIO45-C. Avoid TOCTOU race conditions while accessing files" for more information about TOCTOU race conditions).

Essentially, an attacker can switch out a file for one of the file types shown in Table 9–1 with the specified effect.

Table 9–1. File Types and Effects

Type	Note on Effect
Another regular file	The fstat() verification fails.
FIFO	Either open() returns -1 and sets errno to ENXIO, or open() succeeds and the fstat() verification fails.
Symbolic link	open() returns -1 if O_NOFOLLOW is available; otherwise, the fstat() verification fails.
Special device	Usually the fstat() verification fails on st_mode. This can still be a problem if the device is one for which just opening (or closing) it causes a side effect. If st_mode compares equal, then the device is one that, after opening, appears to be a regular file. It would then fail the fstat() verification on st_dev and st_ino (unless it happens to be the *same* file, as can happen with /dev/fd/* on Solaris, but this would not be a problem).

To be compliant with this rule and to prevent this TOCTOU race condition, file_name must refer to a file in a secure directory (see "FIO15-C. Ensure that file operations are performed in a secure directory").

Noncompliant Code Example (Windows)

This noncompliant code example uses the GetFileType() function to attempt to prevent opening a special file:

```
#include <Windows.h>

void func(const TCHAR *file_name) {
  HANDLE hFile = CreateFile(
    file_name,
    GENERIC_READ | GENERIC_WRITE, 0,
    NULL, OPEN_EXISTING,
    FILE_ATTRIBUTE_NORMAL, NULL
  );
  if (hFile == INVALID_HANDLE_VALUE) {
    /* Handle error */
  } else if (GetFileType(hFile) != FILE_TYPE_DISK) {
    /* Handle error */
    CloseHandle(hFile);
```

```
  } else {
    /* Operate on the file */
    CloseHandle(hFile);
  }
}
```

Although tempting, the Win32 `GetFileType()` function is dangerous in this case. If the file name given identifies a named pipe that is currently blocking on a read request, the call to `GetFileType()` will block until the read request completes. This provides an effective attack vector for a denial-of-service attack on the application. Furthermore, the act of opening a file handle may cause side effects, such as line states being set to their default voltage when opening a serial device.

Compliant Solution (Windows)

Microsoft documents a list of reserved identifiers that represent devices and have a device namespace to be used specifically by devices [MSDN]. In this compliant solution, `isReservedName()` function can be used to determine if a specified path refers to a device. Care must be taken to avoid a TOCTOU race condition when first testing a pathname using the `isReservedName()` function and then later operating on that pathname.

```
#include <ctype.h>
#include <stdbool.h>
#include <stdlib.h>
#include <string.h>
#include <stdio.h>

static bool isReservedName(const char *path) {
  /* This list of reserved names comes from MSDN */
  static const char *reserved[] = {
    "nul", "con", "prn", "aux", "com1", "com2", "com3",
    "com4", "com5", "com6", "com7", "com8", "com9",
    "lpt1", "lpt2", "lpt3", "lpt4", "lpt5", "lpt6",
    "lpt7", "lpt8", "lpt9"
  };
  bool ret = false;

  /*
   * First, check to see if this is a device namespace, which
   * always starts with \\.\, because device namespaces are not
   * valid file paths.
   */
```

```
if (!path || 0 == strncmp(path, "\\\\.\\", 4)) {
  return true;
}

/* Compare against the list of ancient reserved names */
for (size_t i = 0; !ret &&
     i < sizeof(reserved) / sizeof(*reserved); ++i) {
 /*
  * Because Windows uses a case-insensitive file system, operate on
  * a lowercase version of the given filename. Note: This ignores
  * globalization issues and assumes ASCII characters.
  */
  if (0 == _stricmp(path, reserved[i])) {
    ret = true;
  }
}
return ret;
}
```

Risk Assessment

Allowing operations that are appropriate only for regular files to be performed on devices can result in denial-of-service attacks or more serious exploits depending on the platform.

Rule	Severity	Likelihood	Remediation Cost	Priority	Level
FIO32-C	Medium	Unlikely	Medium	P4	L3

Related Guidelines

MITRE CWE	CWE-67, Improper Handling of Windows Device Names

Bibliography

[Garfinkel 1996]	Section 5.6, "Device Files"
[Howard 2002]	Chapter 11, "Canonical Representation Issues"
[IEEE Std 1003.1-2013]	XSH, System Interfaces, open
[MSDN]	

■ FIO34-C. Distinguish between characters read from a file and EOF or WEOF

The EOF macro represents a negative value that is used to indicate that the file is exhausted and no data remains when reading data from a file. EOF is an example of an in-band error indicator. In-band error indicators are problematic to work with, and the creation of new in-band-error indicators is discouraged by "ERR02-C. Avoid in-band error indicators."

The byte I/O functions fgetc(), getc(), and getchar() all read a character from a stream and return it as an unsigned char that has been converted to an int (see "STR00-C. Represent characters using an appropriate type" for more information on character types). If the stream is at the end of the file, the end-of-file indicator for the stream is set and the function returns EOF. If a read error occurs, the error indicator for the stream is set and the function returns EOF. If these functions succeed, they cast the character returned into an unsigned char. Because EOF is negative, it should not match any unsigned character value. However, this is true only for implementations where the int type is wider than char. On an implementation where int and char have the same width, a character-reading function can read and return a valid character that has the same bit-pattern as EOF. This could occur, for example, if an attacker inserted a value that looked like EOF into the file or data stream to alter the behavior of the program. The C Standard requires only that the int type be able to represent a maximum value of +32767 and that a char type be no larger than an int. Although uncommon, this situation can result in the integer constant expression EOF being indistinguishable from a valid character; that is, (int)(unsigned char)65535 == –1. Consequently, failing to use feof() and ferror() to detect end-of-file and file errors can result in incorrectly identifying the EOF character on rare implementations where sizeof(int) == sizeof(char).

This problem is much more common when reading wide characters. The fgetwc(), getwc(), and getwchar() functions return a value of type wint_t. This value can represent the next wide character read, or it can represent WEOF, which indicates end-of-file for wide character streams. On most implementations, the wchar_t type has the same width as wint_t, and so these functions can return a character indistinguishable from WEOF.

The C Standard feof() and ferror() functions are not subject to the problems associated with character and integer sizes and should be used to verify end-of-file and file errors for susceptible implementations [Kettlewell 2002].

Calling both functions on each iteration of a loop adds significant overhead, so a good strategy is to temporarily trust EOF and WEOF within the loop but verify them with feof() and ferror() following the loop.

Noncompliant Code Example

This noncompliant code example loops while the character c is not EOF:

```c
#include <stdio.h>

void func(void) {
  int c;

  do {
    c = getchar();
  } while (c != EOF);
}
```

Although EOF is guaranteed to be negative and distinct from the value of any unsigned character, it is not guaranteed to be different from any such value when converted to an int. Consequently, when int has the same width as char, this loop may terminate prematurely.

Compliant Solution

This compliant solution uses feof() to test for end-of-file and ferror() to test for errors:

```c
#include <stdio.h>

void func(void) {
  int c;

  do {
    c = getchar();
  } while (c != EOF);
  if (feof(stdin)) {
    /* Handle end of file */
  } else if (ferror(stdin)) {
    /* Handle file error */
  } else {
    /* Received a character that resembles EOF; handle error */
  }
}
```

Noncompliant Code Example (Nonportable)

This noncompliant code example uses an assertion to ensure that the code is executed only on architectures where int is wider than char and EOF is guaranteed not to be a valid character value. However, this code example is noncompliant because the variable c is declared as a char rather than an int, making it possible for a valid character value to compare equal to the value of the EOF macro when char is signed because of sign extension:

```
#include <assert.h>
#include <limits.h>
#include <stdio.h>

void func(void) {
  char c;
  static_assert(UCHAR_MAX < UINT_MAX, "FIO34-C violation");

  do {
    c = getchar();
  } while (c != EOF);
}
```

Assuming that a char is a signed 8-bit type and an int is a 32-bit type, if getchar() returns the character value '\xff' (decimal 255), it will be interpreted as EOF because this value is sign-extended to 0xFFFFFFFF (the value of EOF) to perform the comparison (see "STR34-C. Cast characters to unsigned char before converting to larger integer sizes").

Compliant Solution (Nonportable)

This compliant solution declares c to be an int. Consequently, the loop will terminate only when the file is exhausted.

```
#include <assert.h>
#include <stdio.h>
#include <limits.h>

void func(void) {
  int c;
  static_assert(UCHAR_MAX < UINT_MAX, "FIO34-C violation");

  do {
    c = getchar();
  } while (c != EOF);
}
```

Noncompliant Code Example (Wide Characters)

In this noncompliant example, the result of the call to the C standard library function getwc() is stored into a variable of type wchar_t and is subsequently compared with WEOF:

```
#include <stddef.h>
#include <stdio.h>
#include <wchar.h>

enum { BUFFER_SIZE = 32 };

void g(void) {
  wchar_t buf[BUFFER_SIZE];
  wchar_t wc;
  size_t i = 0;

  while ((wc = getwc(stdin)) != L'\n' && wc != WEOF) {
    if (i < (BUFFER_SIZE - 1)) {
      buf[i++] = wc;
    }
  }

  buf[i] = L'\0';
}
```

This code suffers from two problems. First, the value returned by getwc() is immediately converted to wchar_t before being compared with WEOF. Second, there is no check to ensure that wint_t is wider than wchar_t. Both of these problems make it possible for an attacker to terminate the loop prematurely by supplying the wide-character value matching WEOF in the file.

Compliant Solution

This compliant solution declares c to be a wint_t to match the integer type returned by getwc(). Furthermore, it does not rely on WEOF to determine end-of-file definitively.

```
#include <stddef.h>
#include <stdio.h>
#include <wchar.h>

enum { BUFFER_SIZE = 32 };

void g(void) {
  wchar_t buf[BUFFER_SIZE];
```

```
    wint_t wc;
    size_t i = 0;

    while ((wc = getwc(stdin)) != L'\n' && wc != WEOF) {
      if (i < BUFFER_SIZE - 1) {
        buf[i++] = wc;
      }
    }

    if (feof(stdin) || ferror(stdin)) {
     buf[i] = L'\0';
    } else {
      /* Received a wide character that resembles WEOF; handle error */
    }
}
```

Exceptions

FIO34-EX1: A number of C functions do not return characters but can return EOF as a status code. These functions include fclose(), fflush(), fputs(), fscanf(), puts(), scanf(), sscanf(), vfscanf(), and vscanf(). These return values can be compared to EOF without validating the result.

Risk Assessment

Incorrectly assuming characters from a file cannot match EOF or WEOF has resulted in significant vulnerabilities, including command injection attacks (see the *CA-1996-22 advisory).

Rule	Severity	Likelihood	Remediation Cost	Priority	Level
FIO34-C	High	Probable	Medium	P12	L1

Related Guidelines

ISO/IEC TS 17961:2013	Using character values that are indistinguishable from EOF [chreof]

Bibliography

[Kettlewell 2002]	Section 1.2, "<stdio.h> and Character Types"
[NIST 2006]	SAMATE Reference Dataset Test Case ID 000-000-088
[Summit 2005]	Question 12.2

■ FIO37-C. Do not assume that `fgets()` or `fgetws()` returns a nonempty string when successful

Errors can occur when incorrect assumptions are made about the type of data being read. These assumptions may be violated, for example, when binary data has been read from a file instead of text from a user's terminal or the output of a process is piped to `stdin` (see "FIO14-C. Understand the difference between text mode and binary mode with file streams"). On some systems, it may also be possible to input a null byte (as well as other binary codes) from the keyboard.

Subclause 7.21.7.2 of the C Standard [ISO/IEC 9899:2011] says,

> The `fgets` function returns `s` if successful. If end-of-file is encountered and no characters have been read into the array, the contents of the array remain unchanged and a null pointer is returned.

The wide-character function `fgetws()` has the same behavior. Therefore, if `fgets()` or `fgetws()` returns a non-null pointer, it is safe to assume that the array contains data. However, it is erroneous to assume that the array contains a nonempty string because the data may contain null characters.

Noncompliant Code Example

This noncompliant code example attempts to remove the trailing new-line (`\n`) from an input line. The `fgets()` function is typically used to read a new-line-terminated line of input from a stream. It takes a size parameter for the destination buffer and copies, at most, `size - 1` characters from a stream to a character array.

```
#include <stdio.h>
#include <string.h>

enum { BUFFER_SIZE = 1024 };

void func(void) {
  char buf[BUFFER_SIZE];

  if (fgets(buf, sizeof(buf), stdin) == NULL) {
    /* Handle error */
  }
  buf[strlen(buf) - 1] = '\0';
}
```

The `strlen()` function computes the length of a string by determining the number of characters that precede the terminating null character. A problem occurs if the first character read from the input by `fgets()` happens to be a null character. This may occur, for example, if a binary data file is read by the fgets() call [Lai 2006]. If the first character in buf is a null character, strlen(buf) returns 0, the expression strlen(buf) − 1 wraps around to a large positive value, and a write-outside-array-bounds error occurs.

Compliant Solution

This compliant solution uses strchr() to replace the new-line character in the string if it exists:

```
#include <stdio.h>
#include <string.h>

enum { BUFFER_SIZE = 1024 };

void func(void) {
  char buf[BUFFER_SIZE];
  char *p;

  if (fgets(buf, sizeof(buf), stdin)) {
    p = strchr(buf, '\n');
    if (p) {
      *p = '\0';
    }
  } else {
    /* Handle error */
  }
}
```

Risk Assessment

Incorrectly assuming that character data has been read can result in an out-of-bounds memory write or other flawed logic.

Rule	Severity	Likelihood	Remediation Cost	Priority	Level
FIO37-C	High	Probable	Medium	P12	L1

Related Guidelines

MITRE CWE	CWE-119, Improper Restriction of Operations within the Bounds of a Memory Buffer
	CWE-241, Improper Handling of Unexpected Data Type

Bibliography

[ISO/IEC 9899:2011]	7.21.7.2, "The fgets Function"
	7.29.3.2, "The fgetws Function"
[Lai 2006]	
[Seacord 2013b]	Chapter 2, "Strings"

■ FIO38-C. Do not copy a FILE object

According to the C Standard, 7.21.3, paragraph 6 [ISO/IEC 9899:2011]:

> The address of the FILE object used to control a stream may be significant; a copy of a FILE object need not serve in place of the original.

Consequently, do not copy a FILE object.

Noncompliant Code Example

This noncompliant code example can fail because a by-value copy of stdout is being used in the call to fputs():

```
#include <stdio.h>

int main(void) {
  FILE my_stdout = *stdout;
  if (fputs("Hello, World!\n", &my_stdout) == EOF) {
    /* Handle error */
  }
  return 0;
}
```

This noncompliant example raises an "access violation" exception at runtime when compiled with Microsoft Visual Studio 2013 and run on Windows.

Compliant Solution

In this compliant solution, a copy of the stdout pointer to the FILE object is used in the call to fputs():

```
#include <stdio.h>

int main(void) {
  FILE *my_stdout = stdout;
```

```
  if (fputs("Hello, World!\n", my_stdout) == EOF) {
    /* Handle error */
  }
  return 0;
}
```

Risk Assessment

Using a copy of a FILE object in place of the original may result in a crash, which can be used in a denial-of-service attack.

Rule	Severity	Likelihood	Remediation Cost	Priority	Level
FIO38-C	Low	Probable	Medium	P4	L3

Related Guidelines

ISO/IEC TS 17961:2013	Copying a FILE object [filecpy]

Bibliography

[ISO/IEC 9899:2011]	7.21.3, "Files"

■ FIO39-C. Do not alternately input and output from a stream without an intervening flush or positioning call

The C Standard, 7.21.5.3, paragraph 7 [ISO/IEC 9899:2011], places the following restrictions on update streams:

> When a file is opened with update mode . . ., both input and output may be performed on the associated stream. However, output shall not be directly followed by input without an intervening call to the fflush function or to a file positioning function (fseek, fsetpos, or rewind), and input shall not be directly followed by output without an intervening call to a file positioning function, unless the input operation encounters end-of-file. Opening (or creating) a text file with update mode may instead open (or create) a binary stream in some implementations.

The following scenarios can result in undefined behavior (see undefined behavior 151 in Appendix B):

- Receiving input from a stream directly following an output to that stream without an intervening call to fflush(), fseek(), fsetpos(), or rewind() if the file is not at end-of-file

- Outputting to a stream after receiving input from that stream without a call to fseek(), fsetpos(), or rewind() if the file is not at end-of-file

Consequently, a call to fseek(), fflush(), or fsetpos() is necessary between input and output to the same stream. See "ERR07-C. Prefer functions that support error checking over equivalent functions that don't" for more information on why fseek() is preferred over rewind().

Noncompliant Code Example

This noncompliant code example appends data to a file and then reads from the same file:

```c
#include <stdio.h>

enum { BUFFERSIZE = 32 };

extern void initialize_data(char *data, size_t size);

void func(const char *file_name) {
  char data[BUFFERSIZE];
  char append_data[BUFFERSIZE];
  FILE *file;

  file = fopen(file_name, "a+");
  if (file == NULL) {
    /* Handle error */
  }

  initialize_data(append_data, BUFFERSIZE);

  if (fwrite(append_data, 1, BUFFERSIZE, file) != BUFFERSIZE) {
    /* Handle error */
  }
  if (fread(data, 1, BUFFERSIZE, file) < BUFFERSIZE) {
    /* Handle there not being data */
  }
```

```
  if (fclose(file) == EOF) {
    /* Handle error */
  }
}
```

Because there is no intervening flush or positioning call between the call to fread() and fwrite(), the behavior is undefined.

Compliant Solution

In this compliant solution, fseek() is called between the output and input, eliminating the undefined behavior:

```c
#include <stdio.h>

enum { BUFFERSIZE = 32 };

extern void initialize_data(char *data, size_t size);

void func(const char *file_name) {
  char data[BUFFERSIZE];
  char append_data[BUFFERSIZE];
  FILE *file;

  file = fopen(file_name, "a+");
  if (file == NULL) {
    /* Handle error */
  }

  initialize_data(append_data, BUFFERSIZE);
  if (fwrite(append_data, BUFFERSIZE, 1, file) != BUFFERSIZE) {
    /* Handle error */
  }

  if (fseek(file, 0L, SEEK_SET) != 0) {
    /* Handle error */
  }

  if (fread(data, BUFFERSIZE, 1, file) != 0) {
    /* Handle there not being data */
  }

  if (fclose(file) == EOF) {
    /* Handle error */
  }
}
```

Risk Assessment

Alternately inputting and outputting from a stream without an intervening flush or positioning call is undefined behavior.

Rule	Severity	Likelihood	Remediation Cost	Priority	Level
FIO39-C	Low	Likely	Medium	P6	L2

Related Guidelines

ISO/IEC TS 17961:2013	Interleaving stream inputs and outputs without a flush or positioning call [ioileave]

Bibliography

[ISO/IEC 9899:2011]	7.21.5.3, "The `fopen` Function"

■ FIO40-C. Reset strings on `fgets()` or `fgetws()` failure

If either of the C Standard `fgets()` or `fgetws()` functions fail, the contents of the array being written is indeterminate (see undefined behavior 170 in Appendix B.) It is necessary to reset the string to a known value to avoid errors on subsequent string manipulation functions.

Noncompliant Code Example

In this noncompliant code example, an error flag is set if `fgets()` fails. However, buf is not reset and has indeterminate contents:

```c
#include <stdio.h>

enum { BUFFER_SIZE = 1024 };

void func(FILE *file) {
  char buf[BUFFER_SIZE];

  if (fgets(buf, sizeof(buf), file) == NULL) {
    /* Set error flag and continue */
  }
}
```

Compliant Solution

In this compliant solution, `buf` is set to an empty string if `fgets()` fails. The equivalent solution for `fgetws()` would set `buf` to an empty wide string.

```
#include <stdio.h>

enum { BUFFER_SIZE = 1024 };

void func(FILE *file) {
  char buf[BUFFER_SIZE];

  if (fgets(buf, sizeof(buf), file) == NULL) {
    /* Set error flag and continue */
    *buf = '\0';
  }
}
```

Exceptions

FIO40-EX1: If the string goes out of scope immediately following the call to `fgets()` or `fgetws()`, or is not referenced in the case of a failure, it need not be reset.

Risk Assessment

Making invalid assumptions about the contents of an array modified by `fgets()` or `fgetws()` can result in undefined behavior and abnormal program termination.

Rule	Severity	Likelihood	Remediation Cost	Priority	Level
FIO40-C	Low	Probable	Medium	P4	L3

▪ FIO41-C. Do not call getc(), putc(), getwc(), or putwc() with a stream argument that has side effects

Do not invoke `getc()` or `putc()`, or their wide-character analogues `getwc()` and `putwc()`, with a stream argument that has side effects. The stream argument passed to these macros may be evaluated more than once if these functions are implemented as unsafe macros (see "PRE31-C. Avoid side effects in arguments to unsafe macros" for more information).

This rule does not apply to the character argument in putc() or the wide-character argument in putwc(), which are guaranteed to be evaluated exactly once.

Noncompliant Code Example (getc())

This noncompliant code example calls the getc() function with an expression as the stream argument. If getc() is implemented as a macro, the file may be opened multiple times (see "FIO31-C. Do not open a file that is already open").

```
#include <stdio.h>

void func(const char *file_name) {
  FILE *fptr;

  int c = getc(fptr = fopen(file_name, "r"));
  if (c == EOF) {
    /* Handle error */
  }

  if (fclose(fptr) == EOF) {
    /* Handle error */
  }
}
```

This noncompliant code example also violates "ERR33-C. Detect and handle standard library errors" because the value returned by fopen() is not checked for errors.

Compliant Solution (getc())

In this compliant solution, fopen() is called before getc() and its return value is checked for errors:

```
#include <stdio.h>

void func(const char *file_name) {
  int c;
  FILE *fptr;

  fptr = fopen(file_name, "r");
  if (fptr == NULL) {
    /* Handle error */
  }
```

```
    c = getc(fptr);
    if (c == EOF) {
      /* Handle error */
    }

    if (fclose(fptr) == EOF) {
      /* Handle error */
    }
}
```

Noncompliant Code Example (`putc()`)

In this noncompliant example, `putc()` is called with an expression as the stream argument. If `putc()` is implemented as a macro, this expression might be evaluated multiple times.

```
#include <stdio.h>

void func(const char *file_name) {
  FILE *fptr = NULL;
  int c = 'a';

  while (c <= 'z') {
    if (putc(c++, fptr ? fptr :
        (fptr = fopen(file_name, "w"))) == EOF) {
      /* Handle error */
    }
  }

  if (fclose(fptr) == EOF) {
    /* Handle error */
  }
}
```

This noncompliant code example might appear safe even if the `putc()` macro evaluates its stream argument multiple times, as the ternary conditional expression ostensibly prevents multiple calls to `fopen()`. However, the assignment to `fptr` and the evaluation of `fptr` as the controlling expression of the ternary conditional expression can take place between the same sequence points, resulting in undefined behavior (a violation of "EXP30-C. Do not depend on the order of evaluation for side effects"). This code also violates "ERR33-C. Detect and handle standard library errors" because it fails to check the return value from `fopen()`.

Compliant Solution (putc())

In this compliant solution, the stream argument to putc() no longer has side effects:

```c
#include <stdio.h>

void func(const char *file_name) {
  int c = 'a';
  FILE *fptr = fopen(file_name, "w");

  if (fptr == NULL) {
    /* Handle error */
  }

  while (c <= 'z') {
    if (putc(c++, fptr) == EOF) {
      /* Handle error */
    }
  }

  if (fclose(fptr) == EOF) {
    /* Handle error */
  }
}
```

The expression c++ is safe because putc() evaluates its character argument exactly once.

> NOTE The output of this compliant solution differs depending on the character set. For example, when run on a machine using an ASCII-derived code set such as ISO-8859 or Unicode, this solution will print out the 26 lowercase letters of the English alphabet. However, if run with an EBCDIC-based code set, such as Codepage 037 or Codepage 285, punctuation marks or symbols may be output between the letters.

Risk Assessment

Using an expression that has side effects as the stream argument to getc(), putc(), getwc(), or putwc() can result in unexpected behavior and abnormal program termination.

Rule	Severity	Likelihood	Remediation Cost	Priority	Level
FIO41-C	Low	Unlikely	Medium	P2	L3

■ FIO42-C. Close files when they are no longer needed

A call to the fopen() or freopen() function must be matched with a call to fclose() before the lifetime of the last pointer that stores the return value of the call has ended or before **normal program termination**, whichever occurs first.

In general, this rule should also be applied to other functions with open and close resources, such as the POSIX open() and close() functions, or the Microsoft Windows CreateFile() and CloseHandle() functions.

Noncompliant Code Example

This code example is noncompliant because the file opened by the call to fopen() is not closed before function func() returns:

```
#include <stdio.h>

int func(const char *filename) {
  FILE *f = fopen(filename, "r");
  if (NULL == f) {
    return -1;
  }
  /* ... */
  return 0;
}
```

Compliant Solution

In this compliant solution, the file pointed to by f is closed before returning to the caller:

```
#include <stdio.h>

int func(const char *filename) {
  FILE *f = fopen(filename, "r");
  if (NULL == f) {
    return -1;
  }
  /* ... */
  if (fclose(f) == EOF) {
    return -1;
  }
  return 0;
}
```

Noncompliant Code Example (exit())

This code example is noncompliant because the resource allocated by the call to fopen() is not closed before the program terminates. Although exit() closes the file, the program has no way of determining if an error occurs while flushing or closing the file.

```
#include <stdio.h>
#include <stdlib.h>

int main(void) {
  FILE *f = fopen(filename, "w");
  if (NULL == f) {
    exit(EXIT_FAILURE);
  }
  /* ... */
  exit(EXIT_SUCCESS);
}
```

Compliant Solution (exit())

In this compliant solution, the program closes f explicitly before calling exit(), allowing any error that occurs when flushing or closing the file to be handled appropriately:

```
#include <stdio.h>
#include <stdlib.h>

int main(void) {
  FILE *f = fopen(filename, "w");
  if (NULL == f) {
    /* Handle error */
  }
  /* ... */
  if (fclose(f) == EOF) {
    /* Handle error */
  }

  exit(EXIT_SUCCESS);
}
```

Noncompliant Code Example (POSIX)

This code example is noncompliant because the resource allocated by the call to open() is not closed before function func() returns:

```
#include <stdio.h>
#include <fcntl.h>

int func(const char *filename) {
  int fd = open(filename, O_RDONLY, S_IRUSR);
  if (-1 == fd) {
    return -1;
  }
  /* ... */
  return 0;
}
```

Compliant Solution (POSIX)

In this compliant solution, fd is closed before returning to the caller:

```
#include <stdio.h>
#include <fcntl.h>
#include <unistd.h>

int func(const char *filename) {
  int fd = open(filename, O_RDONLY, S_IRUSR);
  if (-1 == fd) {
    return -1;
  }
  /* ... */
  if (-1 == close(fd)) {
    return -1;
  }
  return 0;
}
```

Noncompliant Code Example (Windows)

In this noncompliant code example, the file opened by the Microsoft Windows CreateFile() function is not closed before func() returns:

```
#include <Windows.h>

int func(LPCTSTR filename) {
  HANDLE hFile = CreateFile(filename, GENERIC_READ, 0, NULL,
                            OPEN_EXISTING,
                            FILE_ATTRIBUTE_NORMAL, NULL);
```

```
  if (INVALID_HANDLE_VALUE == hFile) {
    return -1;
  }
  /* ... */
  return 0;
}
```

Compliant Solution (Windows)

In this compliant solution, hFile is closed by invoking the CloseHandle()
function before returning to the caller:

```
#include <Windows.h>
int func(LPCTSTR filename) {
  HANDLE hFile = CreateFile(filename, GENERIC_READ, 0, NULL,
                            OPEN_EXISTING,
                            FILE_ATTRIBUTE_NORMAL, NULL);
  if (INVALID_HANDLE_VALUE == hFile) {
    return -1;
  }
  /* ... */
  if (!CloseHandle(hFile)) {
    return -1;
  }

  return 0;
}
```

Risk Assessment

Failing to properly close files may allow an attacker to exhaust system
resources and can increase the risk that data written into in-memory file buffers will not be flushed in the event of abnormal program termination.

Rule	Severity	Likelihood	Remediation Cost	Priority	Level
FIO42-C	Medium	Unlikely	Medium	P4	L3

Related Guidelines

ISO/IEC TS 17961:2013	Failing to close files or free dynamic memory when they are no longer needed [fileclose]
MITRE CWE	CWE-404, Improper Resource Shutdown or Release

Bibliography

[IEEE Std 1003.1-2013]	XSH, System Interfaces, open

■ FIO44-C. Only use values for `fsetpos()` that are returned from `fgetpos()`

The C Standard, 7.21.9.3 [ISO/IEC 9899:2011], defines the following behavior for `fsetpos()`:

> The `fsetpos` function sets the `mbstate_t` object (if any) and file position indicator for the stream pointed to by `stream` according to the value of the object pointed to by `pos`, which shall be a value obtained from an earlier successful call to the `fgetpos` function on a stream associated with the same file.

Invoking the `fsetpos()` function with any other values for `pos` is undefined behavior.

Noncompliant Code Example

This noncompliant code example attempts to read three values from a file and then set the file position pointer back to the beginning of the file:

```
#include <stdio.h>
#include <string.h>

int opener(FILE *file) {
  int rc;
  fpos_t offset;

  memset(&offset, 0, sizeof(offset));

  if (file == NULL) {
    return -1;
  }

  /* Read in data from file */

  rc = fsetpos(file, &offset);
  if (rc != 0 ) {
```

```
        return rc;
    }

    return 0;
}
```

Only the return value of an `fgetpos()` call is a valid argument to `fsetpos()`; passing a value of type `fpos_t` that was created in any other way is undefined behavior.

Compliant Solution

In this compliant solution, the initial file position indicator is stored by first calling `fgetpos()`, which is used to restore the state to the beginning of the file in the later call to `fsetpos()`:

```c
#include <stdio.h>
#include <string.h>

int opener(FILE *file) {
    int rc;
    fpos_t offset;

    if (file == NULL) {
        return -1;
    }

    rc = fgetpos(file, &offset);
    if (rc != 0 ) {
        return rc;
    }

    /* Read in data from file */

    rc = fsetpos(file, &offset);
    if (rc != 0 ) {
        return rc;
    }

    return 0;
}
```

Risk Assessment

Misuse of the `fsetpos()` function can position a file position indicator to an unintended location in the file.

Rule	Severity	Likelihood	Remediation Cost	Priority	Level
FIO44-C	Medium	Unlikely	Medium	P4	L3

Related Guidelines

ISO/IEC TS 17961:2013	Using a value for `fsetpos` other than a value returned from `fgetpos` [xfilepos]

Bibliography

[ISO/IEC 9899:2011]	7.21.9.3, "The `fsetpos` Function"

■ FIO45-C. Avoid TOCTOU race conditions while accessing files

A TOCTOU (time-of-check, time-of-use) race condition is possible when two or more concurrent processes are operating on a shared file system [Seacord 2013b]. Typically, the first access is a check to verify some attribute of the file, followed by a call to use the file. An attacker can alter the file between the two accesses, or replace the file with a symbolic or hard link to a different file. These TOCTOU conditions can be exploited when a program performs two or more file operations on the same file name or path name.

A program that performs two or more file operations on a single file name or path name creates a race window between the two file operations. This race window comes from the assumption that the file name or path name refers to the same resource both times. If an attacker can modify the file, remove it, or replace it with a different file, then this assumption will not hold.

Noncompliant Code Example

If an existing file is opened for writing with the w mode argument, the file's previous contents (if any) are destroyed. This noncompliant code example tries to prevent an existing file from being overwritten by first opening it for reading before opening it for writing. An attacker can exploit the race window between the two calls to `fopen()` to overwrite an existing file.

```
#include <stdio.h>

void open_some_file(const char *file) {
```

```
    FILE *f = fopen(file, "r");
    if (NULL != f) {
      /* File exists, handle error */
    } else {
      if (fclose(f) == EOF) {
        /* Handle error */
      }
      f = fopen(file, "w");
      if (NULL == f) {
        /* Handle error */
      }

      /* Write to file */
      if (fclose(f) == EOF) {
        /* Handle error */
      }
    }
}
```

Compliant Solution

This compliant solution invokes the fopen() at a single location, and uses the x mode of fopen(), which was added in C11. This mode causes fopen() to fail if the file exists. This check and subsequent open is performed without creating a race window.

```
#include <stdio.h>

void open_some_file(const char *file) {
  FILE *f = fopen(file, "wx")
  if (NULL == f) {
    /* Handle error */
  }
  /* Write to file */
  if (fclose(f) == EOF) {
    /* Handle error */
  }
}
```

Compliant Solution (POSIX)

This compliant solution uses the O_CREAT and O_EXCL flags of POSIX's open() function. These flags cause open() to fail if the file exists.

```
#include <stdio.h>
#include <unistd.h>
#include <fcntl.h>
```

```
void open_some_file(const char *file) {
  int fd = open(file, O_CREAT | O_EXCL | O_WRONLY);
  if (-1 != fd) {
    FILE *f = fdopen(fd, "w");
    if (NULL != f) {
      /* Write to file */

      if (fclose(f) == EOF) {
        /* Handle error */
      }
    }
    else {
      if (close(fd) == -1) {
        /* Handle error */
      }
    }
  }
}
```

Exceptions

FIO45-EX1: TOCTOU race conditions require that the vulnerable process is more privileged than the attacker; otherwise there is nothing to be gained from a successful attack. An unprivileged process is not subject to this rule.

FIO45-EX2: Accessing a file name or path name multiple times is permitted if the file referenced resides in a secure directory (for more information, see "FIO15-C. Ensure that file operations are performed in a secure directory").

FIO45-EX3: Accessing a file name or path name multiple times is permitted if the program can verify that every operation operates on the same file.

This POSIX code example verifies that each subsequent file access operates on the same file. In POSIX, every file can be uniquely identified by using its device and i-node attributes. This code example checks that a file name refers to a regular file (and not a directory, symbolic link, or other special file) by invoking lstat(). This call also retrieves its device and i-node. The file is subsequently opened. Finally, the program verifies that the file that was opened is the same one (matching device and i-nodes) as the file that was confirmed as a regular file.

```
#include <sys/stat.h>
#include <fcntl.h>
```

```
int open_regular_file(char *filename, int flags) {
  struct stat lstat_info;
  struct stat fstat_info;
  int f;

  if (lstat(filename, &lstat_info) == -1) {
    /* File does not exist, handle error */
  }

  if (!S_ISREG(lstat_info.st_mode)) {
    /* File is not a regular file, handle error */
  }

  if ((f = open(filename, flags)) == -1) {
    /* File has disappeared, handle error */
  }

  if (fstat(f, &fstat_info) == -1) {
    /* Handle error */
  }

  if (lstat_info.st_ino != fstat_info.st_ino  ||
      lstat_info.st_dev != fstat_info.st_dev) {
    /* Open file is not the expected regular file, handle error */
  }

  /* f is the expected regular open file */
  return f;
}
```

Risk Assessment

TOCTOU race conditions can result in unexpected behavior, including privilege escalation.

Rule	Severity	Likelihood	Remediation Cost	Priority	Level
FIO45-C	High	Probable	High	P6	L2

Bibliography

[Seacord 2013b]	Chapter 7, "Files"

■ FIO46-C. Do not access a closed file

Using the value of a pointer to a FILE object after the associated file is closed is undefined behavior (see undefined behavior 148 in Appendix B). Programs that close the standard streams (especially stdout, but also stderr and stdin) must be careful not to use these streams in subsequent function calls, particularly those that implicitly operate on them (such as printf(), perror(), and getc()).

This rule can be generalized to other file representations.

Noncompliant Code Example

In this noncompliant code example, the stdout stream is used after it is closed:

```c
#include <stdio.h>

int close_stdout(void) {
  if (fclose(stdout) == EOF) {
    return -1;
  }

  puts("stdout successfully closed.");
  return 0;
}
```

Compliant Solution

In this compliant solution, stdout is not used again after it is closed. This must remain true for the remainder of the program, or stdout must be assigned the address of an open file object.

```c
#include <stdio.h>

int close_stdout(void) {
  if (fclose(stdout) == EOF) {
    return -1;
  }

  fputs("stdout successfully closed.", stderr);
  return 0;
}
```

Risk Assessment

Using the value of a pointer to a FILE object after the associated file is closed is undefined behavior.

Rule	Severity	Likelihood	Remediation Cost	Priority	Level
FIO46-C	Medium	Unlikely	Medium	P4	L3

Bibliography

[IEEE Std 1003.1-2013]	XSH, System Interfaces, open
[ISO/IEC 9899:2011]	7.21.3, "Files" 7.21.5.1, "The fclose Function"

■ FIO47-C. Use valid format strings

The formatted output functions (fprintf() and related functions) convert, format, and print their arguments under control of a *format* string, which the C Standard, 7.21.6.1, paragraph 3 [ISO/IEC 9899:2011], specifies:

> The format shall be a multibyte character sequence, beginning and ending in its initial shift state. The format is composed of zero or more directives: ordinary multibyte characters (not %), which are copied unchanged to the output stream; and conversion specifications, each of which results in fetching zero or more subsequent arguments, converting them, if applicable, according to the corresponding conversion specifier, and then writing the result to the output stream.

Each *conversion specification* is introduced by the % character followed (in order) by

- Zero or more flags (in any order), which modify the meaning of the conversion specification
- An optional minimum field *width*
- An optional *precision* that gives the minimum number of digits to appear for certain conversion specifiers

■ An optional *length modifier* that specifies the size of the argument

■ A *conversion specifier character* that indicates the type of conversion to be applied

Common mistakes in creating format strings include

■ Providing an incorrect number of arguments for the format string

■ Using invalid conversion specifiers

■ Using a flag character that is incompatible with the conversion specifier

■ Using a length modifier that is incompatible with the conversion specifier

■ Mismatching the argument type and conversion specifier

■ Using an argument of type other than int for *width* or *precision*

Table 9–2, on page 302, summarizes the compliance of various conversion specifications. The first column contains one or more conversion specifier characters. The next four columns consider the combination of the specifier characters with the various flags (the apostrophe ['], -, +, the space character, #, and 0). The next eight columns consider the combination of the specifier characters with the various length modifiers (h, hh, l, ll, j, z, t, and L). Valid combinations are marked with a type name; arguments matched with the conversion specification are interpreted as that type. For example, an argument matched with the specifier %hd is interpreted as a short, so short appears in the cell where d and h intersect. The last column denotes the expected type of arguments matched with the original specifier characters. Valid and meaningful combinations are marked by the ✓ symbol (save for the length modifier columns, as described previously). Valid combinations that have no effect are labeled *N/E*. Using a combination marked by the ✗ symbol, using a specification not represented in the table, or using an argument of an unexpected type is undefined behavior (see undefined behaviors 153, 155, 157, 158, 161, and 162 in Appendix B).

The formatted input functions (fscanf() and related functions) use similarly specified format strings and impose similar restrictions on their format strings and arguments.

Do not supply an unknown or invalid conversion specification or an invalid combination of flag character, precision, length modifier, conversion specifier to a formatted IO function. Likewise, do not provide a number or type of arguments that do not match the argument type of the conversion specifier used in the format string.

Format strings are usually string literals specified at the call site, but they need not be. However, they should not contain tainted values (see "FIO30-C. Exclude user input from format strings" for more information).

Noncompliant Code Example

Mismatches between arguments and conversion specifications may result in undefined behavior. Compilers may diagnose type mismatches in formatted output function invocations. In this noncompliant code example, the error_type argument to printf() is incorrectly matched with the s specifier rather than with the d specifier. Likewise, the error_msg argument is incorrectly matched with the d specifier instead of the s specifier. These usages result in undefined behavior. One possible result of this invocation is that printf() will interpret the error_type argument as a pointer and try to read a string from the address that error_type contains, possibly resulting in an access violation.

```c
#include <stdio.h>

void func(void) {
  const char *error_msg = "Resource not available to user.";
  int error_type = 3;
  /* ... */
  printf("Error (type %s): %d\n", error_type, error_msg);
  /* ... */
}
```

Compliant Solution

This compliant solution ensures that the arguments to the printf() function match their respective conversion specifications:

```c
#include <stdio.h>

void func(void) {
  const char *error_msg = "Resource not available to user.";
  int error_type = 3;
  /* ... */
  printf("Error (type %d): %s\n", error_type, error_msg);

  /* ... */
}
```

Table 9-2. Compliance of Conversion Specifications

Conversion Specifier Character	'XSI	-, +, SPACE	#	o	h	hh	l	ll	j	z	t	L	Argument Type
d, i	✓	✓	X	✓	short	signed char	long	long long	intmax_t	size_t	ptrdiff_t	X	Signed integer
o	X	✓	✓	✓	unsigned short	unsigned char	unsigned long	unsigned long long	uintmax_t	size_t	ptrdiff_t	X	Unsigned integer
u	✓	✓	X	✓	unsigned short	unsigned char	unsigned long	unsigned long long	uintmax_t	size_t	ptrdiff_t	X	Unsigned integer
x, X	X	✓	✓	✓	unsigned short	unsigned char	unsigned long	unsigned long long	uintmax_t	size_t	ptrdiff_t	X	Unsigned integer
f, F	✓	✓	✓	✓	X	X	N/E	N/E	X	X	X	long double	double or long double
e, E	X	✓	✓	✓	X	X	N/E	N/E	X	X	X	long double	double or long double
g, G	✓	✓	✓	✓	X	X	N/E	N/E	X	X	X	long double	double or long double
a, A	✓	✓	✓	✓	X	X	N/E	N/E	X	X	X	long double	double or long double

									Type
c	×	×	×	wint_t	×	×	×	×	int or wint_t
s	✓	×	×	NTWS	×	×	×	×	NTCS or NTWS
p	✓	×	×	×	×	×	×	×	void*
n	✓	short*	char*	long*	long long*	intmax_t*	size_t*	ptrdiff_t*	Pointer to integer
c ^{XSI}	✓	×	×	×	×	×	×	×	wint_t
s ^{XSI}	✓	×	×	×	×	×	×	×	NTWS
%	✓	×	×	×	×	×	×	×	None

SPACE: The space (" ") character

N/E: No effect

NTCS: char * argument pointing to a null-terminated character string

NTWS: wchar_t * argument pointing to a null-terminated wide character string

XSI: ISO/IEC 9945-2003 XSI extension

Risk Assessment

Incorrectly specified format strings can result in memory corruption or abnormal program termination.

Rule	Severity	Likelihood	Remediation Cost	Priority	Level
FIO47-C	High	Unlikely	Medium	P6	L2

Related Guidelines

ISO/IEC TS 17961:2013	Using invalid format strings [invfmtstr]
MITRE CWE	CWE-686, Function Call with Incorrect Argument Type

Bibliography

[ISO/IEC 9899:2011]	7.21.6.1, "The `fprintf` Function"

Chapter 10

Environment (ENV)

Chapter Contents

Risk Assessment Summary

Rule	Severity	Likelihood	Remediation Cost	Priority	Level
ENV30-C	Low	Probable	Medium	P4	L3
ENV31-C	Low	Probable	Medium	P4	L3
ENV32-C	Medium	Likely	Medium	P12	L1
ENV33-C	High	Probable	Medium	P12	L1
ENV34-C	Low	Probable	Medium	P4	L3

■ ENV30-C. Do not modify the object referenced by the return value of certain functions

Some functions return a pointer to an object that cannot be modified without causing undefined behavior. These functions include `getenv()`, `setlocale()`, `localeconv()`, `asctime()`, and `strerror()`. In such cases, the function call results must be treated as being `const`-qualified.

The C Standard, 7.22.4.6, paragraph 4 [ISO/IEC 9899:2011], defines `getenv()` as follows:

> The `getenv` function returns a pointer to a string associated with the matched list member. The string pointed to shall not be modified by the program, but may be overwritten by a subsequent call to the `getenv` function. If the specified name cannot be found, a null pointer is returned.

If the string returned by `getenv()` must be altered, a local copy should be created. Altering the string returned by `getenv()` is undefined behavior (see undefined behavior 184 in Appendix B).

Similarly, subclause 7.11.1.1, paragraph 8 [ISO/IEC 9899:2011], defines `setlocale()` as follows:

> The pointer to string returned by the `setlocale` function is such that a subsequent call with that string value and its associated category will restore that part of the program's locale. The string pointed to shall not be modified by the program, but may be overwritten by a subsequent call to the `setlocale` function.

And subclause 7.11.2.1, paragraph 8 [ISO/IEC 9899:2011], defines `localeconv()` as follows:

> The `localeconv` function returns a pointer to the filled-in object. The structure pointed to by the return value shall not be modified by the program, but may be overwritten by a subsequent call to the `localeconv` function. In addition, calls to the `setlocale` function with categories LC_ALL, LC_MONETARY, or LC_NUMERIC may overwrite the contents of the structure.

Altering the string returned by `setlocale()` or the structure returned by `localeconv()` are undefined behaviors (see undefined behaviors 120 and 121 in Appendix B). Furthermore, the C Standard imposes no requirements on the contents of the string by `setlocale()`. Consequently, no assumptions can be made as to the string's internal contents or structure.

Finally, subclause 7.24.6.2, paragraph 4 [ISO/IEC 9899:2011], states:

> The strerror function returns a pointer to the string, the contents of which are locale-specific. The array pointed to shall not be modified by the program, but may be overwritten by a subsequent call to the strerror function.

Altering the string returned by strerror() is undefined behavior (see undefined behavior 184 in Appendix B).

Noncompliant Code Example (getenv())

This noncompliant code example modifies the string returned by getenv() by replacing all double quotation marks (") with underscores (_):

```
#include <stdlib.h>

void trstr(char *c_str, char orig, char rep) {
  while (*c_str != '\0') {
    if (*c_str == orig) {
      *c_str = rep;
    }
    ++c_str;
  }
}

void func(void) {
  char *env = getenv("TEST_ENV");
  if (env == NULL) {
  /* Handle error */
  }
  trstr(env,'"', '_');
}
```

Compliant Solution (getenv()) (Environment Not Modified)

If the programmer does not intend to modify the environment, this compliant solution demonstrates modifying a copy of the return value:

```
#include <stdlib.h>
#include <string.h>

void trstr(char *c_str, char orig, char rep) {
  while (*c_str != '\0') {
    if (*c_str == orig) {
      *c_str = rep;
```

```
    }
    ++c_str;
  }
}

void func(void) {
  const char *env;
  char *copy_of_env;

  env = getenv("TEST_ENV");
  if (env == NULL) {
    /* Handle error */
  }

  copy_of_env = (char *)malloc(strlen(env) + 1);
  if (copy_of_env == NULL) {
    /* Handle error */
  }

  strcpy(copy_of_env, env);
  trstr(copy_of_env,'"', '_');
  /* ... */
  free(copy_of_env);
}
```

Compliant Solution (getenv()) (Modifying the Environment in POSIX)

If the programmer's intent is to modify the environment, this compliant solution, which saves the altered string back into the environment by using the POSIX setenv() and strdup() functions, can be used:

```
#include <stdlib.h>
#include <string.h>

void trstr(char *c_str, char orig, char rep) {
  while (*c_str != '\0') {
    if (*c_str == orig) {
      *c_str = rep;
    }
    ++c_str;
  }
}

void func(void) {
  const char *env;
  char *copy_of_env;
```

```
      env = getenv("TEST_ENV");
      if (env == NULL) {
        /* Handle error */
      }

      copy_of_env = strdup(env);
      if (copy_of_env == NULL) {
        /* Handle error */
      }

      trstr(copy_of_env,'"', '_');

      if (setenv("TEST_ENV", copy_of_env, 1) != 0) {
        /* Handle error */
      }
      /* ... */
      free(copy_of_env);
    }
```

Noncompliant Code Example (`localeconv()`)

In this noncompliant example, the object returned by `localeconv()` is directly modified:

```
#include <locale.h>

void f2(void) {
  struct lconv *conv = localeconv();

  if ('\0' == conv->decimal_point[0]) {
    conv->decimal_point = ".";
  }
}
```

Compliant Solution (`localeconv()`) (Copy)

This compliant solution modifies a copy of the object returned by `localeconv()`:

```
#include <locale.h>
#include <stdlib.h>
#include <string.h>

void f2(void) {
  const struct lconv *conv = localeconv();
  if (conv == NULL) {
    /* Handle error */
  }
```

```
  struct lconv *copy_of_conv = (struct lconv *)malloc(
    sizeof(struct lconv));
  if (copy_of_conv == NULL) {
    /* Handle error */
  }

  memcpy(copy_of_conv, conv, sizeof(struct lconv));

  if ('\0' == copy_of_conv->decimal_point[0]) {
    copy_of_conv->decimal_point = ".";
  }
  /* ... */
  free(copy_of_conv);
}
```

Risk Assessment

Modifying the object pointed to by the return value of getenv(), setlocale(), localeconv(), asctime(), or strerror() is undefined behavior. Even if the modification succeeds, the modified object can be overwritten by a subsequent call to the same function.

Rule	Severity	Likelihood	Remediation Cost	Priority	Level
ENV30-C	Low	Probable	Medium	P4	L3

Related Guidelines

ISO/IEC TS 17961:2013	Modifying the string returned by getenv, localeconv, setlocale, and strerror [libmod]

Bibliography

[IEEE Std 1003.1-2013]	XSH, System Interfaces, setenv XSH, System Interfaces, strdup
[ISO/IEC 9899:2011]	7.11.1.1, "The setlocale Function" 7.11.2.1, "The localeconv Function" 7.22.4.6, "The getenv Function" 7.24.6.2, "The strerror Function"

■ ENV31-C. Do not rely on an environment pointer following an operation that may invalidate it

Some implementations provide a nonportable environment pointer that is valid when main() is called but may be invalidated by operations that modify the environment.

The C Standard, J.5.1 [ISO/IEC 9899:2011], states:

> In a hosted environment, the main function receives a third argument, char *envp[], that points to a null-terminated array of pointers to char, each of which points to a string that provides information about the environment for this execution of the program.

Consequently, under a hosted environment supporting this common extension, it is possible to access the environment through a modified form of main():

```
int main(int argc, char *argv[], char *envp[]){ /* ... */ }
```

However, modifying the environment by any means may cause the environment memory to be reallocated, with the result that envp now references an incorrect location. For example, when compiled with GCC 4.8.1 and run on a 32-bit Intel GNU/Linux machine, the following code,

```
#include <stdio.h>
#include <stdlib.h>

extern char **environ;

int main(int argc, const char *argv[], const char *envp[]) {
  printf("environ:  %p\n", environ);
  printf("envp:     %p\n", envp);
  setenv("MY_NEW_VAR", "new_value", 1);
  puts("--Added MY_NEW_VAR--");
  printf("environ:  %p\n", environ);
  printf("envp:     %p\n", envp);
  return 0;
}
```

yields:

```
% ./envp-environ
environ: 0xbf8656ec
envp:    0xbf8656ec
```

```
--Added MY_NEW_VAR--
environ: 0x804a008
envp:    0xbf8656ec
```

It is evident from these results that the environment has been relocated as a result of the call to setenv(). The external variable environ is updated to refer to the current environment; the envp parameter is not.

An environment pointer may also become invalidated by subsequent calls to getenv() (see "ENV34-C. Do not store pointers returned by certain functions" for more information).

Noncompliant Code Example (POSIX)

After a call to the POSIX setenv() function, or to another function that modifies the environment, the envp pointer may no longer reference the current environment. The *Portable Operating System Interface (POSIX®), Base Specifications, Issue 7* [IEEE Std 1003.1-2013], states:

> Unanticipated results may occur if setenv() changes the external variable environ. In particular, if the optional envp argument to main() is present, it is not changed, and thus may point to an obsolete copy of the environment (as may any other copy of environ).

This noncompliant code example accesses the envp pointer after calling setenv():

```
#include <stdio.h>
#include <stdlib.h>

int main(int argc, const char *argv[], const char *envp[]) {
  if (setenv("MY_NEW_VAR", "new_value", 1) != 0) {
    /* Handle error */
  }
  if (envp != NULL) {
    for (size_t i = 0; envp[i] != NULL; ++i) {
      puts(envp[i]);
    }
  }
  return 0;
}
```

Because envp may no longer point to the current environment, this program has undefined behavior.

Compliant Solution (POSIX)

On POSIX platforms, the external variable `environ` can be used in place of `envp`, as in this compliant solution:

```
#include <stdio.h>
#include <stdlib.h>

extern char **environ;

int main(void) {
  if (setenv("MY_NEW_VAR", "new_value", 1) != 0) {
    /* Handle error */
  }
  if (environ != NULL) {
    for (size_t i = 0; environ[i] != NULL; ++i) {
      puts(environ[i]);
    }
  }
  return 0;
}
```

Noncompliant Code Example (Windows)

After a call to the Windows `_putenv_s()` function or to another function that modifies the environment, the `envp` pointer may no longer reference the environment.

According to the Visual C++ reference [MSDN],

> The environment block passed to `main` and `wmain` is a "frozen" copy of the current environment. If you subsequently change the environment via a call to _putenv or _wputenv, the current environment (as returned by getenv / _wgetenv and the _environ / _wenviron variable) will change, but the block pointed to by envp will not change.

This noncompliant code example accesses the `envp` pointer after calling `_putenv_s()`:

```
#include <stdio.h>
#include <stdlib.h>

int main(int argc, const char *argv[], const char *envp[]) {
  if (_putenv_s("MY_NEW_VAR", "new_value") != 0) {
    /* Handle error */
  }
```

```
  if (envp != NULL) {
    for (size_t i = 0; envp[i] != NULL; ++i) {
      puts(envp[i]);
    }
  }
  return 0;
}
```

Because envp no longer points to the current environment, this program has undefined behavior.

Compliant Solution (Windows)

This compliant solution uses the _environ variable in place of envp:

```
#include <stdio.h>
#include <stdlib.h>

_CRTIMP extern char **_environ;

int main(int argc, const char *argv[]) {
  if (_putenv_s("MY_NEW_VAR", "new_value") != 0) {
    /* Handle error */
  }
  if (_environ != NULL) {
    for (size_t i = 0; _environ[i] != NULL; ++i) {
      puts(_environ[i]);
    }
  }
  return 0;
}
```

Compliant Solution

This compliant solution can reduce remediation time when a large amount of noncompliant envp code exists. It replaces

```
int main(int argc, char *argv[], char *envp[]) {
  /* ... */
}
```

with:

```
#if defined (_POSIX_) || defined (__USE_POSIX)
  extern char **environ;
  #define envp environ
```

```
#elif defined(_WIN32)
  _CRTIMP extern char **_environ;
  #define envp _environ
#endif

int main(int argc, char *argv[]) {
  /* ... */
}
```

This compliant solution may need to be extended to support other implementations that support forms of the external variable environ.

Risk Assessment

Using the envp environment pointer after the environment has been modified can result in undefined behavior.

Rule	Severity	Likelihood	Remediation Cost	Priority	Level
ENV31-C	Low	Probable	Medium	P4	L3

Bibliography

[IEEE Std 1003.1-2013]	XSH, System Interfaces, setenv
[ISO/IEC 9899:2011]	J.5.1, "Environment Arguments"
[MSDN]	_environ, _wenviron, getenv, _wgetenv, _putenv_s, _wputenv_s

■ ENV32-C. All exit handlers must return normally

The C Standard provides three functions that cause an application to terminate normally: _Exit(), exit(), and quick_exit(). These are collectively called *exit functions*. When the exit() function is called, or control transfers out of the main() entry point function, functions registered with atexit() (but not at_quick_exit()) are called. When the quick_exit() function is called, functions registered with at_quick_exit() (but not atexit()) are called. These functions are collectively called *exit handlers*. When the _Exit() function is called, no exit handlers or signal handlers are called.

Exit handlers must terminate by returning. It is important and potentially safety-critical for all exit handlers to be allowed to perform their cleanup actions. This is particularly true because the application programmer does not always know about handlers that may have been installed by support libraries. Two specific issues include nested calls to an exit function and terminating a call to an exit handler by invoking longjmp().

A nested call to an exit function is undefined behavior (see undefined behavior 182 in Appendix B). This behavior can occur only when an exit function is invoked from an exit handler or when an exit function is called from within a signal handler (see "SIG30-C. Call only asynchronous-safe functions within signal handlers").

If a call to the longjmp() function is made that would terminate the call to an exit handler, the behavior is undefined.

Noncompliant Code Example

In this noncompliant code example, the exit1() and exit2() functions are registered by atexit() to perform required cleanup upon program termination. However, if some_condition evaluates to true, exit() is called a second time, resulting in undefined behavior.

```
#include <stdlib.h>

void exit1(void) {
  /* ... Cleanup code ... */
  return;
}

void exit2(void) {
  extern int some_condition;
  if (some_condition) {
    /* ... More cleanup code ... */
    exit(0);
  }
  return;
}

int main(void) {
  if (atexit(exit1) != 0) {
    /* Handle error */
  }
  if (atexit(exit2) != 0) {
    /* Handle error */
  }
  /* ... Program code ... */
  return 0;
}
```

Functions registered by the `atexit()` function are called in the reverse order from which they were registered. Consequently, if `exit2()` exits in any way other than by returning, `exit1()` will not be executed. The same may also be true for `atexit()` handlers installed by support libraries.

Compliant Solution

A function that is registered as an exit handler by `atexit()` must exit by returning, as in this compliant solution:

```
#include <stdlib.h>

void exit1(void) {
  /* ... Cleanup code ... */
  return;
}

void exit2(void) {
  extern int some_condition;
  if (some_condition) {
    /* ... More cleanup code ... */
  }
  return;
}

int main(void) {
  if (atexit(exit1) != 0) {
    /* Handle error */
  }
  if (atexit(exit2) != 0) {
    /* Handle error */
  }
  /* ... Program code ... */
  return 0;
}
```

Noncompliant Code Example

In this noncompliant code example, `exit1()` is registered by `atexit()` so that upon program termination, `exit1()` is called. The `exit1()` functions jumps back to `main()` to return, with undefined results.

```
#include <stdlib.h>
#include <setjmp.h>

jmp_buf env;
int val;
```

```
void exit1(void) {
  longjmp(env, 1);
}

int main(void) {
  if (atexit(exit1) != 0) {
    /* Handle error */
  }
  if (setjmp(env) == 0) {
    exit(0);
  } else {
    return 0;
  }
}
```

Compliant Solution

This compliant solution does not call `longjmp()` but instead returns from the exit handler normally:

```
#include <stdlib.h>

void exit1(void) {
  return;
}

int main(void) {
  if (atexit(exit1) != 0) {
    /* Handle error */
  }
  return 0;
}
```

Risk Assessment

Terminating a call to an exit handler in any way other than by returning is undefined behavior and may result in abnormal program termination or other unpredictable behavior. It may also prevent other registered handlers from being invoked.

Rule	Severity	Likelihood	Remediation Cost	Priority	Level
ENV32-C	Medium	Likely	Medium	P12	L1

Related Guidelines

ISO/IEC TR 24772:2013	Structured Programming [EWD]
	Termination Strategy [REU]
MITRE CWE	CWE-705, Incorrect Control Flow Scoping

■ ENV33-C. Do not call system()

The C Standard system() function executes a specified command by invoking an implementation-defined command processor, such as a UNIX shell or CMD.EXE in Microsoft Windows. The POSIX popen() function also invokes a command processor but creates a pipe between the calling program and the executed command, returning a pointer to a stream that can be used to either read from or write to the pipe [IEEE Std 1003.1-2013].

Use of the system() function can result in exploitable vulnerabilities, in the worst case allowing execution of arbitrary system commands. Situations in which calls to system() have high risk include the following:

- When passing an unsanitized or improperly sanitized command string originating from a tainted source
- If a command is specified without a path name and the command processor path name resolution mechanism is accessible to an attacker
- If a relative path to an executable is specified and control over the current working directory is accessible to an attacker
- If the specified executable program can be spoofed by an attacker

Noncompliant Code Example

In this noncompliant code example, the system() function is used to execute any_cmd in the host environment. Invocation of a command processor is not required.

```
#include <string.h>
#include <stdlib.h>

enum { BUFFERSIZE = 512 };
```

```
void func(const char *input) {
  char cmdbuf[BUFFERSIZE];
  int len_wanted = snprintf(cmdbuf, BUFFERSIZE,
                            "any_cmd '%s'", input);
  if (len_wanted >= BUFFERSIZE) {
    /* Handle error */
  } else if (len_wanted < 0) {
    /* Handle error */
  } else if (system(cmdbuf) == -1) {
    /* Handle error */
  }
}
```

If this code is compiled and run with elevated privileges on a Linux system, for example, an attacker can create an account by entering the following string:

```
happy'; useradd 'attacker
```

The shell would interpret this string as two separate commands,

```
any_cmd 'happy';
useradd 'attacker'
```

and create a new user account that the attacker can use to access the compromised system.

This noncompliant code example also violates "STR02-C. Sanitize data passed to complex subsystems."

Compliant Solution (POSIX)

In this compliant solution, the call to system() is replaced with a call to execve(). The exec family of functions does not use a full shell interpreter, so these functions are not vulnerable to command-injection attacks, such as the one illustrated in the noncompliant code example.

The execlp(), execvp(), and (nonstandard) execvP() functions duplicate the actions of the shell in searching for an executable file if the specified file name does not contain a forward slash (/) character. As a result, they should be used without a forward slash character (/) only if the PATH environment variable is set to a safe value, as described in "ENV03-C. Sanitize the environment when invoking external programs."

The execl(), execle(), execv(), and execve() functions do not perform path name substitution.

Additionally, precautions should be taken to ensure the external executable cannot be modified by an untrusted user, for example, by ensuring the executable is not writable by the user.

```c
#include <sys/types.h>
#include <sys/wait.h>
#include <unistd.h>

void func(char *input) {
  pid_t pid;
  int status;
  pid_t ret;
  char *const args[3] = {"any_exe", input, NULL};
  char **env;
  extern char **environ;

  /* ... Sanitize arguments ... */

  pid = fork();
  if (pid == -1) {
    /* Handle error */
  } else if (pid != 0) {
    while ((ret = waitpid(pid, &status, 0)) == -1) {
      if (errno != EINTR) {
        /* Handle error */
        break;
      }
    }
    if ((ret != -1) &&
      (!WIFEXITED(status) || !WEXITSTATUS(status)) ) {
      /* Report unexpected child status */
    }
  } else {
    /* ... Initialize env as a sanitized copy of environ ... */
    if (execve("/usr/bin/any_cmd", args, env) == -1) {
      /* Handle error */
      _Exit(127);
    }
  }
}
```

This compliant solution is significantly different from the preceding non-compliant code example. First, input is incorporated into the args array and passed as an argument to execve(), eliminating any concerns about buffer overflow or string truncation while forming the command string. Second, this compliant solution forks a new process before executing "/usr/bin/any_cmd" in the child process. Although this method is more complicated than calling system(), the added security is worth the additional effort.

The exit status of 127 is the value set by the shell when a command is not found, and POSIX recommends that applications should do the same. XCU, section 2.8.2, of the POSIX standard [IEEE Std 1003.1-2013], says:

> If a command is not found, the exit status shall be 127. If the command name is found, but it is not an executable utility, the exit status shall be 126. Applications that invoke utilities without using the shell should use these exit status values to report similar errors.

Compliant Solution (Windows)

This compliant solution uses the Microsoft Windows `CreateProcess()` API:

```c
#include <Windows.h>

void func(TCHAR *input) {
  STARTUPINFO si = { 0 };
  PROCESS_INFORMATION pi;
  si.cb = sizeof(si);
  if (!CreateProcess(TEXT("any_cmd.exe"), input, NULL, NULL, FALSE,
                     0, 0, 0, &si, &pi)) {
    /* Handle error */
  }
  CloseHandle(pi.hThread);
  CloseHandle(pi.hProcess);
}
```

This compliant solution relies on the `input` parameter being non-`const`. If it were `const`, the solution would need to create a copy of the parameter because the `CreateProcess()` function can modify the command-line arguments to be passed into the newly created process.

This solution creates the process such that the child process does not inherit any handles from the parent process, in compliance with "WIN03-C. Understand `HANDLE` inheritance."

Noncompliant Code Example (POSIX)

This noncompliant code invokes the C `system()` function to remove the `.config` file in the user's home directory:

```c
#include <stdlib.h>

void func(void) {
  system("rm ~/.config");
}
```

If the vulnerable program has elevated privileges, an attacker can manipulate the value of the HOME environment variable such that this program can remove any file named .config anywhere on the system.

Compliant Solution (POSIX)

An alternative to invoking the system() call to execute an external program to perform a required operation is to implement the functionality directly in the program using existing library calls. This compliant solution calls the POSIX unlink() function to remove a file without invoking the system() function [IEEE Std 1003.1-2013]:

```c
#include <pwd.h>
#include <unistd.h>
#include <string.h>

void func(void) {
  const char *file_format = "%s/.config";
  size_t len;
  char *file;
  struct passwd *pwd;

  /* Get /etc/passwd entry for current user */
  pwd = getpwuid(getuid());
  if (pwd == NULL) {
    /* Handle error */
  }

  /* Build full path name home dir from pw entry */

  len = strlen(pwd->pw_dir) + strlen(file_format) + 1;
  file = (char *)malloc(len);
  if (NULL == file) {
    /* Handle error */
  }
  int r = snprintf(file, len, file_format, pwd->pw_dir);
  if (r < 0 || r >= len) {
    /* Handle error */
  }
  if (unlink(file) != 0) {
    /* Handle error */
  }

  free(file);
}
```

The unlink() function is not susceptible to file-related race conditions (see "FIO01-C. Be careful using functions that use file names for identification") because if file names a symbolic link, unlink() will remove the symbolic link named by file and not affect any file or directory named by the contents of the symbolic link.

Compliant Solution (Windows)

This compliant solution uses the Microsoft Windows SHGetKnownFolderPath() API to get the current user's My Documents folder, which is then combined with the file name to create the path to the file to be deleted. The file is then removed using the DeleteFile() API.

```
#include <Windows.h>
#include <ShlObj.h>
#include <Shlwapi.h>

#if defined(_MSC_VER)
  #pragma comment(lib, "Shlwapi")
#endif

void func(void) {
  HRESULT hr;
  LPWSTR path = 0;
  WCHAR full_path[MAX_PATH];

  hr = SHGetKnownFolderPath(&FOLDERID_Documents, 0, NULL, &path);
  if (FAILED(hr)) {
    /* Handle error */
  }
  if (!PathCombineW(full_path, path, L".config")) {
    /* Handle error */
  }
  CoTaskMemFree(path);
  if (!DeleteFileW(full_path)) {
    /* Handle error */
  }
}
```

Risk Assessments

If the command string passed to system(), popen(), or other function that invokes a command processor is not fully sanitized, the risk of exploitation is high. In the worst case scenario, an attacker can execute arbitrary system commands on the compromised machine with the privileges of the vulnerable process.

Rule	Severity	Likelihood	Remediation Cost	Priority	Level
ENV33-C	High	Probable	Medium	P12	L1

Related Guidelines

ISO/IEC TR 24772:2013	Unquoted Search Path or Element [XZQ]
ISO/IEC TS 17961:2013	Calling system [syscall]
MITRE CWE	CWE-78, Improper Neutralization of Special Elements used in an OS Command ("OS Command Injection") CWE-88, Argument Injection or Modification

Bibliography

[IEEE Std 1003.1-2013]	XSH, System Interfaces, exec XSH, System Interfaces, popen XSH, System Interfaces, unlink
[Wheeler 2004]	

■ ENV34-C. Do not store pointers returned by certain functions

The C Standard, 7.22.4.6, paragraph 4 [ISO/IEC 9899:2011], states:

> The getenv function returns a pointer to a string associated with the matched list member. The string pointed to shall not be modified by the program but may be overwritten by a subsequent call to the getenv function.

This paragraph gives an implementation the latitude, for example, to return a pointer to a statically allocated buffer. Consequently, do not store this pointer because it may be overwritten by a subsequent call to the getenv() function or invalidated by modifications to the environment. This string should be referenced immediately and discarded. If later use is anticipated, the string should be copied so the copy can be safely referenced as needed.

The `getenv()` function is not thread-safe. Make sure to address any possible race conditions resulting from the use of this function.

The `asctime()`, `localeconv()`, `setlocale()`, and `strerror()` functions have similar restrictions. Do not access the objects returned by any of these functions after a subsequent call.

Noncompliant Code Example

This noncompliant code example attempts to compare the value of the TMP and TEMP environment variables to determine if they are the same:

```
#include <stdlib.h>
#include <string.h>
#include <stdio.h>

void func(void) {
  char *tmpvar;
  char *tempvar;

  tmpvar = getenv("TMP");
  if (!tmpvar) {
    /* Handle error */
  }
  tempvar = getenv("TEMP");
  if (!tempvar) {
    /* Handle error */
  }
  if (strcmp(tmpvar, tempvar) == 0) {
    printf("TMP and TEMP are the same.\n");
  } else {
    printf("TMP and TEMP are NOT the same.\n");
  }
}
```

This code example is noncompliant because the string referenced by tmpvar may be overwritten as a result of the second call to the `getenv()` function. As a result, it is possible that both tmpvar and tempvar will compare equal even if the two environment variables have different values.

Compliant Solution

This compliant solution uses the `malloc()` and `strcpy()` functions to copy the string returned by `getenv()` into a dynamically allocated buffer:

```
#include <stdlib.h>
#include <string.h>
```

```c
#include <stdio.h>

void func(void) {
  char *tmpvar;
  char *tempvar;

  const char *temp = getenv("TMP");
  if (temp != NULL) {
    tmpvar = (char *)malloc(strlen(temp)+1);
    if (tmpvar != NULL) {
      strcpy(tmpvar, temp);
    } else {
      /* Handle error */
    }
  } else {
    /* Handle error */
  }

  temp = getenv("TEMP");
  if (temp != NULL) {
    tempvar = (char *)malloc(strlen(temp)+1);
    if (tempvar != NULL) {
      strcpy(tempvar, temp);
    } else {
      /* Handle error */
    }
  } else {
    /* Handle error */
  }

  if (strcmp(tmpvar, tempvar) == 0) {
    printf("TMP and TEMP are the same.\n");
  } else {
    printf("TMP and TEMP are NOT the same.\n");
  }
  free(tmpvar);
  free(tempvar);
}
```

Compliant Solution (Annex K)

The C Standard, Annex K, provides the `getenv_s()` function for getting a value from the current environment. However, `getenv_s()` can still have **data races** with other threads of execution that modify the environment list.

```c
#define __STDC_WANT_LIB_EXT1__ 1
#include <errno.h>
#include <stdlib.h>
```

```c
#include <string.h>
#include <stdio.h>

void func(void) {
  char *tmpvar;
  char *tempvar;
  size_t requiredSize;
  errno_t err;
  err = getenv_s(&requiredSize, NULL, 0, "TMP");

  if (err) {
    /* Handle error */
  }

  tmpvar = (char *)malloc(requiredSize);
  if (!tmpvar) {
    /* Handle error */
  }
  err = getenv_s(&requiredSize, tmpvar, requiredSize, "TMP" );

  if (err) {
    /* Handle error */
  }
  err = getenv_s(&requiredSize, NULL, 0, "TEMP");
  if (err) {
    /* Handle error */
  }

  tempvar = (char *)malloc(requiredSize);
  if (!tempvar) {
    /* Handle error */
  }
  err = getenv_s(&requiredSize, tempvar, requiredSize, "TEMP" );

  if (err) {
    /* Handle error */
  }
  if (strcmp(tmpvar, tempvar) == 0) {
    printf("TMP and TEMP are the same.\n");
  } else {
    printf("TMP and TEMP are NOT the same.\n");
  }
  free(tmpvar);
  tmpvar = NULL;
  free(tempvar);
  tempvar = NULL;
}
```

Compliant Solution (Windows)

Microsoft Windows provides the _dupenv_s() and wdupenv_s() functions for getting a value from the current environment [MSDN]. The _dupenv_s() function searches the list of environment variables for a specified name. If the name is found, a buffer is allocated; the variable's value is copied into the buffer, and the buffer's address and number of elements are returned. The _dupenv_s() and _wdupenv_s() functions provide more convenient alternatives to getenv_s() and _wgetenv_s() because each function handles buffer allocation directly.

The caller is responsible for freeing any allocated buffers returned by these functions by calling free().

```c
#include <stdlib.h>
#include <errno.h>
#include <string.h>
#include <stdio.h>

void func(void) {
  char *tmpvar;
  char *tempvar;
  size_t len;

  errno_t err = _dupenv_s(&tmpvar, &len, "TMP");
  if (err) {
    /* Handle error */
  }
  err = _dupenv_s(&tempvar, &len, "TEMP");
  if (err) {
    /* Handle error */
  }

  if (strcmp(tmpvar, tempvar) == 0) {
    printf("TMP and TEMP are the same.\n");
  } else {
    printf("TMP and TEMP are NOT the same.\n");
  }
  free(tmpvar);
  tmpvar = NULL;
  free(tempvar);
  tempvar = NULL;
}
```

Compliant Solution (POSIX)

POSIX provides the strdup() function, which can make a copy of the environment variable string [IEEE Std 1003.1-2013]. The strdup() function is also included in *Extensions to the C Library—Part II* [ISO/IEC TR 24731-2:2010].

```
#include <stdlib.h>
#include <string.h>
#include <stdio.h>

void func(void) {
  char *tmpvar;
  char *tempvar;

  const char *temp = getenv("TMP");
  if (temp != NULL) {
    tmpvar = strdup(temp);
    if (tmpvar == NULL) {
      /* Handle error */
    }
  } else {
    /* Handle error */
  }

  temp = getenv("TEMP");
  if (temp != NULL) {
    tempvar = strdup(temp);
    if (tempvar == NULL) {
      /* Handle error */
    }
  } else {
    /* Handle error */
  }

  if (strcmp(tmpvar, tempvar) == 0) {
    printf("TMP and TEMP are the same.\n");
  } else {
    printf("TMP and TEMP are NOT the same.\n");
  }
  free(tmpvar);
  tmpvar = NULL;
  free(tempvar);
  tempvar = NULL;
}
```

Risk Assessment

Storing the pointer to the string returned by getenv(), localeconv(), setlocale(), or strerror() can result in overwritten data.

Rule	Severity	Likelihood	Remediation Cost	Priority	Level
ENV34-C	Low	Probable	Medium	P4	L3

Related Guidelines

ISO/IEC TR 24731-2	5.3.1.1, "The strdup Function"
ISO/IEC TS 17961:2013	Using an object overwritten by getenv, localeconv, setlocale, and strerror [libuse]

Bibliography

[IEEE Std 1003.1-2013]	Chapter 8, "Environment Variables" XSH, System Interfaces, strdup
[ISO/IEC 9899:2011]	7.22.4, "Communication with the Environment" 7.22.4.6, "The getenv Function" K.3.6.2.1, "The getenv_s Function"
[MSDN]	_dupenv_s() and _wdupenv_s()
[Viega 2003]	Section 3.6, "Using Environment Variables Securely"

Chapter 11

Signals (SIG)

Chapter Contents

Risk Assessment Summary

Rule	Severity	Likelihood	Remediation Cost	Priority	Level
SIG30-C	High	Likely	Medium	P18	L1
SIG31-C	High	Likely	High	P9	L2
SIG34-C	Low	Unlikely	Low	P3	L3
SIG35-C	Low	Unlikely	High	P1	L3

■ SIG30-C. Call only asynchronous-safe functions within signal handlers

Call only **asynchronous-safe functions** within signal handlers. For strictly conforming programs, only the C standard library functions abort(), _Exit(), quick_exit(), and signal() can be safely called from within a signal handler.

The C Standard, 7.14.1.1, paragraph 5 [ISO/IEC 9899:2011], states that if the signal occurs other than as the result of calling the abort() or raise() function, the behavior is undefined if

> the signal handler calls any function in the standard library other than the abort function, the _Exit function, the quick_exit function, or the signal function with the first argument equal to the signal number corresponding to the signal that caused the invocation of the handler.

Implementations may define a list of additional asynchronous-safe functions. These functions can also be called within a signal handler. This restriction applies to library functions as well as application-defined functions.

According to the C Rationale, 7.14.1.1 [C99 Rationale 2003],

> When a signal occurs, the normal flow of control of a program is interrupted. If a signal occurs that is being trapped by a signal handler, that handler is invoked. When it is finished, execution continues at the point at which the signal occurred. This arrangement can cause problems if the signal handler invokes a library function that was being executed at the time of the signal.

In general, it is not safe to invoke I/O functions from within signal handlers. Programmers should ensure a function is included in the list of an implementation's asynchronous-safe functions for all implementations their code will run on before using them in signal handlers.

Noncompliant Code Example

In this noncompliant example, the C standard library functions fprintf() and free() are called from the signal handler via the function log_message(). Neither function is asynchronous-safe.

```
#include <signal.h>
#include <stdio.h>
#include <stdlib.h>
```

```
enum { MAXLINE = 1024 };
char *info = NULL;

void log_message(void) {
  fprintf(stderr, info);
}

void handler(int signum) {
  log_message();
  free(info);
  info = NULL;
}

int main(void) {
  if (signal(SIGINT, handler) == SIG_ERR) {
    /* Handle error */
  }
  info = (char *)malloc(MAXLINE);
  if (info == NULL) {
    /* Handle Error */
  }

  while (1) {
    /* Main loop program code */

    log_message();

    /* More program code */
  }
  return 0;
}
```

Compliant Solution

Signal handlers should be as concise as possible—ideally by unconditionally setting a flag and returning. This compliant solution sets a flag of type volatile sig_atomic_t and returns; the log_message() and free() functions are called directly from main():

```
#include <signal.h>
#include <stdio.h>
#include <stdlib.h>

enum { MAXLINE = 1024 };
volatile sig_atomic_t eflag = 0;
char *info = NULL;
```

```
void log_message(void) {
  fprintf(stderr, info);
}

void handler(int signum) {
  eflag = 1;
}

int main(void) {
  if (signal(SIGINT, handler) == SIG_ERR) {
    /* Handle error */
  }
  info = (char *)malloc(MAXLINE);
  if (info == NULL) {
    /* Handle error */
  }

  while (!eflag) {
    /* Main loop program code */

    log_message();

    /* More program code */
  }

  log_message();
  free(info);
  info = NULL;

  return 0;
}
```

Noncompliant Code Example (longjmp())

Invoking the longjmp() function from within a signal handler can lead to undefined behavior if it results in the invocation of any non-asynchronous-safe functions. Consequently, neither longjmp() nor the POSIX siglongjmp() functions should ever be called from within a signal handler.

This noncompliant code example is similar to a vulnerability in an old version of Sendmail [VU#834865]. The intent is to execute code in a main() loop, which also logs some data. Upon receiving a SIGINT, the program transfers out of the loop, logs the error, and terminates.

However, an attacker can exploit this noncompliant code example by generating a SIGINT just before the second if statement in log_message(). The result is that longjmp() transfers control back to main(), where log_message() is called again. However, the first if statement would not be executed this time (because buf is not set to NULL as a result of the interrupt), and the program would write to the invalid memory location referenced by buf0.

```c
#include <setjmp.h>
#include <signal.h>
#include <stdlib.h>

enum { MAXLINE = 1024 };
static jmp_buf env;

void handler(int signum) {
  longjmp(env, 1);
}

void log_message(char *info1, char *info2) {
  static char *buf = NULL;
  static size_t bufsize;
  char buf0[MAXLINE];

  if (buf == NULL) {
    buf = buf0;
    bufsize = sizeof(buf0);
  }

  /*
   * Try to fit a message into buf, else reallocate
   * it on the heap and then log the message.
   */

  /* Program is vulnerable if SIGINT is raised here */

  if (buf == buf0) {
    buf = NULL;
  }
}

int main(void) {
  if (signal(SIGINT, handler) == SIG_ERR) {
    /* Handle error */
  }
  char *info1;
  char *info2;

  /* info1 and info2 are set by user input here */

  if (setjmp(env) == 0) {
    while (1) {
      /* Main loop program code */
```

```
        log_message(info1, info2);
        /* More program code */
      }
    } else {
      log_message(info1, info2);
    }

    return 0;
}
```

Compliant Solution

In this compliant solution, the call to longjmp() is removed; the signal handler sets an error flag instead:

```
#include <signal.h>
#include <stdlib.h>

enum { MAXLINE = 1024 };
volatile sig_atomic_t eflag = 0;

void handler(int signum) {
  eflag = 1;
}

void log_message(char *info1, char *info2) {
  static char *buf = NULL;
  static size_t bufsize;
  char buf0[MAXLINE];

  if (buf == NULL) {
    buf = buf0;
    bufsize = sizeof(buf0);
  }

  /*
   * Try to fit a message into buf, else reallocate
   * it on the heap and then log the message.
   */
  if (buf == buf0) {
    buf = NULL;
  }
}

int main(void) {
  if (signal(SIGINT, handler) == SIG_ERR) {
    /* Handle error */
  }
```

```
  char *info1;
  char *info2;

  /* info1 and info2 are set by user input here */

  while (!eflag) {
    /* Main loop program code */
    log_message(info1, info2);
    /* More program code */
  }

  log_message(info1, info2);

  return 0;
}
```

Noncompliant Code Example (raise())

In this noncompliant code example, the `int_handler()` function is used to carry out tasks specific to SIGINT and then raises SIGTERM. However, there is a nested call to the `raise()` function, which is undefined behavior.

```
#include <signal.h>
#include <stdlib.h>

void term_handler(int signum) {
  /* SIGTERM handler */
}

void int_handler(int signum) {
  /* SIGINT handler */
  if (raise(SIGTERM) != 0) {
    /* Handle error */
  }
}

int main(void) {
  if (signal(SIGTERM, term_handler) == SIG_ERR) {
    /* Handle error */
  }
  if (signal(SIGINT, int_handler) == SIG_ERR) {
    /* Handle error */
  }

  /* Program code */
  if (raise(SIGINT) != 0) {
```

```
    /* Handle error */
  }
  /* More code */

  return EXIT_SUCCESS;
}
```

Compliant Solution

In this compliant solution, `int_handler()` invokes `term_handler()` instead of raising SIGTERM:

```c
#include <signal.h>
#include <stdlib.h>

void term_handler(int signum) {
  /* SIGTERM handler */
}

void int_handler(int signum) {
  /* SIGINT handler */
  /* Pass control to the SIGTERM handler */
  term_handler(SIGTERM);
}

int main(void) {
  if (signal(SIGTERM, term_handler) == SIG_ERR) {
    /* Handle error */
  }
  if (signal(SIGINT, int_handler) == SIG_ERR) {
    /* Handle error */
  }

  /* Program code */
  if (raise(SIGINT) != 0) {
    /* Handle error */
  }
  /* More code */

  return EXIT_SUCCESS;
}
```

Risk Assessment

Invoking functions that are not asynchronous-safe from within a signal handler is undefined behavior.

Rule	Severity	Likelihood	Remediation Cost	Priority	Level
SIG30-C	High	Likely	Medium	P18	L1

Related Vulnerabilities

For an overview of software vulnerabilities resulting from improper signal handling, see Michal Zalewski's paper "Delivering Signals for Fun and Profit" [Zalewski 2001].

CERT Vulnerability Note VU#834865 "Sendmail signal I/O race condition" describes a vulnerability resulting from a violation of this rule. Another notable case where using the `longjmp()` function in a signal handler caused a serious vulnerability is wu-ftpd 2.4 [Greenman 1997]. The effective user ID is set to 0 in one signal handler. If a second signal interrupts the first, a call is made to `longjmp()`, returning the program to the main thread but without lowering the user's privileges. These escalated privileges can be used for further exploitation.

Related Guidelines

ISO/IEC TS 17961:2013	Calling functions in the C Standard Library other than `abort`, `_Exit`, and `signal` from within a signal handler [asyncsig]
MITRE CWE	CWE-479, Signal Handler Use of a Non-reentrant Function

Bibliography

[C99 Rationale 2003]	5.2.3, "Signals and Interrupts" 7.14.1.1, "The `signal` Function"
[Dowd 2006]	Chapter 13, "Synchronization and State"
[Greenman 1997]	
[IEEE Std 1003.1-2013]	XSH, System Interfaces, `longjmp` XSH, System Interfaces, `raise`
[ISO/IEC 9899:2011]	7.14.1.1, "The `signal` Function"
[OpenBSD]	`signal()` Man Page
[VU#834365]	
[Zalewski 2001]	"Delivering Signals for Fun and Profit"

■ SIG31-C. Do not access shared objects in signal handlers

Accessing or modifying shared objects in signal handlers can result in race conditions that can leave data in an inconsistent state. The two exceptions (C Standard, 5.1.2.3, paragraph 5) to this rule are the ability to read and write to lock-free atomic objects or to read from or write to variables of type `volatile sig_atomic_t`. Accessing any other type of object from a signal handler is undefined behavior (see undefined behavior 131 in Appendix B).

The need for the `volatile` keyword is described in "DCL22-C. Use volatile for data that cannot be cached."

The type `sig_atomic_t` is the integer type of an object that can be accessed as an atomic entity even in the presence of asynchronous interrupts. The type of `sig_atomic_t` is implementation-defined, though it provides some guarantees. Integer values ranging from `SIG_ATOMIC_MIN` through `SIG_ATOMIC_MAX`, inclusive, may be safely stored to a variable of the type. In addition, when `sig_atomic_t` is a signed integer type, `SIG_ATOMIC_MIN` must be no greater than -127 and `SIG_ATOMIC_MAX` no less than 127. Otherwise, `SIG_ATOMIC_MIN` must be 0 and `SIG_ATOMIC_MAX` must be no less than 255. The macros `SIG_ATOMIC_MIN` and `SIG_ATOMIC_MAX` are defined in the header `<stdint.h>`.

According to the C99 Rationale [C99 Rationale 2003], other than calling a limited, prescribed set of library functions,

> the C89 Committee concluded that about the only thing a strictly conforming program can do in a signal handler is to assign a value to a `volatile static` variable which can be written uninterruptedly and promptly return.

This issue was discussed at the April 2008 meeting of ISO/IEC WG14, and it was agreed that there are no known implementations in which it would be an error to read a value from a `volatile sig_atomic_t` variable, and the original intent of the committee was that both reading and writing variables of `volatile sig_atomic_t` would be strictly conforming.

The signal handler may also call a handful of functions, including `abort()` (see "SIG30-C. Call only asynchronous-safe functions within signal handlers" for more information).

Noncompliant Code Example

In this noncompliant code example, `err_msg` is updated to indicate that the `SIGINT` signal was delivered. The `err_msg` variable is a character pointer and not a variable of type `volatile sig_atomic_t`.

```c
#include <signal.h>
#include <stdlib.h>
#include <string.h>

enum { MAX_MSG_SIZE = 24 };
char *err_msg;

void handler(int signum) {
  strcpy(err_msg, "SIGINT encountered.");
}

int main(void) {
  signal(SIGINT, handler);

  err_msg = (char *)malloc(MAX_MSG_SIZE);
  if (err_msg == NULL) {
    /* Handle error */
  }
  strcpy(err_msg, "No errors yet.");
  /* Main code loop */
  return 0;
}
```

Compliant Solution (Writing volatile sig_atomic_t)

For maximum portability, signal handlers should only unconditionally set a variable of type volatile sig_atomic_t and return, as in this compliant solution:

```c
#include <signal.h>
#include <stdlib.h>
#include <string.h>

enum { MAX_MSG_SIZE = 24 };
volatile sig_atomic_t e_flag = 0;

void handler(int signum) {
  e_flag = 1;
}

int main(void) {
  char *err_msg = (char *)malloc(MAX_MSG_SIZE);
  if (err_msg == NULL) {
    /* Handle error */
  }

  signal(SIGINT, handler);
  strcpy(err_msg, "No errors yet.");
```

```
  /* Main code loop */
  if (e_flag) {
    strcpy(err_msg, "SIGINT received.");
  }
  return 0;
}
```

Compliant Solution (Lock-Free Atomic Access)

Signal handlers can refer to objects with static or thread storage duration that are lock-free atomic objects, as in this compliant solution:

```
#include <signal.h>
#include <stdlib.h>
#include <string.h>
#include <stdatomic.h>

#if __STDC_NO_ATOMICS__ == 1
#error "Atomics is not supported"
#elif ATOMIC_INT_LOCK_FREE == 0
#error "int is never lock-free"
#endif

atomic_int e_flag = ATOMIC_VAR_INIT(0);

void handler(int signum) {
  eflag = 1;
}

int main(void) {
  enum { MAX_MSG_SIZE = 24 };
  char err_msg[MAX_MSG_SIZE];
#if ATOMIC_INT_LOCK_FREE == 1
  if (!atomic_is_lock_free(&e_flag)) {
    return EXIT_FAILURE;
  }
#endif
  if (signal(SIGINT, handler) == SIG_ERR) {
    return EXIT_FAILURE;
  }
  strcpy(err_msg, "No errors yet.");
  /* Main code loop */
  if (e_flag) {
    strcpy(err_msg, "SIGINT received.");
  }
  return EXIT_SUCCESS;
}
```

Exceptions

SIG31-EX1: The C Standard, 7.14.1.1, paragraph 5, makes a special exception for errno when a valid call to the `signal()` function results in a SIG_ERR return, allowing errno to take an indeterminate value (see "ERR32-C. Do not rely on indeterminate values of errno").

Risk Assessment

Accessing or modifying shared objects in signal handlers can result in accessing data in an inconsistent state. "Delivering Signals for Fun and Profit" [Zalewski 2001] provides some examples of vulnerabilities that can result from violating this rule and other signal-handling rules.

Rule	Severity	Likelihood	Remediation Cost	Priority	Level
SIG31-C	High	Likely	High	P9	L2

Related Guidelines

ISO/IEC TS 17961:2013	Accessing shared objects in signal handlers [accsig]
MITRE CWE	CWE-662, Improper Synchronization

Bibliography

[C99 Rationale 2003]	5.2.3, "Signals and Interrupts"
[ISO/IEC 9899:2011]	7.14.1.1, "The `signal` Function"
[Zalewski 2001]	

■ SIG34-C. Do not call `signal()` from within interruptible signal handlers

A signal handler should not reassert its desire to handle its own signal. This is often done on *nonpersistent* platforms—that is, platforms that, upon receiving a signal, reset the handler for the signal to a default value before calling the bound signal handler. Calling `signal()` under these conditions presents a race condition (see "SIG01-C. Understand implementation-specific details regarding signal handler persistence").

A signal handler may call signal() only if it does not need to be asynchronous-safe (that is, if all relevant signals are masked so that the handler cannot be interrupted).

Noncompliant Code Example (POSIX)

On nonpersistent platforms, this noncompliant code example contains a race window, starting when the host environment resets the signal and ending when the handler calls signal(). During that time, a second signal sent to the program will trigger the default signal behavior, consequently defeating the persistent behavior implied by the call to signal() from within the handler to reassert the binding.

If the environment is persistent (that is, it does not reset the handler when the signal is received), the signal() call from within the handler() function is redundant.

```
#include <signal.h>

void handler(int signum) {
  if (signal(signum, handler) == SIG_ERR) {
    /* Handle error */
  }
  /* Handle signal */
}

void func(void) {
  if (signal(SIGUSR1, handler) == SIG_ERR) {
    /* Handle error */
  }
}
```

Compliant Solution (POSIX)

Calling the signal() function from within the signal handler to reassert the binding is unnecessary for persistent platforms, as in this compliant solution:

```
#include <signal.h>

void handler(int signum) {
  /* Handle signal */
}

void func(void) {
  if (signal(SIGUSR1, handler) == SIG_ERR) {
    /* Handle error */
  }
}
```

Compliant Solution (POSIX)

POSIX defines the `sigaction()` function, which assigns handlers to signals in a similar manner to `signal()` but allows the caller to explicitly set persistence. Consequently, the `sigaction()` function can be used to eliminate the race window on nonpersistent platforms, as in this compliant solution:

```
#include <signal.h>

void handler(int signum) {
  /* Handle signal */
}

void func(void) {
  struct sigaction act;
  act.sa_handler = handler;
  act.sa_flags = 0;
  if (sigemptyset(&act.sa_mask) != 0) {
    /* Handle error */
  }
  if (sigaction(SIGUSR1, &act, NULL) != 0) {
    /* Handle error */
  }
}
```

Although the handler in this example does not call `signal()`, it could do so safely because the signal is masked and the handler cannot be interrupted. If the same handler is installed for more than one signal, the signals must be masked explicitly in `act.sa_mask` to ensure that the handler cannot be interrupted because the system masks only the signal being delivered.

POSIX recommends that new applications should use `sigaction()` rather than `signal()`. The `sigaction()` function is not defined by the C Standard and is not supported on some platforms, including Windows.

Compliant Solution (Windows)

There are two classes of signals in the Visual C++ implementation:

- SIGSEGV, SIGILL, and SIGFPE have per-thread handlers, so each thread may register its own handler for these signals.
- SIGABRT, SIGBREAK, SIGTERM, and SIGINT have global handlers and access to these handlers is synchronized via a global lock.

For the signals with global handlers, the handler is reset to SIG_DFL and the handler is called under a lock, so there is no race if `signal()` is called again from the handler to reassert itself as the handler. For the signals with per-thread handlers, the state is local to the thread and resultantly there is no opportunity for a race.

Exceptions

SIG34-EX1: For implementations with persistent signal handlers, it is safe for a handler to modify the behavior of its own signal. Behavior modifications include ignoring the signal, resetting to the default behavior, and having the signal handled by a different handler. A handler reasserting its binding is also safe but unnecessary.

The following code example resets a signal handler to the system's default behavior:

```
#include <signal.h>

void handler(int signum) {
#if !defined(_WIN32)
  if (signal(signum, SIG_DFL) == SIG_ERR) {
    /* Handle error */
  }
#endif
  /* Handle signal */
}

void func(void) {
  if (signal(SIGUSR1, handler) == SIG_ERR) {
    /* Handle error */
  }
}
```

Risk Assessment

Two signals in quick succession can trigger a race condition on nonpersistent platforms, causing the signal's default behavior despite a handler's attempt to override it.

Rule	Severity	Likelihood	Remediation Cost	Priority	Level
SIG34-C	Low	Unlikely	Low	P3	L3

Related Guidelines

ISO/IEC TS 17961:2013	Calling signal from interruptible signal handlers [sigcall]
MITRE CWE	CWE-479, Signal Handler Use of a Non-reentrant Function

■ SIG35-C. Do not return from a computational exception signal handler

According to the C Standard, 7.14.1.1 [ISO/IEC 9899:2011], if a signal handler returns when it has been entered as a result of a computational exception (that is, with the value of its argument of SIGFPE, SIGILL, SIGSEGV, or any other implementation-defined value corresponding to such an exception), then the behavior is undefined (see undefined behavior 130 in Appendix B).

The *Portable Operating System Interface (POSIX®), Base Specifications, Issue 7* [IEEE Std 1003.1-2013], adds SIGBUS to the list of computational exception signal handlers:

> The behavior of a process is undefined after it returns normally from a signal-catching function for a SIGBUS, SIGFPE, SIGILL, or SIGSEGV signal that was not generated by kill(), sigqueue(), or raise().

Do not return from a signal handler that is invoked by SIGFPE, SIGILL, or SIGSEGV, or any other implementation-defined value corresponding to a computational exception such as SIGBUS on POSIX systems, regardless of how the signal was generated.

Noncompliant Code Example

In this noncompliant code example, the division operation has undefined behavior if denom equals 0 (see "INT33-C. Ensure that division and remainder operations do not result in divide-by-zero errors") and may result in a SIGFPE signal to the program:

```
#include <signal.h>
#include <stdlib.h>

volatile sig_atomic_t denom;

void sighandle(int s) {
  /* Fix the offending volatile */
  if (denom == 0) {
    denom = 1;
  }
}

int main(int argc, char *argv[]) {
  int result;
```

```
  if (argc < 2) {
    return 0;
  }
  denom = (sig_atomic_t)strtol(argv[1], NULL, 10);
  signal(SIGFPE, sighandle);
  result = 100 / (int)denom;
  return 0;
}
```

When compiled with some implementations, this noncompliant code example will loop infinitely if given the input 0. It illustrates that even when a SIGFPE handler attempts to fix the error condition while obeying all other rules of signal handling, the program still does not behave as expected.

Compliant Solution

The only portably safe way to leave a SIGFPE, SIGILL, or SIGSEGV handler is to invoke abort(), quick_exit(), or _Exit(). In the case of SIGFPE, the default action is abnormal termination, so no user-defined handler is required:

```
#include <signal.h>
#include <stdlib.h>

int main(int argc, char *argv[]) {
  int result;
  int denom;

  if (argc < 2) {
    return 0;
  }
  denom = strtol(argv[1], NULL, 10);
  result = 100 / denom;
  return 0;
}
```

Assigning the result of strtol() to denom without checking to make sure it fits violates "INT31-C. Ensure that integer conversions do not result in lost or misinterpreted data." See "INT06-C. Use strtol() or a related function to convert a string token to an integer" for a proper example of how to convert a string token to an integer and ensure that the value is in the range of int.

Risk Assessment

Returning from a computational exception signal handler is undefined behavior.

Rule	Severity	Likelihood	Remediation Cost	Priority	Level
SIG35-C	Low	Unlikely	High	P1	L3

Bibliography

[IEEE Std 1003.1-2013]	2.4.1 Signal Generation and Delivery
[ISO/IEC 9899:2011]	7.14.1.1, "The `signal` Function"

Chapter 12

Error Handling (ERR)

Chapter Contents

Risk Assessment Summary

Rule	Severity	Likelihood	Remediation Cost	Priority	Level
ERR30-C	Medium	Probable	Medium	P8	L2
ERR32-C	Low	Unlikely	Low	P3	L3
ERR33-C	High	Likely	Medium	P18	L1

■ ERR30-C. Set errno to zero before calling a library function known to set errno, and check errno only after the function returns a value indicating failure

The value of errno is initialized to zero at program startup, but it is never subsequently set to zero by any C standard library function. The value of errno may be set to nonzero by a C standard library function call whether or not there is an error, provided the use of errno is not documented in the description of the function. It is meaningful for a program to inspect the contents of errno only after an error might have occurred. More precisely, errno is meaningful only after a library function that sets errno on error has returned an error code.

According to Question 20.4 of C-FAQ [Summit 2005]:

> In general, you should detect errors by checking return values, and use errno only to distinguish among the various causes of an error, such as "File not found" or "Permission denied." (Typically, you use perror or strerror to print these discriminating error messages.) It's only necessary to detect errors with errno when a function does not have a unique, unambiguous, out-of-band error return (that is, because all of its possible return values are valid; one example is atoi [sic]). In these cases (and in these cases only; check the documentation to be sure whether a function allows this), you can detect errors by setting errno to 0, calling the function, and then testing errno. (Setting errno to 0 first is important, as no library function ever does that for you.)

Note that atoi() is not required to set the value of errno.

Library functions fall into the following categories:

- Those that set errno and return an **out-of-band error indicator**
- Those that set errno and return an in-band error indicator
- Those that do not promise to set errno
- Those with differing standards documentation

Library Functions That Set errno and Return an Out-of-Band Error Indicator. The C Standard specifies that the functions listed in Table 12–1 set errno and return an out-of-band error indicator. That is, their return value on error can never be returned by a successful call.

Table 12–1. Functions That Set errno and Return an Out-of-Band Error Indicator

Function Name	Return Value	errno **Value**
ftell()	–1L	Positive
fgetpos(), fsetpos()	Nonzero	Positive
mbrtowc(), mbsrtowcs()	(size_t)(-1)	EILSEQ
signal()	SIG_ERR	Positive
wcrtomb(), wcsrtombs()	(size_t)(-1)	EILSEQ
mbrtoc16(), mbrtoc32()	(size_t)(-1)	EILSEQ
c16rtomb(), cr32rtomb()	(size_t)(-1)	EILSEQ

A program may set and check errno for these library functions but is not required to do so. The program should not check the value of errno without first verifying that the function returned an error indicator. For example, errno should not be checked after calling signal() without first ensuring that signal() actually returned SIG_ERR.

Library Functions That Set errno and Return an In-Band Error Indicator. The C Standard specifies that the functions listed in Table 12–2 occasionally set errno and return an in-band error indicator. That is, the return value when an error occurs is also a valid return value for successful calls. For example, the strtoul() function returns ULONG_MAX and sets errno to ERANGE if an error occurs. Because ULONG_MAX is a valid return value, errno must be used to check whether an error actually occurred. A program that uses errno for error checking must set it to 0 before calling one of these library functions and then inspect errno before a subsequent library function call.

The fgetwc() and fputwc() functions return WEOF in multiple cases, only one of which results in setting errno. The string conversion functions will return the maximum or minimum representable value and set errno to ERANGE if the converted value cannot be represented by the data type. However, if the conversion cannot happen because the input is invalid, the function will return 0, and the output pointer parameter will be assigned the value of the input pointer parameter, provided the output parameter is non-null.

Table 12–2. Functions That Set errno and Return an In-Band Error Indicator

Function Name	Return Value	errno **Value**
fgetwc(), fputwc()	WEOF	EILSEQ
strtol(), wcstol()	LONG_MIN or LONG_MAX	ERANGE
strtoll(), wcstoll()	LLONG_MIN or LLONG_MAX	ERANGE
strtoul(), wcstoul()	ULONG_MAX	ERANGE
strtoull(), wcstoull()	ULLONG_MAX	ERANGE
strtoumax(), wcstoumax()	UINTMAX_MAX	ERANGE
strtod(), wcstod()	0 or ±HUGE_VAL	ERANGE
strtof(), wcstof()	0 or ±HUGE_VALF	ERANGE
strtold(), wcstold()	0 or ±HUGE_VALL	ERANGE
strtoimax(), wcstoimax()	INTMAX_MIN, INTMAX_MAX	ERANGE

Library Functions That Do Not Promise to Set errno. The C Standard fails to document the behavior of errno for some functions. For example, the setlocale() function normally returns a null pointer in the event of an error but no guarantees are made about setting errno.

After calling one of these functions, a program should not rely solely on the value of errno to determine if an error occurred. The function might have altered errno, but this does not ensure that errno will properly indicate an error condition.

Library Functions with Differing Standards Documentation. Some functions behave differently regarding errno in various standards. The fopen() function is one such example. When fopen() encounters an error, it returns a null pointer. The C Standard makes no mention of errno when describing fopen(). However, POSIX.1 declares that when fopen() encounters an error, it returns a null pointer and sets errno to a value indicating the error [IEEE Std 1003.1-2013]. The implication is that a program conforming to C but not to POSIX (such as a Windows program) should not check errno after calling fopen(), but a POSIX program may check errno if fopen() returns a null pointer.

Library Functions and errno

The following uses of errno are documented in the C Standard:

- Functions defined in <complex.h> may set errno but are not required to.

- For numeric conversion functions in the strtod, strtol, wcstod, and wcstol families, if the correct result is outside the range of representable values, an appropriate minimum or maximum value is returned, and the value ERANGE is stored in errno. For floating-point conversion functions in the strtod and wcstod families, if an underflow occurs, whether errno acquires the value ERANGE is implementation-defined. If the conversion fails, 0 is returned and errno is not set.

- The numeric conversion function atof() and those in the atoi family "need not affect the value of" errno.

- For mathematical functions in <math.h>, if the integer expression math_errhandling & MATH_ERRNO is nonzero, on a domain error, errno acquires the value EDOM; on an overflow with default rounding or if the mathematical result is an exact infinity from finite arguments, errno acquires the value ERANGE; and on an underflow, whether errno acquires the value ERANGE is implementation-defined.

- If a request made by calling signal() cannot be honored, a value of SIG_ERR is returned and a positive value is stored in errno.

- The byte I/O functions, wide-character I/O functions, and multibyte conversion functions store the value of the macro EILSEQ in errno if and only if an encoding error occurs.

- On failure, fgetpos() and fsetpos() return nonzero and store an implementation-defined positive value in errno.

- On failure, ftell() returns –1L and stores an implementation-defined positive value in errno.

- The perror() function maps the error number in errno to a message and writes it to stderr.

The POSIX.1 standard defines the use of errno by many more functions (including C standard library functions). POSIX also has a small set of functions that are exceptions to the rule. These functions have no return value reserved to indicate an error, but they still set errno on error. To detect an error, an application must set errno to 0 before calling the function and check whether it is nonzero after the call. Affected functions include strcoll(), strxfrm(), strerror(), wcscoll(), wcsxfrm(), and fwide(). Note that the C Standard allows these functions to set errno to a nonzero value on success. Consequently, this type of error checking should be performed only on POSIX systems.

Noncompliant Code Example (strtoul())

This noncompliant code example fails to set errno to 0 before invoking strtoul(). If an error occurs, strtoul() returns a valid value (ULONG_MAX), so errno is the only means of determining if strtoul() ran successfully.

```
#include <errno.h>
#include <limits.h>
#include <stdlib.h>

void func(const char *c_str) {
  unsigned long number;
  char *endptr;

  number = strtoul(c_str, &endptr, 0);
  if (endptr == c_str || (number == ULONG_MAX
                          && errno == ERANGE)) {
    /* Handle error */
  } else {
    /* Computation succeeded */
  }
}
```

Any error detected in this manner may have occurred earlier in the program or may not represent an actual error.

Compliant Solution (strtoul())

This compliant solution sets errno to 0 before the call to strtoul() and inspects errno after the call:

```
#include <errno.h>
#include <limits.h>
#include <stdlib.h>

void func(const char *c_str) {
  unsigned long number;
  char *endptr;

  errno = 0;
  number = strtoul(c_str, &endptr, 0);
```

```
    if (endptr == c_str || (number == ULONG_MAX
                            && errno == ERANGE)) {
      /* Handle error */
    } else {
      /* Computation succeeded */
    }
}
```

Noncompliant Code Example (fopen())

This noncompliant code example may fail to diagnose errors because fopen() might not set errno even if an error occurs:

```
#include <errno.h>
#include <stdio.h>

void func(const char *filename) {
  FILE *fileptr;

  errno = 0;
  fileptr = fopen(filename, "rb");
  if (errno != 0) {
    /* Handle error */
  }
}
```

Compliant Solution (fopen(), C)

The C Standard makes no mention of errno when describing fopen(). In this compliant solution, the results of the call to fopen() are used to determine failure, and errno is not checked:

```
#include <stdio.h>

void func(const char *filename) {
  FILE *fileptr = fopen(filename, "rb");
  if (fileptr == NULL) {
    /* An error occurred in fopen() */
  }
}
```

Compliant Solution (fopen(), POSIX)

In this compliant solution, errno is checked only after an error has already been detected by another means:

```
#include <errno.h>
#include <stdio.h>
```

```
void func(const char *filename) {
  FILE *fileptr;

  errno = 0;
  fileptr = fopen(filename, "rb");
  if (fileptr == NULL)  {
    /*
     * An error occurred in fopen(); now it's valid
     * to examine errno.
     */
    perror("func");
  }
}
```

Risk Assessment

The improper use of errno may result in failing to detect an error condition or in incorrectly identifying an error condition when none exists.

Rule	Severity	Likelihood	Remediation Cost	Priority	Level
ERR30-C	Medium	Probable	Medium	P8	L2

Related Guidelines

ISO/IEC TS 17961:2013	Incorrectly setting and using errno [inverrno]
MITRE CWE	CWE-456, Missing Initialization of a Variable

Bibliography

[Brainbell.com]	Macros and Miscellaneous Pitfalls
[Horton 1990]	Section 11, p. 168 Section 14, p. 254
[IEEE Std 1003.1-2013]	XSH, System Interfaces, fopen
[Koenig 1989]	Section 5.4, p. 73
[Summit 2005]	

■ ERR32-C. Do not rely on indeterminate values of errno

According to the C Standard [ISO/IEC 9899:2011], the behavior of a program is undefined when

> the value of errno is referred to after a signal occurred other than as the result of calling the abort or raise function and the corresponding signal handler obtained a SIG_ERR return from a call to the signal function.

See undefined behavior 133 in Appendix B.

A signal handler is allowed to call signal(), and if that fails, signal() returns SIG_ERR and sets errno to a positive value. However, if the event that caused a signal was external (not the result of the program calling abort() or raise()), the only functions the signal handler may call are _Exit() or abort(), or it may call signal() on the signal currently being handled, and if signal() fails, the value of errno is indeterminate.

This rule is also a special case of "SIG31-C. Do not access shared objects in signal handlers." The object designated by errno is of static storage duration and is not a volatile sig_atomic_t. As a result, performing any action that would require errno to be set would normally cause undefined behavior. The C Standard, 7.14.1.1, paragraph 5, makes a special exception for errno in this case, allowing errno to take on an indeterminate value but specifying that there is no other undefined behavior. This special exception makes it possible to call signal() from within a signal handler without risking undefined behavior, but the handler, and any code executed after the handler returns, must not depend on the value of errno being meaningful.

Noncompliant Code Example

The handler() function in this noncompliant code example attempts to restore default handling for the signal indicated by signum. If the request to set the signal to default can be honored, the signal() function returns the value of the signal handler for the most recent successful call to the signal() function for the specified signal. Otherwise, a value of SIG_ERR is returned and a positive value is stored in errno. Unfortunately, the value of errno is indeterminate because the handler() function is called when an external signal is raised, so any attempt to read errno (for example, by the perror() function) is undefined behavior:

```
#include <signal.h>
#include <stdlib.h>
#include <stdio.h>
```

```
typedef void (*pfv)(int);

void handler(int signum) {
  pfv old_handler = signal(signum, SIG_DFL);
  if (old_handler == SIG_ERR) {
    perror("SIGINT handler"); /* Undefined behavior */
    /* Handle error */
  }
}

int main(void) {
  pfv old_handler = signal(SIGINT, handler);
  if (old_handler == SIG_ERR) {
    perror("SIGINT handler");
    /* Handle error */
  }

  /* Main code loop */

  return EXIT_SUCCESS;
}
```

The call to `perror()` from `handler()` also violates "SIG30-C. Call only asynchronous-safe functions within signal handlers."

Compliant Solution

This compliant solution does not reference `errno` and does not return from the signal handler if the `signal()` call fails:

```
#include <signal.h>
#include <stdlib.h>
#include <stdio.h>

typedef void (*pfv)(int);

void handler(int signum) {
  pfv old_handler = signal(signum, SIG_DFL);
  if (old_handler == SIG_ERR) {
    abort();
  }
}

int main(void) {
  pfv old_handler = signal(SIGINT, handler);
```

```
    if (old_handler == SIG_ERR) {
      perror("SIGINT handler");
      /* Handle error */
    }

    /* Main code loop */

    return EXIT_SUCCESS;
}
```

Noncompliant Code Example (POSIX)

POSIX is less restrictive than C about what applications can do in signal handlers. It has a long list of asynchronous-safe functions that can be called (see "SIG30-C. Call only asynchronous-safe functions within signal handlers"). Many of these functions set errno on error, which can lead to a signal handler being executed between a call to a failed function and the subsequent inspection of errno. Consequently, the value inspected is not the one set by that function but the one set by a function call in the signal handler. POSIX applications can avoid this problem by ensuring that signal handlers containing code that might alter errno always save the value of errno on entry and restore it before returning.

The signal handler in this noncompliant code example alters the value of errno, and as a result, it can cause incorrect error handling if executed between a failed function call and the subsequent inspection of errno:

```
#include <signal.h>
#include <stdlib.h>
#include <errno.h>
#include <sys/wait.h>

void reaper(int signum) {
  errno = 0;
  for (;;) {
    int rc = waitpid(-1, NULL, WNOHANG);
    if ((0 == rc) || (-1 == rc && EINTR != errno)) {
      break;
    }
  }
  if (ECHILD != errno) {
    /* Handle error */
  }
}
```

```
int main(void) {
  struct sigaction act;
  act.sa_handler = reaper;
  act.sa_flags = 0;
  if (sigemptyset(&act.sa_mask) != 0) {
    /* Handle error */
  }
  if (sigaction(SIGCHLD, &act, NULL) != 0) {
    /* Handle error */
  }

  /* ... */

  return EXIT_SUCCESS;
}
```

Compliant Solution (POSIX)

This compliant solution saves and restores the value of errno in the signal handler:

```
#include <signal.h>
#include <stdlib.h>
#include <errno.h>
#include <sys/wait.h>

void reaper(int signum) {
  errno_t save_errno = errno;
  errno = 0;
  for (;;) {
    int rc = waitpid(-1, NULL, WNOHANG);
    if ((0 == rc) || (-1 == rc && EINTR != errno)) {
      break;
    }
  }
  if (ECHILD != errno) {
    /* Handle error */
  }
  errno = save_errno;
}

int main(void) {
  struct sigaction act;
  act.sa_handler = reaper;
  act.sa_flags = 0;
```

```
    if (sigemptyset(&act.sa_mask) != 0) {
      /* Handle error */
    }
    if (sigaction(SIGCHLD, &act, NULL) != 0) {
      /* Handle error */
    }

    /* ... */

    return EXIT_SUCCESS;
}
```

Risk Assessment

Referencing indeterminate values of errno is undefined behavior.

Rule	Severity	Likelihood	Remediation Cost	Priority	Level
ERR32-C	Low	Unlikely	Low	P3	L3

Bibliography

[ISO/IEC 9899:2011]	7.14.1.1, "The signal Function"

■ ERR33-C. Detect and handle standard library errors

The majority of the standard library functions, including I/O functions and memory allocation functions, return either a valid value or a value of the correct return type that indicates an error (for example, –1 or a null pointer). Assuming that all calls to such functions will succeed and failing to check the return value for an indication of an error is a dangerous practice that may lead to unexpected or undefined behavior when an error occurs. It is essential that programs detect and appropriately handle all errors in accordance with an error-handling policy, as discussed in "ERR00-C. Adopt and implement a consistent and comprehensive error-handling policy."

The successful completion or failure of each of the standard library functions listed in Table 12–3 shall be determined either by comparing the function's return value with the value listed in the column labeled "Error Return" or by calling one of the library functions mentioned in the footnotes.

The `ungetc()` function does not set the error indicator even when it fails, so it is not possible to check for errors reliably unless it is known that the argument is not equal to EOF. The C Standard [ISO/IEC 9899:2011] states that "one character of pushback is guaranteed," so this should not be an issue if, at

Table 12–3. Standard Library Functions

Function	Successful Return	Error Return
aligned_alloc()	Pointer to space	NULL
asctime_s()	0	Nonzero
at_quick_exit()	0	Nonzero
atexit()	0	Nonzero
bsearch()	Pointer to matching element	NULL
bsearch_s()	Pointer to matching element	NULL
btowc()	Converted wide character	WEOF
c16rtomb()	Number of bytes	(size_t)(-1)
c32rtomb()	Number of bytes	(size_t)(-1)
calloc()	Pointer to space	NULL
clock()	Processor time	(clock_t)(-1)
cnd_broadcast()	thrd_success	thrd_error
cnd_init()	thrd_success	thrd_nomem or thrd_error
cnd_signal()	thrd_success	thrd_error
cnd_timedwait()	thrd_success	thrd_timedout or thrd_error
cnd_wait()	thrd_success	thrd_error
ctime_s()	0	Nonzero
fclose()	0	EOF (negative)
fflush()	0	EOF (negative)
fgetc()	Character read	EOF[1]
fgetpos()	0	Nonzero, errno > 0
fgets()	Pointer to string	NULL
fgetwc()	Wide character read	WEOF[1]

Table 12–3. Standard Library Functions (Continued)

Function	Successful Return	Error Return
fopen()	Pointer to stream	NULL
fopen_s()	0	Nonzero
fprintf()	Number of characters (nonnegative)	Negative
fprintf_s()	Number of characters (nonnegative)	Negative
fputc()	Character written	EOF[2]
fputs()	Nonnegative	EOF (negative)
fputwc()	Wide character written	WEOF
fputws()	Non-negative	EOF (negative)
fread()	Elements read	Elements read
freopen()	Pointer to stream	NULL
freopen_s()	0	Nonzero
fscanf()	Number of conversions (nonnegative)	EOF (negative)
fscanf_s()	Number of conversions (nonnegative)	EOF (negative)
fseek()	0	Nonzero
fsetpos()	0	Nonzero, errno > 0
ftell()	File position	-1L, errno > 0
fwprintf()	Number of wide characters (nonnegative)	Negative
fwprintf_s()	Number of wide characters (nonnegative)	Negative
fwrite()	Elements written	Elements written
fwscanf()	Number of conversions (nonnegative)	EOF (negative)
fwscanf_s()	Number of conversions (nonnegative)	EOF (negative)
getc()	Character read	EOF[1]
getchar()	Character read	EOF[1]

continues

Table 12–3. Standard Library Functions (Continued)

Function	Successful Return	Error Return
getenv()	Pointer to string	NULL
getenv_s()	Pointer to string	NULL
gets_s()	Pointer to string	NULL
getwc()	Wide character read	WEOF
getwchar()	Wide character read	WEOF
gmtime()	Pointer to broken-down time	NULL
gmtime_s()	Pointer to broken-down time	NULL
localtime()	Pointer to broken-down time	NULL
localtime_s()	Pointer to broken-down time	NULL
malloc()	Pointer to space	NULL
mblen(), s != NULL	Number of bytes	–1
mbrlen(), s != NULL	Number of bytes or status	(size_t)(-1)
mbrtoc16()	Number of bytes or status	(size_t)(-1), errno == EILSEQ
mbrtoc32()	Number of bytes or status	(size_t)(-1), errno == EILSEQ
mbrtowc(), s != NULL	Number of bytes or status	(size_t)(-1), errno == EILSEQ
mbsrtowcs()	Number of non-null elements	(size_t)(-1), errno == EILSEQ
mbsrtowcs_s()	0	Nonzero
mbstowcs()	Number of non-null elements	(size_t)(-1)
mbstowcs_s()	0	Nonzero
mbtowc(), s != NULL	Number of bytes	–1
memchr()	Pointer to located character	NULL
mktime()	Calendar time	(time_t)(-1)
mtx_init()	thrd_success	thrd_error
mtx_lock()	thrd_success	thrd_error
mtx_timedlock()	thrd_success	thrd_timedout or thrd_error

Table 12–3. Standard Library Functions (Continued)

Function	Successful Return	Error Return
mtx_trylock()	thrd_success	thrd_busy or thrd_error
mtx_unlock()	thrd_success	thrd_error
printf_s()	Number of characters (nonnegative)	Negative
putc()	Character written	EOF[2]
putwc()	Wide character written	WEOF
raise()	0	Nonzero
realloc()	Pointer to space	NULL
remove()	0	Nonzero
rename()	0	Nonzero
setlocale()	Pointer to string	NULL
setvbuf()	0	Nonzero
scanf()	Number of conversions (nonnegative)	EOF (negative)
scanf_s()	Number of conversions (nonnegative)	EOF (negative)
signal()	Pointer to previous function	SIG_ERR, errno > 0
snprintf()	Number of characters that would be written (nonnegative)	Negative
snprintf_s()	Number of characters that would be written (nonnegative)	Negative
sprintf()	Number of non-null characters written	Negative
sprintf_s()	Number of non-null characters written	Negative
sscanf()	Number of conversions (nonnegative)	EOF (negative)
sscanf_s()	Number of conversions (nonnegative)	EOF (negative)
strchr()	Pointer to located character	NULL
strerror_s()	0	Nonzero

continues

Table 12–3. Standard Library Functions (Continued)

Function	Successful Return	Error Return
strftime()	Number of non-null characters	0
strpbrk()	Pointer to located character	NULL
strrchr()	Pointer to located character	NULL
strstr()	Pointer to located string	NULL
strtod()	Converted value	0, errno == ERANGE
strtof()	Converted value	0, errno == ERANGE
strtoimax()	Converted value	INTMAX_MAX or INTMAX_MIN, errno == ERANGE
strtok()	Pointer to first character of a token	NULL
strtok_s()	Pointer to first character of a token	NULL
strtol()	Converted value	LONG_MAX or LONG_MIN, errno == ERANGE
strtold()	Converted value	0, errno == ERANGE
strtoll()	Converted value	LLONG_MAX or LLONG_MIN, errno == ERANGE
strtoumax()	Converted value	UINTMAX_MAX, errno == ERANGE
strtoul()	Converted value	ULONG_MAX, errno == ERANGE
strtoull()	Converted value	ULLONG_MAX, errno == ERANGE
strxfrm()	Length of transformed string	>= n
swprintf()	Number of non-null wide characters	Negative
swprintf_s()	Number of non-null wide characters	Negative
swscanf()	Number of conversions (nonnegative)	EOF (negative)
swscanf_s()	Number of conversions (nonnegative)	EOF (negative)
thrd_create()	thrd_success	thrd_nomem or thrd_error
thrd_detach()	thrd_success	thrd_error
thrd_join()	thrd_success	thrd_error

Table 12–3. Standard Library Functions (Continued)

Function	Successful Return	Error Return
thrd_sleep()	0	Negative
time()	Calendar time	(time_t)(-1)
timespec_get()	Base	0
tmpfile()	Pointer to stream	NULL
tmpfile_s()	0	Nonzero
tmpnam()	Non-null pointer	NULL
tmpnam_s()	0	Nonzero
tss_create()	thrd_success	thrd_error
tss_get()	Value of thread-specific storage	0
tss_set()	thrd_success	thrd_error
ungetc()	Character pushed back	EOF
ungetwc()	Character pushed back	WEOF
vfprintf()	Number of characters (nonnegative)	Negative
vfprintf_s()	Number of characters (nonnegative)	Negative
vfscanf()	Number of conversions (nonnegative)	EOF (negative)
vfscanf_s()	Number of conversions (nonnegative)	EOF (negative)
vfwprintf()	Number of wide characters (nonnegative)	Negative
vfwprintf_s()	Number of wide characters (nonnegative)	Negative
vfwscanf()	Number of conversions (nonnegative)	EOF (negative)
vfwscanf_s()	Number of conversions (nonnegative)	EOF (negative)
vprintf_s()	Number of characters (nonnegative)	Negative
vscanf()	Number of conversions (nonnegative)	EOF (negative)
vscanf_s()	Number of conversions (nonnegative)	EOF (negative)

continues

Table 12–3. Standard Library Functions (Continued)

Function	Successful Return	Error Return
vsnprintf()	Number of characters that would be written (nonnegative)	Negative
vsnprintf_s()	Number of characters that would be written (nonnegative)	Negative
vsprintf()	Number of non-null characters (nonnegative)	Negative
vsprintf_s()	Number of non-null characters (nonnegative)	Negative
vsscanf()	Number of conversions (nonnegative)	EOF (negative)
vsscanf_s()	Number of conversions (nonnegative)	EOF (negative)
vswprintf()	Number of non-null wide characters	Negative
vswprintf_s()	Number of non-null wide characters	Negative
vswscanf()	Number of conversions (nonnegative)	EOF (negative)
vswscanf_s()	Number of conversions (nonnegative)	EOF (negative)
vwprintf_s()	Number of wide characters (nonnegative)	Negative
vwscanf()	Number of conversions (nonnegative)	EOF (negative)
vwscanf_s()	Number of conversions (nonnegative)	EOF (negative)
wcrtomb()	Number of bytes stored	(size_t)(-1)
wcschr()	Pointer to located wide character	NULL
wcsftime()	Number of non-null wide characters	0
wcspbrk()	Pointer to located wide character	NULL
wcsrchr()	Pointer to located wide character	NULL
wcsrtombs()	Number of non-null bytes	(size_t)(-1), errno == EILSEQ

Table 12–3. Standard Library Functions (Continued)

Function	Successful Return	Error Return
wcsrtombs_s()	0	Nonzero
wcsstr()	Pointer to located wide string	NULL
wcstod()	Converted value	0, errno == ERANGE
wcstof()	Converted value	0, errno == ERANGE
wcstoimax()	Converted value	INTMAX_MAX or INTMAX_MIN, errno == ERANGE
wcstok()	Pointer to first wide character of a token	NULL
wcstok_s()	Pointer to first wide character of a token	NULL
wcstol()	Converted value	LONG_MAX or LONG_MIN, errno == ERANGE
wcstold()	Converted value	0, errno == ERANGE
wcstoll()	Converted value	LLONG_MAX or LLONG_MIN, errno == ERANGE
wcstombs()	Number of non-null bytes	(size_t)(-1)
wcstombs_s()	0	Nonzero
wcstoumax()	Converted value	UINTMAX_MAX, errno == ERANGE
wcstoul()	Converted value	ULONG_MAX, errno == ERANGE
wcstoull()	Converted value	ULLONG_MAX, errno == ERANGE
wcsxfrm()	Length of transformed wide string	>= n
wctob()	Converted character	EOF
wctomb(), s != NULL	Number of bytes stored	–1
wctomb_s(), s != NULL	Number of bytes stored	–1
wctrans()	Valid argument to towctrans()	0
wctype()	Valid argument to iswctype()	0
wmemchr()	Pointer to located wide character	NULL

continues

Table 12–3. Standard Library Functions (Continued)

Function	Successful Return	Error Return
wprintf_s()	Number of wide characters (nonnegative)	Negative
wscanf()	Number of conversions (nonnegative)	EOF (negative)
wscanf_s()	Number of conversions (nonnegative)	EOF (negative)

Note: According to "FIO34-C. Distinguish between characters read from a file and EOF or WEOF," callers should verify end-of-file and file errors for the functions in this table as follows:
1. By calling ferror() and feof()
2. By calling ferror()

most, one character is ever pushed back before reading again (see "FIO13-C. Never push back anything other than one read character").

Noncompliant Code Example (setlocale())

In this noncompliant code example, the function utf8_to_wcs() attempts to convert a sequence of UTF-8 characters to wide characters. It first invokes setlocale() to set the global locale to the implementation-defined value "en_US.UTF-8" but does not check for failure. The setlocale() function will fail by returning a null pointer, for example, when the locale is not installed. The function may fail for other reasons as well, such as the lack of resources. Depending on the sequence of characters pointed to by utf8, the subsequent call to mbstowcs() may fail or result in the function storing an unexpected sequence of wide characters in the supplied buffer wcs.

```
#include <locale.h>
#include <stdlib.h>

int utf8_to_wcs(wchar_t *wcs, size_t n, const char *utf8,
                size_t *size) {
  if (NULL == size) {
    return -1;
  }
  setlocale(LC_CTYPE, "en_US.UTF-8");
  *size = mbstowcs(wcs, utf8, n);
  return 0;
}
```

Compliant Solution (`setlocale()`)

This compliant solution checks the value returned by `setlocale()` and avoids calling `mbstowcs()` if the function fails. The function also takes care to restore the locale to its initial setting before returning control to the caller.

```
#include <locale.h>
#include <stdlib.h>

int utf8_to_wcs(wchar_t *wcs, size_t n, const char *utf8,
                size_t *size) {
  if (NULL == size) {
    return -1;
  }
  const char *save = setlocale(LC_CTYPE, "en_US.UTF-8");
  if (NULL == save) {
    return -1;
  }

  *size = mbstowcs(wcs, utf8, n);
  if (NULL == setlocale(LC_CTYPE, save)) {
    return -1;
  }
  return 0;
}
```

Noncompliant Code Example (`calloc()`)

In this noncompliant code example, `temp_num`, `tmp2`, and `num_of_records` are derived from a tainted source. Consequently, an attacker can cause `calloc()` to fail by providing a large value for `num_of_records`.

```
#include <stdlib.h>
#include <string.h>

enum { SIG_DESC_SIZE = 32 };

typedef struct {
  char sig_desc[SIG_DESC_SIZE];
} signal_info;

void func(size_t num_of_records, size_t temp_num,
          const char *tmp2) {
  signal_info *start = (signal_info *)calloc(num_of_records,
                                      sizeof(signal_info));
```

```
  signal_info *point = start + temp_num - 1;
  if (tmp2 == NULL) {
    /* Handle error */
  }
  memcpy(point->sig_desc, tmp2, SIG_DESC_SIZE);
  /* ... */
}
```

When calloc() fails, it returns a null pointer that is assigned to start. If start is null, an attacker can provide a value for temp_num that, when scaled by sizeof(signal_info), references a writable address to which control is eventually transferred. The contents of the string referenced by tmp2 can then be used to overwrite the address, resulting in an arbitrary code execution vulnerability.

Compliant Solution (calloc())

To correct this error, ensure the pointer returned by calloc() is not null:

```
#include <stdlib.h>
#include <string.h>

enum { SIG_DESC_SIZE = 32 };

typedef struct {
  char sig_desc[SIG_DESC_SIZE];
} signal_info;

void func(size_t num_of_records, size_t temp_num,
          const char *tmp2) {
  signal_info *point;
  signal_info *start = (signal_info *)calloc(num_of_records,
                                        sizeof(signal_info));
  if (start == NULL) {
    /* Handle allocation error */
  } else if (tmp2 == NULL) {
    /* Handle error */
  }
  point = start + temp_num - 1;
  memcpy(point->sig_desc, tmp2, SIG_DESC_SIZE);
  point->sig_desc[SIG_DESC_SIZE - 1] = '\0';
  /* ... */
}
```

Noncompliant Code Example (`realloc()`)

This noncompliant code example calls `realloc()` to resize the memory referred to by p. However, if `realloc()` fails, it returns a null pointer and the connection between the original block of memory and p is lost, resulting in a memory leak.

```
#include <stdlib.h>

void *p;
void func(size_t new_size) {
  if (new_size == 0) {
    /* Handle error */
  }
  p = realloc(p, new_size);
  if (p == NULL) {
   /* Handle error */
  }
}
```

This code example does comply with "MEM04-C. Beware of zero-length allocations."

Compliant Solution (`realloc()`)

In this compliant solution, the result of `realloc()` is assigned to the temporary pointer q and validated before it is assigned to the original pointer p:

```
#include <stdlib.h>

void *p;
void func(size_t new_size) {
  void *q;

  if (new_size == 0) {
    /* Handle error */
  }

  q = realloc(p, new_size);
  if (q == NULL) {
    /* Handle error */
  } else {
    p = q;
  }
}
```

Noncompliant Code Example (fseek())

In this noncompliant code example, the fseek() function is used to set the file position to a location offset in the file referred to by file prior to reading a sequence of bytes from the file. However, if an I/O error occurs during the seek operation, the subsequent read will fill the buffer with the wrong contents.

```
#include <stdio.h>

size_t read_at(FILE *file, long offset,
               void *buf, size_t nbytes) {
  fseek(file, offset, SEEK_SET);
  return fread(buf, 1, nbytes, file);
}
```

Compliant Solution (fseek())

According to the C Standard, the fseek() function returns a nonzero value to indicate that an error occurred. This compliant solution tests for this condition before reading from a file to eliminate the chance of operating on the wrong portion of the file if fseek() fails:

```
#include <stdio.h>

size_t read_at(FILE *file, long offset,
               void *buf, size_t nbytes) {
  if (fseek(file, offset, SEEK_SET) != 0) {
    /* Indicate error to caller */
    return 0;
  }
  return fread(buf, 1, nbytes, file);
}
```

Noncompliant Code Example (snprintf())

In this noncompliant code example, snprintf() is assumed to succeed. However, if the call fails (for example, because of insufficient memory, as described in GNU libc bug 441945), the subsequent call to log_message() has undefined behavior because the character buffer is uninitialized and need not be null-terminated.

```
#include <stdio.h>

extern void log_message(const char *);

void f(int i, int width, int prec) {
```

```
      char buf[40];
      snprintf(buf, sizeof(buf), "i = %*.*i", width, prec, i);
      log_message(buf);
      /* ... */
}
```

Compliant Solution (snprintf())

This compliant solution does not assume that snprintf() will succeed regardless of its arguments. It tests the return value of snprintf() before subsequently using the formatted buffer. This compliant solution also treats the case where the static buffer is not large enough for snprintf() to append the terminating null character as an error.

```
#include <stdio.h>
#include <string.h>

extern void log_message(const char *);

void f(int i, int width, int prec) {
    char buf[40];
    int n;
    n = snprintf(buf, sizeof(buf), "i = %*.*i", width, prec, i);
    if (n < 0 || n >= sizeof(buf)) {
        /* Handle snprintf() error */
        strcpy(buf, "unknown error");
    }
    log_message(buf);
}
```

Compliant Solution (snprintf(null))

If unknown, the length of the formatted string can be discovered by invoking snprintf() with a null buffer pointer to determine the size required for the output, then dynamically allocating a buffer of sufficient size, and finally calling snprintf() again to format the output into the dynamically allocated buffer. Even with this approach, the success of all calls still needs to be tested, and any errors must be appropriately handled. A possible optimization is to first attempt to format the string into a reasonably small buffer allocated on the stack and, only when the buffer turns out to be too small, dynamically allocate one of a sufficient size:

```
#include <stdio.h>
#include <stdlib.h>
#include <string.h>
```

```
extern void log_message(const char *);

void f(int i, int width, int prec) {
  char buffer[20];
  char *buf = buffer;
  int n  = sizeof(buffer);
  const char fmt[] = "i = %*.*i";

  n = snprintf(buf, n, fmt, width, prec, i);
  if (n < 0) {
    /* Handle snprintf() error */
    strcpy(buffer, "unknown error");
    goto write_log;
  }

  if (n < sizeof(buffer)) {
    goto write_log;
  }

  buf = (char *)malloc(n + 1);
  if (NULL == buf) {
    /* Handle malloc() error */
    strcpy(buffer, "unknown error");
    goto write_log;
  }

  n = snprintf(buf, n, fmt, width, prec, i);
  if (n < 0) {
    /* Handle snprintf() error */
    strcpy(buffer, "unknown error");
  }

write_log:
  log_message(buf);

  if (buf != buffer) {
    free(buf);
  }
}
```

Note that this solution uses the goto statement, as suggested in "MEM12-C. Consider using a goto chain when leaving a function on error when using and releasing resources."

Exceptions

ERR33-EX1: It is acceptable to ignore the return value of a function that cannot fail, or a function whose return value is inconsequential, or if an error

Table 12–4. Functions the Return Values of Which Need Not Be Checked

Function	Successful Return	Error Return
putchar()	Character written	EOF
putwchar()	Wide character written	WEOF
puts()	Nonnegative	EOF (negative)
printf(), vprintf()	Number of characters (nonnegative)	Negative
wprintf(), vwprintf()	Number of wide characters (nonnegative)	Negative
kill_dependency()	The input parameter	NA
memcpy(), wmemcpy()	The destination input parameter	NA
memmove(), wmemmove()	The destination input parameter	NA
strcpy(), wcscpy()	The destination input parameter	NA
strncpy(), wcsncpy()	The destination input parameter	NA
strcat(), wcscat()	The destination input parameter	NA
strncat(), wcsncat()	The destination input parameter	NA
memset(), wmemset()	The destination input parameter	NA

condition need not be diagnosed. The function's results should be explicitly cast to void to signify programmer intent. Return values from the functions in Table 12–4 do not need to be checked because their historical use has overwhelmingly omitted error checking, and the repercussions have been inconsequential.

Risk Assessment

Failing to detect error conditions can lead to unpredictable results, including abnormal program termination and denial-of-service attacks or, in some situations, could even allow an attacker to run arbitrary code.

Rule	Severity	Likelihood	Remediation Cost	Priority	Level
ERR33-C	High	Likely	Medium	P18	L1

Related Vulnerabilities

The vulnerability in Adobe Flash [VU#159523] arises because Flash neglects to check the return value from calloc(). Even when calloc() returns a null pointer, Flash writes to an offset from the return value. Dereferencing a null pointer usually results in a program crash, but dereferencing an offset from a null pointer allows an exploit to succeed without crashing the program.

Related Guidelines

ISO/IEC TS 17961:2013	Failing to detect and handle standard library errors [liberr]
MITRE CWE	CWE-252, Unchecked Return Value CWE-253, Incorrect Check of Function Return Value CWE-390, Detection of Error Condition without Action CWE-391, Unchecked Error Condition

Bibliography

[DHS 2006]	Handle All Errors Safely
[Henricson 1992]	Recommendation 12.1, "Check for All Errors Reported from Functions"
[ISO/IEC 9899:2011]	7.21.7.10, "The ungetc Function"
[VU#159523]	

Chapter 13

Concurrency (CON)

Chapter Contents

Risk Assessment Summary

Rule	Severity	Likelihood	Remediation Cost	Priority	Level
CON30-C	Medium	Unlikely	Medium	P4	L3
CON31-C	Medium	Probable	High	P4	L3
CON32-C	Medium	Probable	Medium	P8	L2
CON33-C	Medium	Probable	High	P4	L3
CON34-C	Medium	Probable	High	P4	L3
CON35-C	Low	Probable	Medium	P4	L3
CON36-C	Low	Unlikely	Medium	P2	L3
CON37-C	Low	Probable	Low	P6	L2
CON38-C	Low	Unlikely	Medium	P2	L3
CON39-C	Low	Likely	Medium	P6	L2
CON40-C	Medium	Probable	Medium	P8	L2
CON41-C	Low	Unlikely	Medium	P2	L3

■ CON30-C. Clean up thread-specific storage

The `tss_create()` function creates a thread-specific storage pointer identified by a key. Threads can allocate thread-specific storage and associate the storage with a key that uniquely identifies the storage by calling the `tss_set()` function. If not properly freed, this memory may be leaked. Ensure that thread-specific storage is freed.

Noncompliant Code Example

In this noncompliant code example, each thread dynamically allocates storage in the `get_data()` function, which is then associated with the global key by the call to `tss_set()` in the `add_data()` function. This memory is subsequently leaked when the threads terminate.

```
#include <threads.h>
#include <stdlib.h>

/* Global key to the thread-specific storage */
tss_t key;
enum { MAX_THREADS = 3 };
```

```
int *get_data(void) {
  int *arr = (int *)malloc(2 * sizeof(int));
  if (arr == NULL) {
    return arr;  /* Report error */
  }
  arr[0] = 10;
  arr[1] = 42;
  return arr;
}

int add_data(void) {
  int *data = get_data();
  if (data == NULL) {
    return -1;  /* Report error */
  }

  if (thrd_success != tss_set(key, (void *)data)) {
    /* Handle error */
  }
  return 0;
}

void print_data(void) {
  /* Get this thread's global data from key */
  int *data = tss_get(key);

  if (data != NULL) {
    /* Print data */
  }
}

int function(void *dummy) {
  if (add_data() != 0) {
    return -1;  /* Report error */
  }
  print_data();
  return 0;
}

int main(void) {
  thrd_t thread_id[MAX_THREADS];

  /* Create the key before creating the threads */
  if (thrd_success != tss_create(&key, NULL)) {
    /* Handle error */
  }

  /* Create threads that would store specific storage */
  for (size_t i = 0; i < MAX_THREADS; i++) {
```

```
    if (thrd_success != thrd_create(&thread_id[i],
                                function, NULL)) {
      /* Handle error */
    }
  }

  for (size_t i = 0; i < MAX_THREADS; i++) {
    if (thrd_success != thrd_join(thread_id[i], NULL)) {
      /* Handle error */
    }
  }

  tss_delete(key);
  return 0;
}
```

Compliant Solution

In this compliant solution, each thread explicitly frees the thread-specific storage returned by the `tss_get()` function before terminating:

```
#include <threads.h>
#include <stdlib.h>

/* Global key to the thread-specific storage */
tss_t key;

int function(void *dummy) {
  if (add_data() != 0) {
    return -1;  /* Report error */
  }
  print_data();
  free(tss_get(key));
  return 0;
}

/* ... Other functions are unchanged */
```

Compliant Solution

This compliant solution invokes a destructor function registered during the call to `tss_create()` to automatically free any thread-specific storage:

```
#include <threads.h>
#include <stdlib.h>
```

```
/* Global key to the thread-specific storage */
tss_t key;
enum { MAX_THREADS = 3 };

/* ... Other functions are unchanged */

void destructor(void *data) {
  free(data);
}

int main(void) {
  thrd_t thread_id[MAX_THREADS];

  /* Create the key before creating the threads */
  if (thrd_success != tss_create(&key, destructor)) {
    /* Handle error */
  }

  /* Create threads that would store specific storage */
  for (size_t i = 0; i < MAX_THREADS; i++) {
    if (thrd_success != thrd_create(&thread_id[i],
                                    function, NULL)) {
      /* Handle error */
    }
  }

  for (size_t i = 0; i < MAX_THREADS; i++) {
    if (thrd_success != thrd_join(thread_id[i], NULL)) {
      /* Handle error */
    }
  }

  tss_delete(key);
  return 0;
}
```

Defect Report #416 (http://www.open-std.org/jtc1/sc22/wg14/www/docs/dr_
416.htm) states that "the standard does not specify if or when destructors
for thread-specific data keys (created with the `tss_create` function) are
invoked." The key observation from WG14 committee discussion concerns
the deliberate underspecification of threads to allow the greatest opportunity for implementation on a variety of operating systems. Consequently, it
is important to consult the documentation for the specific implementation
before adopting this or similar solutions using destructors for thread-specific
data keys.

Risk Assessment

Failing to free thread-specific objects results in memory leaks and could result in a denial-of-service attack.

Rule	Severity	Likelihood	Remediation Cost	Priority	Level
CON30-C	Medium	Unlikely	Medium	P4	L3

■ CON31-C. Do not destroy a mutex while it is locked

Mutexes are used to protect shared data structures being concurrently accessed. If a mutex is destroyed while a thread is blocked waiting for that mutex, **critical sections** (shared data that would otherwise be protected from data races) are no longer protected.

The C Standard, 7.26.4.1, paragraph 2 [ISO/IEC 9899:2011], states:

> The mtx_destroy function releases any resources used by the mutex pointed to by mtx. No threads can be blocked waiting for the mutex pointed to by mtx.

This statement implies that destroying a mutex while a thread is waiting on it is undefined behavior.

Noncompliant Code Example

This noncompliant code example creates several threads that each invoke the do_work() function, passing a unique number as an ID. The do_work() function initializes the lock mutex if the argument is 0 and destroys the mutex if the argument is max_threads - 1. In all other cases, the do_work() function provides normal processing. Each thread, except the final cleanup thread, increments the atomic completed variable when it is finished.

Unfortunately, this code contains several race conditions, allowing the mutex to be destroyed before it is unlocked. Additionally, there is no guarantee that lock will be initialized before it is passed to mtx_lock(). Each of these behaviors is undefined.

```
#include <stdatomic.h>
#include <threads.h>

mtx_t lock;
/* Atomic so multiple threads can modify safely */
atomic_int completed = ATOMIC_VAR_INIT(0);
enum { max_threads = 5 };
```

```
int do_work(void *arg) {
  int *i = (int *)arg;

  if (*i == 0) { /* Creation thread */
    if (thrd_success != mtx_init(&lock, mtx_plain)) {
      /* Handle error */
    }
    atomic_store(&completed, 1);
  } else if (*i < max_threads - 1) { /* Worker thread */
    if (thrd_success != mtx_lock(&lock)) {
      /* Handle error */
    }
    /* Access data protected by the lock */
    atomic_fetch_add(&completed, 1);
    if (thrd_success != mtx_unlock(&lock)) {
      /* Handle error */
    }
  } else { /* Destruction thread */
    mtx_destroy(&lock);
  }
  return 0;
}

int main(void) {
  thrd_t threads[max_threads];

  for (size_t i = 0; i < max_threads; i++) {
    if (thrd_success != thrd_create(&threads[i], do_work, &i)) {
      /* Handle error */
    }
  }
  for (size_t i = 0; i < max_threads; i++) {
    if (thrd_success != thrd_join(threads[i], 0)) {
      /* Handle error */
    }
  }
  return 0;
}
```

Compliant Solution

This compliant solution eliminates the race conditions by initializing the mutex in main() before creating the threads and by destroying the mutex in main() after joining the threads:

```
#include <stdatomic.h>
#include <threads.h>
```

```
mtx_t lock;
/* Atomic so multiple threads can increment safely */
atomic_int completed = ATOMIC_VAR_INIT(0);
enum { max_threads = 5 };

int do_work(void *dummy) {
  if (thrd_success != mtx_lock(&lock)) {
    /* Handle error */
  }
  /* Access data protected by the lock */
  atomic_fetch_add(&completed, 1);
  if (thrd_success != mtx_unlock(&lock)) {
    /* Handle error */
  }

  return 0;
}

int main(void) {
  thrd_t threads[max_threads];

  if (thrd_success != mtx_init(&lock, mtx_plain)) {
    /* Handle error */
  }
  for (size_t i = 0; i < max_threads; i++) {
    if (thrd_success != thrd_create(&threads[i], do_work, NULL)) {
      /* Handle error */
    }
  }
  for (size_t i = 0; i < max_threads; i++) {
    if (thrd_success != thrd_join(threads[i], 0)) {
      /* Handle error */
    }
  }

  mtx_destroy(&lock);
  return 0;
}
```

Risk Assessment

Destroying a mutex while it is locked may result in invalid control flow and data corruption.

Rule	Severity	Likelihood	Remediation Cost	Priority	Level
CON31-C	Medium	Probable	High	P4	L3

Related Guidelines

MITRE CWE	CWE-667, Improper Locking

Bibliography

[ISO/IEC 9899:2011]	7.26.4.1, "The `mtx_destroy` Function"

■ CON32-C. Prevent data races when accessing bit-fields from multiple threads

When accessing a bit-field, a thread may inadvertently access a separate bit-field in adjacent memory. This is because compilers are required to store multiple adjacent bit-fields in one storage unit whenever they fit. Consequently, data races may exist not just on a bit-field accessed by multiple threads but also on other bit-fields sharing the same byte or word. A similar problem is discussed in "CON00-C. Avoid race conditions with multiple threads," but the issue described by this rule can be harder to diagnose because it may not be obvious that the same memory location is being modified by multiple threads.

One approach for preventing data races in concurrent programming is to use a mutex. When properly observed by all threads, a mutex can provide safe and secure access to a shared object. However, mutexes provide no guarantees with regard to other objects that might be accessed when the mutex is not controlled by the accessing thread. Unfortunately, there is no portable way to determine which adjacent bit-fields may be stored along with the desired bit-field.

Another approach is to insert a non-bit-field member between any two bit-fields to ensure that each bit-field is the only one accessed within its storage unit. This technique effectively guarantees that no two bit-fields are accessed simultaneously.

Noncompliant Code Example (Bit-Field)

Adjacent bit-fields may be stored in a single memory location. Consequently, modifying adjacent bit-fields in different threads is undefined behavior, as shown in this noncompliant code example:

```
struct multi_threaded_flags {
  unsigned int flag1 : 2;
  unsigned int flag2 : 2;
};
```

```
struct multi_threaded_flags flags;

int thread1(void *arg) {
  flags.flag1 = 1;
  return 0;
}

int thread2(void *arg) {
  flags.flag2 = 2;
  return 0;
}
```

The C Standard, 3.14, paragraph 3 [ISO/IEC 9899:2011], states:

NOTE 2 A bit-field and an adjacent non-bit-field member are in separate memory locations. The same applies to two bit-fields, if one is declared inside a nested structure declaration and the other is not, or if the two are separated by a zero-length bit-field declaration, or if they are separated by a non-bit-field member declaration. It is not safe to concurrently update two non-atomic bit-fields in the same structure if all members declared between them are also (non-zero-length) bit-fields, no matter what the sizes of those intervening bit-fields happen to be.

For example, the following instruction sequence is possible:

```
Thread 1: register 0 = flags
Thread 1: register 0 &= ~mask(flag1)
Thread 2: register 0 = flags
Thread 2: register 0 &= ~mask(flag2)
Thread 1: register 0 |= 1 << shift(flag1)
Thread 1: flags = register 0
Thread 2: register 0 |= 2 << shift(flag2)
Thread 2: flags = register 0
```

Compliant Solution (Bit-Field, C11, Mutex)

This compliant solution protects all accesses of the flags with a mutex, thereby preventing any data races:

```
#include <threads.h>

struct multi_threaded_flags {
  unsigned int flag1 : 2;
  unsigned int flag2 : 2;
};

struct mtf_mutex {
  struct multi_threaded_flags s;
```

```
  mtx_t mutex;
};

struct mtf_mutex flags;

int thread1(void *arg) {
  if (thrd_success != mtx_lock(&flags.mutex)) {
    /* Handle error */
  }
  flags.s.flag1 = 1;
  if (thrd_success != mtx_unlock(&flags.mutex)) {
    /* Handle error */
  }
  return 0;
}

int thread2(void *arg) {
  if (thrd_success != mtx_lock(&flags.mutex)) {
    /* Handle error */
  }
  flags.s.flag2 = 2;
  if (thrd_success != mtx_unlock(&flags.mutex)) {
    /* Handle error */
  }
  return 0;
}
```

Compliant Solution (C11)

In this compliant solution, two threads simultaneously modify two distinct
non-bit-field members of a structure. Because the members occupy different
bytes in memory, no concurrency protection is required.

```
struct multi_threaded_flags {
  unsigned char flag1;
  unsigned char flag2;
};

struct multi_threaded_flags flags;

int thread1(void *arg) {
  flags.flag1 = 1;
  return 0;
}

int thread2(void *arg) {
  flags.flag2 = 2;
  return 0;
}
```

Unlike C99, C11 explicitly defines a memory location and provides the following note in subclause 3.14.2 [ISO/IEC 9899:2011]:

> NOTE 1 Two threads of execution can update and access separate memory locations without interfering with each other.

Using a compiler that conforms to C99 or earlier, it is possible that flag1 and flag2 are stored in the same word. If both assignments occur on a thread-scheduling interleaving that ends with both stores occurring after one another, it is possible that only one of the flags will be set as intended, and the other flag will contain its previous value, because both members are represented by the same word, which is the smallest unit the processor can work on. Before the changes made to the C Standard for C11, there were no guarantees that these flags could be modified concurrently.

Risk Assessment

Although the race window is narrow, an assignment or an expression can evaluate improperly because of misinterpreted data resulting in a corrupted running state or unintended information disclosure.

Rule	Severity	Likelihood	Remediation Cost	Priority	Level
CON32-C	Medium	Probable	Medium	P8	L2

Bibliography

[ISO/IEC 9899:2011]	3.14, "Memory Location"

■ CON33-C. Avoid race conditions when using library functions

Some C standard library functions are not guaranteed to be **reentrant** with respect to threads. Functions such as strtok() and asctime() return a pointer to the result stored in function-allocated memory on a per-process basis. Other functions such as rand() store state information in function-allocated memory on a per-process basis. Multiple threads invoking the same function can cause concurrency problems, which often result in abnormal behavior and can cause more serious vulnerabilities, such as abnormal termination, denial-of-service attack, and data integrity violations.

According to the C Standard, the library functions listed in Table 13–1 may contain data races when invoked by multiple threads.

Table 13–1. Library Functions Subject to Data Races

Function	Remediation
rand(), srand()	MSC30-C. Do not use the rand() function for generating pseudorandom numbers
getenv(), getenv_s()	ENV34-C. Do not store pointers returned by certain functions
strtok()	strtok_s() in C11 Annex K strtok_r() in POSIX
strerror()	strerror_s() in C11 Annex K strerror_r() in POSIX
asctime(), ctime(), localtime(), gmtime()	asctime_s(), ctime_s(), localtime_s(), gmtime_s() in C11 Annex K
setlocale()	Protect multithreaded access to locale-specific APIs with a mutex
ATOMIC_VAR_INIT, atomic_init()	Do not attempt to initialize an atomic variable from multiple threads
tmpnam()	tmpnam_s() in C11 Annex K tmpnam_r() in POSIX
mbrtoc16(), c16rtomb(), mbrtoc32(), c32rtomb()	Do not call with a null mbstate_t * argument

Section 2.9.1 of the *Portable Operating System Interface (POSIX®), Base Specifications, Issue 7* [IEEE Std 1003.1-2013] extends the list of functions that are not required to be thread-safe.

Noncompliant Code Example

In this noncompliant code example, the function f() is called from within a multithreaded application but encounters an error while calling a system function. The strerror() function returns a human-readable error string given an error number. The C Standard, 7.24.6.2 [ISO/IEC 9899:2011], specifically states that strerror() is not required to avoid data races. An implementation could write the error string into a static array and return a pointer to it, and that array might be accessible and modifiable by other threads.

```
#include <errno.h>
#include <stdio.h>
#include <string.h>

void f(FILE *fp) {
  fpos_t pos;
  errno = 0;
```

```
  if (0 != fgetpos(fp, &pos)) {
    char *errmsg = strerror(errno);
    printf("Couldn't get the file position: %s\n", errmsg);
  }
}
```

Note that this code first sets errno to 0 to comply with "ERR30-C. Set errno to zero before calling a library function known to set errno, and check errno only after the function returns a value indicating failure."

Compliant Solution (strerror_s())

This compliant solution uses the strerror_s() function from Annex K of the C Standard, which has the same functionality as strerror() but guarantees thread safety:

```
#define __STDC_WANT_LIB_EXT1__ 1
#include <errno.h>
#include <stdio.h>
#include <string.h>

enum { BUFFERSIZE = 64 };
void f(FILE *fp) {
  fpos_t pos;
  errno = 0;

  if (0 != fgetpos(fp, &pos)) {
    char errmsg[BUFFERSIZE];
    if (strerror_s(errmsg, BUFFERSIZE, errno) != 0) {
      /* Handle error */
    }
    printf("Could not get the file position: %s\n", errmsg);
  }
}
```

Note that because Annex K is optional, strerror_s() may not be available in all implementations.

Compliant Solution (POSIX, strerror_r())

This compliant solution uses the POSIX strerror_r() function, which has the same functionality as strerror() but guarantees thread safety:

```
#include <errno.h>
#include <stdio.h>
```

```
enum { BUFFERSIZE = 64 };

void f(FILE *fp) {
  fpos_t pos;
  errno = 0;

  if (0 != fgetpos(fp, &pos)) {
    char errmsg[BUFFERSIZE];
    if (strerror_r(errno, errmsg, BUFFERSIZE) != 0) {
      /* Handle error */
    }
    printf("Could not get the file position because of %s\n",
           errmsg);
  }
}
```

Linux provides two versions of strerror_r(), known as the *XSI-compliant version* and the *GNU-specific version*. This compliant solution assumes the XSI-compliant version, which is the default when an application is compiled as required by POSIX (that is, by defining _POSIX_C_SOURCE or _XOPEN_SOURCE appropriately). The strerror_r() manual page lists version(s) that are available on a particular system.

Risk Assessment

Race conditions caused by multiple threads invoking the same library function can lead to abnormal termination of the application, data integrity violations, or denial-of-service attack.

Rule	Severity	Likelihood	Remediation Cost	Priority	Level
CON33-C	Medium	Probable	High	P4	L3

Bibliography

[IEEE Std 1003.1-2013]	Section 2.9.1, "Thread Safety"
[ISO/IEC 9899:2011]	7.24.6.2, "The strerror Function"
[Open Group 1997]	Section 10.12, "Thread-Safe POSIX.1 and C-Language Functions"

■ CON34-C. Declare objects shared between threads with appropriate storage durations

Accessing the automatic or thread-local variables of one thread from another thread is implementation-defined [ISO/IEC 9899:2011] and can cause invalid memory accesses because the execution of threads can be interwoven within the constraints of the synchronization model. As a result, the referenced stack frame or thread-local variable may no longer be valid when another thread tries to access it. Shared static variables can be protected by thread synchronization mechanisms. However, automatic (local) variables cannot be shared in the same manner because the referenced stack frame's thread would need to stop executing, or some other mechanism must be employed to ensure that the referenced stack frame is still valid. Do not access automatic or thread-local objects from a thread other than the one with which the object is associated. See "DCL30-C. Declare objects with appropriate storage durations" for information on how to declare objects with appropriate storage durations when data is not being shared between threads.

Noncompliant Code Example (Automatic Storage Duration)

This noncompliant code example passes the address of a variable to a child thread, which prints it out. The variable has automatic storage duration. Depending on the execution order, the child thread might reference the variable after the variable's lifetime in the parent thread. This would cause the child thread to access an invalid memory location.

```
#include <threads.h>
#include <stdio.h>

int child_thread(void *val) {
  int *res = (int *)val;
  printf("Result: %d\n", *res);
  return 0;
}

void create_thread(thrd_t *tid) {
  int val = 1;
  if (thrd_success != thrd_create(tid, child_thread, &val)) {
    /* Handle error */
  }
}

int main(void) {
  thrd_t tid;
  create_thread(&tid);
```

```
    if (thrd_success != thrd_join(tid, NULL)) {
      /* Handle error */
    }
    return 0;
}
```

Noncompliant Code Example (Automatic Storage Duration)

One solution is to ensure that all objects with automatic storage duration shared between threads are declared such that their lifetime extends past the lifetime of the threads. This can be accomplished using a thread synchronization mechanism, such as thrd_join(). For example, in this compliant solution, val is declared in main(), where thrd_join() is called. Because the parent thread waits until the child thread completes before continuing its execution, the shared objects have a lifetime at least as great as the thread. However, this example relies on implementation-defined behavior and is nonportable.

```
#include <threads.h>
#include <stdio.h>

int child_thread(void *val) {
  int *result = (int *)val;
  printf("Result: %d\n", *result);  /* Correctly prints 1 */
  return 0;
}

void create_thread(thrd_t *tid, int *val) {
  if (thrd_success != thrd_create(tid, child_thread, val)) {
    /* Handle error */
  }
}

int main(void) {
  int val = 1;
  thrd_t tid;
  create_thread(&tid, &val);
  if (thrd_success != thrd_join(tid, NULL)) {
    /* Handle error */
  }
  return 0;
}
```

Compliant Solution (Static Storage Duration)

This compliant solution stores the value in an object having static storage duration. The lifetime of this object is the entire execution of the program; consequently, it can be safely accessed by any thread.

```
#include <threads.h>
#include <stdio.h>

int child_thread(void *v) {
  int *result = (int *)v;
  printf("Result: %d\n", *result);  /* Correctly prints 1 */
  return 0;
}

void create_thread(thrd_t *tid) {
  static int val = 1;
  if (thrd_success != thrd_create(tid, child_thread, &val)) {
    /* Handle error */
  }
}

int main(void) {
  thrd_t tid;
  create_thread(&tid);
  if (thrd_success != thrd_join(tid, NULL)) {
    /* Handle error */
  }
  return 0;
}
```

Compliant Solution (Allocated Storage Duration)

This compliant solution stores the value passed to the child thread in a dynamically allocated object. Because this object will persist until explicitly freed, the child thread can safely access its value.

```
#include <threads.h>
#include <stdio.h>
#include <stdlib.h>

int child_thread(void *val) {
  int *result = (int *)val;
  printf("Result: %d\n", *result); /* Correctly prints 1 */
  return 0;
}

void create_thread(thrd_t *tid, int *value) {
  *value = 1;
  if (thrd_success != thrd_create(tid, child_thread,
                                  value)) {
    /* Handle error */
  }
}
```

```
int main(void) {
  thrd_t tid;
  int *value = (int *)malloc(sizeof(int));
  if (!value) {
    /* Handle error */
  }
  create_thread(&tid, value);
  if (thrd_success != thrd_join(tid, NULL)) {
    /* Handle error */
  }
  free(value);
  return 0;
}
```

Noncompliant Code Example (Thread-Specific Storage)

In this noncompliant code example, the value is stored in thread-specific storage of the parent thread. However, because thread-specific data is available only to the thread that stores it, the child_thread() function will set result to a null value.

```
#include <threads.h>
#include <stdio.h>
#include <stdlib.h>

static tss_t key;

int child_thread(void *v) {
  int *result = tss_get(*(tss_t *)v);
  printf("Result: %d\n", *result);
  return 0;
}

int create_thread(void *thrd) {
  int *val = (int *)malloc(sizeof(int));
  if (val == NULL) {
    /* Handle error */
  }
  *val = 1;
  if (thrd_success != tss_set(key, val) {
    /* Handle error */
  }
  if (thrd_success != thrd_create((thrd_t *)thrd,
                                  child_thread, &key)) {
    /* Handle error */
  }
  return 0;
}
```

```
int main(void) {
  thrd_t parent_tid, child_tid;

  if (thrd_success != tss_create(&key, free)) {
    /* Handle error */
  }
  if (thrd_success != thrd_create(&parent_tid, create_thread,
                                  &child_tid)) {
    /* Handle error */
  }
  if (thrd_success != thrd_join(parent_tid, NULL)) {
    /* Handle error */
  }
  if (thrd_success != thrd_join(child_tid, NULL)) {
    /* Handle error */
  }
  if (thrd_success != tss_delete(key)) {
    /* Handle error */
  }
  return 0;
}
```

Compliant Solution (Thread-Specific Storage)

This compliant solution illustrates how thread-specific storage can be combined with a call to a thread synchronization mechanism, such as thrd_ join(). Because the parent thread waits until the child thread completes before continuing its execution, the child thread is guaranteed to access a valid live object.

```
#include <threads.h>
#include <stdio.h>
#include <stdlib.h>

static tss_t key;

int child_thread(void *v) {
  int *result = v;
  printf("Result: %d\n", *result);  /* Correctly prints 1 */
  return 0;
}

int create_thread(void *thrd) {
  int *val = (int *)malloc(sizeof(int));
  if (val == NULL) {
    /* Handle error */
  }
  val = 1;
```

```
    if (thrd_success != tss_set(key, val)) {
      /* Handle error */
    }
    /* ... */
    void *v = tss_get(key);
    if (thrd_success != thrd_create((thrd_t *)thrd,
                                    child_thread, v)) {
      /* Handle error */
    }
    return 0;
}

int main(void) {
  thrd_t parent_tid, child_tid;

  if (thrd_success != tss_create(&key, free)) {
    /* Handle error */
  }
  if (thrd_success != thrd_create(&parent_tid, create_thread,
                                  &child_tid)) {
    /* Handle error */
  }
  if (thrd_success != thrd_join(parent_tid, NULL)) {
    /* Handle error */
  }
  if (thrd_success != thrd_join(child_tid, NULL)) {
    /* Handle error */
  }
  if (thrd_success != tss_delete(key)) {
    /* Handle error */
  }
  return 0;
}
```

This compliant solution uses pointer-to-integer and integer-to-pointer conversions, which have implementation-defined behavior (see "INT36-C. Converting a pointer to integer or integer to pointer").

Compliant Solution (Thread-Local Storage, Windows, Visual Studio)

Similar to the preceding compliant solution, this compliant solution uses thread-local storage combined with thread synchronization to ensure the child thread is accessing a valid live object. It uses the Visual Studio–specific __declspec(thread) language extension to provide the thread-local storage and the WaitForSingleObject() API to provide the synchronization.

```
#include <Windows.h>
#include <stdio.h>

DWORD WINAPI child_thread(LPVOID v) {
  int *result = (int *)v;
  printf("Result: %d\n", *result);  /* Correctly prints 1 */
  return NULL;
}

int create_thread(HANDLE *tid) {
  /* Declare val as a thread-local value */
  __declspec(thread) int val = 1;
  *tid = create_thread(NULL, 0, child_thread, &val, 0, NULL);
  return *tid == NULL;
}

int main(void) {
  HANDLE tid;

  if (create_thread(&tid)) {
    /* Handle error */
  }

  if (WAIT_OBJECT_0 != WaitForSingleObject(tid, INFINITE)) {
    /* Handle error */
  }
  CloseHandle(tid);

  return 0;
}
```

Noncompliant Code Example (OpenMP, `parallel`)

It is important to note that local data can be used securely with threads when using other thread interfaces, so the programmer need not always copy data into nonlocal memory when sharing data with threads. For example, the `shared` keyword in "The OpenMP® API Specification for Parallel Programming" [OpenMP] can be used in combination with OpenMP's threading interface to share local memory without having to worry about whether local automatic variables remain valid.

In this noncompliant code example, a variable j is declared outside a `parallel` #pragma and not listed as a private variable. In OpenMP, variables outside a `parallel` #pragma are shared unless designated as `private`.

```
#include <omp.h>
#include <stdio.h>
```

```
int main(void) {
  int j = 0;
  #pragma omp parallel
  {
    int t = omp_get_thread_num();
    printf("Running thread - %d\n", t);
    for (int i = 0; i < 5050; i++) {
      j++;  /* j not private; could be a race condition */
    }
    printf("Just ran thread - %d\n", t);
    printf("loop count %d\n", j);
  }
  return 0;
}
```

Compliant Solution (OpenMP, `parallel`, `private`)

In this compliant solution, the variable j is declared outside of the `parallel` `#pragma` but is explicitly labeled as `private`:

```
#include <omp.h>
#include <stdio.h>

int main(void) {
  int j = 0;
  #pragma omp parallel private(j)
  {
    int t = omp_get_thread_num();
    printf("Running thread - %d\n", t);
    for (int i = 0; i < 5050; i++) {
      j++;
    }
    printf("Just ran thread - %d\n", t);
    printf("loop count %d\n", j);
  }
  return 0;
}
```

Risk Assessment

Threads that reference the stack of other threads can potentially overwrite important information on the stack, such as function pointers and return addresses. The compiler may not generate warnings if the programmer allows one thread to access another thread's local variables, so a programmer may not catch a potential error at compile time. The remediation cost for this error is high because analysis tools have difficulty diagnosing problems with concurrency and race conditions.

Recommendation	Severity	Likelihood	Remediation Cost	Priority	Level
CON34-C	Medium	Probable	High	P4	L3

Bibliography

[ISO/IEC 9899:2011]	6.2.4, "Storage Durations of Objects"
[OpenMP]	The OpenMP® API Specification for Parallel Programming

■ CON35-C. Avoid deadlock by locking in a predefined order

Mutexes are used to prevent multiple threads from causing a data race by accessing shared resources at the same time. Sometimes, when locking mutexes, multiple threads hold each other's lock, and the program consequently deadlocks. Four conditions are required for deadlock to occur:

- Mutual exclusion
- Hold and wait
- No preemption
- Circular wait

Deadlock needs all four conditions, so preventing deadlock requires preventing any one of the four conditions. One simple solution is to lock the mutexes in a predefined order, which prevents circular wait.

Noncompliant Code Example

The behavior of this noncompliant code example depends on the runtime environment and the platform's scheduler. The program is susceptible to deadlock if thread `thr1` attempts to lock `ba2`'s mutex at the same time thread `thr2` attempts to lock `ba1`'s mutex in the `deposit()` function.

```
#include <stdlib.h>
#include <threads.h>

typedef struct {
  int balance;
  mtx_t balance_mutex;
} bank_account;

typedef struct {
  bank_account *from;
```

```
    bank_account *to;
    int amount;
} transaction;

void create_bank_account(bank_account **ba,
                         int initial_amount) {
    bank_account *nba = (bank_account *)malloc(
        sizeof(bank_account)
    );
    if (nba == NULL) {
        /* Handle error */
    }

    nba->balance = initial_amount;
    if (thrd_success
        != mtx_init(&nba->balance_mutex, mtx_plain)) {
        /* Handle error */
    }

    *ba = nba;
}

int deposit(void *ptr) {
    transaction *args = (transaction *)ptr;

    if (thrd_success != mtx_lock(&args->from->balance_mutex)) {
        /* Handle error */
    }

    /* Not enough balance to transfer */
    if (args->from->balance < args->amount) {
        if (thrd_success
            != mtx_unlock(&args->from->balance_mutex)) {
            /* Handle error */
        }
        return -1;  /* Indicate error */
    }

    if (thrd_success != mtx_lock(&args->to->balance_mutex)) {
        /* Handle error */
    }

    args->from->balance -= args->amount;
    args->to->balance += args->amount;

    if (thrd_success
        != mtx_unlock(&args->from->balance_mutex)) {
        /* Handle error */
    }
```

```
      if (thrd_success
          != mtx_unlock(&args->to->balance_mutex)) {
        /* Handle error */
      }

      free(ptr);
      return 0;
    }

int main(void) {
      thrd_t thr1, thr2;
      transaction *arg1;
      transaction *arg2;
      bank_account *ba1;
      bank_account *ba2;

      create_bank_account(&ba1, 1000);
      create_bank_account(&ba2, 1000);

      arg1 = (transaction *)malloc(sizeof(transaction));
      if (arg1 == NULL) {
        /* Handle error */
      }
      arg2 = (transaction *)malloc(sizeof(transaction));
      if (arg2 == NULL) {
        /* Handle error */
      }

      arg1->from = ba1;
      arg1->to = ba2;
      arg1->amount = 100;

      arg2->from = ba2;
      arg2->to = ba1;
      arg2->amount = 100;

      /* Perform the deposits */
      if (thrd_success
          != thrd_create(&thr1, deposit, (void *)arg1)) {
        /* Handle error */
      }
      if (thrd_success
          != thrd_create(&thr2, deposit, (void *)arg2)) {
        /* Handle error */
      }
      return 0;
    }
```

Compliant Solution

This compliant solution eliminates the circular wait condition by establishing a predefined order for locking in the deposit() function. Each thread will lock on the basis of the bank_account ID, which is set when the bank_account struct is initialized.

```
#include <stdlib.h>
#include <threads.h>

typedef struct {
  int balance;
  mtx_t balance_mutex;

  /* Should not change after initialization */
  unsigned int id;
} bank_account;

typedef struct {
  bank_account *from;
  bank_account *to;
  int amount;
} transaction;

unsigned int global_id = 1;

void create_bank_account(bank_account **ba,
                         int initial_amount) {
  bank_account *nba = (bank_account *)malloc(
    sizeof(bank_account)
  );
  if (nba == NULL) {
    /* Handle error */
  }

  nba->balance = initial_amount;
  if (thrd_success
      != mtx_init(&nba->balance_mutex, mtx_plain)) {
    /* Handle error */
  }

  nba->id = global_id++;
  *ba = nba;
}
```

```c
int deposit(void *ptr) {
  transaction *args = (transaction *)ptr;
  int result = -1;
  mtx_t *first;
  mtx_t *second;

  if (args->from->id == args->to->id) {
    return -1;  /* Indicate error */
  }

  /* Ensure proper ordering for locking */
  if (args->from->id < args->to->id) {
    first = &args->from->balance_mutex;
    second = &args->to->balance_mutex;
  } else {
    first = &args->to->balance_mutex;
    second = &args->from->balance_mutex;
  }
  if (thrd_success != mtx_lock(first)) {
    /* Handle error */
  }
  if (thrd_success != mtx_lock(second)) {
    /* Handle error */
  }

  /* Not enough balance to transfer */
  if (args->from->balance >= args->amount) {
    args->from->balance -= args->amount;
    args->to->balance += args->amount;
    result = 0;
  }

  if (thrd_success != mtx_unlock(second)) {
    /* Handle error */
  }
  if (thrd_success != mtx_unlock(first)) {
    /* Handle error */
  }
  free(ptr);
  return result;
}
```

Risk Assessment

Deadlock prevents multiple threads from progressing, halting program execution. A denial-of-service attack is possible if the attacker can create the conditions for deadlock.

Rule	Severity	Likelihood	Remediation Cost	Priority	Level
CON35-C	Low	Probable	Medium	P4	L3

Related Guidelines

MITRE CWE	CWE-764, Multiple Locks of a Critical Resource

■ CON36-C. Wrap functions that can spuriously wake up in a loop

The cnd_wait() and cnd_timedwait() functions temporarily cede possession of a mutex so that other threads that may be requesting the mutex can proceed. These functions must always be called from code that is protected by locking a mutex. The waiting thread resumes execution only after it has been notified, generally as the result of the invocation of the cnd_signal() or cnd_broadcast() function invoked by another thread. The cnd_wait() function must be invoked from a loop that checks whether a **condition predicate** holds. A condition predicate is an expression constructed from the variables of a function that must be true for a thread to be allowed to continue execution. The thread pauses execution, via cnd_wait(), cnd_timedwait(), or some other mechanism, and is resumed later, presumably when the condition predicate is true and the thread is notified.

```
#include <threads.h>
#include <stdbool.h>

extern bool until_finish(void);
extern mtx_t lock;
extern cnd_t condition;

void func(void) {
  if (thrd_success != mtx_lock(&lock)) {
    /* Handle error */
  }

  while (until_finish()) {  /* Predicate does not hold */
    if (thrd_success != cnd_wait(&condition, &lock)) {
      /* Handle error */
    }
  }

  /* Resume when condition holds */
```

```
    if (thrd_success != mtx_unlock(&lock)) {
      /* Handle error */
    }
  }
}
```

The notification mechanism notifies the waiting thread and allows it to check its condition predicate. The invocation of `cnd_broadcast()` in another thread cannot precisely determine which waiting thread will be resumed. Condition predicate statements allow notified threads to determine whether they should resume upon receiving the notification.

Noncompliant Code Example

This noncompliant code example monitors a linked list and assigns one thread to consume list elements when the list is nonempty.

This thread pauses execution using `cnd_wait()` and resumes when notified, presumably when the list has elements to be consumed. It is possible for the thread to be notified even if the list is still empty, perhaps because the notifying thread used `cnd_broadcast()`, which notifies all threads. Notification using `cnd_broadcast()` is frequently preferred over using `cnd_signal()` (see "CON38-C. Preserve thread-safety and liveness when using condition variables" for more information).

Note that a condition predicate is typically the negation of the condition expression in the loop. In this noncompliant code example, the condition predicate for removing an element from a linked list is (`list->next != NULL`), whereas the condition expression for the `while` loop condition is (`list->next == NULL`).

This noncompliant code example nests the `cnd_wait()` function inside an `if` block and consequently fails to check the condition predicate after the notification is received. If the notification was spurious or malicious, the thread would wake up prematurely.

```
#include <threads.h>

struct node_t {
  void *node;
  struct node_t *next;
};

struct node_t list;
static mtx_t lock;
static cnd_t condition;

void consume_list_element(void) {
  if (thrd_success != mtx_lock(&lock)) {
```

```
      /* Handle error */
    }

    if (list.next == NULL) {
      if (thrd_success != cnd_wait(&condition, &lock)) {
        /* Handle error */
      }
    }

    /* Proceed when condition holds */

    if (thrd_success != mtx_unlock(&lock)) {
      /* Handle error */
    }
}
```

Compliant Solution

This compliant solution calls the cnd_wait() function from within a while loop to check the condition both before and after the call to cnd_wait():

```
#include <threads.h>

struct node_t {
  void *node;
  struct node_t *next;
};

struct node_t list;
static mtx_t lock;
static cnd_t condition;

void consume_list_element(void) {
  if (thrd_success != mtx_lock(&lock)) {
    /* Handle error */
  }

  while (list.next == NULL) {
    if (thrd_success != cnd_wait(&condition, &lock)) {
      /* Handle error */
    }
  }

  /* Proceed when condition holds */

  if (thrd_success != mtx_unlock(&lock)) {
    /* Handle error */
  }
}
```

Risk Assessment

Failure to enclose calls to the `cnd_wait()` or `cnd_timedwait()` functions inside a `while` loop can lead to indefinite blocking and denial of service (DoS).

Rule	Severity	Likelihood	Remediation Cost	Priority	Level
CON36-C	Low	Unlikely	Medium	P2	L3

Bibliography

[ISO/IEC 9899:2011]	7.17.7.4, "The `atomic_compare_exchange` Generic Functions"
[Lea 2000]	1.3.2, "Liveness" 3.2.2, "Monitor Mechanics"

■ CON37-C. Do not call `signal()` in a multithreaded program

Calling the `signal()` function in a multithreaded program is undefined behavior (see undefined behavior 135 in Appendix B).

Noncompliant Code Example

This noncompliant code example invokes the `signal()` function from a multithreaded program:

```
#include <signal.h>
#include <threads.h>

volatile sig_atomic_t flag = 0;

void handler(int signum) {
  flag = 1;
}

/* Runs until user sends SIGUSR1 */
int func(void *data) {
  while (!flag) {
    /* ... */
  }
  return 0;
}
```

```
int main(void) {
  signal(SIGUSR1, handler); /* Undefined! */
  thrd_t tid;

  if (thrd_success != thrd_create(&tid, func, NULL)) {
    /* Handle error */
  }
  /* ... */
  return 0;
}
```

NOTE The SIGUSR1 signal value is not defined in the C Standard; consequently, this is not a C-compliant code example.

Compliant Solution

This compliant solution uses an object of type `atomic_flag` to indicate when the child thread should terminate its loop:

```
#include <stdatomic.h>
#include <threads.h>

atomic_flag flag = ATOMIC_VAR_INIT(0);

int func(void *data) {
  while (!flag) {
    /* ... */
  }
  return 0;
}

int main(void) {
  int result;
  thrd_t tid;

  if (thrd_success != thrd_create(&tid, func, NULL)) {
    /* Handle error */
  }
  /* ... */
  /* Set flag when done */
  while (!atomic_flag_test_and_set(&flag))
    ; /* Continue attempts */

  return 0;
}
```

Exceptions

CON37-EX1: Implementations such as POSIX that provide defined behavior when multithreaded programs use custom signal handlers are exempt from this rule [IEEE Std 1003.1-2013].

Risk Assessment

Mixing signals and threads is undefined behavior.

Rule	Severity	Likelihood	Remediation Cost	Priority	Level
CON37-C	Low	Probable	Low	P6	L2

Bibliography

[IEEE Std 1003.1-2013]	XSH 2.9.1, "Thread-Safety"

■ CON38-C. Preserve thread-safety and liveness when using condition variables

Both thread-safety and **liveness** are concerns when using condition variables. The *thread-safety* property requires that all objects maintain consistent states in a multithreaded environment [Lea 2000]. The *liveness* property requires that every operation or function invocation execute to completion without interruption; for example, there is no deadlock.

Condition variables must be used inside a `while` loop (see "CON36-C. Wrap functions that can spuriously wake up in a loop" for more information). To guarantee liveness, programs must test the `while` loop condition before invoking the `cnd_wait()` function. This early test checks whether another thread has already satisfied the condition predicate and sent a notification. Invoking the `cnd_wait()` function after the notification has been sent results in indefinite blocking.

To guarantee thread safety, programs must test the `while` loop condition after returning from the `cnd_wait()` function. When a given thread invokes the `cnd_wait()` function, it will attempt to block until its condition variable is signaled by a call to `cnd_broadcast()` or to `cnd_signal()`.

The `cnd_signal()` function unblocks one of the threads that are blocked on the specified condition variable at the time of the call. If multiple threads are waiting on the same condition variable, the scheduler can select any of those threads to be awakened (assuming that all threads have the same priority level). The `cnd_broadcast()` function unblocks all of the threads that are blocked on the specified condition variable at the time of the call. The order in which threads execute following a call to `cnd_broadcast()` is unspecified. Consequently, an unrelated thread could start executing, discover that its condition predicate is satisfied, and resume execution even though it was supposed to remain dormant. For these reasons, threads must check the condition predicate after the `cnd_wait()` function returns. A `while` loop is the best choice for checking the condition predicate both before and after invoking `cnd_wait()`.

The use of `cnd_signal()` is safe if each thread uses a unique condition variable. If multiple threads share a condition variable, the use of `cnd_signal()` is safe only if the following conditions are met:

- All threads must perform the same set of operations after waking up, which means that any thread can be selected to wake up and resume for a single invocation of `cnd_signal()`.
- Only one thread is required to wake upon receiving the signal.

The `cnd_broadcast()` function can be used to unblock all of the threads that are blocked on the specified condition variable if the use of `cnd_signal()` is unsafe.

Noncompliant Code Example (`cnd_signal()`)

This noncompliant code example uses five threads that are intended to execute sequentially according to the step level assigned to each thread when it is created (serialized processing). The `current_step` variable holds the current step level and is incremented when the respective thread completes. Finally, another thread is signaled so that the next step can be executed. Each thread waits until its step level is ready, and the `cnd_wait()` function call is wrapped inside a `while` loop, in compliance with "CON36-C. Wrap functions that can spuriously wake up in a loop."

```
#include <stdio.h>
#include <threads.h>

enum { NTHREADS = 5 };

mtx_t mutex;
cnd_t cond;

int run_step(void *t) {
  static int current_step = 0;
  size_t my_step = *(size_t *)t;
```

```
  if (thrd_success != mtx_lock(&mutex)) {
    /* Handle error */
  }

  printf("Thread %d has the lock\n", my_step);

  while (current_step != my_step) {
    printf("Thread %d is sleeping...\n", my_step);

    if (thrd_success != cnd_wait(&cond, &mutex)) {
      /* Handle error */
    }

    printf("Thread %d woke up\n", my_step);
  }

  /* Do processing ... */
  printf("Thread %d is processing...\n", my_step);
  current_step++;

  /* Signal a waiting task */
  if (thrd_success != cnd_signal(&cond)) {
    /* Handle error */
  }

  printf("Thread %d is exiting...\n", my_step);

  if (thrd_success != mtx_unlock(&mutex)) {
    /* Handle error */
  }
  return 0;
}

int main(void) {
  thrd_t threads[NTHREADS];
  size_t step[NTHREADS];

  if (thrd_success != mtx_init(&mutex, mtx_plain)) {
    /* Handle error */
  }

  if (thrd_success != cnd_init(&cond)) {
    /* Handle error */
  }

  /* Create threads */
  for (size_t i = 0; i < NTHREADS; ++i) {
    step[i] = i;
```

```
        if (thrd_success != thrd_create(&threads[i], run_step,
                                        &step[i])) {
          /* Handle error */
        }
      }

      /* Wait for all threads to complete */
      for (size_t i = NTHREADS; i != 0; --i) {
        if (thrd_success != thrd_join(threads[i-1], NULL)) {
          /* Handle error */
        }
      }

      mtx_destroy(&mutex);
      cnd_destroy(&cond);
      return 0;
    }
```

In this example, all threads share a condition variable. Each thread has its own distinct condition predicate because each thread requires current_ step to have a different value before proceeding. When the condition variable is signaled, any of the waiting threads can wake up. Table 13–2 illustrates a possible scenario in which the liveness property is violated. If, by chance, the notified thread is not the thread with the next step value, that thread will wait again. No additional notifications can occur, and eventually the pool of available threads will be exhausted.

Table 13–2. Deadlock: Out-of-Sequence Step Value

Time	Thread # (my_step)	current_ step	Action
0	3	0	Thread 3 executes first time: predicate is FALSE -> wait()
1	2	0	Thread 2 executes first time: predicate is FALSE -> wait()
2	4	0	Thread 4 executes first time: predicate is FALSE -> wait()
3	0	0	Thread 0 executes first time: predicate is TRUE -> current_step++; cnd_signal()
4	1	1	Thread 1 executes first time: predicate is TRUE -> current_step++; cnd_signal()
5	3	2	Thread 3 wakes up (scheduler choice): predicate is FALSE -> wait()
6	—	—	**Thread exhaustion!** No more threads to run, and a conditional variable signal is needed to wake up the others

Compliant Solution (cnd_broadcast())

This compliant solution uses the cnd_broadcast() function to signal all wait-ing threads instead of a single random thread. Only the run_step() thread code from the noncompliant code example is modified, as follows:

```c
#include <stdio.h>
#include <threads.h>

int run_step(void *t) {
  static size_t current_step = 0;
  size_t my_step = *(size_t *)t;

  if (thrd_success != mtx_lock(&mutex)) {
    /* Handle error */
  }

  printf("Thread %d has the lock\n", my_step);

  while (current_step != my_step) {
    printf("Thread %d is sleeping...\n", my_step);

    if (thrd_success != cnd_wait(&cond, &mutex)) {
      /* Handle error */
    }

    printf("Thread %d woke up\n", my_step);
  }

  /* Do processing ... */
  printf("Thread %d is processing...\n", my_step);

  current_step++;

  /* Signal ALL waiting tasks */
  if (thrd_success != cnd_broadcast(&cond)) {
    /* Handle error */
  }

  printf("Thread %d is exiting...\n", my_step);

  if (thrd_success != mtx_unlock(&mutex)) {
    /* Handle error */
  }
  return 0;
}
```

Awakening all threads guarantees the liveness property because each thread will execute its condition predicate test, and exactly one will succeed and continue execution.

Compliant Solution (Using `cnd_signal()` with a Unique Condition Variable per Thread)

Another compliant solution is to use a unique condition variable for each thread (all associated with the same mutex). In this case, `cnd_signal()` wakes up only the thread that is waiting on it. This solution is more efficient than using `cnd_broadcast()` because only the desired thread is awakened.

Note that the condition predicate of the signaled thread must be true; otherwise, a deadlock will occur.

```c
#include <stdio.h>
#include <threads.h>

enum { NTHREADS = 5 };

mtx_t mutex;
cnd_t cond[NTHREADS];

int run_step(void *t) {
  static size_t current_step = 0;
  size_t my_step = *(size_t *)t;

  if (thrd_success != mtx_lock(&mutex)) {
    /* Handle error */
  }

  printf("Thread %d has the lock\n", my_step);

  while (current_step != my_step) {
    printf("Thread %d is sleeping...\n", my_step);

    if (thrd_success != cnd_wait(&cond[my_step], &mutex)) {
      /* Handle error */
    }

    printf("Thread %d woke up\n", my_step);
  }

  /* Do processing ... */
  printf("Thread %d is processing...\n", my_step);
```

```
    current_step++;

    /* Signal next step thread */
    if ((my_step + 1) < NTHREADS) {
      if (thrd_success != cnd_signal(&cond[my_step + 1])) {
        /* Handle error */
      }
    }

    printf("Thread %d is exiting...\n", my_step);

    if (thrd_success != mtx_unlock(&mutex)) {
      /* Handle error */
    }
    return 0;
}

int main(void) {
  thrd_t threads[NTHREADS];
  size_t step[NTHREADS];

  if (thrd_success != mtx_init(&mutex, mtx_plain)) {
    /* Handle error */
  }

  for (size_t i = 0; i< NTHREADS; ++i) {
    if (thrd_success != cnd_init(&cond[i])) {
      /* Handle error */
    }
  }

  /* Create threads */
  for (size_t i = 0; i < NTHREADS; ++i) {
    step[i] = i;
    if (thrd_success != thrd_create(&threads[i], run_step,
                                    &step[i])) {
      /* Handle error */
    }
  }

  /* Wait for all threads to complete */
  for (size_t i = NTHREADS; i != 0; --i) {
    if (thrd_success != thrd_join(threads[i-1], NULL)) {
      /* Handle error */
    }
  }

  mtx_destroy(&mutex);
```

```
    for (size_t i = 0; i < NTHREADS; ++i) {
      cnd_destroy(&cond[i]);
    }
    return 0;
}
```

Compliant Solution (Windows, Condition Variables)

This compliant solution uses a CONDITION_VARIABLE object, available on Microsoft Windows (Vista and later):

```
#include <Windows.h>
#include <stdio.h>

CRITICAL_SECTION lock;
CONDITION_VARIABLE cond;

DWORD WINAPI run_step(LPVOID t) {
  static size_t current_step = 0;
  size_t my_step = (size_t)t;

  EnterCriticalSection(&lock);
  printf("Thread %d has the lock\n", my_step);

  while (current_step != my_step) {
    printf("Thread %d is sleeping...\n", my_step);

    if (!SleepConditionVariableCS(&cond, &lock, INFINITE)) {
      /* Handle error */
    }

    printf("Thread %d woke up\n", my_step);
  }

  /* Do processing ... */
  printf("Thread %d is processing...\n", my_step);

  current_step++;

  LeaveCriticalSection(&lock);

  /* Signal ALL waiting tasks */
  WakeAllConditionVariable(&cond);

  printf("Thread %d is exiting...\n", my_step);
  return 0;
}
```

```
enum { NTHREADS = 5 };

int main(void) {
  HANDLE threads[NTHREADS];

  InitializeCriticalSection(&lock);
  InitializeConditionVariable(&cond);

  /* Create threads */
  for (size_t i = 0; i < NTHREADS; ++i) {
    threads[i] = CreateThread(NULL, 0, run_step,
                              (LPVOID)i, 0, NULL);
  }

  /* Wait for all threads to complete */
  WaitForMultipleObjects(NTHREADS, threads, TRUE, INFINITE);

  DeleteCriticalSection(&lock);

  return 0;
}
```

Risk Assessment

Failing to preserve the thread-safety and liveness of a program when using condition variables can lead to indefinite blocking and denial of service (DoS).

Rule	Severity	Likelihood	Remediation Cost	Priority	Level
CON38-C	Low	Unlikely	Medium	P2	L3

Bibliography

[IEEE Std 1003.1-2013]	XSH, System Interfaces, pthread_cond_broadcast XSH, System Interfaces, pthread_cond_signal
[Lea 2000]	

■ CON39-C. Do not join or detach a thread that was previously joined or detached

The C Standard, 7.26.5.6 [ISO/IEC 9899:2011], states that a thread shall not be joined once it was previously joined or detached. Similarly, subclause 7.26.5.3 states that a thread shall not be detached once it was previously joined or detached. Violating either of these subclauses results in undefined behavior.

Noncompliant Code Example

This noncompliant code example detaches a thread that is later joined:

```c
#include <threads.h>

int thread_func(void *arg) {
  /* Do work */
  thrd_detach(thrd_current());
  return 0;
}

int main(void) {
  thrd_t t;

  if (thrd_success != thrd_create(&t, thread_func, NULL)) {
    /* Handle error */
    return 0;
  }

  if (thrd_success != thrd_join(t, 0)) {
    /* Handle error */
    return 0;
  }
  return 0;
}
```

Compliant Solution

This compliant solution does not detach the thread. Its resources are released upon successfully joining with the main thread:

```c
#include <threads.h>

int thread_func(void *arg) {
  /* Do work */
  return 0;
}

int main(void) {
  thrd_t t;

  if (thrd_success != thrd_create(&t, thread_func, NULL)) {
    /* Handle error */
    return 0;
  }

  if (thrd_success != thrd_join(t, 0)) {
```

```
    /* Handle error */
    return 0;
  }
  return 0;
}
```

Risk Assessment

Joining or detaching a previously joined or detached thread is undefined behavior.

Rule	Severity	Likelihood	Remediation Cost	Priority	Level
CON39-C	Low	Likely	Medium	P6	L2

Bibliography

[ISO/IEC 9899:2011]	7.26.5.3, "The `thrd_detach` Function" 7.26.5.6, "The `thrd_join` Function"

■ CON40-C. Do not refer to an atomic variable twice in an expression

A consistent locking policy guarantees that multiple threads cannot simultaneously access or modify shared data. Atomic variables eliminate the need for locks by guaranteeing thread safety when certain operations are performed on them. The thread-safe operations on atomic variables are specified in the C Standard, subclauses 7.17.7 and 7.17.8 [ISO/IEC 9899:2011]. While atomic operations can be combined, combined operations do not provide the thread safety provided by individual atomic operations.

Every time an atomic variable appears on the left-hand side of an assignment operator, including a compound assignment operator such as `*=`, an atomic write is performed on the variable. The use of the increment (++) or decrement (--) operators on an atomic variable constitutes an atomic read-and-write operation and is consequently thread-safe. Any reference of an atomic variable anywhere else in an expression indicates a distinct atomic read on the variable.

If the same atomic variable appears twice in an expression, then two atomic reads, or an atomic read and an atomic write, are required. Such a pair of atomic operations is not thread-safe, as another thread can modify the atomic variable between the two operations. Consequently, an atomic variable must not be referenced twice in the same expression.

Noncompliant Code Example (atomic_bool)

This noncompliant code example declares a shared `atomic_bool` flag variable and provides a `toggle_flag()` method that negates the current value of flag:

```c
#include <stdatomic.h>
#include <stdbool.h>

static atomic_bool flag;

void init_flag(void) {
  atomic_init(&flag, false);
}

void toggle_flag(void) {
  bool temp_flag = atomic_load(&flag);
  temp_flag = !temp_flag;
  atomic_store(&flag, temp_flag);
}

bool get_flag(void) {
  return atomic_load(&flag);
}
```

Execution of this code may result in a data race because the value of flag is read, negated, and written back. This occurs even though the read and write are both atomic.

Consider, for example, two threads that call `toggle_flag()`. The expected effect of toggling flag twice is that it is restored to its original value. However, the scenario in Table 13–3 leaves flag in the incorrect state.

Table 13–3. Toggle_Flag() without Compare-and-Exchange

Time	flag	Thread	Action
1	true	t_1	Reads the current value of flag, true, into a cache
2	true	t_2	Reads the current value of flag, (still) true, into a different cache
3	true	t_1	Toggles the temporary variable in the cache to false
4	true	t_2	Toggles the temporary variable in the different cache to false
5	false	t_1	Writes the cache variable's value to flag
6	false	t_2	Writes the different cache variable's value to flag

As a result, the effect of the call by t_2 is not reflected in `flag`; the program behaves as if `toggle_flag()` were called only once, not twice.

Compliant Solution (`atomic_compare_exchange_weak()`)

This compliant solution uses a compare-and-exchange to guarantee that the correct value is stored in `flag`. All updates are visible to other threads. The call to `atomic_compare_exchange_weak()` is in a loop in conformance with "CON41-C. Wrap functions that can fail spuriously in a loop."

```
#include <stdatomic.h>
#include <stdbool.h>

static atomic_bool flag;

void init_flag(void) {
  atomic_init(&flag, false);
}

void toggle_flag(void) {
  bool old_flag = atomic_load(&flag);
  bool new_flag;
  do {
    new_flag = !old_flag;
  } while (!atomic_compare_exchange_weak(&flag, &old_flag, new_flag));
}

bool get_flag(void) {
  return atomic_load(&flag);
}
```

An alternative solution is to use the `atomic_flag` data type for managing Boolean values atomically. However, `atomic_flag` does not support a toggle operation.

Compliant Solution (Compound Assignment)

This compliant solution uses the `^=` assignment operation to toggle `flag`. This operation is guaranteed to be atomic, according to the C Standard, 6.5.16.2, paragraph 3. This operation performs a bitwise-exclusive-or between its arguments, but for Boolean arguments, this is equivalent to negation.

```
#include <stdatomic.h>
#include <stdbool.h>
```

```
static atomic_bool flag;

void toggle_flag(void) {
  flag ^= 1;
}

bool get_flag(void) {
  return flag;
}
```

Another alternative solution is to use a mutex to protect the atomic operation, but this solution loses the performance benefits of atomic variables.

Noncompliant Code Example

This noncompliant code example takes an atomic global variable n and computes n + (n-1) + (n-2) + ... + 1, using the formula n * (n + 1) / 2:

```
#include <stdatomic.h>

atomic_int n;

void compute_sum(void) {
  return n * (n + 1) / 2;
}
```

The value of n may change between the two atomic reads of n in the expression, yielding an incorrect result.

Compliant Solution

This compliant solution passes the atomic variable as a function parameter, forcing the variable to be copied, and guaranteeing a correct result:

```
#include <stdatomic.h>

void compute_sum(atomic_int n) {
  return n * (n + 1) / 2;
}
```

Risk Assessment

When operations on atomic variables are assumed to be atomic, but are not atomic, surprising data races can occur, leading to corrupted data and invalid control flow.

Rule	Severity	Likelihood	Remediation Cost	Priority	Level
CON40-C	Medium	Probable	Medium	P8	L2

Related Guidelines

MITRE CWE	CWE-366, Race Condition within a Thread
	CWE-413, Improper Resource Locking
	CWE-567, Unsynchronized Access to Shared Data in a Multithreaded Context
	CWE-667, Improper locking

Bibliography

[ISO/IEC 14882:2011]	6.5.16.2, "Compound Assignment"
	7.17, "Atomics"

■ CON41-C. Wrap functions that can fail spuriously in a loop

Functions that can fail spuriously should be wrapped in a loop. The `atomic_compare_exchange_weak()` and `atomic_compare_exchange_weak_explicit()` functions both attempt to set an atomic variable to a new value but only if it currently possesses a known old value. Unlike the related functions `atomic_compare_exchange_strong()` and `atomic_compare_exchange_strong_explicit()`, these functions are permitted to *fail spuriously*. This makes these functions faster on some platforms—for example, on architectures that implement compare-and-exchange using load-linked/store-conditional instructions, such as Alpha, ARM, MIPS, and PowerPC. The C Standard, 7.17.7.4, paragraph 4 [ISO/IEC 9899:2011], describes this behavior:

> A weak compare-and-exchange operation may fail spuriously. That is, even when the contents of memory referred to by `expected` and `object` are equal, it may return zero and store back to `expected` the same memory contents that were originally there.

Noncompliant Code Example

In this noncompliant code example, `reorganize_data_structure()` is to be used as an argument to `thrd_create()`. After reorganizing, the function attempts to replace the head pointer so that it points to the new version. If no other thread has changed the head pointer since it was originally loaded, reorganize_data_structure() is intended to exit the thread with a result of true, indicating success. Otherwise, the new reorganization attempt is discarded and the thread is exited with a result of false. However, atomic_compare_exchange_weak() may fail even when the head pointer has not changed. Therefore, reorganize_data_structure() may perform the work and then discard it unnecessarily.

```
#include <stdatomic.h>
#include <stdbool.h>

struct data {
  struct data *next;
  /* ... */
};

extern void cleanup_data_structure(struct data *head);

int reorganize_data_structure(void *thread_arg) {
  struct data *_Atomic *ptr_to_head = thread_arg;
  struct data *old_head = atomic_load(ptr_to_head);
  struct data *new_head;
  bool success;

  /* ... Reorganize the data structure ... */

  success = atomic_compare_exchange_weak(ptr_to_head,
                                  &old_head, new_head);
  if (!success) {
    cleanup_data_structure(new_head);
  }
  return success; /* Exit the thread */
}
```

Compliant Solution (atomic_compare_exchange_weak())

To recover from spurious failures, a loop must be used. However, atomic_compare_exchange_weak() might fail because the head pointer changed, or the failure may be spurious. In either case, the thread must perform the work repeatedly until the compare-and-exchange succeeds, as shown in this compliant solution:

```
#include <stdatomic.h>
#include <stdbool.h>
```

```
struct data {
  struct data *next;
  /* ... */
};

extern void cleanup_data_structure(struct data *head);

int reorganize_data_structure(void *thread_arg) {
  struct data *_Atomic *ptr_to_head = thread_arg;
  struct data *old_head = atomic_load(ptr_to_head);
  struct data *new_head = NULL;
  struct data *saved_old_head;
  bool success;

  do {
    if (new_head != NULL) {
      cleanup_data_structure(new_head);
    }
    saved_old_head = old_head;
/* ... Reorganize the data structure ... */
  }
  while (!(success = atomic_compare_exchange_weak(
             ptr_to_head, &old_head, new_head
             )) && old_head == saved_old_head);
  return success; /* Exit the thread */
}
```

This loop could also be part of a larger control flow; for example, the thread from the noncompliant code example could be retried if it returns false.

Compliant Solution (`atomic_compare_exchange_strong()`)

When a weak compare-and-exchange would require a loop and a strong one would not, the strong one is preferable, as in this compliant solution:

```
#include <stdatomic.h>
#include <stdbool.h>

struct data {
  struct data *next;
  /* ... */
};

extern void cleanup_data_structure(struct data *head);

int reorganize_data_structure(void *thread_arg) {
  struct data *_Atomic *ptr_to_head = thread_arg;
```

```
    struct data *old_head = atomic_load(ptr_to_head);
    struct data *new_head;
    bool success;

    /* ... Reorganize the data structure ... */

    success = atomic_compare_exchange_strong(
      ptr_to_head, &old_head, new_head
    );
    if (!success) {
      cleanup_data_structure(new_head);
    }
    return success; /* Exit the thread */
}
```

Risk Assessment

Failing to wrap the `atomic_compare_exchange_weak()` and `atomic_compare_exchange_weak_explicit()` functions in a loop can result in incorrect values and control flow.

Rule	Severity	Likelihood	Remediation Cost	Priority	Level
CON41-C	Low	Unlikely	Medium	P2	L3

Bibliography

[ISO/IEC 9899:2011]	7.17.7.4, "The `atomic_compare_exchange` Generic Functions"
[Lea 2000]	1.3.2, "Liveness" 3.2.2, "Monitor Mechanics"

Chapter 14

Miscellaneous (MSC)

Chapter Contents

Risk Assessment Summary

Rule	Severity	Likelihood	Remediation Cost	Priority	Level
MSC30-C	Medium	Unlikely	Low	P6	L2
MSC32-C	Medium	Likely	Low	P18	L1

continues

Rule	Severity	Likelihood	Remediation Cost	Priority	Level
MSC33-C	High	Likely	Low	P27	L1
MSC37-C	High	Unlikely	Low	P9	L2
MSC38-C	Low	Unlikely	Medium	P2	L3
MSC39-C	Low	Unlikely	Low	P3	L3
MSC40-C	Low	Unlikely	Medium	P2	L3

■ MSC30-C. Do not use the rand() function for generating pseudorandom numbers

Pseudorandom number generators use mathematical algorithms to produce a sequence of numbers with good statistical properties, but the numbers produced are not genuinely random.

The C Standard rand() function makes no guarantees as to the quality of the random sequence produced. The numbers generated by some implementations of rand() have a comparatively short cycle, and the numbers can be predictable. Applications that have strong pseudorandom number requirements must use a generator that is known to be sufficient for their needs.

Noncompliant Code Example

The following noncompliant code generates an ID with a numeric part produced by calling the rand() function. The IDs produced are predictable and have limited randomness.

```
#include <stdio.h>
#include <stdlib.h>

enum { len = 12 };

void func(void) {
  /*
   * id will hold the ID, starting with the characters
   * "ID" followed by a random integer.
   */
  char id[len];
  int r;
  int num;
```

```c
/* ... */
r = rand(); /* Generate a random integer */
num = snprintf(id, len, "ID % d", r); /* Generate the ID */
/* ... */
}
```

Compliant Solution (POSIX)

This compliant solution replaces the rand() function with the POSIX random() function:

```c
#include <stdio.h>
#include <stdlib.h>
#include <time.h>

enum { len = 12 };

void func(void) {
  /*
   * id will hold the ID, starting with the characters
   * "ID" followed by a random integer.
   */
  char id[len];
  int r;
  int num;
  /* ... */
  struct timespec ts;
  if (timespec_get(&ts, TIME_UTC) == 0) {
    /* Handle error */
  }
  srandom(ts.tv_nsec ^ ts.tv_sec); /* Seed the PRNG */
  /* ... */
  r = random(); /* Generate a random integer */
  num = snprintf(id, len, "ID%d", r); /* Generate the ID */
  /* ... */
}
```

The POSIX random() function is a better pseudorandom number generator. Although on some platforms the low dozen bits generated by rand() go through a cyclic pattern, all the bits generated by random() are usable. The rand48 family of functions provides another alternative for pseudorandom numbers.

Although not specified by POSIX, arc4random() is another possibility for systems that support it. The arc4random(3) manual page [OpenBSD] states:

> arc4random() fits into a middle ground not covered by other subsystems such as the strong, slow, and resource-expensive random devices described

in random(4) versus the fast but poor-quality interfaces described in rand(3), random(3), and drand48(3).

To achieve the best random numbers possible, an implementation-specific function must be used. When unpredictability is crucial and speed is not an issue, as in the creation of strong cryptographic keys, use a true entropy source such as /dev/random, or a hardware device capable of generating random numbers. Note that the /dev/random device can block for a long time if there are not enough events going on to generate sufficient entropy.

Compliant Solution (Windows)

On Windows platforms, the CryptGenRandom() function can be used to generate cryptographically strong random numbers. Note that the exact details of the implementation are unknown, including, for example, what source of entropy CryptGenRandom() uses. From the Microsoft Developer Network CryptGenRandom() reference [MSDN]:

> If an application has access to a good random source, it can fill the pbBuffer buffer with some random data before calling CryptGenRandom(). The CSP [cryptographic service provider] then uses this data to further randomize its internal seed. It is acceptable to omit the step of initializing the pbBuffer buffer before calling CryptGenRandom().

```
#include <Windows.h>
#include <wincrypt.h>
#include <stdio.h>

void func(void) {
  HCRYPTPROV prov;
  if (CryptAcquireContext(&prov, NULL, NULL,
                          PROV_RSA_FULL, 0)) {
    long int li = 0;
    if (CryptGenRandom(prov, sizeof(li), (BYTE *)&li)) {
      printf("Random number: %ld\n", li);
    } else {
      /* Handle error */
    }
    if (!CryptReleaseContext(prov, 0)) {
      /* Handle error */
    }
  } else {
    /* Handle error */
  }
}
```

Risk Assessment

The use of the `rand()` function can result in predictable random numbers.

Rule	Severity	Likelihood	Remediation Cost	Priority	Level
MSC30-C	Medium	Unlikely	Low	P6	L2

Related Guidelines

MITRE CWE	CWE-327, Use of a Broken or Risky Cryptographic Algorithm CWE-330, Use of Insufficiently Random Values

Bibliography

[MSDN]	"CryptGenRandom Function"
[OpenBSD]	`arc4random()`

◾ MSC32-C. Properly seed pseudorandom number generators

A pseudorandom number generator (PRNG) is a deterministic algorithm capable of generating sequences of numbers that approximate the properties of random numbers. Each sequence is completely determined by the initial state of the PRNG and the algorithm for changing the state. Most PRNGs make it possible to set the initial state, also called the *seed state*. Setting the initial state is called *seeding* the PRNG.

Calling a PRNG in the same initial state, either without seeding it explicitly or by seeding it with the same value, results in generating the same sequence of random numbers in different runs of the program. If a PRNG function is called 10 times consecutively to produce a sequence of 10 random numbers without being seeded, running the code for the first time produces the sequence S = {r1, r2, r3, r4, r5, r6, r7, r8, r9, r10}. If the PRNG is subsequently seeded with the same initial seed value, then it will generate the same sequence S.

As a result, after the first run of an improperly seeded PRNG, an attacker can predict the sequence of random numbers that will be generated in future runs. Improperly seeding or failing to seed the PRNG can lead to vulnerabilities, especially in security protocols.

The solution is to ensure that the PRNG is always properly seeded. A properly seeded PRNG will generate a different sequence of random numbers each time it is run.

Not all random number generators can be seeded. True random number generators that rely on hardware to produce completely unpredictable results do not need to be and cannot be seeded. Some high-quality PRNGs, such as the /dev/random device on some UNIX systems, also cannot be seeded. This rule applies only to algorithmic pseudorandom number generators that can be seeded.

Noncompliant Code Example (POSIX)

This noncompliant code example generates a sequence of 10 pseudorandom numbers using the random() function. When random() is not seeded, it behaves like rand(), producing the same sequence of random numbers each time any program that uses it is run.

```
#include <stdio.h>
#include <stdlib.h>

void func(void) {
  for (unsigned int i = 0; i < 10; ++i) {
    /* Always generates the same sequence */
    printf("%ld, ", random());
  }
}
```

The output is as follows:

```
1st run: 1804289383, 846930886, 1681692777, 1714636915, 1957747793,
         424238335, 719885386, 1649760492,596516649, 1189641421,
2nd run: 1804289383, 846930886, 1681692777, 1714636915, 1957747793,
         424238335, 719885386, 1649760492, 596516649, 1189641421,
...
nth run: 1804289383, 846930886, 1681692777, 1714636915, 1957747793,
         424238335, 719885386, 1649760492, 596516649, 1189641421,
```

Compliant Solution (POSIX)

Call srandom() before invoking random() to seed the random sequence generated by random(). This compliant solution produces different random number sequences each time the program is run:

```c
#include <stdio.h>
#include <stdlib.h>
#include <time.h>

void func(void) {
  struct timespec ts;
  if (timespec_get(&ts, TIME_UTC) == 0) {
   /* Handle error */
  }
  else {
   srandom(ts.tv_nsec ^ ts.tv_sec);
   for (unsigned int i = 0; i < 10; ++i) {
     /* Generates different sequences at different runs */
     printf("%ld, ", random());
   }
  }
}
```

The output is as follows:

```
1st run: 198682410, 2076262355, 910374899, 428635843, 2084827500,
         1558698420, 4459146, 733695321, 2044378618, 1649046624,
2nd run: 1127071427, 252907983, 1358798372, 2101446505, 1514711759,
         229790273, 954268511, 1116446419, 368192457, 1297948050,
3rd run: 2052868434, 1645663878, 731874735, 1624006793, 938447420,
         1046134947, 1901136083, 418123888, 836428296, 2017467418,
```

This may not be sufficiently random for concurrent execution, where it may lead to correlated generated series in different threads, or for small embedded systems that have an unsigned int type with a width of 16 bits. Depending on the application and the desirable level of security, a programmer may choose alternative ways to seed PRNGs. In general, hardware is more capable than software of generating real random numbers (for example, by sampling the thermal noise of a diode).

Compliant Solution (Windows)

The CryptGenRandom() function does not run the risk of not being properly seeded because its arguments serve as seeders:

```c
#include <Windows.h>
#include <wincrypt.h>
```

```c
#include <stdio.h>

void func(void) {
  HCRYPTPROV hCryptProv;
  long rand_buf;
  /* Example of instantiating the CSP */
  if (CryptAcquireContext(&hCryptProv, NULL, NULL,
                          PROV_RSA_FULL, 0)) {
    printf("CryptAcquireContext succeeded.\n");
  } else {
    printf("Error during CryptAcquireContext!\n");
  }

  for (unsigned int i = 0; i < 10; ++i) {
    if (!CryptGenRandom(hCryptProv, sizeof(rand_buf),
                        (BYTE *)&rand_buf)) {
      printf("Error\n");
    } else {
      printf("%ld, ", rand_buf);
    }
  }
}
```

The output is as follows:

```
1st run: -1597837311, 906130682, -1308031886, 1048837407, -931041900,
         -658114613, -1709220953, -1019697289, 1802206541, 406505841,
2nd run: 885904119, -687379556, -1782296854, 1443701916, -624291047,
         2049692692, -990451563, -142307804, 1257079211, 897185104,
3rd run: 190598304, -1537409464, 1594174739, -424401916, -1975153474,
         826912927, 1705549595, -1515331215, 474951399, 1982500583,
```

Risk Assessment

Rule	Severity	Likelihood	Remediation Cost	Priority	Level
MSC32-C	Medium	Likely	Low	P18	L1

Related Guidelines

MITRE CWE	CWE-327, Use of a Broken or Risky Cryptographic Algorithm
	CWE-330, Use of Insufficiently Random Values

Bibliography

[MSDN]   "CryptGenRandom Function"

■ MSC33-C. Do not pass invalid data to the asctime() function

The C Standard, 7.27.3.1 [ISO/IEC 9899:2011], provides the following sample implementation of the asctime() function:

```
char *asctime(const struct tm *timeptr) {
  static const char wday_name[7][3] = {
    "Sun", "Mon", "Tue", "Wed", "Thu", "Fri", "Sat"
  };
  static const char mon_name[12][3] = {
    "Jan", "Feb", "Mar", "Apr", "May", "Jun",
    "Jul", "Aug", "Sep", "Oct", "Nov", "Dec"
  };
  static char result[26];
  sprintf(
    result,
    "%.3s %.3s%3d %.2d:%.2d:%.2d %d\n",
    wday_name[timeptr->tm_wday],
    mon_name[timeptr->tm_mon],
    timeptr->tm_mday, timeptr->tm_hour,
    timeptr->tm_min, timeptr->tm_sec,
    1900 + timeptr->tm_year
  );
  return result;
}
```

This function is supposed to output a character string of 26 characters at most, including the terminating null character. If we count the length indicated by the format directives, we arrive at 25. Taking into account the terminating null character, the array size of the string appears sufficient.

However, this implementation assumes that the values of the struct tm data in timepiece are within normal ranges and does nothing to enforce the range limit. If any of the values print more characters than expected, the sprintf() function may overflow the result array. For example, if tm_year has the value 12345, then 27 characters (including the terminating null character) are printed, resulting in a buffer overflow.

The *POSIX® Base Specifications* [IEEE Std 1003.1-2013] says the following about the `asctime()` and `asctime_r()` functions:

> These functions are included only for compatibility with older implementations. They have undefined behavior if the resulting string would be too long, so the use of these functions should be discouraged. On implementations that do not detect output-string-length overflow, it is possible to overflow the output buffers in such a way as to cause applications to fail, or possible system security violations. Also, these functions do not support localized date and time formats. To avoid these problems, applications should use `strftime()` to generate strings from broken-down times.

The C Standard, Annex K, also defines `asctime_s()`, which can be used as a secure substitute for `asctime()`.

The `asctime()` function appears in the list of obsolescent functions in "MSC24-C. Do not use deprecated or obsolescent functions."

Noncompliant Code Example

This noncompliant code example invokes the `asctime()` function with potentially unsanitized data:

```
#include <time.h>

void func(struct tm *time_tm) {
  char *time = asctime(time_tm);
  /* ... */
}
```

Compliant Solution (`strftime()`)

The `strftime()` function allows the programmer to specify a more rigorous format and also to specify the maximum size of the resulting time string:

```
#include <time.h>

enum { maxsize = 26 };

void func(struct tm *time) {
  char s[maxsize];
  /* Current time representation for locale */
  const char *format = "%c";
```

```
    size_t size = strftime(s, maxsize, format, time);
}
```

This call has the same effects as asctime() but also ensures that no more than maxsize characters are printed, preventing buffer overflow.

Compliant Solution (asctime_s())

The C Standard, Annex K, defines the asctime_s() function, which serves as a close replacement for the asctime() function but requires an additional argument that specifies the maximum size of the resulting time string:

```
#define __STDC_WANT_LIB_EXT1__ 1
#include <time.h>

enum { maxsize = 26 };

void func(struct tm *time_tm) {
  char buffer[maxsize];

  if (asctime_s(buffer, maxsize, &time_tm)) {
    /* Handle error */
  }
}
```

Risk Assessment

On implementations that do not detect output-string-length overflow, it is possible to overflow the output buffers.

Rule	Severity	Likelihood	Remediation Cost	Priority	Level
MSC33-C	High	Likely	Low	P27	L1

Bibliography

[IEEE Std 1003.1-2013]	XSH, System Interfaces, asctime
[ISO/IEC 9899:2011]	7.27.3.1, "The asctime Function"

■ MSC37-C. Ensure that control never reaches the end of a non-void function

If control reaches the closing curly brace (}) of a non-void function without evaluating a return statement, using the return value of the function call is undefined behavior (see undefined behavior 88 in Appendix B).

Noncompliant Code Example

In this noncompliant code example, control reaches the end of the checkpass() function when the two strings passed to strcmp() are not equal, resulting in undefined behavior. Many compilers will generate code for the checkpass() function, returning various values along the execution path where no return statement is defined.

```
#include <string.h>
#include <stdio.h>

int checkpass(const char *password) {
  if (strcmp(password, "pass") == 0) {
    return 1;
  }
}

void func(const char *userinput) {
  if (checkpass(userinput)) {
    printf("Success\n");
  }
}
```

This error is frequently diagnosed by compilers (see "MSC00-C. Compile cleanly at high warning levels").

Compliant Solution

This compliant solution ensures that the checkpass() function always returns a value:

```
#include <string.h>
#include <stdio.h>

int checkpass(const char *password) {
  if (strcmp(password, "pass") == 0) {
    return 1;
```

```
  }
  return 0;
}

void func(const char *userinput) {
  if (checkpass(userinput)) {
    printf("Success!\n");
  }
}
```

Noncompliant Code Example

In this noncompliant code example, control reaches the end of the getlen()
function when input does not contain the integer delim. Because the potentially undefined return value of getlen() is later used as an index into an
array, a buffer overflow may occur.

```
#include <stddef.h>

size_t getlen(const int *input, size_t maxlen, int delim) {
  for (size_t i = 0; i < maxlen; ++i) {
    if (input[i] == delim) {
      return i;
    }
  }
}

void func(int userdata) {
  size_t i;
  int data[] = { 1, 1, 1 };
  i = getlen(data, sizeof(data), 0);
  data[i] = userdata;
}
```

Compliant Solution

This compliant solution changes the interface of getlen() to store the result in
a user-provided pointer and return an error code to indicate any error conditions. The best method for handling this type of error is specific to the application and the type of error (see "ERR00-C. Adopt and implement a consistent
and comprehensive error-handling policy" for more on error handling).

```
int getlen(const int *input, size_t maxlen, int delim,
           size_t *result) {
  for (size_t i = 0; i < maxlen; ++i) {
```

```
    if (input[i] == delim) {
      if (result != NULL) {
        *result = i;
      }
      return 0;
    }
  }
  return -1;
}

void func(int userdata) {
  size_t i;
  int data[] = {1, 1, 1};
  if (getlen(data, sizeof(data), 0, &i) != 0) {
    /* Handle error */
  } else {
    data[i] = userdata;
  }
}
```

Exceptions

MSC37-EX1: According to the C Standard, 5.1.2.2.3, paragraph 1 [ISO/IEC 9899:2011], "Reaching the } that terminates the main function returns a value of 0." As a result, it is permissible for control to reach the end of the main() function without executing a return statement.

Risk Assessment

Using the return value from a non-void function where control reaches the end of the function can lead to buffer overflow vulnerabilities as well as other unexpected program behaviors.

Rule	Severity	Likelihood	Remediation Cost	Priority	Level
MSC37-C	High	Unlikely	Low	P9	L2

Bibliography

[ISO/IEC 9899:2011]   5.1.2.2.3, "Program Termination"

■ MSC38-C. Do not treat a predefined identifier as an object if it might only be implemented as a macro

The C Standard, 7.1.4, paragraph 1, states [ISO/IEC 9899:2011]:

> Any function declared in a header may be additionally implemented as a function-like macro defined in the header, so if a library function is declared explicitly when its header is included, one of the techniques shown below can be used to ensure the declaration is not affected by such a macro. Any macro definition of a function can be suppressed locally by enclosing the name of the function in parentheses, because the name is then not followed by the left parenthesis that indicates expansion of a macro function name. For the same syntactic reason, it is permitted to take the address of a library function even if it is also defined as a macro.[185]
>
> 185) This means that an implementation shall provide an actual function for each library function, even if it also provides a macro for that function.

However, the C Standard enumerates specific exceptions in which the behavior of accessing an object or function expanded to be a standard library macro definition is undefined. The macros are `assert`, `errno`, `math_errhandling`, `setjmp`, `va_start`, `va_arg`, `va_copy`, and `va_end`. These cases are described by undefined behaviors 110, 114, 122, 124, and 138 (see Appendix B). Programmers must not suppress these macros to access the underlying object or function.

Noncompliant Code Example (`assert`)

In this noncompliant code example, the standard `assert()` macro is suppressed in an attempt to pass it as a function pointer to the `execute_handler()` function. Attempting to suppress the `assert()` macro is undefined behavior.

```
#include <assert.h>

typedef void (*handler_type)(int);

void execute_handler(handler_type handler, int value) {
   handler(value);
}

void func(int e) {
   execute_handler(&(assert), e < 0);
}
```

Compliant Solution (`assert`)

In this compliant solution, the `assert()` macro is wrapped in a helper function, removing the undefined behavior:

```
#include <assert.h>

typedef void (*handler_type)(int);

void execute_handler(handler_type handler, int value) {
  handler(value);
}

static void assert_handler(int value) {
  assert(value);
}

void func(int e) {
  execute_handler(&assert_handler, e < 0);
}
```

Noncompliant Code Example (Redefining `errno`)

Legacy code is apt to include an incorrect declaration, such as the following in this noncompliant code example:

```
extern int errno;
```

Compliant Solution (Declaring `errno`)

This compliant solution demonstrates the correct way to declare `errno` by including the header `<errno.h>`:

```
#include <errno.h>
```

C-conforming implementations are required to declare `errno` in `<errno.h>`, although some historic implementations failed to do so.

Risk Assessment

Accessing objects or functions underlying the specific macros enumerated in this rule is undefined behavior.

Rule	Severity	Likelihood	Remediation Cost	Priority	Level
MSC38-C	Low	Unlikely	Medium	P2	L3

Bibliography

ISO/IEC 9899:2011   7.1.4, "Use of Library Functions"

■ MSC39-C. Do not call va_arg() on a va_list that has an indeterminate value

Variadic functions access their variable arguments by using va_start() to initialize an object of type va_list, iteratively invoking the va_arg() macro, and finally calling va_end(). The va_list may be passed as an argument to another function, but calling va_arg() within that function causes the va_list to have an indeterminate value in the calling function. As a result, attempting to read variable arguments without reinitializing the va_list can have unexpected behavior. According to the C Standard, 7.16, paragraph 3 [ISO/IEC 9899:2011]:

> If access to the varying arguments is desired, the called function shall declare an object (generally referred to as **ap** in this subclause) having type va_list. The object ap may be passed as an argument to another function; if that function invokes the va_arg macro with parameter ap, the value of ap in the calling function is indeterminate and shall be passed to the va_end macro prior to any further reference to ap.[253]
>
> 253) It is permitted to create a pointer to a va_list and pass that pointer to another function, in which case the original function may take further use of the original list after the other function returns.

Noncompliant Code Example

This noncompliant code example attempts to check that none of its variable arguments are zero by passing a va_list to helper function contains_zero(). After the call to contains_zero(), the value of ap is indeterminate.

```
#include <stdarg.h>
#include <stdio.h>

int contains_zero(size_t count, va_list ap) {
  for (size_t i = 1; i < count; ++i) {
    if (va_arg(ap, double) == 0.0) {
      return 1;
    }
  }
}
```

```
    return 0;
}

int print_reciprocals(size_t count, ...) {
  va_list ap;
  va_start(ap, count);

  if (contains_zero(count, ap)) {
    va_end(ap);
    return 1;
  }

  for (size_t i = 0; i < count; ++i) {
    printf("%f ", 1.0 / va_arg(ap, double));
  }

  va_end(ap);
  return 0;
}
```

Compliant Solution

This compliant solution modifies `contains_zero()` to take a pointer to a `va_list`. It then uses the `va_copy` macro to copy the list, traverses the copy, and cleans it up. Consequently, the `print_reciprocals()` function is free to traverse the original `va_list`.

```
#include <stdarg.h>
#include <stdio.h>

int contains_zero(size_t count, va_list *ap) {
  va_list ap1;
  va_copy(ap1, *ap);
  for (size_t i = 1; i < count; ++i) {
    if (va_arg(ap1, double) == 0.0) {
      return 1;
    }
  }
  va_end(ap1);
  return 0;
}

int print_reciprocals(size_t count, ...) {
  int status;
```

```
    va_list ap;
    va_start(ap, count);

    if (contains_zero(count, &ap)) {
      printf("0 in arguments!\n");
      status = 1;
    } else {
      for (size_t i = 0; i < count; i++) {
        printf("%f ", 1.0 / va_arg(ap, double));
      }
      printf("\n");
      status = 0;
    }

    va_end(ap);
    return status;
}
```

Risk Assessment

Reading variable arguments using a va_list that has an indeterminate value can have unexpected results.

Rule	Severity	Likelihood	Remediation Cost	Priority	Level
MSC39-C	Low	Unlikely	Low	P3	L3

Bibliography

[ISO/IEC 9899:2011]　　7.16, "Variable Arguments <stdarg.h>"

■ MSC40-C. Do not violate constraints

According to the C Standard, 3.8 [ISO/IEC 9899:2011], a constraint is a "restriction, either syntactic or semantic, by which the exposition of language elements is to be interpreted." Despite the similarity of the terms, a runtime constraint is not a kind of constraint.

Violating any *shall* statement within a constraint clause in the C Standard requires an implementation to issue a diagnostic message. The C Standard, 5.1.1.3 [ISO/IEC 9899:2011], states:

> A conforming implementation shall produce at least one diagnostic message (identified in an implementation-defined manner) if a preprocessing translation unit or translation unit contains a violation of any syntax rule or constraint, even if the behavior is also explicitly specified as undefined or implementation-defined. Diagnostic messages need not be produced in other circumstances.

The C Standard further explains in a footnote:

> The intent is that an implementation should identify the nature of, and where possible localize, each violation. Of course, an implementation is free to produce any number of diagnostics as long as a valid program is still correctly translated. It may also successfully translate an invalid program.

Any constraint violation is a violation of this rule because it can result in an invalid program.

Noncompliant Code Example (Inline, Internal Linkage)

The C Standard, 6.7.4, paragraph 3 [ISO/IEC 9899:2011], states:

> An inline definition of a function with external linkage shall not contain a definition of a modifiable object with static or thread storage duration, and shall not contain a reference to an identifier with internal linkage.

The motivation behind this constraint lies in the semantics of inline definitions. Paragraph 7 of subclause 6.7.4 reads, in part:

> An inline definition provides an alternative to an external definition, which a translator may use to implement any call to the function in the same translation unit. It is unspecified whether a call to the function uses the inline definition or the external definition.

That is, if a function has an external and inline definition, implementations are free to choose which definition to invoke (two distinct invocations of the function may call different definitions, one the external definition, the other the inline definition). Therefore, issues can arise when these definitions reference internally linked objects or mutable objects with static or thread storage duration.

This noncompliant code example refers to a static variable with file scope and internal linkage from within an external inline function:

```
static int I = 12;
extern inline void func(int a) {
  int b = a * I;
  /* ... */
}
```

Compliant Solution (Inline, Internal Linkage)

This compliant solution omits the `static` qualifier; consequently, the variable I has external linkage by default:

```
int I = 12;
extern inline void func(int a) {
  int b = a * I;
  /* ... */
}
```

Noncompliant Code Example (Inline, Modifiable Static)

This noncompliant code example defines a modifiable `static` variable within an `extern inline` function:

```
extern inline void func(void) {
  static int I = 12;
  /* Perform calculations which may modify I */
}
```

Compliant Solution (Inline, Modifiable Static)

This compliant solution removes the `static` keyword from the local variable definition. If the modifications to I must be retained between invocations of func(), it must be declared at file scope so that it will be defined with external linkage.

```
extern inline void func(void) {
  int I = 12;
  /* Perform calculations which may modify I */
}
```

Noncompliant Code Example (Inline, Modifiable `static`)

This noncompliant code example includes two translation units: `file1.c` and `file2.c`. The first file, `file1.c`, defines a pseudorandom number generation function:

```
/* file1.c */

/* Externally linked definition of the function get_random() */
extern unsigned int get_random(void) {
  /* Initialize the seeds */
  static unsigned int m_z = 0xdeadbeef;
  static unsigned int m_w = 0xbaddecaf;

  /* Compute the next pseudorandom value and update the seeds */
  m_z = 36969 * (m_z & 65535) + (m_z >> 16);
  m_w = 18000 * (m_w & 65535) + (m_w >> 16);
  return (m_z << 16) + m_w;
}
```

The left-shift operation on the last line may wrap, but this is permitted by exception INT30-EX3 to rule "INT30-C. Ensure that unsigned integer operations do not wrap."

The second file, `file2.c`, defines an `inline` version of this function that references mutable `static` objects—namely, objects that maintain the state of the pseudorandom number generator. Separate invocations of the `get_random()` function can call different definitions, each operating on separate static objects, resulting in a faulty pseudorandom number generator.

```
/* file2.c */

/* Inline definition of get_random function */
inline unsigned int get_random(void) {
  /*
   * Initialize the seeds
   * Constraint violation: static duration storage referenced
   * in non-static inline definition
   */
  static unsigned int m_z = 0xdeadbeef;
  static unsigned int m_w = 0xbaddecaf;

  /* Compute the next pseudorandom value and update the seeds */
  m_z = 36969 * (m_z & 65535) + (m_z >> 16);
  m_w = 18000 * (m_w & 65535) + (m_w >> 16);
  return (m_z << 16) + m_w;
}

int main(void) {
  unsigned int rand_no;
```

```
    for (int ii = 0; ii < 100; ii++) {
      /*
       * Get a pseudorandom number. Implementation defined whether
       * the inline definition in this file or the external
       * definition in file2.c is called.
       */
      rand_no = get_random();
      /* Use rand_no... */
    }

    /* ... */

    /*
     * Get another pseudorandom number. Behavior is
     * implementation defined.
     */
    rand_no = get_random();
    /* Use rand_no... */
    return 0;
}
```

Compliant Solution (Inline, Modifiable static)

This compliant solution adds the static modifier to the inline function definition in file2.c, giving it internal linkage. All references to get_random() in file.2.c will now reference the internally linked definition. The first file, which was not changed, is not shown here.

```
/* file2.c */

/* Static inline definition of get_random function */
static inline unsigned int get_random(void) {
  /* Initialize the seeds.
   * No more constraint violation; the inline function is now
   * internally linked.
   */
  static unsigned int m_z = 0xdeadbeef;
  static unsigned int m_w = 0xbaddecaf;

  /* Compute next pseudorandom value and update the seeds */
  m_z = 36969 * (m_z & 65535) + (m_z >> 16);
  m_w = 18000 * (m_w & 65535) + (m_w >> 16);
  return (m_z << 16) + m_w;
}

int main(void) {
  /* Generate pseudorandom numbers using get_random()... */
  return 0;
}
```

2

8

Risk Assessment

Constraint violations are a broad category of errors that can result in unexpected control flow and corrupted data.

Rule	Severity	Likelihood	Remediation Cost	Priority	Level
MSC40-C	Low	Unlikely	Medium	P2	L3

Bibliography

[ISO/IEC 9899:2011]	4, "Conformance"
	5.1.1.3, "Diagnostics"
	6.7.4, "Function Specifiers"

Appendix  A

Glossary

abnormal end [ISO/IEC/IEEE 24765:2010] Termination of a process prior to completion.

abnormal program termination See *abnormal end*.

analyzer [ISO/IEC 9899:2011] Mechanism that diagnoses coding flaws in software programs.

> NOTE Analyzers may include static analysis tools, tools within a compiler suite, or tools in other contexts.

asynchronous-safe function [GNU Pth] A function is asynchronous-safe, or asynchronous-signal safe, if it can be called safely and without side effects from within a signal handler context. That is, it must be able to be interrupted at any point to run linearly out of sequence without causing an inconsistent state. It must also function properly when global data might itself be in an inconsistent state. Some asynchronous-safe operations are listed here:

- Call the `signal()` function to reinstall a signal handler
- Unconditionally modify a `volatile sig_atomic_t` variable (as modification to this type is atomic)
- Call the `_Exit()` function to immediately terminate program execution
- Invoke an asynchronous-safe function, as specified by the implementation

Few functions are portably asynchronous-safe.

availability [IEEE Std 610.12-1990] The degree to which a system or component is operational and accessible when required for use. Often expressed as a probability.

condition predicate An expression constructed from the variables of a function that must be true for a thread to be allowed to continue execution.

conforming [ISO/IEC 9899:2011] Conforming programs may depend on nonportable features of a conforming implementation.

critical sections Shared data that would otherwise be protected from data races.

dangling pointer A pointer to deallocated memory.

data race [ISO/IEC 9899:2011] The execution of a program contains a data race if it contains two conflicting actions in different threads, at least one of which is not atomic, and neither happens before the other. Any such data race results in undefined behavior.

denial-of-service attack Also *DoS attack*. An attempt to make a computer resource unavailable to its intended users.

diagnostic message [ISO/IEC 9899:2011] A diagnostic message is a message belonging to an implementation-defined subset of the implementation's message output. A diagnostic message may indicate a constraint violation or a valid but questionable language construct. Messages typically include the file name and line number pointing to the offending code construct. In addition, implementations also often indicate the severity of the problem. Although the C Standard does not specify any such requirement, the most severe problems often cause implementations to fail to fully translate a translation unit. Diagnostics output in such cases are termed *errors*. Other problems may cause implementations simply to issue a warning message and continue translating the rest of the program. See also *error message* and *warning message*.

double-free vulnerability An exploitable error resulting from the same allocated object being freed more than once.

error message A diagnostic message generated when source code is encountered that prevents an implementation from translating a translation unit. See also *diagnostic message* and *warning message*.

exploit [ISO/IEC TS 17961:2013] Technique that takes advantage of a security vulnerability to violate an explicit or implicit security policy.

function-like macro [ISO/IEC 9899:2011] A `#define` preprocessing directive that defines an identifier immediately followed by zero or more parameters, the ellipsis (...), or a combination of the two, enclosed in parentheses, similar syntactically to a function call. Subsequent instances of the macro name followed by a parenthesized list of arguments in a translation unit are replaced by the replacement list of preprocessing tokens that constitute the remainder of the directive. See also *unsafe function-like macro*.

hosted environment [ISO/IEC 9899:2011] An environment that is not freestanding. Program startup occurs at main(), complex types are implemented, and all C standard library facilities are available.

implementation [ISO/IEC 9899:2011] Particular set of software, running in a particular translation environment under particular control options, that performs translation of programs for, and supports execution of functions in, a particular execution environment.

implementation-defined behavior [ISO/IEC 9899:2011] Unspecified behavior whereby each implementation documents how the choice is made.

in-band error indicator [ISO/IEC 9899:2011] A library function return value on error that can never be returned by a successful call to that library function.

indeterminate value [ISO/IEC 9899:2011] Either an unspecified value or a trap representation.

invalid pointer A pointer that is not a valid pointer. See *valid pointer*.

liveness Every operation or method invocation executes to completion without interruptions, even if it goes against safety.

lvalue [ISO/IEC 9899:2011] An expression with an object type or an incomplete type other than void. The name *lvalue* comes originally from the assignment expression E1 = E2, in which the left operand E1 is required to be a (modifiable) lvalue. It is perhaps better considered as representing an object "locator value."

normal program termination [IEEE Std 1003.1-2013] Normal termination occurs by a return from main(), when requested with the exit(), _exit(), or _Exit() functions, or when the last thread in the process terminates by returning from its start function, by calling the pthread_exit() function, or through cancellation. See also *abnormal termination*.

object-like macro [ISO/IEC 9899:2011] A #define preprocessing directive that defines an identifier with no parentheses. Subsequent instances of the macro name in a translation unit are replaced by the replacement list of preprocessing tokens that constitute the remainder of the directive. See also *function-like macro*.

out-of-band error indicator [ISO/IEC TS 17961:2013] A library function return value used to indicate nothing but the error status.

out-of-domain value [ISO/IEC TS 17961:2013] One of a set of values that is not in the domain of a particular operator or function.

reentrant [ISO/IEC/IEEE 24765:2010] Pertaining to a software module that can be entered as part of one process while also in execution as part of another process and still achieve the desired results.

reliability [IEEE Std 610.12-1990] The ability of a system or component to perform its required functions under stated conditions for a specified period of time.

restricted sink [ISO/IEC TS 17961:2013] Operands and arguments whose domain is a subset of the domain described by their types.

sanitize [ISO/IEC TS 17961:2013] Assure by testing or replacement that a tainted or other value conforms to the constraints imposed by one or more restricted sinks into which it may flow.

> NOTE If the value does not conform, either the path is diverted to avoid using the value or a different, known-conforming value is substituted. For example, adding a null character to the end of a buffer before passing it as an argument to the `strlen` function.

security flaw [ISO/IEC TS 17961:2013] Defect that poses a potential security risk.

security policy [Internet Society 2000] Set of rules and practices that specify or regulate how a system or organization provides security services to protect sensitive and critical system resources.

sequence point [ISO/IEC 9899:2011] Evaluation of an expression may produce side effects. At specific points in the execution sequence called *sequence points*, all side effects of previous evaluations have completed, and no side effects of subsequent evaluations have yet taken place.

side effect [ISO/IEC 9899:2011] Changes in the state of the execution environment achieved by accessing a volatile object, modifying an object, modifying a file, or calling a function that does any of those operations.

> NOTE The IEC 60559 standard for binary floating-point arithmetic requires certain user-accessible status flags and control modes. Floating-point operations implicitly set the status flags; modes affect result values of floating-point operations. Implementations that support such floating-point state are required to regard changes to it as side effects. These are detailed in Annex F of the C Standard.

static analysis [ISO/IEC TS 17961:2013] Any process for assessing code without executing it.

strictly conforming [ISO/IEC 9899:2011] A strictly conforming program is one that uses only those features of the language and library specified in the international standard. Strictly conforming programs are intended to be maximally portable among conforming implementations and cannot, for example, depend on implementation-defined behavior.

string [ISO/IEC 9899:2011] A string is a contiguous sequence of characters terminated by and including the first null character.

tainted source [ISO/IEC TS 17961:2013] External source of untrusted data.

> NOTE Tainted sources include
>
> ■ parameters to the main() function,
> ■ the returned values from localeconv(), fgetc(), getc(), getchar(), fgetwc(), getwc(), and getwchar(), and
> ■ the strings produced by getenv(), fscanf(), vfscanf(), vscanf(), fgets(), fread(), fwscanf(), vfwscanf(), vwscanf(), wscanf(), and fgetws().

tainted value [ISO/IEC TS 17961:2013] Value derived from a tainted source that has not been sanitized.

target implementation [ISO/IEC TS 17961:2013] Implementation of the C programming language whose environmental limits and implementation-defined behavior are assumed by the analyzer during the analysis of a program.

TOCTOU, TOCTTOU Time-of-check, time-of-use (TOCTOU), also referred to as *time-of-check-to-time-of-use (TOCTTOU)*, represents a vulnerability in which access control checks are nonatomic with the operations they protect, allowing an attacker to violate access control rules.

trap representation [ISO/IEC 9899:2011] Object representation that does not represent a value of the object type. Attempting to read the value of an object that has a trap representation other than by an expression that has a character type is undefined. Producing such a representation by a side effect that modifies all or any part of the object other than by an expression that has a character type is undefined.

undefined behavior (UB) [ISO/IEC 9899:2011] Behavior, upon use of a nonportable or erroneous program construct or of erroneous data, for which the C Standard imposes no requirements. An example of undefined behavior is the behavior on integer overflow.

unexpected behavior Well-defined behavior that may be unexpected or unanticipated by the programmer; incorrect programming assumptions.

unsafe function-like macro A function-like macro whose expansion causes one or more of its arguments not to be evaluated exactly once. See also *function-like macro*.

unsigned integer wrapping Computation involving unsigned operands whose result is reduced modulo the number that is one greater than the largest value that can be represented by the resulting type.

unspecified behavior [ISO/IEC 9899:2011] Behavior for which the C Standard provides two or more possibilities and imposes no further requirements on which is chosen in any instance.

unspecified value [ISO/IEC 9899:2011] A valid value of the relevant type where the C Standard imposes no requirements on which value is chosen in any instance. An unspecified value cannot be a trap representation.

untrusted data [ISO/IEC 11889-1:2009] Data originating from outside of a trust boundary.

valid pointer [ISO/IEC TS 17961:2013] Pointer that refers to an element within an array or one past the last element of an array. See also *invalid pointer.*

> NOTE For the purposes of this definition, a pointer to an object that is not an element of an array behaves the same as a pointer to the first element of an array of length one with the type of the object as its element type (see C Standard, 6.5.8, paragraph 4).
>
> For the purposes of this definition, an object can be considered to be an array of a certain number of bytes; that number is the size of the object, as produced by the `sizeof` operator (see C Standard, 6.3.2.3, paragraph 7).

validation [IEC 61508-4] Confirmation by examination and provision of objective evidence that the particular requirements for a specific intended use are fulfilled.

vulnerability [ISO/IEC TS 17961:2013] Set of conditions that allows an attacker to violate an explicit or implicit security policy.

warning message A diagnostic message generated when source code is encountered that does not prevent an implementation from translating a translation unit. See *diagnostic message* and *error message.*

Appendix B

Undefined Behavior

According to the C Standard, Annex J, J.2 [ISO/IEC 9899:2011], the behavior of a program is undefined in the circumstances outlined in the following table. The "Guideline" column in the table identifies the coding practices that address the specific case of undefined behavior (UB). The descriptions of undefined behaviors in the "Description" column are direct quotes from the standard. The parenthesized numbers refer to the subclause of the C Standard (C11) that identifies the undefined behavior.

UB	Description	Guideline
1	A "shall" or "shall not" requirement that appears outside of a constraint is violated (clause 4).	MSC15-C
2	A nonempty source file does not end in a new-line character which is not immediately preceded by a backslash character or ends in a partial preprocessing token or comment (5.1.1.2).	
3	Token concatenation produces a character sequence matching the syntax of a universal character name (5.1.1.2).	PRE30-C
4	A program in a hosted environment does not define a function named main using one of the specified forms (5.1.2.2.1).	
5	The execution of a program contains a data race (5.1.2.4).	
6	A character not in the basic source character set is encountered in a source file, except in an identifier, a character constant, a string literal, a header name, a comment, or a preprocessing token that is never converted to a token (5.2.1).	

continues

UB	Description	Guideline
7	An identifier, comment, string literal, character constant, or header name contains an invalid multibyte character or does not begin and end in the initial shift state (5.2.1.2).	
8	The same identifier has both internal and external linkage in the same translation unit (6.2.2).	DCL36-C
9	An object is referred to outside of its lifetime (6.2.4).	DCL21-C, DCL30-C
10	The value of a pointer to an object whose lifetime has ended is used (6.2.4).	DCL30-C, EXP33-C
11	The value of an object with automatic storage duration is used while it is indeterminate (6.2.4, 6.7.8, 6.8).	EXP33-C, MSC22-C
12	A trap representation is read by an lvalue expression that does not have character type (6.2.6.1).	EXP33-C
13	A trap representation is produced by a side effect that modifies any part of the object using an lvalue expression that does not have character type (6.2.6.1).	
14	The operands to certain operators are such that they could produce a negative zero result, but the implementation does not support negative zeros (6.2.6.2).	
15	Two declarations of the same object or function specify types that are not compatible (6.2.7).	DCL23-C, DCL40-C
16	A program requires the formation of a composite type from a variable length array type whose size is specified by an expression that is not evaluated (6.2.7).	
17	Conversion to or from an integer type produces a value outside the range that can be represented (6.3.1.4).	FLP34-C
18	Demotion of one real floating type to another produces a value outside the range that can be represented (6.3.1.5).	FLP34-C
19	An lvalue does not designate an object when evaluated (6.3.2.1).	
20	A non-array lvalue with an incomplete type is used in a context that requires the value of the designated object (6.3.2.1).	
21	An lvalue designation an object of automatic storage duration that could have been declared with the `register` storage class is used in a context that requires the value of the designated object, but the object is uninitialized (6.3.2.1).	
22	An lvalue having array type is converted to a pointer to the initial element of the array, and the array object has `register` storage class (6.3.2.1).	

UB	Description	Guideline
23	An attempt is made to use the value of a void expression, or an implicit or explicit conversion (except to **void**) is applied to a void expression (6.3.2.2).	
24	Conversion of a pointer to an integer type produces a value outside the range that can be represented (6.3.2.3).	INT36-C
25	Conversion between two pointer types produces a result that is incorrectly aligned (6.3.2.3).	EXP36-C
26	A pointer is used to call a function whose type is not compatible with the pointed-to type (6.3.2.3).	EXP37-C
27	An unmatched ' or " character is encountered on a logical source line during tokenization (6.4).	
28	A reserved keyword token is used in translation phase 7 or 8 for some purpose other than as a keyword (6.4.1).	
29	A universal character name in an identifier does not designate a character whose encoding falls into one of the specified ranges (6.4.2.1).	
30	The initial character of an identifier is a universal character name designating a digit (6.4.2.1).	
31	Two identifiers differ only in nonsignificant characters (6.4.2.1).	DCL23-C, DCL40-C
32	The identifier **func{}** is explicitly declared (6.4.2.2).	
33	The program attempts to modify a string literal (6.4.5).	STR30-C
34	The characters ', back-slash, ", /, or /* occur in the sequence between the < and > delimiters, or the characters ', back-slash, //, or /* occur in the sequence between the " delimiters, in a header name preprocessing token (6.4.7).	EXP39-C
35	A side effect on a scalar object is unsequenced relative to either a different side effect on the same scalar object or a value computation using the value of the same scalar object (6.5).	EXP30-C
36	An exceptional condition occurs during the evaluation of an expression (6.5).	INT32-C
37	An object has its stored value accessed other than by an lvalue of an allowable type (6.5).	DCL40-C, EXP39-C
38	For a call to a function without a function prototype in scope, the number of arguments does not equal the number of parameters (6.5.2.2).	EXP37-C

continues

UB	Description	Guideline
39	For call to a function without a function prototype in scope where the function is defined with a function prototype, either the prototype ends with an ellipsis or the types of the arguments after promotion are not compatible with the types of the parameters (6.5.2.2).	EXP37-C
40	For a call to a function without a function prototype in scope where the function is not defined with a function prototype, the types of the arguments after promotion are not compatible with those of the parameters after promotion (with certain exceptions) (6.5.2.2).	EXP37-C
41	A function is defined with a type that is not compatible with the type (of the expression) pointed to by the expression that denotes the called function (6.5.2.2).	DCL40-C, EXP37-C
42	A member of an atomic structure or union is accessed (6.5.2.3).	
43	The operand of the unary * operator has an invalid value (6.5.3.2).	
44	A pointer is converted to other than an integer or pointer type (6.5.4).	
45	The value of the second operand of the / or % operator is zero (6.5.5).	INT33-C
46	Addition or subtraction of a pointer into, or just beyond, an array object and an integer type produces a result that does not point into, or just beyond, the same array object (6.5.6).	ARR30-C
47	Addition or subtraction of a pointer into, or just beyond, an array object and an integer type produces a result that points just beyond the array object and is used as the operand of a unary * operator that is evaluated (6.5.6).	ARR30-C
48	Pointers that do not point into, or just beyond, the same array object are subtracted (6.5.6).	ARR36-C
49	An array subscript is out of range, even if an object is apparently accessible with the given subscript (as in the lvalue expression a[1][7] given the declaration int a[4][5]) (6.5.6).	ARR30-C
50	The result of subtracting two pointers is not representable in an object of type ptrdiff_t (6.5.6).	
51	An expression is shifted by a negative number or by an amount greater than or equal to the width of the promoted expression (6.5.7).	INT34-C
52	An expression having signed promoted type is left-shifted and either the value of the expression is negative or the result of shifting would not be representable in the promoted type (6.5.7).	

UB	Description	Guideline
53	Pointers that do not point to the same aggregate or union (nor just beyond the same array object) are compared using relational operators (6.5.8).	ARR36-C
54	An object is assigned to an inexactly overlapping object or to an exactly overlapping object with incompatible type (6.5.16.1).	
55	An expression that is required to be an integer constant expression does not have an integer type; has operands that are not integer constants, enumeration constants, character constants, sizeof expressions whose results are integer constants, or immediately-cast floating constants; or contains casts (outside operands to sizeof operators) other than conversions of arithmetic types to integer types (6.6).	
56	A constant expression in an initializer is not, or does not evaluate to, one of the following: an arithmetic constant expression, a null pointer constant, an address constant, or an address constant for an object type plus or minus an integer constant expression (6.6).	
57	An arithmetic constant expression does not have arithmetic type; has operands that are not integer constants, floating constants, enumeration constants, character constants, or sizeof expressions; or contains casts (outside operands to sizeof operators) other than conversions of arithmetic types to arithmetic types (6.6).	
58	The value of an object is accessed by an array-subscript [], member-access . or ->, address &, or indirection * operator or a pointer cast in creating an address constant (6.6).	
59	An identifier for an object is declared with no linkage and the type of the object is incomplete after its declarator, or after its init-declarator if it has an initializer (6.7).	
60	A function is declared at block scope with an explicit storage-class specifier other than extern (6.7.1).	
61	A structure or union is defined as containing no named members (6.7.2.1).	
62	An attempt is made to access, or generate a pointer to just past, a flexible array member of a structure when the referenced object provides no elements for that array (6.7.2.1).	ARR30-C
63	When the complete type is needed, an incomplete structure or union type is not completed in the same scope by another declaration of the tag that defines the content (6.7.2.3).	
64	An attempt is made to modify an object defined with a const-qualified type through use of an lvalue with non-const-qualified type (6.7.3).	EXP05-C, EXP40-C

continues

UB	Description	Guideline
65	An attempt is made to refer to an object defined with a `volatile`-qualified type through use of an lvalue with non-`volatile`-qualified type (6.7.3).	EXP32-C
66	The specification of a function type includes any type qualifiers (6.7.3).	
67	Two qualified types that are required to be compatible do not have the identically qualified version of a compatible type (6.7.3).	
68	An object which has been modified is accessed through a `restrict`-qualified pointer to a `const`-qualified type, or through a `restrict`-qualified pointer and another pointer that are not both based on the same object (6.7.3.1).	EXP43-C
69	A `restrict`-qualified pointer is assigned a value based on another restricted pointer whose associated block neither began execution before the block associated with this pointer, nor ended before the assignment (6.7.3.1).	
70	A function with external linkage is declared with an `inline` function specifier, but is not also defined in the same translation unit (6.7.4).	
71	A function declared with a `_Noreturn` function specifier returns to its caller (6.7.4).	
72	The definition of an object has an alignment specifier and another declaration of that object has a different alignment specifier (6.7.5).	
73	Declarations of an object in different translation units have different alignment specifiers (6.7.5).	
74	Two pointer types that are required to be compatible are not identically qualified, or are not pointers to compatible types (6.7.6.1).	
75	The size expression in an array declaration is not a constant expression and evaluates at program execution time to a nonpositive value (6.7.6.2).	ARR32-C
76	In a context requiring two array types to be compatible, they do not have compatible element types, or their size specifiers evaluate to unequal values (6.7.6.2).	
77	A declaration of an array parameter includes the keyword `static` within the [and] and the corresponding argument does not provide access to the first element of an array with at least the specified number of elements (6.7.6.3).	
78	A storage-class specifier or type qualifier modifies the keyword `void` as a function parameter type list (6.7.6.3).	

UB	Description	Guideline
79	In a context requiring two function types to be compatible, they do not have compatible return types, or their parameters disagree in use of the ellipsis terminator or the number and type of parameters (after default argument promotion, when there is no parameter type list or when one type is specified by a function definition with an identifier list) (6.7.6.3).	
80	The value of an unnamed member of a structure or union is used (6.7.9).	
81	The initializer for a scalar is neither a single expression nor a single expression enclosed in braces (6.7.9).	
82	The initializer for a structure or union object that has automatic storage duration is neither an initializer list nor a single expression that has compatible structure or union type (6.7.9).	
83	The initializer for an aggregate or union, other than an array initialized by a string literal, is not a brace-enclosed list of initializers for its elements or members (6.7.9).	
84	An identifier with external linkage is used, but in the program there does not exist exactly one external definition for the identifier, or the identifier is not used and there exist multiple external definitions for the identifier (6.9).	
85	A function definition includes an identifier list, but the types of the parameters are not declared in a following declaration list (6.9.1).	
86	An adjusted parameter type in a function definition is not an object type (6.9.1).	
87	A function that accepts a variable number of arguments is defined without a parameter type list that ends with the ellipsis notation (6.9.1).	
88	The } that terminates a function is reached, and the value of the function call is used by the caller (6.9.1).	MSC37-C
89	An identifier for an object with internal linkage and an incomplete type is declared with a tentative definition (6.9.2).	
90	The token defined is generated during the expansion of a #if or #elif preprocessing directive, or the use of the defined unary operator does not match one of the two specified forms prior to macro replacement (6.10.1).	
91	The #include preprocessing directive that results after expansion does not match one of the two header name forms (6.10.2).	
92	The character sequence in an #include preprocessing directive does not start with a letter (6.10.2).	

continues

UB	Description	Guideline
93	There are sequences of preprocessing tokens within the list of macro arguments that would otherwise act as preprocessing directives (6.10.3).	PRE32-C
94	The result of the preprocessing operator # is not a valid character string literal (6.10.3.2).	
95	The result of the preprocessing operator ## is not a valid preprocessing token (6.10.3.3).	
96	The #line preprocessing directive that results after expansion does not match one of the two well-defined forms, or its digit sequence specifies zero or a number greater than 2147483647 (6.10.4).	
97	A non-STDC #pragma preprocessing directive that is documented as causing translation failure or some other form of undefined behavior is encountered (6.10.6).	
98	A #pragma STDC preprocessing directive does not match one of the well-defined forms (6.10.6).	
99	The name of a predefined macro, or the identifier defined, is the subject of a #define or #undef preprocessing directive (6.10.8).	
100	An attempt is made to copy an object to an overlapping object by use of a library function, other than as explicitly allowed (e.g., memmove) (clause 7).	
101	A file with the same name as one of the standard headers, not provided as part of the implementation, is placed in any of the standard places that are searched for included source files (7.1.2).	
102	A header is included within an external declaration or definition (7.1.2).	
103	A function, object, type, or macro that is specified as being declared or defined by some standard header is used before any header that declares or defines it is included (7.1.2).	
104	A standard header is included while a macro is defined with the same name as a keyword (7.1.2).	
105	The program attempts to declare a library function itself, rather than via a standard header, but the declaration does not have external linkage (7.1.2).	
106	The program declares or defines a reserved identifier, other than as allowed by 7.1.4 (7.1.3).	DCL37-C
107	The program removes the definition of a macro whose name begins with an underscore and either an uppercase letter or another underscore (7.1.3).	

UB	Description	Guideline
108	An argument to a library function has an invalid value or a type not expected by a function with a variable number of arguments (7.1.4).	
109	The pointer passed to a library function array parameter does not have a value such that all address computations and object accesses are valid (7.1.4).	ARR30-C, ARR38-C
110	The macro definition of `assert` is suppressed in order to access an actual function (7.2).	MSC38-C
111	The argument to the `assert` macro does not have a scalar type (7.2).	
112	The `CX_LIMITED_RANGE`, `FENV_ACCESS`, or `FP_CONTRACT` pragma is used in any context other than outside all external declarations or preceding all explicit declarations and statements inside a compound statement (7.3.4, 7.6.1, 7.12.2).	
113	The value of an argument to a character handling function is neither equal to the value of `EOF` nor representable as an `unsigned char` (7.4).	STR37-C
114	A macro definition of `errno` is suppressed in order to access an actual object, or the program defines an identifier with the name `errno` (7.5).	DCL37-C, MSC38-C
115	Part of the program tests floating-point status flags, sets floating-point control modes, or runs under non-default mode settings, but was translated with the state for the `FENV_ACCESS` pragma "off" (7.6.1).	
116	The exception-mask argument for one of the functions that provide access to the floating-point status flags has a nonzero value not obtained by bitwise OR of the floating-point exception macros (7.6.2).	
117	The `fesetexceptflag` function is used to set floating-point status flags that were not specified in the call to the `fegetexceptflag` function that provided the value of the corresponding `fexcept_t` object (7.6.2.4).	
118	The argument to `fesetenv` or `feupdateenv` is neither an object set by a call to `fegetenv` or `feholdexcept`, nor is it an environment macro (7.6.4.3, 7.6.4.4).	
119	The value of the result of an integer arithmetic or conversion function cannot be represented (7.8.2.1, 7.8.2.2, 7.8.2.3, 7.8.2.4, 7.22.6.1, 7.22.6.2, 7.22.1).	ERR07-C
120	The program modifies the string pointed to by the value returned by the `setlocale` function (7.11.1.1).	ENV30-C

continues

UB	Description	Guideline
121	The program modifies the structure pointed to by the value returned by the localeconv function (7.11.2.1).	ENV30-C
122	A macro definition of math_errhandling is suppressed or the program defines an identifier with the name math_errhandling (7.12).	MSC38-C
123	An argument to a floating-point classification or comparison macro is not of real floating type (7.12.3, 7.12.14).	
124	A macro definition of setjmp is suppressed in order to access an actual function, or the program defines an external identifier with the name setjmp (7.13).	MSC38-C
125	An invocation of the setjmp macro occurs other than in an allowed context (7.13.2.1).	MSC22-C
126	The longjmp function is invoked to restore a nonexistent environment (7.13.2.1).	MSC22-C
127	After a longjmp, there is an attempt to access the value of an object of automatic storage class with non-volatile-qualified type, local to the function containing the invocation of the corresponding setjmp macro, which was changed between the setjmp invocation and longjmp call (7.13.2.1).	MSC22-C
128	The program specifies an invalid pointer to a signal handler function (7.14.1.1).	
129	A signal handler returns when the signal corresponded to a computational exception (7.14.1.1).	SIG31-C
130	A signal handler called in response to SIGFPE, SIGILL, SIGSEGV, or any other implementation-defined value corresponding to a computational exception returns (7.14.1.1).	SIG35-C
131	A signal occurs as the result of calling the abort or raise function, and the signal handler calls the raise function (7.14.1.1).	SIG30-C, SIG31-C
132	A signal occurs other than as the result of calling the abort or raise function, and the signal handler refers to an object with static or thread storage duration that is not a lock-free atomic object other than by assigning a value to an object declared as volatile sig_atomic_t, or calls any function in the standard library other than the abort function, the _Exit function, the quick_exit function, or the signal function (for the same signal number) (7.14.1.1).	SIG31-C
133	The value of errno is referred to after a signal occurred other than as the result of calling the abort or raise function and the corresponding signal handler obtained a SIG_ERR return from a call to the signal function (7.14.1.1).	ERR32-C

UB	Description	Guideline
134	A signal is generated by an asynchronous signal handler (7.14.1.1).	
135	The `signal` function is used in a multithreaded program (7.14.1.1).	CON37-C
136	A function with a variable number of arguments attempts to access its varying arguments other than through a properly declared and initialized `va_list` object, or before the `va_start` macro is invoked (7.16, 7.16.1.1, 7.16.1.4).	
137	The macro `va_arg` is invoked using the parameter `ap` that was passed to a function that invoked the macro `va_arg` with the same parameter (7.16).	
138	A macro definition of `va_start`, `va_arg`, `va_copy`, or `va_end` is suppressed in order to access an actual function, or the program defines an external identifier with the name `va_copy` or `va_end` (7.16.1).	MSC38-C
139	The `va_start` or `va_copy` macro is invoked without a corresponding invocation of the `va_end` macro in the same function, or vice versa (7.16.1, 7.16.1.2, 7.16.1.3, 7.16.1.4).	
140	The type parameter to the `va_arg` macro is not such that a pointer to an object of that type can be obtained simply by postfixing a * (7.16.1.1).	
141	The `va_arg` macro is invoked when there is no actual next argument, or with a specified type that is not compatible with the promoted type of the actual next argument, with certain exceptions (7.16.1.1).	DCL10-C
142	The `va_copy` or `va_start` macro is called to initialize a `va_list` that was previously initialized by either macro without an intervening invocation of the `va_end` macro for the same `va_list` (7.16.1.2, 7.16.1.4).	
143	The parameter *parmN* of a `va_start` macro is declared with the register storage class, with a function or array type, or with a type that is not compatible with the type that results after application of the default argument promotions (7.16.1.4).	
144	The member designator parameter of an `offsetof` macro is an invalid right operand of the . operator for the type parameter, or designates a bit-field (7.19).	
145	The argument in an instance of one of the integer-constant macros is not a decimal, octal, or hexadecimal constant, or it has a value that exceeds the limits for the corresponding type (7.20.4).	
146	A byte input/output function is applied to a wide-oriented stream, or a wide character input/output function is applied to a byte-oriented stream (7.21.2).	

continues

UB	Description	Guideline
147	Use is made of any portion of a file beyond the most recent wide character written to a wide-oriented stream (7.21.2).	
148	The value of a pointer to a FILE object is used after the associated file is closed (7.21.3).	FIO42-C, FIO46-C
149	The stream for the fflush function points to an input stream or to an update stream in which the most recent operation was input (7.21.5.2).	
150	The string pointed to by the mode argument in a call to the fopen function does not exactly match one of the specified character sequences (7.21.5.3).	
151	An output operation on an update stream is followed by an input operation without an intervening call to the fflush function or a file positioning function, or an input operation on an update stream is followed by an output operation with an intervening call to a file positioning function (7.21.5.3).	FIO39-C
152	An attempt is made to use the contents of the array that was supplied in a call to the setvbuf function (7.21.5.6).	
153	There are insufficient arguments for the format in a call to one of the formatted input/output functions, or an argument does not have an appropriate type (7.21.6.1, 7.21.6.2, 7.29.2.1, 7.29.2.2).	FIO47-C
154	The format in a call to one of the formatted input/output functions or to the strftime or wcsftime function is not a valid multibyte character sequence that begins and ends in its initial shift state (7.21.6.1, 7.121.6.2, 7.27.3.5, 7.229.2.1, 7.29.2.2, 7.29.5.1).	
155	In a call to one of the formatted output functions, a precision appears with a conversion specifier other than those described (7.21.6.1, 7.29.2.1).	FIO47-C
156	A conversion specification for a formatted output function uses an asterisk to denote an argument-supplied field width or precision, but the corresponding argument is not provided (7.21.6.1, 7.29.2.1).	
157	A conversion specification for a formatted output function uses a # or 0 flag with a conversion specifier other than those described (7.21.6.1, 7.29.2.1).	FIO47-C
158	A conversion specification for one of the formatted input/output functions uses a length modifier with a conversion specifier other than those described (7.21.6.1, 7.21.6.2, 7.29.2.1, 7.29.2.2).	FIO47-C
159	An s conversion specifier is encountered by one of the formatted output functions, and the argument is missing the null terminator (unless a precision is specified that does not require null termination) (7.21.6.1, 7.29.2.1).	

UB	Description	Guideline
160	An n conversion specification for one of the formatted input/ output functions includes any flags, an assignment-suppressing character, a field width, or a precision (7.21.6.1, 7.21.6.2, 7.29.2.1, 7.29.2.2).	
161	A % conversion specifier is encountered by one of the formatted input/output functions, but the complete conversion specification is not exactly %% (7.21.6.1, 7.21.6.2, 7.29.2.1, 7.29.2.2).	FIO47-C
162	An invalid conversion specification is found in the format for one of the formatted input/output functions, or the strftime or wcsftime function (7.21.6.1, 7.21.6.2, 7.27.3.5, 7.29.2.1, 7.29.2.2, 7.29.5.1).	FIO47-C
163	The number of characters or wide characters transmitted by a formatted output function (or written to an array, or that would have been written to an array) is greater than INT_MAX (7.21.6.1, 7.29.2.1).	
164	The number of input items assigned by a formatted input function is greater than INT_MAX (7.21.6.2, 7.29.2.2).	
165	The result of a conversion by one of the formatted input functions cannot be represented in the corresponding object, or the receiving object does not have an appropriate type (7.21.6.2, 7.29.2.2).	
166	A c, s, or [conversion specifier is encountered by one of the formatted input functions, and the array pointed to by the corresponding argument is not large enough to accept the input sequence (and a null terminator if the conversion specifier is s or [) (7.21.6.2, 7.29.2.2).	
167	A c, s, or [conversion specifier with an l qualifier is encountered by one of the formatted input functions, but the input is not a valid multibyte character sequence that begins in the initial shift state (7.21.6.2, 7.29.2.2).	
168	The input item for a %p conversion by one of the formatted input functions is not a value converted earlier during the same program execution (7.21.6.2, 7.29.2.2).	
169	The vfprintf, vfscanf, vprintf, vscanf, vsnprintf, vsprintf, vsscanf, vfwprintf, vfwscanf, vswprintf, vswscanf, vwprintf, or vwscanf function is called with an improperly initialized va_list argument, or the argument is used (other than in an invocation of va_end) after the function returns (7.21.6.8, 7.21.6.9, 7.21.6.10, 7.21.6.11, 7.21.6.12, 7.21.6.13, 7.21.6.14, 7.29.2.5, 7.29.2.6, 7.29.2.7, 7.29.2.8, 7.29.2.9, 7.29.2.10).	

continues

UB	Description	Guideline
170	The contents of the array supplied in a call to the fgets, gets, or fgetws function are used after a read error occurred (7.21.7.2, 7.21.7.7, 7.293.2).	FIO40-C
171	The file position indicator for a binary stream is used after a call to the ungetc function where its value was zero before the call (7.21.7.11).	
172	The file position indicator for a stream is used after an error occurred during a call to the fread or fwrite function (7.21.8.1, 7.21.8.2).	
173	A partial element read by a call to the fread function is used (7.21.8.1).	
174	The fseek function is called for a text stream with a nonzero offset and either the offset was not returned by a previous successful call to the ftell function on a stream associated with the same file or whence is not SEEK_SET (7.21.9.2).	
175	The fsetpos function is called to set a position that was not returned by a previous successful call to the fgetpos function on a stream associated with the same file (7.21.9.3).	
176	A non-null pointer returned by a call to the calloc, malloc, or realloc function with a zero requested size is used to access an object (7.22.3).	MEM04-C
177	The value of a pointer that refers to space deallocated by a call to the free or realloc function is used (7.22.3).	MEM30-C
178	The alignment requested of the aligned_alloc function is not valid or not supported by the implementation, or the size requested is not an integral multiple of the alignment (7.22.3.1).	
179	The pointer argument to the free or realloc function does not match a pointer earlier returned by calloc, malloc, or realloc, or the space has been deallocated by a call to free or realloc (7.22.3.3, 7.22.3.5).	MEM34-C
180	The value of the object allocated by the malloc function is used (7.22.3.4).	
181	The values of any bytes in a new object allocated by the realloc function beyond the size of the old object are used (7.22.3.5).	EXP33-C
182	The program calls the exit or quick_exit function more than once, or calls both functions (7.22.4.4, 7.22.4.7).	ENV32-C, ERR04-C
183	During the call to a function registered with the atexit or at_quick_exit function, a call is made to the longjmp function that would terminate the call to the registered function (7.22.4.4, 7.22.4.7).	ENV32-C

UB	Description	Guideline
184	The string set up by the `getenv` or `strerror` function is modified by the program (7.22.4.6, 7.24.6.2).	ENV30-C
185	A signal is raised while the `quick_exit` function is executing (7.22.4.7).	
186	A command is executed through the `system` function in a way that is documented as causing termination or some other form of undefined behavior (7.22.4.8).	
187	A searching or sorting utility function is called with an invalid pointer argument, even if the number of elements is zero (7.22.5).	
188	The comparison function called by a searching or sorting utility function alters the contents of the array being searched or sorted, or returns ordering values inconsistently (7.22.5).	
189	The array being searched by the `bsearch` function does not have its elements in proper order (7.22.5.1).	
190	The current conversion state is used by a multibyte/wide character conversion function after changing the LC_CTYPE category (7.22.7).	
191	A string or wide string utility function is instructed to access an array beyond the end of an object (7.24.1, 7.29.4).	
192	A string or wide string utility function is called with an invalid pointer argument, even if the length is zero (7.24.1, 7.29.4).	
193	The contents of the destination array are used after a call to the `strxfrm`, `strftime`, `wcsxfrm`, or `wcsftime` function in which the specified length was too small to hold the entire null-terminated result (7.24.4.5, 7.27.3.5, 7.29.4.4.4, 7.29.5.1).	
194	The first argument in the very first call to the `strtok` or `wcstok` is a null pointer (7.24.5.8, 7.29.4.5.7).	
195	The type of an argument to a type-generic macro is not compatible with the type of the corresponding parameter of the selected function (7.25).	
196	A complex argument is supplied for a generic parameter of a type-generic macro that has no corresponding complex function (7.25).	
197	At least one member of the broken-down time passed to `asctime` contains a value outside its normal range, or the calculated year exceeds four digits or is less than the year 1000 (7.27.3.1).	
198	The argument corresponding to an `s` specifier without an `l` qualifier in a call to the `fwprintf` function does not point to a valid multibyte character sequence that begins in the initial shift state (7.29.2.11).	

continues

UB	Description	Guideline
199	In a call to the `wcstok` function, the object pointed to by `ptr` does not have the value stored by the previous call for the same wide string (7.29.4.5.7).	
200	An `mbstate_t` object is used inappropriately (7.29.6).	EXP33-C
201	The value of an argument of type `wint_t` to a wide character classification or case mapping function is neither equal to the value of `WEOF` nor representable as a `wchar_t` (7.230.1).	
202	The `iswctype` function is called using a different `LC_CTYPE` category from the one in effect for the call to the `wctype` function that returned the description (7.30.2.2.1).	
203	The `towctrans` function is called using a different `LC_CTYPE` category from the one in effect for the call to the `wctrans` function that returned the description (7.30.3.2.1).	

Appendix C

Unspecified Behavior

According to the C Standard, Annex J, J.1 [ISO/IEC 9899:2011], the behavior of a program is unspecified in the circumstances outlined in the following table. The descriptions of unspecified behaviors in the "Description" column are direct quotes from the standard. The parenthesized numbers refer to the subclause of the C Standard (C11) that identifies the unspecified behavior. The "Guideline" column in the table identifies the coding practices that address the specific case of unspecified behavior (USB).

USB	Description	Guideline
1	The manner and timing of static initialization (5.1.2).	
2	The termination status returned to the hosted environment if the return type of main is not compatible with int (5.1.2.2.3).	
3	The values of objects that are neither lock-free atomic objects nor of type volatile sig_atomic_t and the state of the floating-point environment when the processing of the abstract machine is interrupted by receipt of a signal (5.1.2.3).	
4	The behavior of the display device if a printing character is written when the active position is at the final position of a line (5.2.2).	
5	The behavior of the display device if a backspace character is written when the active position is at the initial position of a line (5.2.2).	

continues

481

USB	Description	Guideline
6	The behavior of the display device if a horizontal tab character is written when the active position is at or past the last defined horizontal tabulation position (5.2.2).	
7	The behavior of the display device if a vertical tab character is written when the active position is at or past the last defined vertical tabulation position (5.2.2).	
8	How an extended source character that does not correspond to a universal character name counts toward the significant initial characters in an external identifier (5.2.4.1).	
9	Many aspects of the representations of types (6.2.6).	
10	The value of padding bytes when storing values in structures or unions (6.2.6.1).	
11	The values of bytes that correspond to union members other than the one last stored into (6.2.6.1).	EXP-39C
12	The representation used when storing a value in an object that has more than one object representation for that value (6.2.6.1).	
13	The values of any padding bits in integer representations (6.2.6.2).	
14	Whether certain operators can generate negative zeros and whether a negative zero becomes a normal zero when stored in an object (6.2.6.2).	
15	Whether two string literals result in distinct arrays (6.4.5).	
16	The order in which subexpressions are evaluated and the order in which side effects take place, except as specified for the function-call (), &&, ||, ?:, and comma operators (6.5).	EXP30-C
17	The order in which the function designator, arguments, and subexpressions within the arguments are evaluated in a function call (6.5.2.2).	
18	The order of side effects among compound literal initialization list expressions (6.5.2.5).	
19	The order in which the operands of an assignment operator are evaluated (6.5.16).	
20	The alignment of the addressable storage unit allocated to hold a bit-field (6.7.2.1).	
21	Whether a call to an inline function uses the inline definition or the external definition of the function (6.7.4).	

USB	Description	Guideline
22	Whether or not a size expression is evaluated when it is part of the operand of a `sizeof` operator and changing the value of the size expression would not affect the result of the operator (6.7.6.2).	EXP44-C
23	The order in which any side effects occur among the initialization list expressions in an initializer (6.7.9).	
24	The layout of storage for function parameters (6.9.1).	
25	When a fully expanded macro replacement list contains a function-like macro name as its last preprocessing token and the next preprocessing token from the source file is a (, and the fully expanded replacement of that macro ends with the name of the first macro and the next preprocessing token from the source file is again a (, whether that is considered a nested replacement (6.10.3).	
26	The order in which # and ## operations are evaluated during macro substitution (6.10.3.2, 6.10.3.3).	
27	The state of the floating-point status flags when execution passes from a part of the program translated with FENV_ACCESS "off" to a part translated with FENV_ACCESS "on" (7.6.1).	
28	The order in which `feraiseexcept` raises floating-point exceptions, except as stated in F.8.6 (7.6.2.3).	
29	Whether `math_errhandling` is a macro or an identifier with external linkage (7.12).	DCL37-C
30	The results of the `frexp` functions when the specified value is not a floating-point number (7.12.6.4).	
31	The numeric result of the `ilogb` functions when the correct value is outside the range of the return type (7.12.6.5, F.10.3.5).	
32	The result of rounding when the value is out of range (7.12.9.5, 7.12.9.7, F.10.6.5).	
33	The value stored by the `remquo` functions in the object pointed to by quo when y is zero (7.12.10.3).	
34	Whether a comparison macro argument that is represented in a format wider than its semantic type is converted to the semantic type (7.12.14).	
35	Whether `setjmp` is a macro or an identifier with external linkage (7.13).	DCL37-C
36	Whether `va_copy` and `va_end` are macros or identifiers with external linkage (7.16.1).	DCL37-C

continues

USB	Description	Guideline
37	The hexadecimal digit before the decimal point when a non-normalized floating-point number is printed with an **a** or A conversion specifier (7.21.6.1, 7.29.2.1).	
38	The value of the file position indicator after a successful call to the ungetc function for a text stream, or the ungetwc function for any stream, until all pushed-back characters are read or discarded (7.21.7.10, 7.29.3.10).	
39	The details of the value stored by the fgetpos function (7.21.9.1).	
40	The details of the value returned by the ftell function for a text stream (7.21.9.4).	
41	Whether the strtod, strtof, strtold, wcstod, wcstof, and wcstold functions convert a minus-signed sequence to a negative number directly or by negating the value resulting from converting the corresponding unsigned sequence (7.22.1.3, 7.29.4.1.1).	
42	The order and contiguity of storage allocated by successive calls to the calloc, malloc, and realloc functions (7.22.3).	
43	The amount of storage allocated by a successful call to the calloc, malloc, and realloc function when 0 bytes was requested (7.22.3).	MEM04-C
44	Whether a call to the atexit function that does not happen before the exit function is called will succeed (7.22.4.2).	
45	Whether a call to the at_quick_exit function that does not happen before the quick_exit function is called will succeed (7.22.4.3).	
46	Which of two elements that compare as equal is matched by the bsearch function (7.22.5.1).	
47	The order of two elements that compare as equal in an array sorted by the qsort function (7.22.5.2).	
48	The encoding of the calendar time returned by the time function (7.27.2.4).	MSC05-C
49	The characters stored by the strftime or wcsftime function if any of the time values being converted is outside the normal range (7.27.3.5, 7.29.5.1).	
50	Whether an encoding error occurs if a wchar_t value that does not correspond to a member of the extended character set appears in the format string for a function in 7.29.2 or 7.29.5 and the specified semantics do not require that value to be processed by wcrtomb (7.29.1).	

USB	Description	Guideline
51	The conversion state after an encoding error occurs (7.28.1.1, 7.28.1.2, 7.28.1.3, 7.28.1.4, 7.29.6.3.2, 7.29.6.3.3, 7.29.6.4.1, 7.29.6.4.2).	
52	The resulting value when the "invalid" floating-point exception is raised during IEC 60559 floating to integer conversion (F.4).	
53	Whether conversion of non-integer IEC 60559 floating values to integer raises the "inexact" floating-point exception (F.4).	
54	Whether or when library functions in <math.h> raise the "inexact" floating-point exception in an IEC 60559 conformant implementation (F.10).	
55	Whether or when library functions in <math.h> raise an undeserved "underflow" floating-point exception in an IEC 60559 conformant implementation (F.10).	
56	The exponent value stored by frexp for a NaN or infinity (F.10.3.4).	
57	The numeric result returned by the lrint, llrint, lround, and llround functions if the rounded value is outside the range of the return type (F.10.6.5, F.10.6.7).	
58	The sign of one part of the complex result of several math functions for certain exceptional values in IEC 60559–compatible implementations (G.6.1.1, G.6.2.2, G.6.2.3, G.6.2.4, G.6.2.5, G.6.2.6, G.6.3.1, G.6.4.2).	

Bibliography

[Acton 2006] Acton, Mike. Understanding Strict Aliasing. *CellPerformance*, June 1, 2006.

[Banahan 2003] Banahan, Mike, Declan Brady, and Mark Doran. *The C Book, Second Edition*. Originally published by Addison-Wesley in 1991. Published by Mike Banahan as an e-book in 2003. http://www.phy.duke.edu/~rgb/General/c_book/c_book/index.html

[Brainbell.com] Brainbell.com. "Advice and Warnings for C Tutorials." http://www.brainbell.com/tutors/c/Advice_and_Warnings_for_C/

[Bryant 2003] Bryant, Randal E., and Dave O'Halloran. *Computer Systems: A Programmer's Perspective*. Upper Saddle River, NJ: Prentice Hall, 2003.

[C99 Rationale 2003] *Rationale for International Standard—Programming Languages—C, Revision 5.10* (C99 Rationale), April 2003. http://www.open-std.org/jtc1/sc22/wg14/www/C99RationaleV5.10.pdf

[Chess 2007] Chess, Brian, and Jacob West. *Secure Programming with Static Analysis*. Boston: Addison-Wesley, 2007.

[Coverity 2007] *Coverity Prevent User's Manual* (3.3.0). 2007.

[CVE] Common Vulnerabilities and Exposures. http://cve.mitre.org/

[Dewhurst 2002] Dewhurst, Stephen C. *C++ Gotchas: Avoiding Common Problems in Coding and Design*. Boston: Addison-Wesley, 2002.

[DHS 2006] U.S. Department of Homeland Security. "Build Security In." 2006. https://buildsecurityin.us-cert.gov/

[DISA 2008] DISA. *Application Security and Development Security Technical Implementation Guide,* Version 2, Release 1. July 2008. http://citeseerx.ist.psu.edu/viewdoc/download?rep=rep1&type=pdf&doi=10.1.1.184.4979

[Dowd 2006] Dowd, Mark, John McDonald, and Justin Schuh. *The Art of Software Security Assessment: Identifying and Preventing Software Vulnerabilities.* Boston: Addison-Wesley, 2006. See http://taossa.com for updates and errata.

[Drepper 2006] Drepper, Ulrich. "Defensive Programming for Red Hat Enterprise Linux (and What To Do If Something Goes Wrong)." May 3, 2006. http://people.redhat.com/drepper/defprogramming.pdf

[Finlay 2003] Finlay, Ian A. CERT Advisory CA-2003-16, "Buffer Overflow in Microsoft RPC." CERT/CC, July 2003. http://www.cert.org/advisories/CA-2003-16.html

[Flake 2006] Flake, Halvar. "Attacks on Uninitialized Local Variables." Black Hat Federal, 2006. http://www.blackhat.com/presentations/bh-europe-06/bh-eu-06-Flake.pdf

[Garfinkel 1996] Garfinkel, Simson, and Gene Spafford. *Practical UNIX & Internet Security, Second Edition.* Sebastopol, CA: O'Reilly Media, 1996.

[GCC Bugs] GCC Team. "GCC Bugs." Free Software Foundation, Inc., 2013. http://gcc.gnu.org/bugs/#nonbugs_c

[GNU Pth] Engelschall, Ralf S. GNU Portable Threads, 2006. http://www.gnu.org/software/pth/

[Goodin 2009] Goodin, Dan. "Clever Attack Exploits Fully-Patched Linux Kernel." *The Register,* July 2009. http://www.theregister.co.uk/2009/07/17/linux_kernel_exploit/

[Graff 2003] Graff, Mark G., and Kenneth R. Van Wyk. *Secure Coding: Principles and Practices.* Cambridge, MA: O'Reilly, 2003.

[Greenman 1997] Greenman, David. "Serious Security Bug in wu-ftpd v2.4." BUGTRAQ Mailing List (bugtraq@securityfocus.com), January 2, 1997. http://seclists.org/bugtraq/1997/Jan/0011.html

[Griffiths 2006] Griffiths, Andrew. "Clutching at Straws: When You Can Shift the Stack Pointer." 2006. http://felinemenace.org/papers/p63-0x0e_Shifting_the_Stack_Pointer.txt

[Hatton 1995] Hatton, Les. *Safer C: Developing Software for High-Integrity and Safety-Critical Systems.* New York: McGraw-Hill, 1995.

[Henricson 1992] Henricson, Mats, and Erik Nyquist. "Programming in C++, Rules and Recommendations." Ellemtel Telecommunication Systems Laboratories, 1992. http://www.doc.ic.ac.uk/lab/cplus/c++.rules/

[Horton 1990] Horton, Mark R. *Portable C Software.* Upper Saddle River, NJ: Prentice Hall, 1990.

[Howard 2002] Howard, Michael, and David C. LeBlanc. *Writing Secure Code, Second Edition*. Redmond, WA: Microsoft Press, 2002.

[IEC 60812] International Electrotechnical Commission (IEC). *Analysis Techniques for System Reliability—Procedure for Failure Mode and Effects Analysis (FMEA), Second Edition*. (IEC 60812). Geneva, Switzerland: IEC, 2006.

[IEC 61508-4] IEC. *Functional Safety of Electrical/Electronic/Programmable Electronic Safety-Related Systems—Part 4: Definitions and Abbreviations* (IEC 61508-4). Geneva, Switzerland: IEC. 1998.

[IEEE 754] Institute of Electrical and Electronics Engineers (IEEE). *Standard for Binary Floating-Point Arithmetic* (IEEE 754-2008), 2008. http://grouper.ieee.org/groups/754/

[IEEE Std 1003.1-2013] IEEE and The Open Group. *Standard for Information Technology—Portable Operating System Interface (POSIX®), Base Specifications, Issue 7* (IEEE Std 1003.1, 2013 Edition). E-book: http://ieeexplore.ieee.org/servlet/opac?punumber=6506089

[IEEE Std 610.12-1990] IEEE Computer Society. *IEEE Standard Glossary of Software Engineering Terminology*. New York: IEEE, September 1990.

[Internet Society 2000] The Internet Society. *Internet Security Glossary (RFC 2828)*. 2000. ftp://ftp.rfc-editor.org/in-notes/rfc2828.txt

[ISO/IEC 10646:2012] International Organization for Standardization/International Electrotechnical Commission (ISO/IEC). *Information Technology—Universal Multiple-Octet Coded Character Set (UCS)* (ISO/IEC 10646:2012). Geneva, Switzerland: ISO, 2012. http://standards.iso.org/ittf/PubliclyAvailableStandards/index.html

[ISO/IEC 11889-1:2009] ISO/IEC. *Information Technology—Trusted Platform Module—Part 1: Overview* (ISO/IEC 11889-1:2009). Geneva, Switzerland: ISO, 2009.

[ISO/IEC 14882:2011] ISO/IEC. *Information Technology—Programming Languages—C++, Third Edition*. (ISO/IEC 14882-2011). Geneva, Switzerland: ISO, 2011.

[ISO/IEC 9899:1990] ISO/IEC. *Programming Languages—C* (ISO/IEC 9899:1990). Geneva, Switzerland: ISO, 1990.

[ISO/IEC 9899:1999] ISO/IEC. *Programming Languages—C, Second Edition*. (ISO/IEC 9899:1999). Geneva, Switzerland: ISO, 1999.

[ISO/IEC 9899:2011] ISO/IEC. *Programming Languages—C, Third Edition*. (ISO/IEC 9899:2011). Geneva, Switzerland: ISO, 2011.

[ISO/IEC JTC1/SC22/WG14 N791] ISO/IEC. *Solving the Struct Hack Problem* (ISO/IEC JTC1/SC22/WG14 N791). Geneva, Switzerland: ISO, 1997.

[ISO/IEC TR 24731-2:2010] ISO/IEC. *Extensions to the C Library—Part II: Dynamic Allocation Functions* (ISO/IEC TR 24731). Geneva, Switzerland: ISO, April 2010.

[ISO/IEC TR 24772:2013] ISO/IEC. *Information Technology—Programming Languages—Guidance to Avoiding Vulnerabilities in Programming Languages through Language Selection and Use* (ISO/IEC TR 24772:2013). Geneva, Switzerland: ISO, March 2013.

[ISO/IEC TS 17961:2013] ISO/IEC. *Information Technology—Programming Languages, Their Environments and System Software Interfaces—C Secure Coding Rules* (ISO/IEC TS 17961). Geneva, Switzerland: ISO, 2012.

[ISO/IEC/IEEE 24765:2010] ISO/IEC/IEEE. *Systems and Software Engineering—Vocabulary*. Geneva, Switzerland: ISO, 2010.

[Jack 2007] Jack, Barnaby. "Vector Rewrite Attack: Exploitable NULL Pointer Vulnerabilities on ARM and XScale Architectures" (white paper). May 2007. http://cansecwest.com/csw07/Vector-Rewrite-Attack.pdf

[Jones 2008] Jones, Derek M. *The New C Standard: An Economic and Cultural Commentary*. Farnborough, England: Knowledge Software Ltd., 2008. http://www.knosof.co.uk/cbook/

[Kernighan 1988] Kernighan, Brian W., and Dennis M. Ritchie. *The C Programming Language, Second Edition*. Englewood Cliffs, NJ: Prentice Hall, 1988.

[Kettlewell 2002] Kettlewell, Richard. C Language Gotchas. February 2002. http://www.greenend.org.uk/rjk/2001/02/cfu.html

[Kirch-Prinz 2002] Kirch-Prinz, Ulla, and Peter Prinz. *C Pocket Reference*. Sebastopol, CA: O'Reilly, 2002.

[Koenig 1989] Koenig, Andrew. *C Traps and Pitfalls*. Reading, MA: Addison-Wesley, 1989.

[Lai 2006] Lai, Ray. "Reading between the Lines." *OpenBSD Journal*, October 2006. http://undeadly.org/cgi?action=article&sid=20061027031811

[Lea 2000] Lea, Doug. *Concurrent Programming in Java, Second Edition*. Boston: Addison-Wesley, 2000.

[Liu 2009] Liu, Likai. "Making NULL-Pointer Reference Legal." *Life of a Computer Science Student*, January, 2009. http://lifecs.likai.org/2009/01/making-null-pointer-reference-legal.html

[Lockheed Martin 2005] Lockheed Martin. "Joint Strike Fighter Air Vehicle C++ Coding Standards for the System Development and Demonstration Program." Document Number 2RDU00001 Rev C., December 2005. http://www.research.att.com/~bs/JSF-AV-rules.pdf

[McCluskey 2001] McCluskey, Glen. "Fexible Array Members and Designators in C9X." *;login:*, 26, 4 (July 2001): 29–32. http://www.usenix.org/publications/login/2001-07/pdfs/mccluskey.pdf

[Mercy 2006] Mercy. "Exploiting Uninitialized Data." *SecuriTeam*, January 2006. http://www.securiteam.com/securityreviews/5EP040KHFW.html

[Microsoft 2003] Microsoft Security Bulletin MS03-026, "Buffer Overrun In RPC Interface Could Allow Code Execution (823980)." September 2003. http://www.microsoft.com/technet/security/bulletin/MS03-026.mspx

[MISRA C:2012] Motor Industry Software Reliability Association (MISRA). *MISRA C3: Guidelines for the Use of the C Language in Critical Systems 2012*. Nuneaton, UK: MIRA, 2012. http://www.misra.org.uk/

[MIT 2005] Massachusetts Institute of Technology (MIT). "MIT krb5 Security Advisory 2005-003. http://web.mit.edu/kerberos/www/advisories/MITKRB5-SA-2005-003-recvauth.txt

[MITRE 2013] MITRE. Common Weakness Enumeration. 2013. http://cwe.mitre.org

[MSDN] Microsoft Developer Network. http://msdn.microsoft.com/en-us/default.aspx

[Murenin 2007] Murenin, Constantine A. "cnst: 10-Year-Old Pointer-Arithmetic Bug in make(1) Is Now Gone, Thanks to malloc.conf and Some Debugging." *LiveJournal*, June 2007. http://cnst.livejournal.com/24040.html

[NIST 2006] National Institute of Standards and Technology (NIST). *SAMATE Reference Dataset*. 2006. http://samate.nist.gov/SRD/

[Open Group 1997] The Open Group. "Go Solo 2—The Authorized Guide to Version 2 of the Single UNIX Specification" (white paper). May 1997. http://www.unix.org/whitepapers/64bit.html

[OpenBSD] Berkley Software Design, Inc. Manual Pages. June 2008. http://www.openbsd.org/cgi-bin/man.cgi

[OpenMP] OpenMP. "The OpenMP API® Specification for Parallel Programming." http://openmp.org/wp/

[OWASP Freed Memory] Open Web Application Security Project (OWASP). "Using Freed Memory." http://www.owasp.org/index.php/Using_freed_memory

[Pethia 2003] Pethia, Richard D. "Viruses and Worms: What Can We Do about Them?" September 10, 2003. http://www.cert.org/congressional_testimony/Pethia-Testimony-9-10-2003/

[Plum 1985] Plum, Thomas. *Reliable Data Structures in C*. Kamuela, HI: Plum Hall, Inc., 1985.

[Plum 1989] Plum, Thomas, and Dan Saks. *C Programming Guidelines, Second Edition*. Kamuela, HI: Plum Hall, 1989.

[Plum 1991] Plum, Thomas. *C++ Programming*. Kamuela, HI: Plum Hall, 1991.

[Saks 2007] Saks, Dan. "Sequence Points." *Embedded Systems Design*, July 1, 2002. http://www.embedded.com/electronics-blogs/programming-pointers/4023983/Sequence-Points

[Seacord 2013a] Seacord, Robert C. "C Secure Coding Rules: Past, Present, and Future." InformIT, June 26, 2013. http://www.informit.com/articles/article.aspx?p=2088511

[Seacord 2013b] Seacord, Robert C. *Secure Coding in C and C++, Second Edition*. Boston: Addison-Wesley, 2013. See http://www.cert.org/books/secure-coding for news and errata.

[Spinellis 2006] Spinellis, Diomidis. *Code Quality: The Open Source Perspective*. Boston: Addison-Wesley, 2006. http://www.spinellis.gr/codequality

[Summit 1995] Summit, Steve. *C Programming FAQs: Frequently Asked Questions*. Reading, MA: Addison-Wesley, 1995.

[Summit 2005] Summit, Steve. "comp.lang.c Answers to Frequently Asked Questions (FAQ List)." 2005. http://www.faqs.org/faqs/comp.lang.c/C-FAQ-list/

[Sun 1993] Sun Security Bulletin #00122. 1993. http://sunsolve.sun.com/search/document.do?assetkey=1-22-00122-1

[UNIX 1992] UNIX System Laboratories. *System V Interface Definition, Third Edition*. Reading, MA: Addison-Wesley, 1992.

[van Sprundel 2006] van Sprundel, Ilja. "Unusualbugs." 2006. http://2008.ruxcon.org.au/files/2006/unusual_bugs.pdf

[Viega 2003] Viega, John, and Matt Messier. *Secure Programming Cookbook for C and C++: Recipes for Cryptography, Authentication, Networking, Input Validation & More*. Sebastopol, CA: O'Reilly, 2003.

[Viega 2005] Viega, John. *CLASP Reference Guide: Volume 1.1 Training*. Secure Software, 2005.

[VU#159523] Giobbi, Ryan. Vulnerability Note VU#159523, "Adobe Flash Player Integer Overflow Vulnerability." April 2008. http://www.kb.cert.org/vuls/id/159523

[VU#162289] Dougherty, Chad. Vulnerability Note VU#162289, "GCC Silently Discards Some Wraparound Checks." April 2008. http://www.kb.cert.org/vuls/id/162289

[VU#551436] Giobbi, Ryan. Vulnerability Note VU#551436, "Mozilla Firefox SVG Viewer Vulnerable to Buffer Overflow." 2007. http://www.kb.cert.org/vulnotes/id/551436

[VU#623332] Mead, Robert. Vulnerability Note VU#623332, "MIT Kerberos 5 Contains Double-Free Vulnerability in 'krb5_recvauth()' Function." 2005. http://www.kb.cert.org/vuls/id/623332

[VU#834865] Gennari, Jeff. Vulnerability Note VU#834865, "Sendmail Signal I/O Race Condition." March 2008. http://www.kb.cert.org/vuls/id/834865

[VU#925211] Dougherty, Chad. Vulnerability Note VU#925211, "Debian and Ubuntu OpenSSL Packages Contain a Predictable Random Number Generator." June 2008. https://www.kb.cert.org/vuls/id/925211

[Walfridsson 2003] Walfridsson, Krister. "Aliasing, Pointer Casts and GCC 3.3." August 2003. http://mail-index.netbsd.org/tech-kern/2003/08/11/0001.html

[Walls 2006] Walls, Douglas. "How to Use the Qualifier in C." Sun ONE Tools Group, Sun Microsystems. March 2006.

[Wang 2012] Wang, Xi. "More Randomness or Less" (blog entry). June 2012. http://kqueue.org/blog/2012/06/25/more-randomness-or-less/

[Warren 2002] Warren, Henry S. *Hacker's Delight*. Boston: Addison-Wesley, 2002. http://www.hackersdelight.org

[Wheeler 2004] Wheeler, David. "Secure Programmer: Call Components Safely." *SecurityFocus*, December 2004. http://www.securityfocus.com/archive/98/385517/30/150/threaded

[Wojtczuk 2008] Wojtczuk, Rafal. "Analyzing the Linux Kernel vmsplice Exploit." McAfee Avert Labs blog, February 13, 2008. http://www.avertlabs.com/research/blog/index.php/2008/02/13/analyzing-the-linux-kernel-vmsplice-exploit/

[xorl 2009] xorl. "xorl %eax, %eax." 2009. http://xorl.wordpress.com/

[Zalewski 2001] Zalewski, Michal. "Delivering Signals for Fun and Profit: Understanding, Exploiting and Preventing Signal-Handling Related Vulnerabilities." Bindview Corporation, May 2001. http://lcamtuf.coredump.cx/signals.txt

Index

A

A conversion specifier, 303
a conversion specifier, 303
Abnormal program termination
    array contents, 284
    closing files, 291
    defined, 459
    dereferencing null pointers, 65–66
    divide-by-zero errors, 137
    error conditions, 381
    exit handlers, 318
    format string specifiers, 304
    implicit declarations, 19
    misaligned pointers, 73
    pointers to nonallocated memory, 247
    race conditions, 394, 397
    reading freed memory, 238
    stream arguments, 287
    string literal modifications, 205
abort()
    with assert(), 6
    errno, 361
    with signal handlers, 334, 342, 350
Access rights
    access violation exceptions, 279
    uninitialized memory exploits, 64
Accessing
    bit-fields from multiple threads, 391–394
    files
        closed, 298–299
        race conditions in, 294–297

freed memory, 234–239
out-of-range indexes, 175–176
shared objects in signal handlers, 342–345
variables through pointers of incompatible types,
    83–89
acos(), 155
acosh(), 155
Actual arguments for sequence points, 49
Addition
    pointers
        arrays, 170, 184–187
        scaled integers, 196–200
        signed integer overflow, 127–128
    wrapping, 113
afsacl.so library exclusions, 262
Aliases
    C Standard rules, 83–84
    restrict-qualified pointers, 94
alignas(), 74
_Alignas specifiers, 35
aligned_alloc()
    error return values, 366
    memory allocation, 250
    memory freed by, 247
    memory initialization, 56
    object alignment, 253
_aligned_malloc(), 255–256
_aligned_realloc(), 255–256
Alignment
    integer and pointer conversions, 146
    objects, 253–256

495